Nathaniel Shilkret

Sixty Years in the Music Business

By
Nathaniel Shilkret

Edited by
Niel Shell
Barbara Shilkret

The Scarecrow Press, Inc.
Lanham, Maryland • Toronto • Oxford
2005

SCARECROW PRESS, INC.

Published in the United States of America
by Scarecrow Press, Inc.
A wholly owned subsidiary of
The Rowman & Littlefield Publishing Group, Inc.
4501 Forbes Boulevard, Suite 200, Lanham, Maryland 20706
www.scarecrowpress.com

PO Box 317
Oxford
OX2 9RU, UK

British Library Cataloguing in Publication Information Available

Library of Congress Cataloging-in-Publication Data

Shilkret, Nathaniel, 1889–1981.
    Nathaniel Shilkret : sixty years in the music business / edited by Niel Shell,
Barbara Shilkret.
        p. cm.
    Includes bibliographical references (p.), discography (p.), and index.
    ISBN 0-8108-5128-8 (alk. paper)
    1. Shilkret, Nathaniel, 1889–1981. 2. Conductors (Music)—United
States—Biography. I. Shell, Niel. II. Shilkret, Barbara, 1920–2004. III. Title.
ML422.S525A3 2005
780'.92—dc22
                                        2004058928

Niel Shell dedicates this book to Barbara Shilkret (June 21, 1920–October 13, 2004), who was Nathaniel Shilkret's caregiver in his final years.

Nathaniel Shilkret would have wanted this recognition of her selfless efforts on his behalf.

CONTENTS

FOREWORD   vii
INTRODUCTION   x

1   A CHILD PRODIGY   1
2   TEENAGE TO MARRIAGE   10
3   THE VICTOR TALKING MACHINE COMPANY   36
4   RADIO AND RECORDING   62
5   SOUND MOVIES AND RCA   106
6   MOTION PICTURES   164
7   RETURN TO NEW YORK   181
8   MGM AND RKO-PATHÉ   188
9   THE SKINNER TOUR   211
10   CONCLUSION   216

APPENDIX A   COMPOSITIONS AND ARRANGEMENTS   221
APPENDIX B   SELECTIVE RECORD DISCOGRAPHY   235
APPENDIX C   CD DISCOGRAPHY   254
APPENDIX D   RADIO BROADCASTS   279
APPENDIX E   FILMOGRAPHY   286
APPENDIX F   NOTED PERSONALITIES   301
APPENDIX G   GENEALOGY   305
APPENDIX H   CHRONOLOGY   307

BIBLIOGRAPHY   309
ABBREVIATIONS USED IN INDEX   320
INDEX   321

ABOUT THE AUTHOR AND EDITORS   344
CD TRACK LISTING   345

FOREWORD

Nathaniel Shilkret was a clarinet player, pianist, conductor, composer, business executive (A&R man), music director (for Victor, RKO and MGM), and a pioneer in developing the effective use of new recording techniques. He was one of the best-known radio show and recording personalities in the 1920s and 1930s. Perhaps his name is less a household word now than other similar people of his era because his talent was spread over many areas and a portion of his work was "behind the scenes." With this posthumously published autobiography, he is given the opportunity to tell his story.

Nat Shilkret lived in my home from 1956 until his death in 1982. He completed the autobiography presented here around 1965. The manuscript lay untouched until August 1999, when his grandson (my son), also named Nathaniel Shilkret (he has shortened his name to Niel Shell), edited and prepared the manuscript for publication. My son and I annotated the autobiography and added footnotes, illustrations, most section and chapter titles, a bibliography and appendixes, creating an archival edition of this work. Copies of the archival edition have been deposited with the Library of Congress, the archival library at the City College of New York, the Library for the Performing Arts branch of the New York Public Library, and the New York Philharmonic Archives. This published edition contains the complete autobiography, further edited to bring the presentation into better chronological order, and selected material from the appendixes of the archival edition. For historical accuracy editorial changes to the autobiography have been kept to a minimum.

Editorial insertions in the original manuscript are indicated by brackets [like the ones enclosing this statement].

A listing of noted personalities tacitly makes a statement: The individuals listed are "famous" and the others are not. This is only half true.

Although we believe the individuals listed have some legitimate claim to the subjective notions of fame and talent, we do not mean to imply that those not listed were either not well known or not unusually talented. This comment is particularly sincere, since we feel that Nat Shilkret's talents could have placed him on many lists of noted personalities which do not include him.

We expect that this book will appeal to three audiences. First, and foremost, Nat Shilkret's lively commentary, filled with his wonderfully amusing stories, will provide entertainment to a very large general audience. Second, music enthusiasts will be eager to read about one of the great musicians of the first half of the twentieth century. Finally, music historians will, we hope, find something in this work that will help reinforce or extend their historical picture of the period. The enthusiasts we refer to include 78 rpm record collectors of popular, classical, operatic, and ethnic recordings; Old Time Radio buffs; and lovers of cinema, particularly from the era of black and white sound movies.

None of the lists in the appendixes are complete, due to their length or the lack of available data or both. References in the appendixes and footnotes are given by author and date; for example "Rust [1970b]" refers to the second item for 1970 by Rust in the bibliography.

Many of the listings in the bibliography are reference books which are the result of countless hours of research. Collectively, we thank the authors of these works for making the fruit of their efforts available. Among these special thanks go to Richard Spottswood for giving us permission to search the electronic file used to produce his seven volume discography of the approximately 1800 references to Nathaniel Shilkret. Thanks also go to Samuel S. Brylawski (head, Recorded Sound Section of the Motion Picture, Broadcasting and Recorded Sound Division, Library of Congress) for making this electronic file available to us. We thank Ronald Modell for information about the *Paris '90* tour. Thanks go to Diane Hakak for proofreading portions of this book.

We have obtained help in the form of information, copies of documents and clippings from periodicals, bibliographic references, and leads to other sources of information from a number of people who we are pleased to acknowledge: Marilyn Brown (daughter of Nat's brother Jack), Charles Di Cicco, Thomas DeLong, Alasdair Fenton, Richard Freed, Richard Flusser, Tim Gracyk, Albert Haim, Alex Hassan, Edward Jablonski, Ronald Modell, Vicki Ohl, John Peterson, Murray Pfeffer, Jim Pugh, Joan Shilkret (Nat's granddaughter), Adrian Shuman, Natali Kartman (daughter-in-law of Nat's brother Lew), Sidney van Nort, Richard Sudhalter, Bill Utley, Robin Villa, Richard Wandell (associate archivist for the New York Philharmonic Society), Neil Warner (son of Nat's brother Jack), Katharine Weber (granddaughter of Kay Swift), Robert Young (Eveready Battery archivist), and Betty Zehnden.

The following people deserve special thanks for providing, in addition to the type of assistance described above, substantial help with more than just the preparation of the book: Jim Barr, librarian and serious record collector; Harry Friedland, with forty years' experience in sales of specialty records, also a serious record collector and a musicologist; Werner Janssen Jr., a successful attorney and son of composer-conductor Werner Janssen; M. William Krasilovsky, a renowned music attorney and author of *This Business of Music*, a book on music law that, now in its eighth edition, has long been the standard in the field; Keith Marvin, former president of the Historical Automotive Association, author of hundreds of articles on antique automobiles, and a serious record collector; Peter Mintun, cabaret pianist and singer and featured artist on four CDs; Norman Odlum, retired SESAC veteran of more than forty years; Ed Polic, Glenn Miller discographer; Douglas Pomeroy, veteran professional audio engineer; Donald Rose, trombonist for the Miami Symphony Orchestra; Brian Rust, internationally known discographer, whose personal correspondence with us added substantially to the wealth of knowledge in his many discographies; Walter Scott, a Tommy Dorsey archivist for over fifty years; Del and Wayne Shilkret, sons of Nat's brother Harry; Timo Wuori, member of the Finnish Archives of Recorded Sound. We note with sorrow the death of Wayne Shilkret on March 22, 2001, and the death of Harry Friedland on January 13, 2004.

Finally, special thanks are due to a trombonist, who, in his successful effort to revive Nat Shilkret's composition *Concerto for Trombone*, has provided us with limitless assistance and encouragement: Bryan Free, associate principal trombonist of the Royal Scottish National Orchestra.

BARBARA SHILKRET

INTRODUCTION

This list of professional credits can be claimed by only one musician:

Beginning at the age of seven, he was the clarinet soloist for the New York Boys' Orchestra, which toured the country playing at venues such as the Pittsburgh Fair and the famous Willow Grove Park.

As a teenager he played in New York's most prestigious orchestras and bands, including the New York Philharmonic Society (under Vassily Safanov and Gustav Mahler), the New York Symphony Orchestra, the Metropolitan Opera House Orchestra, the Russian Symphony Orchestra, Victor Herbert's Orchestra, Arnold Volpe's Orchestra, the Georges Barrère Ensemble, Sousa's Grand Concert Band, Arthur Pryor's Band, and Edwin Franko Goldman's Band.

In addition to playing clarinet in Walter Damrosch's orchestras, he was Damrosch's rehearsal pianist, playing for luminaries such as Isadora Duncan. He was a member the orchestra when Damrosch toured with Duncan. As a member of the Russian Symphony Orchestra, he provided musical accompaniment for the famed ballerina Anna Pavlova and her partner Mikhael Mordkin.

He made many thousands of recordings for RCA Victor, which for many years was the largest record company in the world; it was known in its early days as the Victor Talking Machine Company. Hundreds of these records had dealers' orders for a half million copies before they were even made. He also recorded for many other companies, including Okeh, Pathé, Edison, Brunswick and Columbia. He conducted the majority of his recordings. He also made recordings playing clarinet, piano, organ, celeste, chimes, trumpet and even whistling. In his book *Pop Memories: 1890–1954*, which lists songs that "made the charts," Whitburn includes more than one hundred recordings conducted by him. Jealousy over his

getting his choice of songs to record is often cited as one of the reasons
Paul Whiteman left Victor and became a Columbia recording artist.

He made thousands of radio broadcasts, sometimes appearing on the
air as many as fifteen times in a single week. His sponsors included Camel,
Carnation, Chesterfield, Esso (now Exxon), Eveready, General Electric,
General Motors, Hire's Root Beer, Knickerbocker, Lysol, Maxwell House,
Mobil Oil, Palmolive, RCA Victor, Salada, and Smith Brothers' Cough
Drops. For one of his broadcasts, the sponsor claimed that the audience
exceeded twenty-five million—more than twenty percent of the U.S. popu-
lation at the time.

One of his scores for a motion picture was nominated for an Academy
Award. Altogether he scored or was musical director for several hun-
dred motion pictures, including Fred Astaire–Ginger Rogers films *Shall We
Dance* and *Swing Time* and half a dozen Laurel and Hardy films.

Other stars of motion pictures which he scored or for which he was
musical director include Edward Arnold, Wallace Beery, Spring Byington,
Leo G. Carroll, Frances Farmer, Cary Grant, Katharine Hepburn, Fredric
March, Burgess Meredith, Colleen Moore, Jack Oakie, Gene Raymond,
Donna Reed, Edward G. Robinson, Ann Sothern, and Spencer Tracy.

In addition to his own musical groups, he conducted John Philip Sousa's
Band (also the United States Marine Band during a 1932 memorial concert
for Sousa), the Philadelphia Symphony Orchestra, and the Los Angeles
Symphony Orchestra. He conducted his own composition at the prestigious
Library of Congress Festival of Chamber Music.

He was a featured attraction at the Mark Strand Theatre, where, as he
put it, he was "given the same marquee lights as Charlie Chaplin." He was
pit orchestra conductor for Cornelia Otis Skinner's *Paris '90* at the Booth
Theater on Broadway and also on two tours through the United States and
Canada.

An almost unbelievable list of the best-known musical talent of the day
performed under his baton. His orchestra members included Jimmy and
Tommy Dorsey, Benny Goodman, Glenn Miller, and Artie Shaw. Jascha
Heifetz and Mischa Elman performed under his direction. Other top mu-
sicians of their day appearing in his orchestras included Jessie Crawford,
Harry Glantz, George Hamilton Green, Joe Green, Ferde Grofé, Chester
Hazlett, Manny Klein, Fud Livingston, Charlie Margulis, Raphael Mendez,
Andy Sannella, Joe Venuti, and Fats Waller.

George Gershwin played under his direction.

He conducted for leading opera stars such as Rose Bampton, Lucrezia
Bori, Feodor Chaliapin, Jon Crain, Richard Crooks, Miguel Fleta, Emilio
De Gorgoza, Amelita Galli-Curci, Mary Garden, Beniamino Gigli, Helen
Jepson, Maria Jeritza, Giovanni Martinelli, Nino Martini, John McCor-
mack, James Melton, Grace Moore, Jan Peerce, Lily Pons, Rosa Ponselle,

Elisabeth Rethberg, Gladys Rice, Tito Schipa, Gladys Swarthout, John Charles Thomas, and Lawrence Tibbett.

He provided orchestral accompaniment for popular singers that included Gene Austin, Franklyn Baur, Henry Burr, Russ Columbo, Sam Coslow, Frank Crumit, Vernon Dalhart, Vaughn DeLeath, Morton Downey, Jane Froman, Sylvia Froos, Wendell Hall, Lewis James, Helen Jepson, Allan Jones, Helen Kane, Dennis King, Scrappy Lambert, Johnny Marvin, Ethel Merman, Helen Morgan, Billy Murray, The Revelers, Paul Robeson, and Aileen Stanley.

He also provided orchestral accompaniment for Edward Arnold, John Barrymore, Fanny Brice, Irene Dunne, Nelson Eddy and Jeannette MacDonald, Gallagher and Shean, Claude Rains, and Van and Schenk.

These lists of stars conducted by him do not include any of the many great artists he recorded in his two thousand or more recordings made to be sold outside the United States. Many of the names mentioned above may not be familiar today to a reader who does not have a special interest in the music of the first half of the twentieth century, but these names were household words to the audiences of their day.

Two of his hundreds of compositions sold in the millions. His best-selling song was *Lonesome Road*, which has been recorded by over a hundred top artists, including the Andrew Sisters (on a Paul Whiteman radio show), Louis Armstrong, Gene Austin, Bing Crosby, Sammy Davis Jr., Tommy Dorsey, Frankie Vallie and the Four Seasons, Benny Goodman, Earl Hines, Al Hirt, Peggy Lee, Julie London, Les Paul and Mary Ford, Paul Robeson, Willard Robison, Frank Sinatra, Muggsy Spanier and Helen Traubel.

His influence on the American musical scene went far beyond the music he composed and the music he played. He was an important executive at Victor during a period when Victor was the leading manufacturer of records, both in terms of quantity and quality of recording artists and in terms of number of records sold. One of his duties was to select the popular and foreign artists who would record for Victor and the songs they would record. This was a position of immense power. For example, he discovered and arranged for Victor to issue a contract to Gene Austin, who estimated that he made over eighty million records in his career. He was the first one that singing cowboy Gene Autry approached when he decided to end his job as a telegraph operator and to begin a singing career. He didn't give Autry a contract at Victor, but the then unknown singer was very glad to get a letter of recommendation. His influence over artists didn't end with the signing of a Victor contract. Songs at the time were assigned by Victor to artists, and the choice of songs artists were assigned had a great impact on their career. Matching artists with songs was another of his duties as a Victor executive. During a recent interview on WNYC, Skitch Henderson described him as "the Czar of RCA."

In addition to having great influence over which artists Victor would feature, his duties as session supervisor shaped the very nature of the music that would be recorded. He allowed jazz musicians to improvise solos; he was progressive and gave musicians the opportunity to express new musical forms. He welcomed black, as well as white, musicians. This was a radical departure from his predecessor Eddie King. King was well known to be authoritarian and very restrictive. The musicians considered King to be a "real square." The "sound of Victor" improved markedly when he replaced King. His promotion of new talent and new forms of music went even beyond his duties with Victor. He commissioned young musicians to compose and, in sharp contrast to some of his colleagues, always fostered an atmosphere that allowed new talent to appear on radio.

There is more yet to his influence. His heavy recording and broadcasting schedules provided employment for many musicians. For years, including those during the Great Depression, he engaged hundreds of musicians on a regular basis. His personal payroll for musicians for 1932, the depth of the Depression, was in excess of $230,000. This was for his radio broadcasts and did not include payments for his Victor recordings.

His work at Victor also had an important technical aspect. Prior to 1925, musicians had to crowd next to "horns" that mechanically reproduced sound. This primitive form of recording required a great deal of skill to successfully transfer the sound onto a disk, and he was a pioneer in recording technique, sometimes challenging the advice of the audio engineers. He credited the engineering aspect of his recording with having an important role in the great popularity of his records.

When the new "electrical" technique for recording came along, he was again in the forefront, working madly to produce a large quantity of the new electrical recordings for a public that was not yet aware of the great technical advance that was coming. The first commercially available electric recording was made under his direction.

The musical genius whose achievements have been described is Nathaniel Shilkret. His career lasted from age seven to age seventy. He had the ability to survive on two or three hours sleep a night, and virtually every waking moment he devoted to music. The results speak for themselves.

Nathaniel Shilkret died in 1982, but his music is very much alive today. Motion pictures to which he contributed music are broadcast almost daily all around the world. Episodes of reruns of the television shows *Gomer Pyle, Andy Griffith, Matlock,* and the *Odd Couple,* which use his composition *Lonesome Road,* air regularly. Well over a hundred commercially produced ˙ CDs contain tracks conducted or composed by Nathaniel Shilkret. Original Shilkret 78 rpm records are readily available, and rarely a days goes by without some collector purchasing one of these records. Since the turn of the millennium, CDs devoted exclusively to works conducted, composed or commissioned by Nathaniel Shilkret have been produced by such mainstream producers as ASV Living Era, NAXOS and Angel Records. New recordings and reissues of old recordings of *Lonesome Road* and *Jeannine, I Dream of Lilac Time* appear regularly.

Four recordings conducted by Nathaniel Shilkret have earned Grammy Awards.

The New York Pops, conducted by Skitch Henderson, performed Nathaniel Shilkret's *Concerto for Trombone* at Carnegie Hall on January 17, 2003. The concerto was commissioned by Tommy Dorsey who played it in 1945 at the New York City Center, with Leopold Stokowski conducting.

Media coverage of the life and work of Nathaniel Shilkret has included several hundred articles in periodicals appearing over a span of more than a century. The coverage was extensive enough that much of his life story has appeared in print in periodicals.

Available for the first time here is his story exactly as he wrote it.

CHAPTER 1
A CHILD PRODIGY

Any one who denies the precociousness of the coming generation in music would find his opinions refuted if he ever heard the Boys' Symphony Orchestra of New York rendering some of the most difficult classics with the freedom and verve of the master musician. ... At the present time there are seventy-five or more who compose the orchestra, and their ages range from that of the clarinet phenomenon Master Nathan Schildkraut, who is scarcely nine years old, to the leader, who has not yet reached his majority.

—**Frank Merritt**, *New York Herald, April 6, 1902*

It was during the tour of 1952–1953 with Miss Cornelia Otis Skinner of her one-woman production of *Paris '90* that she suggested my writing a book of my many experiences in the music business.

While traveling we often had a few hours of riding on the railroad from one city to another, and, with time on our hands, I related many of the happenings in my career as a musician, composer and conductor. With Miss Skinner and myself, there was a young trumpet player, Ronnie Modell, a seventeen-year-old lad, hefty, naive and jolly, who would ask one question after another.

Ronnie was a bright lad from Bronx, New York, with a couple of years experience in the Catskill Borscht circuit and a retentive memory—to hear him imitate and remember all the jokes of well-known comedians was hilarious and highly entertaining.

Personally I did not enjoy answering his many questions like, "How did you start? How was Victor Herbert or Sousa or Toscanini," etc. But Ronnie in his young and eager manner was not easily put off. His uncle was one of the best symphonic trumpeters and Ronnie was anxious to emulate his success.

One day Miss Skinner said, "Nat, why don't you write a book? It would make interesting reading." At first I pooh-poohed the idea, and finally she said, "Nat, tape your stories, and I'll help you put the book together."

Well, it was not until 1956 that I started writing down my stories and, after a few weeks, asked Miss Skinner for her help. By this time she was very busy writing a play that she would star in, and so I laid my notes aside. I found writing easier than taping.

Time went by and now, being retired, I have collected my notes and I hope to put them in shape. Whether it will become a book or not does not interest me too much. I have had many requests for my stories and often debated whether or not to finish them. To me my long association with the music business is like a dream.

Very seldom do I think of the past unless I meet someone who brings up names and incidents. I never kept a diary. Questions like "Were you happy during the many years you worked so hard?" never occur to me as I analyze it. I must have liked my work, otherwise I would not have worked so hard to achieve the success I gained.

Here are some of the questions asked by Ronnie: *"How and when did your first engagement begin?"*

My father was a musician who emigrated to America about 1885— music was his life. He was also a natural teacher, and his likes and dislikes for people depended upon their musical interests and musical talent. Whoever (especially young folks) came into contact with him had to study music.

I was about four and a half years old when he just put a clarinet in my hands and said, "Practice." He would sit with me for hours each day as I blew and blew. I must have been a dumb kid, because I really liked practicing the clarinet—at the age of six I was pretty good at it.

One day he took me to the Grand Street Theater on the east side of New York City and had me play for the musicians. One of the men, Mr. Gruenberg (father of Louis Gruenberg, composer of the opera *Emperor Jones*) listened to me and immediately brought me to the dressing room of the great Jewish actor Jacob Adler.

The play that night was *King Lear*, and, after Adler listened to Gruenberg's enthusiastic report of my ability, he summoned the cast to his dressing room and announced that I would appear and play a clarinet solo. I was assigned to an actress who would be my stage mother.

The Jewish version of *King Lear* did not follow Shakespeare's play too closely. However, the basic idea of the drama was more or less kept. The opening act was a banquet with King Lear at the head of the table, with about twenty actors seated around the table.

For a while there was lively conversation and I hardly understood what they were saying—they spoke Yiddish. In the meantime my stage mother was feeding me candy, nuts, and dates—the fruits were all made of wax. Two things bothered me: one, would I be able to play my clarinet solo with my mouth full of food, and, two, how could I escape the kisses from the women with their heavily painted lips and the men with their beards? After a while King Lear got up and announced my solo.

I was placed near the front headlights in the middle of the stage and played my solo, *Carnival of Venice Variations*. Lots of applause ... and then came the kisses and hugging by the actors. Finally I sat down and, not understanding their rapid conversation, I wondered what my father would think of my performance.

Just about that time King Lear leaped up, banged the table, and then upset the table and all the food—his face distorted with anger—yelling for everyone to get out. My stage mother tried to drag me with her, but I resisted, because I wanted to find my clarinet. I found myself alone with King Lear yelling in a terrifically loud voice.

For a moment I thought that I had done something to anger him. I found my clarinet, quickly ran and picked it up and literally flew off the stage. That, Ronnie, was my first musical experience.

Ronnie: *"What was your next experience?"*.

Playing for Victor Herbert. This was about 1896 at the Musical Headquarters of the Union at 89th Street and 3rd Avenue. It was the beer garden of the Ruppert's Beer. Between 2 p.m. and 3 p.m. musicians met there to receive their job assignments. By almost mutual agreement various groups had fixed spots for symphonic musicians, society works, weddings and affairs of different nationalities, etc.

My father brought me to the union and, with a few musicians around, asked me to open my case and play the clarinet. This I did, and then a fine looking gentleman came over and lifted me onto the bell of a tuba. I played, and, when I was through, he patted me on the cheek and then gave me a silver dollar—the first I had ever seen.

When he left, one of the musicians said to my father, "Do you know who that was? That was the famous musician Victor Herbert."

A few weeks later, a son of my father's friend, Willie Feder, asked me to come with him to a rehearsal on the Bowery. I went with him and there were about seventy boys in an orchestra. They were called the New York Boys' Symphony Orchestra and the leader was Mr. Alfred Pinto—a young man of twenty-two, a pretty good musician and conductor, and a flashy harpist.

Pinto had formed the boys' orchestra—ages six to ten—from East Side Jewish and Italian families. There were lots of talented boys. Mr. Pinto placed me on a table and I played for him. He quickly made me his first clarinetist and soloist. This orchestra lasted six years.

Ronnie: *"Were you born in New York?"*

Yes, but when I was three years old father decided to send my mother, my older brother Lew and myself to Austria to a small village near Lemberg [now Lvov, in the Ukraine]. We stayed there about one year, and I remember clearly my experience there.

Grandfather, on my father's side, was a learned man for the village and made a living as a professional letter writer and teacher. I remember the police, or gendarmes, with their capes and shiny glittering red, white and blue uniforms; a large black dog that jumped on me and scared me; the wagon load of misfits that were hauled away every half year—the diseased, the half-wits and the criminals; and the little boys with their wide slits in their pants on the back, and we used to tease them, pulling their long shirts. American trousers' front buttons slits were safe—they called us Americansky's. They often pulled our ties in retaliation. I also remember the hush of an evening during the sacred holidays; and the brutal and ignorant malameds (teachers) of Hebrew. Thank heavens for the change in today's educated young American rabbis now teaching young children Hebrew.

Above all I recall my good-looking aunt and her barber-doctor in their clean, tiled store. There, anything from a serious illness to a toothache was dispensed with in quick fashion—for most troubles, blood sucking by beetles was administered; for tooth troubles, the tooth was simply yanked out.

As a result of my first experience, my trust in older folks was destroyed: One day when one of my baby teeth became loose, my uncle asked me to open my mouth and said, "Let me put a thread around it so you can play with it." As soon as this was done, he backed up an said, "Come to me." In the meantime someone had opened the door and fastened the other end of the thread to the doorknob. As I walked toward my uncle someone closed the door, and, to my amazement, my tooth was yanked out. It didn't hurt, but I never forgot the resentment that I had been fooled by the people I trusted.

My grandfather's gentle face that shone like the pictures of the patriarchs in the Bible still haunts me. My grandmother was made of a granite disposition, and we never crossed her path when we had done anything naughty. Finally, I remember the sickening trip back to America in some boat that wasn't much larger than a Staten Island ferry boat.

The next year or two is almost lost to me, except for Dad's practicing and teaching me the clarinet. Despite his fiery temper, Father was a good and patient teacher while you paid attention and did your work well. Father had the mid-European idea of children: you brought them up to earn money, so that in the parents' old age the children could support them. This was drilled into me as a child, and I never forgot it.

Ronnie: *"Tell me more about the seventy-two boy orchestra."*

Well, as I said, we lasted six years. The first year we played concerts and vaudeville acts in New York on Saturdays and Sundays—two shows in the afternoons in two different vaudeville houses and two more in the evenings. The first year I received $5 per concert, or $40 for eight shows. The second year I received $10 per show, or $80 for all the shows.

The next year we were engaged for eight weeks in a New Orleans fair. It was quite an open city, to let loose seventy-two boys ranging from the age of seven to the age of twelve. One must remember that some of the boys were pretty tough East Side boys, and their comments were not for the ears of the good boys. One year with that gang and the nice boys who would walk away when they heard "damn" were seasoned regulars. Anyway we were booked at the fair and gave two performances a day. Outside of breaking every window in the French hotel, greasing the floor so that the fat hotel manager slipped down a flight of stairs, and pouring cold water on the beds of the early sleepers, we got into very little trouble for a while.

Some of the society folks took a fancy to the soloists. A violinist, a cellist, a pianist and I were invited to their parties. We were dined, made a fuss over, and received money for our entertainment.

About the seventh week we really got into trouble. We would start our afternoon concerts at about 1:30, play for about one hour, and then have an intermission of a half hour to allow the people to visit the other sites—the zoo, the exhibits, etc.

During the intermission a few of the boys went to the zoo and forced open the cages of the birds, snakes, pigs, etc. About fifteen minutes into our concert we heard screaming, and there was confusion in the audience. The animals had entered the concert spot, and with snakes crawling and pigs running there was terrific confusion.

That did it! We were packed up and sent back to New York in two cars—no sleepers, and that ended our first trip. I still have my letter to my parents. I received $15 per weekend for board, and I apologized for spending fifty cents a week for laundry and candy.

The next year a very nice man, Mr. Pinter, booked the orchestra for a tour into a few southern cities, starting in Washington, D.C., then Raleigh, Atlanta, Richmond and other cities. We would advertise the concerts by marching in the streets like a circus.

We lasted about four weeks, and it was quite a tour. In Atlanta we were invited to a state prison, and some of the older boys got together, and, for two dollars, had a woman do a strip tease act. They were apprehended and were ordered out of the city.

In Richmond, Virginia, right at the Capitol Park, a tough gang of kids hit me with a large melon, right on my silk blouse. (When I think of it now, I don't blame them: me with my Little Lord Fauntleroy suit.) Well, we were pretty rough, and that started a fight. We finally chased them as far as the river, and then we returned to the park of the Capitol. The next morning the paper headlines read, THE YANKEES TAKE RICHMOND AGAIN.

There were other exciting incidents, but finally we landed at Raleigh. Mr. Pinter, manager of the tour, informed Mr. Pinto that he had lost $10,000 to date and wanted to call the trip off. He gave Mr. Pinto enough money to bring the boys back to New York. Mr. Pinto took this to heart and became ill. He was confined to bed for three days.

With seventy-two boys at $3.50 a day for three days, Pinto settled the bill and found himself flat broke. Here he was in a strange city with seventy-two boys and no money—what was he to do? Somehow help came and arranged for us to go to Norfolk, where the Old Dominion Steamship Line would sail us home with the proviso that we must entertain their passengers with a concert.

The boys, having missed breakfast and lunch, were ravenously hungry. We entered the dining room of the ship, and the boys ate double and triple portions of meat, ice cream, etc. We finally started the concert with the *William Tell Overture.* Just as we got to the storm music, we hit Cape Hatteras, and in about five minutes only four boys were left out of the seventy-two. Mr. Pinto was practically carried to his room, and that was the end of the concert.

The next morning we were up bright and early and cured of our seasickness. We started a new game. Outside of the soloists, the boys wore uniforms and caps. The game was to see how many hats we could grab and throw overboard.

We landed in New York on the West Side, and all of us lived on the East Side. Mr. Pinto had just twenty-five cents left, enough to take the four soloists and himself on the Delancey Street horsecar for the four mile drive. The rest of the boys had to walk home through rough neighborhoods, dragging their instruments and baggage. Imagine the poor boys with the basses and drums!

I finally got home and sat down on the stoop of our tenement house and cried because I had not received my $20 week's pay. Mother came along some time after and took me home.

By the next year the New York Boys' Symphony Orchestra became well known. We were engaged for the Pittsburgh Fair, Willow Grove Park, in Philadelphia and for other places—the very attractions that also engaged Sousa's Band, Victor Herbert's Orchestra, and Nahan Franko. We had finally made the grade. There were two performances a day, and I played two solos each day.

At Willow Grove Park (a five-cent car ride from Philadelphia) we played for 20,000 people at each performance. My salary was $50 per week and board. We played in various places for years during the summer months.

The last season must have been very trying for Mr. Pinto. The boys were growing up, and the half fares on the train were getting harder to obtain. Putting on short trousers and standing on their knees didn't always work.

I was about twelve years old then and advertised as a nine-year-old wonder. It was summertime, and I had another job at Bergen Point, on the Kill-van-Kull River in New Jersey. It was a steak and seafood restaurant, and the orchestra was a four-man group. The leader was a young eighteen-year-old fellow with a silken mustache who had engaged me for the whole season, and, when Mr. Pinto asked me to join him for the Willow Grove Park engagement, the young leader insisted that I finish the season.

Mr. Pinto insisted upon having me, and finally the young leader asked me what Pinto was paying me. I answered $50 dollars a week and board. He then said, "If Mr. Pinto will pay me $50 a week and board, I'll let you go." Mr. Pinto agreed, but wanted the young fellow to shave off his mustache. He was too fond of his mustache and refused, and so Pinto engaged him and put him on the last violin stand, so that the audience could not see a boys' orchestra with one of the boys with a mustache.

By this time Mr. Pinto's health was not too good, and the orchestra was disbanded. It had been a wonderful six years' experience—our playing had been very good, sometimes too enthusiastic, and the boys had become good orchestra players. Some of the boys went to Europe, and others entered into the union and became professionals.

In my Bergen Point summer engagement I learned to swim and row, and, since our dinner music started at 6:00 p.m., I had all of the daytime to become a proficient swimmer. One night after our 1:00 a.m. closing session, a friendly waiter asked me to row him to Staten Island, which was about one and a half miles from our restaurant. We landed on Staten Island about 1:30 a.m., and then the waiter visited one bar after another. We finally entered a diner near the river.

As we finished a dish, he threw it in the river. He paid the bill and then the cook noticed the missing dishes. He grabbed a knife and ran for us. Luckily, we managed to shove off before he reached us.

The trip across the river took us over three hours. By this time he was drunk, and insisted upon jumping into the water; and when I asked him if he could swim he replied, "*No.*" At least a dozen times I held him back from jumping and pleaded with him. We finally arrived at our restaurant dock about 5 a.m. Luckily the boat was flat bottomed and solid. Otherwise he would have drowned. By this time the proprietor and three musicians had notified the police. It was a nightmare trip.

During my New York Boys' Orchestra engagement, and especially in New York, I was harassed by the Gerry Society (a society for the prevention of cruelty to children).[1] They were ready to prevent me from performing, and so I was kept in a dressing room until I was ready to play my solo. If the officer stood in the left wing of the steps, I was ushered into and through the right wing. Once on the stage the officer let me perform.

Ronnie: *"When did you start to play the piano?"*

I would say at the age of seven. My older brother studied with two fine teachers, and I would go along and watch the lessons. I would then go to the piano at home, and practice without father knowing. One day Lew [my older brother], who wanted to play baseball, told me to take his place—and for a few weeks I took the lessons. I learned to play the piano without my father knowing it.

Father supplied pianists for dancing school teachers and when he came home one late afternoon tired and exhausted, there being no telephone available in those days, he had trotted from one house to another looking for a pianist.

I worked up enough courage to say, "Dad, send me." Dad said, "I need a pianist, not a clarinetist." I told him that I could play the piano. Father looked at me with a perplexing look, but, being stuck, said, "All right, go to the Clinton Street dancing school at 8 p.m." I arrived at the dancing school a bit frightened and not too confident. You can imagine the look on the dancing teacher when I told him that I was the pianist—a little fellow seven years old.

There was nothing he could do but let me play. He had about fifty pupils, and the lessons were started with the usual easy steps: 123, 123, 123, 123. I had watched my brother, and I was able to play simple rhythms and chords. This went on for one hour, and it was the longest period I had ever played.

After about a five-minute rest I was asked to play a waltz. I had never played a waltz, but of course I knew what a waltz was. I therefore had to make up some waltz melody, and so I started. However I never expected it to last over an hour. My fingers became numb, and my back was terribly painful—luckily a young girl noticed my distress and went over to the dancing master and asked him to give me a rest period. I was given an ice cream soda and received seventy-five cents for my night's effort. Later on my father learned about my substituting for my brother's lessons, and Father did not spare the rod—Lew never tried that again.

I lived on the East Side of New York until I was fifteen years old, and then we moved into our own house in the Bushwick section of Brooklyn. You asked how was living on the East Side—sometimes called the Ghetto.

My recollection is rather pleasant, and there was no lack of food nor lack of fun. Although, as a musician, I saw many wealthy people and lots of rich youngsters, it never occurred to me that I was underprivileged.

There were gang fights between the Jewish, Irish and Italian kids. Knives were not used, just stones and fists. One way to stay out of trouble was to remain in your own neighborhood.

The teachers in school were splendid, and we respected them and their wishes. The parents, especially the Jews, had one great ambition—to have their children educated—boys to become doctors, lawyers, or musicians; girls, teachers.

Popular light books were Frank Merriwell, Horatio Alger, and Nick Carter detective stories. Our teachers recommended the classics. There was plenty of fun in the streets for us as youngsters: street games, open air gyms, Clark House recreational settlements, plus chess, checkers and dominoes. The most important: respect and even fear for our teachers and parents. Strict supervision did not hurt us; we rather expected it.

NOTE

1. Thomas [1964] describes "Elbridge T. Gerry, whose name became an epithet to child performers and their parents. He was a New York lawyer and self-appointed guardian of public morals whose Gerry Society crusaded against cruelty to children. Gerry considered the theater too sinful and exploitive of children, and he persuaded lawmakers in New York and elsewhere to forbid the use of children on the stage until they were sixteen—eighteen in some cities." Fred Astaire, and his sister Adele, were child performers who shared Nat Shilkret's problem with the Gerry Society.

CHAPTER 2

TEENAGE TO MARRIAGE

CLARINETS

Levy, H.

Schildkraut, N.

Gerhardt, J.

WASSILY SAFONOFF, ... *Conductor*

"THUS SPAKE ZARATHUSTRA,"

.... RICHARD STRAUSS

It will be well at the outset for those who wish to get at the poetic purposes of the composer in this colossal piece of programmatic music, to note the full title of the work. It is this: *"Also Sprach Zarathustra:" Tondichtung (frei nach Friedrich Nietsche) für grosses Orchester, von Richard Strauss, Op. 30.* That is: " 'Thus Spake Zarathustra:' A Tone-poem (freely after Friederich Nietsche) for large Orchestra, by Richard Strauss, Op. 30." The large orchestra is composed of [34 violins, 14 violas, 12 cellos, 12 basses,] 1 piccoloflute, 3 flutes, (the third interchangeable with a second piccolo,) 3 oboes, 1 English-horn, 3 clarinets, 1 bass-clarinet, 3 bassoons, 1 double-bassoon, 6 horns, 4 trumpets, 3 trombones, 2 bass-tubas, kettle-drums, bass-drum, cymbals, triangle, [and 2 harps.]

—Program of the Philharmonic Society

of New York, *November 13 and 14, 1908*

10

THE BARON

My next engagement was with a Hungarian or Gypsy orchestra leader—
The Baron! He was a fair violinist, with an imposing figure, monocled and
clicking heels, whose main attractions were women and champagne.

We opened in a new and plush hotel in Atlantic City as a Gypsy orchestra featuring the violin, cimbalom and clarinet. The Baron played like
a jazz-extemporized player. We used no music since all the playing was
done by heart. The Baron could not read music: he learned American
tunes by having one of the violinists play the music while he put his feet
in hot water, repeated what he heard, and in a short while memorized the
melodies. With his repertoire of standard music and American tunes he
was able to perform hundreds of melodies in his Gypsy style.

I had a good ear and plenty of technique, and in a short while became
a professional Gypsy clarinet player.

We arrived at Atlantic City and walked into the palatial hotel in grand
style. The Baron knew how to milk his audience—he would walk up to a
group and play soulful melodies, and, of course, being a titled personality,
click his heels, kiss the ladies' hands and salute the gentlemen.

His experienced eyes picked the most likely group that looked ripe for
a tip. If the money received was large enough, he would hang around a
little longer. If the tip was small, he would quickly turn around and walk
to another group. He was so adept from years of experience that he never
offended his clientele.

However after four weeks he met his Waterloo! One night at about
12:55 a.m. (five minutes before our quitting time) a gentleman came over
and requested a number for one of the ladies in his party. The Baron,
not understanding English, asked one of the violinists to inform him what
the fellow wanted, in a rather vulgar German expression. The Baron said,
"Tell the jerk to get lost"—we started to pack up. The gentleman offered
to pay the Baron anything reasonable if we would stay for one hour. The
Baron's answer was, "Pack up and tell him to go to the devil." Evidently
the Baron had a date with some lady, and, with a contemptuous look at
the man, walked out. Unfortunately the gentleman was the brother of the
hotel owner and understood the German language and had taken in the
Baron's derogatory remarks.

The next morning all our luggage was moved to the back of the hotel,
and we were told to leave the place. Well, we had come in the front entrance,
and now we were standing in the back of the hotel. Counting our cash, we
had just $28—not enough to ride back to New York.

Most of the men were married and sent their monies home—the Baron
had spent all his money on wine and women. I sent my money home.

However the Baron did not seem worried. He looked around, and across the street there was a large saloon. He picked up his violin case and said, "Follow me." I stayed out and the rest went along with him. One half hour later they came out, and they had collected enough money to get home.

A little later I was offered a job at the famous Cafe Boulevard—Twelfth Street and Second Avenue—one of the finest restaurants in New York. They imported prominent Gypsy orchestras from Vienna, and they commanded the highest pay in New York, besides getting over $100 each per week in tips.

It was the rendezvous of society, where great musicians, well-known actors, writers, and opera stars assembled. For some unknown reason the orchestra had not brought a clarinetist or a bass player. My reputation with the Baron's orchestra made me a candidate for the job, and I was asked to join this splendid group. Unluckily I had joined the musicians' union, and, since the Cafe Boulevard was nonunion, I refused the engagement. As for the bass player, Mr. Pasternack, who played piano and viola, accepted the job. Although he had never played the bass, with his quick ear and adaptability he made good. Later he became a conductor at the Metropolitan Opera House, and later Red Seal conductor for the Victor Talking Machine Company.

SHORT STORIES

There was a stocky five-foot boy with Pinto's orchestra who was with us from the age of seven to the age of twelve. He was a trumpet player and his Italian-English expressions were hilarious. His real name was Di Blassi, but we referred to him as "I Tolsch" because he always started his sentences with "I Tolsch," which could mean "I told," "he told," "you told," etc.

Let us skip sixty-five years to 1965. One day in the subway in Long Island I saw a group from an Italian family, and standing in the middle was I Tolsch, and I heard him say to the children, "I Tolsch," practically looking the same as I remembered him. I couldn't believe my eyes.

I walked to the group, and I heard, "I Tolsch you kids to keep together." I was going to speak to him, but just then the train came along and they got on. Evidently he had stuck to his early environment, doing Italian weddings and other jobs for over sixty-five years. I had never run into him during my many years of conducting.

Father played in a beer garden on 125th Street. He took me there, and I saw great wrestling matches. They were not timed TV matches. Sometimes one match took over two hours before a winner was declared.

Pinto's ending was sad. After giving up the boys' orchestra he became harpist for the Ziegfeld Follies shows. One day a new heavy curtain was used, and it swept across the orchestra pit, catching Pinto's fingers. He lost the use of two fingers, and from then on he had to struggle to keep alive.

As I mentioned before, I joined the union. I was fifteen years old, but they were not too strict about ages, and I passed the examination easily.

There was a story about the great cellist Leo Schultz. He came from Germany to join the New York Philharmonic Orchestra, and, when he was told that he had to be examined by the union committee, he thought that was ridiculous and said so. But a rule is a rule, and he was forced to attend the examination board. The committee then proceeded to put a very difficult solo piece written for the violin in front of Schultz.

Realizing their perversity, he contemptuously looked at the examination committee members and proceeded to play the violin solo with the greatest of ease. He not only became the cellist of the symphony orchestra but was picked by the New York Conservatory of Music (directed by Mrs. Thurber) to take the place vacated by the famous Bohemian composer Antonin Dvořák. I had a free scholarship at the conservatory and played in the orchestra conducted by Leo Schultz.

The day after I joined the union I went to the union headquarters, and I was accosted by a man who was a friend of my father—his name was Hyman, leader of the elite Jewish affairs. He asked me if I was busy Saturday night. I said, "No." He then stuck his thumb in his waist coat and stuck four fingers out. He gave me the address, and I played the wedding for him.

Monday afternoon he met me and gave me four dollars. I refused the money and said, "You owe me seven dollars; that is the union price for a wedding." He asked me if I had not seen his four fingers when he offered me the job. I told him that I did not notice his fingers, and he still owed me seven dollars." And so began a week of bargaining. He raised his offer to $4.25, then $4.50, and finally we were up to $6—by this time he was in tears, pleading with me to accept his offer. He said I was depriving his children of food, but finally I received the $7, while his tears were streaming down his beard. That was the last I saw of him.

VICTOR HERBERT

Almost immediately after, I was asked to audition for Victor Herbert for his Saratoga summer engagement at the Grand Hotel. I arrived at my appointed time and found three other clarinet players to be auditioned.

It seemed that the contractor for Herbert had been called down for engaging old-fashioned clarinet players—the contractor then told Mr. Herbert to engage a player without seeing. Herbert said, "Alright—I'll stay in the next room, keep my door open, and I'll be able to hear the player without seeing him."

The four of us played for Herbert, and he dismissed the other three clarinet players. When the contractor brought me into the room Herbert exclaimed, "What is this? I am not engaging a kindergarten!" Then, seeing my disappointed face, he said to me, "Boy, haven't I seen you before?" I answered, "Yes, I was about six years old, and I played for you at the union headquarters and you handed me a silver dollar." He said, "I remember, and, me boy, you are engaged."

A Mr. Lund, who looked like Herbert and had his mannerisms, conducted the thirty-five piece orchestra, and Victor Herbert came up often and conducted. One Sunday he asked me to play a solo. I selected von Weber's *Concertino*, and everything was running smoothly, when suddenly one of my top keys broke, and I could not get a sound out of the instrument. Mr. Herbert understood my dilemma immediately and whispered, "Make believe you are playing; I'll get you out of your troubles, me boy." He found a place to stop within ten seconds, and the audience, not aware of my difficulties, applauded. I was broken hearted, and after the concert I cried.

Herbert soothed me and took me out for a sandwich and milk—he was sympathetic and kind. A week later he had me play another solo, and this time there was no mishap. A dozen years later, when I was connected with the Victor Talking Machine Company as one of the staff conductors, I had charge of his recordings. He would let me take his place, and he would sit in the engineer's booth. I would imitate his style and mannerisms, and he would get a kick out of my results.

When he passed away I was allowed to finish some of his recordings with the permission of his family. I also did a few Sousa Band recordings. I absorbed their styles.

MODEST ALTSCHULER

My next engagement was with the Russian Symphony under Modest Altschuler. He introduced America to Russian composers and artists who were practically unknown. We performed for the first time in America compositions by Rimsky-Korsakov, Moussorgsky, Tchaikovsky, Rachmaninoff, Scriabin, Borodin and many others. The soloists were Mischa Elman,

Josef Lhevinne, Rachmaninoff, Safanov and quite a few more.

Modest Altschuler, besides being a splendid conductor, was a dedicated and natural developer of young talent—especially young American instrumentalists. It was due to his help that, for the first time, young American players ripened into great symphonic musicians.

He invited young men to his home and rehearsed them singly and in groups. One day I was at his house with three other players rehearsing a symphonic poem by Scriabin. Standing near us was a young man with the most soulful and sensitive face—he reminded me of some artist's conception of Christ. He never uttered a word, and we were not introduced to him.

As we finished the rehearsal Modest's brother Jacob Altschuler (manager of the orchestra) walked out with the young man, who seemed embarrassed. When Jacob returned he told Modest, "I asked him to meet me later, and he seemed to hesitate. I asked him the reason, and he told me that all the money he had was ten cents—not enough for carfare."

We also played for the great ballerina Pavlova and her partner Mordkin [1910].

Modest Altschuler, when on a tour, liked to talk to his audience despite his broken English. Often his brother Jacob told him not to speak, but he could not resist the urge. Here is a sample of his speech concerning the third movement of the *Scheherazade Symphonic Suite*: "Ladies and gentlemen, my concertmaster will play the *Scheherazade* beautiful melody on his violin." He would have his violinist stand up, and then he would say, "Here is lovely Scheherazade, a little fat and not so beautiful, but he will make you understand her story by his wonderful tone," etc. We often got a lot of laughs by imitating him.

At a performance of *Midsummer Night's Dream*, the play started with a very low note played by the large and clumsy contrabassoon. There was no music for the contrabassoon in the overture. The cue for the actors to come out was the low contrabassoon note.

We were a bunch of young players seeking to have some fun. We pulled out the bottom of the contrabassoon and kicked it to the other side of the pit. Altschuler gave the downbeat for the bassoonist, but nothing came out. After six downbeats some other player blew a low note, and away went the performance. This sounds rather tame, but it is far from being innocuous. Think of Modest Altschuler's feelings, the stage manager, the actors and the musicians—a fifteen-second wait can feel like an hour.

The poor bassoonist could not explain the disappearance of part of his instrument. We, of course, kept our mouths shut and looked innocent. We acted like angels when Altschuler demanded to know who had removed the lower part of his instrument.

I also played with Arnold Volpe's orchestra [founded in 1904].

OTHER ENGAGEMENTS

Besides the two orchestras mentioned above I played at the sedate Fifth Avenue Hotel at 23rd Street and Broadway. A Chinese ambassador was stopping at the hotel, and he came over to our orchestra, examining our instruments—he was interested in the drums. Finally he sat down and hit the small and large drums and cymbals lightly. He then asked us to play a march.

The large sitting room was filled up by old ladies, and suddenly the ambassador started to bang away at the drums as we played a stirring march. He kept that up for over an hour, and His Highness enjoyed it until we were exhausted.

This reminds me of a story of another Chinese diplomat. He was taken to a symphonic concert, and he listened through the whole program without expressing an opinion whether he liked it or not. After the concert he was asked what number or composition pleased him the most—he said the first number. The opening number was a long symphony, and his choice puzzled our attachés. After discussing his preference, he explained it was the music that brought out the conductor—his choice had been the tuning-up period!

My next summer was spent at Narragansett Pier, Rhode Island. We worked for the beautiful Casino and at social affairs at Newport for the 400; the outstanding lady was Mrs. Hanna, wife of the wealthy shoe manufacturer Hanna. She spent a fortune trying to crash into the Newport set, but never made it because she started as a town girl, working as a chambermaid at a Narragansett hotel.

She was a beautiful and gracious lady, and we musicians liked to please her. She was generous and gave two affairs every season for the town people of Narragansatt. Her son, about thirteen years old, always came along with champagne and two-dollar cigars for us when we played at the Hanna mansion. We would say, "Why do you hand us all these expensive things?" and he would reply, "I am studying to act like a millionaire."

The Casino was catered by the famous Sherry, New York, establishment. The white sandy beach of Narragansett Pier was a great place for swimming—the water smooth, just as a lake, and I could swim out three or four miles on a nice day.

Besides playing at the Casino evenings, we also played for the Polo Games mornings. The little kids hung around our brass section, annoying them by sucking lollipops near them.

THE NEW YORK PHILHARMONIC:
SAFANOV, MAHLER, AND REUTER

The following winter I played with the New York Philharmonic Symphony Orchestra. First, Safanov, the great Russian piano teacher was conductor, and he brought quite a few young musicians into the staid German-controlled orchestra. After Safanov came the famous conductor and composer Gustav Mahler. It was a great experience for me at such a young age to be part of an orchestra with such remarkable musicians. Unfortunately Mahler was a very sick man and did not stay long with us.

Safanov's first concert[1] ended up in confusion due to an accidental mishap. My clarinet partner had a habit of changing his reed often, and we were playing Richard Strauss's *Also Sprach Zarathustra*. We were up to the last six minutes before the ending when my partner decided to change his reed quickly. In his haste his clarinet hit the stand of the first horn player Dutschke and upset his music. Dutschke, with a healthy German swear word, dove for his music and upset the music of the second horn player. With three men trying to pick up their parts, the stand of the bassoon player was upset.

Had this happened near the beginning of the tone-poem most conductors would have stopped and started all over again. But now, with only four minutes left to finish, Safanov hoped that we would get straightened out; but this did not happen. The rest of the piece was played without the woodwind and the horn section—Safanov, with tears running down his beard and his face distorted with anger, kept wringing his hands as if he were in pain. He conducted without a baton.

We finally finished, and the audience applauded. Safanov, instead of acknowledging the applause, made a beeline for our section, ready to tear us to pieces, and he was powerful enough to do this. Never did ten men disappear as fast as we did.

The next morning I bought all the newspapers, and, believe it or not, we received rave notices for our performance.

Mahler, like some other conductors, doubled the woodwind players to compensate for the Beethoven scores in the loud parts because the modern orchestra used so many string players.

Mahler was brought from the Metropolitan Opera House, and when he consented to accept the New York Philharmonic he insisted upon hiring the great horn player Reuter, who had been with the Metropolitan Opera House. Reuter, taking advantage of Mahler's request, demanded what was for then an extravagant price: $300 per week, and he got it.

The reason for Mahler's insistence on Reuter was the difficulty of the horn parts in Wagner's music. Mahler was recognized as the outstanding

Wagnerian conductor. He was a strict disciplinarian, and at times could be almost sadistic.

There was a very fine old gentleman in our bass section who had been instrumental in doing a good deal to help the Philharmonic Orchestra. He was greatly respected by the other musicians and the sponsors.

We were rehearsing the *Ninth Symphony* of Beethoven, and there are some difficult bass passages in the score. As we came to a bass passage Mahler seemed displeased and remarked, "Let me hear each bass player play the passage alone."

For a bass player to play a long passage alone in front of a hundred musicians on such a clumsy instrument is very trying and a nervous experience. A young bass player will have the nerve to try, but for an old man who practically never has to perform as a soloist this could be a very excruciating and humiliating experience.

Mahler was not to be denied; nearly every twenty minutes he would stop the orchestra, turn to the old man [Levy], and ask him, "Are you still too nervous to play?" This went on all through rehearsal. The next morning Mahler walked in and, instead of rehearsing the orchestra, turned to the old bass player and said (in German), "Now that you have had all night to get over your nervousness and have had your rest, play the passage now." The poor bass player, who had practically never performed as a soloist, grew pale and then picked up his bass and walked out of the room. The rest of the men felt terrible, but in those days conductors were Czars, and there was no arguing or reasoning with them.

A few years later Reuter, the horn player, was engaged by Walter Damrosch on our spring tour. After Mahler left the Philharmonic Society, the board did not renew Reuter's contract. They thought his salary too steep, and, besides, the next conductor was not a great Wagnerian specialist. The Metropolitan Opera House did not engage him either, and so, as a freelance musician, he was used by Damrosch for a tour. Reuter was quite a character. His appearance was fantastic—covered with a large and heavy overcoat, a long black beard, and a beaver hat he looked like one of the Wagnerian villains, Hagen.

He never went to a hotel. He would wrap himself in his huge coat and fall asleep at the railroad station on some bench and stay there until the next morning and save the money allowed for lodging.

He ate all his meals in the baggage car. His food consisted of eggs, cheese, and German sausages. He would start with six soft eggs, prick a hole in the top, and then suck the contents. One day, as a joke, we hardboiled three of the eggs and watched Reuter from a distance. He put a hole in one egg and tried to suck it—of course it was one of the hard-boiled eggs. He tried another and the same thing happened. He picked up the third egg and banged it hard in anger. This happened to be one of the non-boiled eggs, and the contents splashed all over his beard and his clothes. He jumped up, mad as hell, and ran to Mr. Damrosch complaining of his treatment. Of course we all blamed it on the dealer who sold the eggs.

Another story was his feud with the Wagnerian conductor Hertz. It seemed that Hertz's criticism of Reuter caused a rift, and after that Reuter ignored Hertz—this went on for some time.

This annoyed Hertz, and at Christmas time he decided to talk the differences over and was even willing to apologize if that would help. Reuter lived about twenty miles from New York City, and he called his place Valhalla— named after Nibelungen, home of the heroes. Hertz took this trip during a storm, and after great difficulties managed to arrive at the Valhalla railroad station. He finally coaxed a horse-driven carriage man to drive him through a heavy snow.

He discovered Reuter sitting on a chair on his porch with a few fierce dogs near him. He shouted Christmas greetings to Reuter. The reply he received from Reuter was, "Get off my property or I'll set my dogs on you." Hertz knew Reuter meant what he said, and he beat a hasty retreat, got into the carriage, and drove away.

MORE ENGAGEMENTS

Besides my symphonic dates I worked at the Park Avenue Hotel with a leader-violinist, Henry Liff. He was an ordinary violinist and was bothered with an asthmatic condition. He would often lean his head on his violin, close his eyes and appear asleep. However, we noticed that he invariably fell asleep whenever he had to play a hard passage. Whether he did it deliberately or fell asleep on account of his condition we never found out.

Later I played at Shanley's restaurant on 42nd Street and Broadway. A young man, Manny Goldstein, was the violinist—he had been in the New York Boys' Orchestra. Manny had a nose that almost hit his mouth, and when we toured with Pinto we would hang a sign on Indian figures that stood in front of cigar stores that read "Goldstein, the Jewish Indian." If you ever saw one of these figures, it showed a nose that almost reached the mouth.

Knowing Manny, I made a dollar bet with one of the musicians that he (Manny) could hardly smell or taste food. The bet was made, and so we contrived to have Manny called to the telephone as soon as the soup was served for our meal.

The soup arrived, Manny was called to the phone, and in his absence we poured and put everything available in his soup—Tabasco sauce, ketchup,

Worcestershire sauce, two heaping spoonfuls of salt, pepper, horseradish, etc. Manny came back and ate his soup without blinking an eye. He finished, and we asked him how the soup tasted. He looked at us and said, "Why do you ask?"—I won my bet.

One winter I remember working in two places in New Jersey. One was at a company that telephoned music to homes and restaurants. To hear the music, people put on earphones. It had been successful in Budapest, and so a gentleman from Hungary thought it would become popular in Newark. It did not go over.

The other place was in East Orange at Thomas Edison's experimental studio. He was working on synchronizing sound with films, and after a while Edison was ready for a showing. The experiments were not adopted then—later on, about twelve or fifteen years later, radio and sound movies came.[2]

Edison was slightly deaf, and in his phonograph record company he judged his acceptance of artists by the looks of electric impulses—the more even or straighter the lines of impression the more he liked the artist. His voice artist was Anna Case; his violin choice Albert Spalding. They both had beautiful tones but were not too emotional in their interpretations. It is partly true that Edison slept very little, but when he grew tired he often laid down on a sofa to relax and perhaps snatch a few minutes of sleep.

The next two summer sessions I joined Arthur Pryor's band at Asbury Park and Willow Grove Park. Pryor had been trombone soloist with Sousa's band, and his tone and technique were so marvelous that, during a Sousa tour in continental Europe, trombone players repeatedly examined his slide trombone, looking for a Yankee trick, being sure that there were hidden valves inside of his instrument.

Pryor's tone was similar to Tommy Dorsey's velvet sound, although their fields were different. Pryor's band was a fine organization. While in Willow Grove Park, the band expanded to fifty men, and it was a fine ensemble. At Asbury Park we worked in a small shell, and the band was reduced to about thirty-five men. As a composer Pryor wrote a few popular pieces—one in particular was *The Whistler and His Dog* that had to be played at each concert as an encore.

As a clarinetist and piano player, I recorded for a few years with many phonograph companies: Victor, Columbia, Okeh, Pathé, Edison and many others. The Pathé Frère's studio never used an orchestra with strings—even their operatic artists were accompanied by band arrangements. Evidently they found recording strings unsatisfactory. Three prominent artists recorded frequently. The dramatic soprano Claudia Muzio recorded for Pathé. Their method puzzled me. I wondered why, on high notes, Muzio had to back up almost ten feet from the horn. If the recording instrument was so sensitive for her voice, why did they use a heavy band instead of the original score of a regular operatic orchestra?

Lucien Muratore, a splendid French tenor, also recorded—and then there was the famous beauty Lina Cavalieri. Although past her prime, she was really a magnificent looking lady and the wife of Muratore.

The contractor for Pathé was a flutist, Paul Heidelberg, who often bragged that he could save the company money because he, as a flute player, had such a tremendously loud tone that he could replace the four flutists used. We heard that so often that at last we started a rumor (of course, not true) that at a recording date Heidelberg had forgotten to engage a flute player for a Pathé date. The number to be recorded was the *William Tell Overture.* Since the flute was necessary for the overture Heidelberg was called up—he lived five miles from the studio in the Bronx. Heidelberg apologized for his mistake but said, "Don't worry. Leave the wire open; my tremendous tone will record even at this distance. Start the overture at noon. I'll be ready." At 12:00 sharp they started, and in a few minutes the manager called Heidelberg and asked, "Is your window open?"

"Yes"—"Then close your window; you are too loud!" The story got around, and after Heidelberg heard it he never bragged about his tremendous tone again.

In my playing days it was customary for most musicians to leave New York for two months during the summer. During a Catskill Mountain hotel engagement we ran into some unusual situations. The hotel was situated on top of a mountain, and we were a seven-man orchestra. The manager was a woman. During the winter we earned good salaries, while in the summertime our salary was not large, but we always stipulated that we must receive adequate rooms and the same food as the guests.

The first meal was served in the same room used to serve the help and was the same meal as was given to the help. We immediately threatened to quit, but the lady claimed that the only way we could cart our belongings from the top of the mountain was through her trucks. When we did not appear at our evening concert, the lady did not know how to act. Besides being the only entertainment available, we had the added endorsement of the guests, and so the lady manager agreed to our request.

Everything went off fine—the meals were good. On the third day Nat Finston, our concertmaster, insisted upon two desserts, claiming that this was his accustomed practice at home. We tried to argue with him, but he insisted, and so the leader, Sam Jospe, had to go back to the manager and ask for the extra dessert.

Luckily she gave in, and in our next meal we received ice cream and strawberry pie. We were so angry at Finston that when we received the pie and ice cream we gave it to him ... not on the table, but all over his tuxedo and face.

That started a real pie throwing contest, and the walls and floor became a mess. Why the manager didn't throw us out I'll never know. After that we finished the season without any more trouble, and we enjoyed ourselves greatly.

The next year we spent at Lake Champlain Hotel. Instead of living at the hotel we chose the boathouse on the lake. The hotel was about a half mile on top of a steep hill, and our first few runs up for meals and concerts exhausted us. By the second week we would make the run and feel exhilarated.

We had a bass player who, during the winter season, played at the Metropolitan Opera House. He was very proud of the bass section, and after listening to his bragging about their power for the fiftieth time we decided to deflate his ego. We picked a French edition by Tavan of Verdi's *Otello* that had a long solo for bass in the arrangement. Luckily, he had not played the arrangement.

We started the selection, and suddenly we came to the solo bass part, and Pfeiffer found himself playing a long one-minute solo. There we were in a large sitting room, with the ladies having their tea and expecting the orchestra to play soothing music. They heard Pfeiffer sawing away at a difficult passage—the longer he played, the more nervous he became, and he sounded like a man sawing at a tree.

The audience at first was surprised to hear their favorite orchestra sounding so terrible, and a few people walked over to us to watch the poor fellow struggling so hard. They started laughing at him, and that upset him entirely. Not only was he nervous, but he became angry at our joke, and his face was livid and his eyes blazed at us. We watched him and acted innocent, despite the fact that in his embarrassment he let out a few swear words at us.

Anyway, we accomplished our purpose. From then until the end of the season we did not hear his favorite words, "When we pitch into a bass passage, the audience thrills," etc.

There was a cellist with us, and on our first night we were all dressed in our tuxedos, ready to climb the steep hill to the hotel for our evening meal and concert. Going to the end of the boathouse the cellist said, "I wonder how deep the water is?" We obliged him by pushing him off the pier. When he came out he set the building on fire. We put it out quickly. The cellist finally put on a new suit, and we went to work. Yes, we were a bit crazy, but we had fun.

There was a man who worked in the kitchen and he loved music. Many nights after work he would come to the boathouse and talk about his experiences. He was a very intelligent man and had traveled to nearly every part of the world. He never stayed in one place more than a season—being a handyman as a cook, carpenter and electrician, he could always find work. In the middle of the season he started to bring down wonderful steaks, and we would start a fire and roast the meal. We furnished the vegetables and salads that we swiped from the hotel farms.

One day we invited the manager of the hotel for one of our barbecues. After the meal the manager asked, "Where did you get these fine steaks? They are as good as the ones we order from New York." We answered, "At Plattsburg."

"What store and what is the address?"

We told him that we did not know the address, and fortunately he did not pursue the subject.

During the next winter Richard Strauss came to America. Coming in the middle of the winter season, his effort to put together a fine orchestra for his concert tour became difficult, since most of the best men were tied up with established organizations.

There was a very fine bassoon player, Benjamin Kohon. He was asked to sign up with the Richard Strauss Orchestra and agreed—but on condition that his father (a poor player) must be hired as the third bassoonist to play contrabassoon—a very large and clumsy instrument. The contractor knew that the old man Kohon was not good, but finally gave in. Besides, the old man was practically the only man left in New York who owned a contrabassoon.

Young Kohon, knowing his father's insatiable habit of asking questions said, "Dad, please, please don't ask questions and especially to Dr. Richard Strauss. If he hears your terrible German accent, he'll really go berserk. So please control yourself and, if he doesn't bother you, keep quiet."

Richard Strauss struggled along with the poor orchestra trying to play his difficult music. At one point he stopped the men and just glared at them. There was complete silence for a few seconds.

Just then a timid voice was heard—it was the old man Kohon. He said, "Herr Doktor, entschuldingen sie mich (Sir doctor, pardon me)." I'll translate the rest. "Can you tell me whether the note in Bar 110 is a G# or F#?"

Strauss, hearing Kohon's poor German accent answered, "Play G#." Kohon blew the note, and, since it was the lowest note of the huge contrabassoon, it sounded like a Bronx cheer. Strauss then asked him to sound F#—again a Bronx cheer. Strauss then came with a remark that went the rounds in orchestral circles: "Take your pick."

THE DAMROSCH CONCERT TOUR

After four weeks of oratorios with singing societies doing Mendelssohn's

Elijah for the twelfth time with amateur conductors, we were really bored. As you know, oratorios are not really interesting for orchestral players, especially if repeated nightly.

So we in the woodwind section decided to have some fun. Sitting near the many sopranos and altos, we started to change our notes to confuse the singers. Barrère, the flutist, played his notes one tone higher; I played my notes one half tone lower; and the other woodwind players also changed their notes.

The ladies, hearing our wrong notes, were unable to keep on pitch— since most of the conductors had little experience with orchestras. We did it for three concerts, and the orchestra men got a great laugh out of this.

However, on the fourth night Mr. Damrosch happened to walk into the concert and listened to our joke. We did not notice him at first, but after a few minutes we spied him and saw the horrified look on his face. Of course, we stopped the nonsense quickly.

We were asked to go to Mr. Damrosch's room by the manager of the orchestra. Although the manager had enjoyed our false notes and laughed as loud as most of the men, he now appeared very angry in front of Mr. Damrosch. He suggested firing at least two of the young Americans, including me. He did not have the nerve to blame Barrère, the great flutist.

Mr. Damrosch did not call us down. In his wonderfully controlled manner he said, "Gentlemen, I regret what you have done—not only to me, but to music. We are down South playing in cities that have never heard a symphony orchestra, and our poor performance cannot spread the love of good music. I appeal to your fine musicianship, your fairness and your love of music, Gentleman. Good night." Of course we were ashamed of ourselves and we stopped the silly fun.

During another tour we played the same program in different cities. Our program consisted of several orchestra numbers and a fine singer, Miss Florence Hinkel, a soprano. The symphony we performed was the *Sixth (Pathétique) Symphony* by Tchaikovsky. In the first movement there are eight notes—four played by the clarinet and four by the bass clarinet, an octave lower. We had performed the work ten times in ten different cities. I played the first four notes, B, A, F#, D, and then I was followed by the same notes, an octave lower by the bass clarinet player.

The bass clarinet is fairly large and heavy, and so a sharp peg is attached to the bottom of the instrument, so that the player can place the peg on the floor. After the sixth or seventh performance I grew annoyed by the noise made by the old bass clarinet player who was extremely nervous. I could hear the clicking of his peg on the wooden floor as his hands shook.

I wondered why Mr. Damrosch, if he was sorry for the old man, did not let the bassoon player take the notes. So for the next two times I played my four notes very softly and very slowly, and all one could hear was knock, knock, knock! . . . at least a dozen times. Damrosch did not say anything the first time I did it. During the next concert I played my four notes so softly that even I could barely hear myself, and I slowed the tempo considerably. The orchestra men, hearing the repeated knocks, began to laugh. After the concert Mr. Damrosch called me into his room and said, "Mr. Shilkret, please play your four notes louder and a bit brighter. The old man is very nervous and," etc. By this time I felt sorry for the poor fellow and cut the nonsense out.

Ronnie: *"Would you have done it if Toscanini conducted?"*

I answered, "Toscanini would not let the old man play in the orchestra."

GEORGES BARRÈRE ENSEMBLE

After the Damrosch tour, Barrère, who created the Barrère Ensemble [in 1914] said, "One flute, one oboe, two clarinets, one bassoon and one horn went on the road playing mostly at colleges and for ladies clubs. Generally, we were very close to our audiences. Irving Cohen, a young oboe player, had taken the place of the greatest oboe player, Tabuteau." This produced a swelled head, and Irving started drinking hard liquor. Not being used to liquor, he was playing worse and worse, and he finally got on my nerves.

Cohen was squeaking often, and a squeak on the oboe sounds like a cat's cry when stepped on. I started to imitate him, and as soon as he squeaked I followed up with a squeak, confusing Cohen more. This made the rest of the men laugh. Barrère, knowing we were close to the audience, turned to me with tears on his beard and whispered, "Cut it out Shilkret; we can't play our instruments and laugh." My kidding stopped Irving Cohen from drinking; it did some good. In fact, Mr. Barrère warned him to stop drinking.

THE SADISTIC TRUMPETER

There was a trumpeter with the Damrosch orchestra who often annoyed me by playing notes one octave higher than written, just to show off. I never understood why Mr. Damrosch let him get away with that. He was German, and from his walk I guessed that, before coming to America, he had served in the German army. He was about five feet, nine inches tall, slightly bald, with pink cheeks and a little mustache curled à la Kaiser Wilhelm.

He bragged about his exercises and weight lifting, and, when he shook
hands with anyone, he would get a lot of pleasure in squeezing their hand
until he heard them wince. Another of his sadistic tricks was to walk up
to some little violinist, suddenly clench his fist, and bang down on the bow
arm. I saw him do it to a fairly old man, and the bow flew away. The poor
fellow could not play for a week without great pain.

One day he caught me unaware and hit me on my right arm—my arm
and fingers were numb, and I could hardly play the piano for my Damrosch
rehearsals—I was playing clarinet with the orchestra and rehearsing singers
and dancers at Mr. Damrosch's house at the piano. I was really angry, and
I told Heinrich that, if he did it again, I'd punch him on the lips so that he
would be unable to play trumpet. He laughed at me.

We were playing a concert at the Century Theater, and it was intermission time. Josef Hofman, the great pianist, was near the exit, quietly
talking to Mr. Damrosch. I was near them, admiring Hofman. Just then
in the corner of my eye I noticed Heinrich coming toward me with a closed
fist. I turned around quickly, and, with all my might, hit him smack on
his lips. He put his hand to his mouth, and, before he could recover, I ran
onto the stage.

He followed me and I ran across the stage, back of the stage, and then
near Hofman and Damrosch. By this time the orchestra men were entering
the stage to get ready for the second part of the program. Heinrich was
slowed down by the men and by many instruments. I finally got to the
front of the stage and stepped on the conductor's podium and grabbed the
baton. We were so close to the audience that Heinrich could do nothing
but glare at me, and I laughed at him, and in a few minutes the concert
began.

My blow did two things: First, it stopped Heinrich from showing off
with his high notes—in fact, he played second trumpet for at least a week.
Second, he never tried to hit me again, although he threatened me a couple
of times. Twenty years passed, and one day at a Victor recording Heinrich
was engaged in a band session. I saw him and asked, "How is your lip?"
He looked at me and did not answer. I noticed that he had lost his swagger
and acted with reduced arrogance. I never saw him after that day. I would
say that while I was with Damrosch, Heinrich was thirty years of age, which
would make him fifty when he played the Victor date.

THE WALDORF-ASTORIA HOTEL

The Waldorf-Astoria was almost a conservatory, rather than a hotel en-

gagement. The manager was Mr. Boldt and Oscar was the famous maî-
tre d'. There were thirty-five men engaged steadily for the dining rooms.
In the Rose Room, Caruso records were played, with our group following
the music of the record.

Week nights there was a concert program from 9 p.m. to 10 p.m. Sundays the orchestra was enlarged to fifty men, and the concert was played
from 9 p.m. to 11 p.m. The extra men were the finest instrumentalists from
symphony orchestras. Mr. Joseph Knecht, a fine musician, was the conductor. There were six composers in the orchestra who would hear their new
compositions performed often. Practically all the young men were students
and developed into splendid symphonic players.

At the night session from 11 p.m. to 1 a.m., we played chamber music.
Being a student at CCNY, I studied my books during that session.

In my last years at the Waldorf, I was a very busy lad indeed. I awoke at
7:30 a.m. and attended special school classes from 8:00 a.m. to 9:30 a.m. My
schedule continued: 10:00 a.m. to 12:30 p.m. at Mr. Damrosch's New York
Symphony rehearsal playing clarinet; 12:45 p.m. to 1:45 p.m. at Damrosch's
home; 2:00 p.m. at various recording studios; dinner at 6:00 p.m.; 7:00 p.m.
to 8:30 p.m. at the Waldorf; 8:45 p.m. to 10:50 p.m. playing at a theater;
back to the Waldorf from 11:00 p.m. to 1:00 a.m.; 1:30 a.m. at an open
air park doing exercises on the bars and running one or two miles; home
studying at 2:30 a.m. until 4:00 a.m.; a short nap and up at 7:30 a.m.

The union prices were not large at the time. However, living was fairly
cheap. I earned about $150 per week. During 1909 to 1914 that was pretty
fair money—with Damrosch about $55, the Waldorf about $50, the Theatre
$28, and recording and extra jobs, the rest.

Damrosch had imported five French musicians: Barrère, flutist; Tabuteau, oboist; Leroy, clarinetist; Mesnard, bassoonist; and a French horn
player (I have forgotten his name). The union fined him $10,000 for that,
but he made up the fine, because the Frenchmen were contracted via franc
standards for two years. It worked well for both, because the men became
well known, and they were able to interest many young American pupils.
They produced many of the best American instrumentalists. Leroy and I
became great friends, and I studied with him. He was a meticulous teacher,
and I gained a lot being with him.

At one time he was engaged by the famous Flonzaley Quartet to play
Brahms' *Quintet*: two violins, a viola, a cello, and a clarinet. Before performing the work for the public they had over one hundred rehearsals on
the work—Leroy rehearsed fifty-seven times with them. When he was busy
I took his place.

Their performance was so perfect that one could almost know when
they breathed. It would be impossible to duplicate their superb achieve-
ment today. First of all, because of the cost of rehearsals, and, second,

because we do not have the time and patience today.

At the Waldorf, as I mentioned before, our concert session was from 9 p.m. to 10 p.m. A splendid trumpeter, Max Schlossberg, played with us. He also played with Arturo Toscanini for the New York Philharmonic Orchestra. Schlossberg, a handsome, six-foot-two, black-haired fine figure of a man, was a very quiet and reserved individual. There was a story about him and Toscanini worth repeating. As I mentioned, Schlossberg was a calm and reserved individual, but he was not a man to take an insult lightly.

At one of Toscanini's rehearsals the trumpet section (three men) had to play a high C together. One of the trumpet players—possibly Schlossberg—cracked on the note. Toscanini turned to them and called them "pigs," in Italian—one of the expressions he used frequently when he was angry. Schlossberg slowly got off his seat and walked over to the podium with his trumpet. Then he blew about eight high C's right into Toscanini's ear. When he finished, he walked back to his seat.

The orchestra men were amazed and startled. This display from such a mild-tempered man! They were sure that Toscanini would order him out of the room. However, Toscanini admired Schlossberg and, no doubt, had to decide what to do with this affront. Besides having respect for Schlossberg, Toscanini knew that Schlossberg was head of the orchestral board and greatly loved by all the men.

It was a great decision to be made by a gifted conductor. Well, he made it: He rapped his baton and continued the rehearsal. The next morning he apologized to Schlossberg for losing his temper and did this in front of all the one hundred musicians. This also proved the greatness of an inspired musician like Toscanini.

Schlossberg's method of teaching young trumpet players produced many of our finest American symphonic trumpeters. His method made it possible for the players to play high notes without too much pressure on the lips.

At one period, when I was married and decided to compose and give up a good deal of my earning capacity, I could always count on Schlossberg's generosity to help me out with a loan. Like most great and dedicated teachers, he never refused a poor pupil for lack of money as long as they showed talent.

The New York Philharmonic Orchestra was dominated by Germans for many years, until Safanov brought in many young Americans. Damrosch's New York Symphony bragged about an orchestra containing more nationalities than any other organization. The Waldorf-Astoria orchestra was mostly Italians and Jews, with about 25 percent being a mix of other nationalities.

I must tell of one of the Italians—Frank Longo. He was a likeable young fellow, a fastidious dresser, and a fairly fine pianist. He loved to talk about his great teacher Joseffy and his idea of hand position—his thumb leaning down and his other fingers pointed upwards. We kidded him a good deal about that, just for the fun of it.

There was a flute player named Marshall who had been soloist with Sousa's band, and he took some pleasure in teasing Frank. Marshall's breakfast consisted of whisky tumblers, and all during the day he was "high." One of his frequent remarks to Longo was, "So, you think you're good? Well, Hambitzer can teach you plenty." Hambitzer played viola, oboe, bassoon, cello, and organ, but [during this period] never piano.

Longo said, "Why, if he is so good, doesn't he play the piano?" Later on I'll speak of Hambitzer.

During one of Longo's spiels on Joseffy's method, Nat Finston said, "Frank, where will all this get you?" Longo turned to him and said, "In ten years, when I am great, you will be glad to kiss my derrière."

Let me get back to Hambitzer. He had been brought up in Cincinnati as a boy prodigy. It was a musical city with a preponderantly German influence. Needing money to further his piano studies, Hambitzer worked at a very large restaurant that featured singers and other attractions.

One time the well-known Boston Fidets were engaged. This was an all girl combination of singers and instrumentalists. One girl, attracted by Hambitzer's playing, often sat near the piano, listening to the seventeen-year-old youth. They became friends, and one night, after his session was through, she asked him to go out with her. He agreed and, probably for the first time in his life, imbibed so much hard liquor that he couldn't recall the next morning what had happened during the night.

That evening the girl told him that they had been married by a minister, and now they were man and wife. Hambitzer could not remember anything, but, being young and very honest, said, "Well, if I married you, then I'll accept you as my wife." The girl thanked Charlie, but said, "No, I cannot accept your offer."

"Why?" asked Hambitzer.

"Well," she said, "I cannot do this to you—I have a venereal disease, and so let's forget the whole thing we are getting into."

Hambitzer never lived with her, but he insisted upon a condition: He said, "I'll support you and take care of you until you are cured and find a job. Then I'll divorce you." This went on for almost ten years. She was then cured and found a position.

About this time the music firm of Witmark (Victor Herbert's publisher) offered Hambitzer a position as composer for operettas. Charlie came to New York, and, for some reason that he never would talk about, he tore up his contract. That is when he joined the Waldorf-Astoria Hotel orchestra, playing oboe, bassoon, viola, cello, and a little organ. It so happened that

Marshall, the flute player, knew him in Cincinnati.

Well, once Frank Longo lost his temper at Marshall's repeated remark that, "Hambitzer can teach you," etc. Longo dared Hambitzer to play the piano. Hambitzer said, "I have not touched the piano for years, but I'll try." He sat down and played one classic composition after another. He could play any number we suggested. He was the most natural pianist I ever heard—barring no one—and his memory was phenomenal. Bach, Beethoven, Mozart, Schubert, Chopin, Schumann, Liszt ... Pieces just poured out of him flawlessly. Poor Longo realized that he was hearing a great pianist, and, after his initial shock, congratulated Charlie, and they became great friends.

Of course, Hambitzer's performance got around, and in a short time he became the busiest teacher in New York. For some reason he had no interest in concertizing. I studied piano with him; another pupil was George Gershwin. George always remembered Hambitzer's influence and praised him highly. Charlie and I often discussed Gershwin at that time. Hambitzer said, "He is a tremendous talent. I have listened to him playing classics with great rhythmic extemporizing, and I have not discouraged him."

Hambitzer, however, insisted that George study classic literature—with that as a background, he thought George would find his medium in time. To get back to Hambitzer, he finally found a beautiful blond girl and married her. He was wonderfully happy, and a girl child was born. Now he was doing well, and, at last, he was at peace. Then a terrible thing happened. His wife became ill and, in a short time, died of cancer.

He would remark, "How could anything like this happen? I was married to a woman who was no good for ten years, and she is still living. Now I married an angel, and she died of a terrible disease." His faith in God was gone, and he started to drink heavily.

I left the Waldorf-Astoria and joined the Victor Talking Machine Company. Later on I heard that Charlie Hambitzer had been picked up in the street handing his money to kids and, on his way to the hospital, passed away. What a calamity; what a pity. His child went back to his wife's family in Cincinnati. Hambitzer, like Schlossberg, never refused a talented pupil who was unable to pay for his lessons. In fact, I've seen him give money to quite a few students who needed help.

Longo was sensitive and easily teased. At every concert there was a couple who always sat near Longo's piano. The man looked like a retired businessman. His wife was a little younger than he was and had a rather good-sized nose. One afternoon we saw Longo and the lady walking on Fifth Avenue. Longo was dressed up in his neat fashion, with a derby, rimless glasses and a rose stuck in his coat.

That evening, as Longo walked in our dressing room, I said, "How are you, Frank?" and then crossed my hand over my nose.

Frank asked, "Why do you do that?"

"Do what?" I asked, again rubbing my nose.

Longo said, "You know what I mean."

This went on all through the first session, and by this time all the boys kept rubbing their noses. By the time the second session was over at 1 a.m., Longo was beside himself. As we were changing into street clothes, Frank came over to me and said, "You have insulted me and a very nice lady." Again I rubbed my nose, and Longo exclaimed, "I challenge you."

I answered, "Okay, what will it be, swords or water pistols?"

He said, "I am not fooling. I will fight a duel." This went on for a while, and then we (about six of us) walked out into a bitter cold snowy night. We walked about three hundred feet to Ditson's Music Store, which had an enclosure. It was a dark and very quiet street, and we were making quite a row with our shouting.

I was still arguing with Frank about whether it would be swords, pistols, or fists, when suddenly an officer appeared and asked, "Who started all this?" The boys pointed to me. The officer took me by the arm and said, "Okay, tell your story to the judge," and walked me off.

He had taken a few steps when Longo suddenly followed us and then cried, "Please, please don't arrest him. He is my best friend; I love him— please let him go."

The officer took a long look at Frank and said, "Well, since you won't charge him for annoying you, I'll let him go." Longo said he was sorry, and we went our way. What Frank did not know was that we were friendly with the officer who had promised to cooperate with our joke!

The grand ballroom at the Waldorf Hotel was often used for many concerts. There was the Bagby morning series that featured operatic stars like Caruso, Chaliapin, Farrar, Galli-Curci, plus instrumentalists like Kreisler and others. There were other societies' musical series that gave recitals. The price for each ticket: $5 (a large sum in those days), and society flocked to them. Tickets were difficult to obtain.

I cannot recall the series involved in this symphonic concert. I was engaged, and Mr. Chapman would conduct a fifty-piece orchestra. There was a couple, Mr. and Mrs. Chapman, who were in charge of the concert. Mrs. Chapman, an enterprising impresario, was able through her large acquaintance with New York's finest society, to give many concerts at a profit. Her husband was a poor musician with an egotistical ambition to be a symphonic conductor.

I can still picture Chapman, a short, stocky figure with a reddish brown goatee beard, cropped hair, perspiration raining down his face, and exaggerated gesticulations as he conducted. At the concert he decided to conduct *Beethoven's Fifth Symphony* as the last number on the program. We got through the first three movements by keeping our eyes from Chapman and following our concertmaster's movements. Then came the fourth and last movement—the Allegro.

There were a few shaky spots, but we managed to keep together. There were thirteen fast bars at the end of the coda, and by this time Chapman, in his excited state, started to beat wildly. The orchestra kept on, hardly looking at the conductor. Then we hit the twelfth bar, and Chapman, hearing this, took a turn about and came down with a terrific downbeat and fell down on his stand. Luckily, he was stopped and held up by the two cellists in front of him.

For weeks every comic musician would reenact the falling Chapman episode, much to the amusement of the musicians. In reading this story, it is hard to see the humor and to appreciate the impact of the real situation. I never think of it without getting a big laugh from it.

Our 7 p.m. Waldorf session required us to wear tuxedos, and Mr. Joseph Knecht would often watch us to notice if we had changed from our brown shoes to our black shoes—sometimes we got away with not changing.

Then there was Judge Gary, head of U.S. Steel, who had many parties, and he gave us orders that we should never play while he and his party dined. This annoyed us greatly, and whenever he came into the dining room, we looked daggers at him. Then came Christmas time, and we were doing our best to have the diners enjoy the music, when in walked Judge Gary and his party.

To our great surprise he asked the waiter to allow us to play. He also gave the waiter a note and an envelope to hand to the leader, a young Cuban fellow. The leader put the envelope in his vest pocket and then announced what we should play. After the number he read the note that told us that Judge did not dislike music—he explained that he liked conversation with his party, and music made it difficult to concentrate on keeping the conversation going. He apologized for his order and wished us a Happy and Merry Christmas.

We then asked the leader what was in the envelope. He pulled out a $10 dollar bill. Of course we believed him. The next day the waiter came over to us and remarked, "Well, Judge Gary is not such a bad guy—he gave you a $100 bill yesterday." You can imagine what we did to that young Cuban leader. He was a stutterer, and his excuses sounded like "tut, tut, tut, tut," etc. We punished him by taking the $100 away from him, and we divided the money between ourselves, and left him out.

Early one morning Hambitzer and I were in the dark ballroom of the Waldorf when we heard wonderful violin playing, and with a tone that could not have come from our own players. An organist was accompanying the violin player. There was enough light at the organ to see: It turned out to be the greatest violin player at that time, Ysaÿe, and a famous French organist. We listened for some time to their heavenly music.

THE ISADORA DUNCAN TOUR

About two or three years before I met Isadora Duncan, I had played for and watched the great Pavlova and Mordkin dance their classic ballet. They were wonderful, and I felt that never would another type of dancing satisfy me.

While with Damrosch on the Isadora Duncan tour, it was a great surprise to see a dancer who looked so different from the slender Pavlova—and her dancing so different. No toe dancing or classic steps or the established routines. However, her movements were natural, without a trace of the accepted formal ballet. At an early age she was fascinated by the dancing figures found on Greek ceramics. She saw a direct and perfect expression of nature. Isadora Duncan was a complete discipline of beauty. Beauty in all its natural manifestations was her religion.

The Greeks usually danced without shoes: bare went the feet of Miss Duncan. She believed that the most beautiful object was the human form in the nude, without much draping. It was M. Mikail Fokine in St. Petersburg that declared Miss Duncan a goddess. He was not concerned with her technical limitations or virtuosity.

She did not have the usual figure of the lithe and trim ballet dancer, but she looked beautiful, and her dancing appearance was wholesome, and her natural movements a satisfying experience. I had played the piano for her rehearsals at Mr. Damrosch's house to save expensive orchestral monies. At the house she wore her street clothes.

The spring tour was in southern U.S. cities, and the climate was very hot. With Miss Duncan clad in very skim drapes and the orchestra in the pit, the brass section, with very little to do, started to rubberneck. Soon some of the men began using their imagination, and there were frequent arguments on "does she or does she not wear undies?" Whether or not she noticed them I'll never know, but when we got back to New York Mr. Damrosch read a letter to us from Isadora Duncan, inviting the orchestra to a private performance at the Carnegie Hall Lyceum to show her appreciation for our splendid playing during her tour.

The music selected by her was Wagner's *Prelude* and *Liebestod* from *Tristan and Isolde*. We started the work, and then Miss Duncan came out with some veils draped around her. She danced for a while, and off came the veils, and this went on and on until we could see her naked body, just covered by a transparent veil.

We were nearing the end when a door of the small balcony opened, and in walked the imposing figure of Mrs. Damrosch (she was the daughter of Senator Blaine, who narrowly missed becoming a U.S. president). Up to then Mr. Damrosch and the orchestra were playing the familiar music with his and our eyes on Miss Duncan. Then, suddenly, we all started looking at our music.

Just what effect the scene had on Mrs. Damrosch we'll never know, but I can say that Miss Duncan never toured with the Damrosch orchestra again. I often wondered how Mr. Damrosch explained this private rehearsal to his wife. Mrs. Damrosch came in, looked for a few minutes, and then walked out before we were finished.

A MAN IN THE CLOUDS

There was a fine pianist, but he was a very strange man—almost a mystic. He was emaciated and very nervous. One day we were starting our dinner session, and just as we were ready he said, "Wait a moment." We asked him why, and he said, "This is Johannes Brahms' birthday, and I will only play his music." We compromised: We would change some pieces to Brahms compositions, provided he would play some pieces by another composer. He shut his eyes, went into sort of a trance, and finally said, "The Master will allow me to play other composers, if you will play four Brahms pieces this session." We agreed; his name was Schendel.

A BRILLIANT CHAP

George Vaughn, a light tan Negro, was a musician, poet and painter. He was highly educated, and a wonderful orator. He played clarinet next to me at the Waldorf-Astoria, and we became friends. He would come to my home during my first year of my marriage, and generally he would bring two or three young painters and girl friends who barely got along by swapping food and clothes for the only thing they had—their paintings. They were well mannered but careless and never helped Anne, my wife, clean up.

They were not lazy, because I knew that most of them spent more than half of the day perfecting their draftsmanship. This went on for a year, and finally, with my son being born and Mrs. Shilkret's time being taken up, I had to part with their company.

Traveling around the cities of the United States, I saw that a few of the paintings made by the painters who visited my house had been accepted by the Chicago and Los Angeles art museums. One of the painters turned to commercial art and made a success of it.

An Overview of 1905 through 1914

The music business, from the time I became a professional by joining the musician's union until the time I joined the Victor Talking Machine Company, ran on an even keel. The recording companies had some impact, but it was the dance craze coming from high society to the masses about 1918 that changed the musician's life.

In 1905 there were society coming-out parties, private home affairs, plus Newport's gala summer season that gave musicians plenty of engagements. In New York the top leader was Van Barr—he would come to the union headquarters daily with a large list of cards, and he would hand instructions out to hundreds of players.

Then there were symphony orchestras, at first controlled by the Germans—not many orchestras, but growing in number. More American youths of foreign parents were getting in symphony orchestras. Practically every hotel, cafe, and theater used live musicians. Weddings, picnics, boats and parks used live musicians.

The prices were not high, but neither were living expenses. The dance craze, considered the exclusive pleasure of the rich, suddenly swept into the middle and lower classes. This gave new ideas to the young American players, and out of this came Joe Smith and his violin and many other so-called jazz styles—perhaps the word jazz was not really used. It was really an exhilarating ragtime pep style.

The popular musician could find plenty of work, especially the young players. It is a fact, and probably always will be, that slackening of work comes with advancing age. It starts during the late forties, except for those who have exceptional talent. I was lucky to quit my playing days at age twenty-five, so I cannot speak personally.

I have watched and taken part in the upheaval of the musician's union. Later on the vast changes in electrical science cut the use of live musicians to a minimum.

Notes

1. Safanov was conductor from 1906 to 1909; he returned to his native Russia in 1911. Mahler became conductor in 1909 and died in 1911 at age fifty.

2. Al Jolson's *The Jazz Singer*, 1927, is the film that revolutionized synchronized sound motion pictures.

CHAPTER 3
THE VICTOR TALKING
MACHINE COMPANY

... the advent of the ... International Novelty Orchestra and The Troubadours culminated in the formation of one of the most outstanding groups ever to grace the grooves of 78 RPM records, and it is safe to say that every one of its monumental accomplishments can be attributed to one man—Nathaniel Shilkret. For elasticity, diversity of type, innovation, intelligence in arranging and execution and sheer brilliance Nat Shilkret and the Victor Orchestra, in the area of the straight dance band, has never been approached, by a considerable margin. They were the only big band that the writer can recall managing to attain and retain an exciting, rhythmic beat when called for, their waltzes were often masterpieces of flowing smoothness and advanced arrangement.

—**John McAndrew**, *Record Research, 1961*

In June 1914 I married Anne Finston, a beautiful and spirited girl, the sister of my best friend Nathaniel W. Finston. A year later I was engaged as an arranger and conductor for the Victor Talking Machine Company by Mr. Eddie King. My earnings at that time were about $150 per week, and I entered into an agreement with Mr. King for about $50 per week,[1] with the allowance to earn my $150 on the outside, if it did not interfere with my Victor work.

What really happened came as a shock. My outside work suddenly took a nosedive. From being an eagerly sought out player, my status as a conductor made me a rival to other leaders, and so I was not engaged. Here I was married with a son, with rising expenses, and suddenly my weekly earnings dropped from $150 to a measly $50. Should I give up my Victor job? No, I couldn't do that because it might be construed that I had not made the grade, and, besides, it had been my ambition for a long time to arrange and conduct.

Then came my interest in my Victor Talking Machine Company work. I was put in the Foreign Department that recorded for thirty-two languages. The prominent nationalities and ethnic groups were Italian, Jewish, Russian, German, Greek, Polish, and Scandinavian. Engaging talent, picking the music, orchestrating, recording, listening to masters and picking the best rendition, translating the title and write-ups for the catalogues, and contracting each artist became my full-time occupation.

There were twelve dates a week—forty-eight separate titles and about two hundred records per month to be filled out. Foreign artists and their repertoire had to be discovered. With other recording companies competing, it was necessary to attend Polish weddings and affairs, Jewish theaters, Italian vaudeville, German cafes, etc.—sometimes meeting immigrants arriving in America for concert tours. It was a hectic department, and I found little time for sleep.

However, it was exciting and interesting, and one day I sat in my New York office when Enrico Caruso walked in. My office was next to the recording room, and he used to spray his throat before entering the recording room. He was accompanied by Mr. Zirato [Caruso's secretary and later associate manager of the New York Philharmonic].

Caruso was a genial and kind man, with a jovial approach. His first greeting was, "Little maestro, you work hard. Are you making enough money?" I answered him in the negative. "Well," he said, "you can never tell—for a long time I used to sing my head off for a week or more and didn't earn enough money for a square meal. Now I just sign a contract and promise to sing, and, without opening my mouth, receive enough advance money for a lifetime of meals. Our profession is a business of 'feast or famine.' I sang as well as now when I was poor. There is no rhyme or reason why artists are underpaid or overpaid."

Between 1915 and 1920 my salary went up slowly, but my work increased greatly. Besides working in the Foreign Department, I was asked to record for the Export Department that was managed by Daniel Mitchell. The Export Department had charge of the catalogues of countries south of the border: Mexico, Cuba, Jamaica, Puerto Rico, and all of Central America and South America. There was such an increase in sales from my first recording release that I was asked to take over the Export Department records.

This added about four hundred titles a year. I never recorded Chinese artists (they were imported), but I often worked with Japanese artists. Partly as an experiment and partly as a gag, I picked a pretty sounding Japanese melody and did an American popular arrangement version. A few weeks later I received a letter with a picture showing that my Japanese record, played on a loudspeaker, caused a tremendous traffic jam. One day a Japanese gentleman came with a record carefully packed. It was a gold-colored labeled record, and I was requested to autograph it for his Highness, the Japanese Emperor.

The importance of the Foreign Department was not only in the sale to those who spoke the language in which the recording was made—Italian, Jewish, Russian and German people were heavy buyers of our Red Seal operatic records—but, also, to the offspring of these people who became interested in our domestic popular singers and dance orchestras.

Our competition was the Columbia Foreign Department. The Jewish clientele found our cantors to their liking. We had the popular Kwartin. Not only did we inherit his old xylophone catalogue, but we issued his latest records when he came to America. His appeal was not so much his voice as his interesting interpretation of the text (of course, in Hebrew). Cantor Josef Rosenblatt had a bel canto voice, technical manipulation of his falsetto, and a matchless florid style. He was a fine composer of Hebrew text. Then there was Cantor Hershman, a newcomer with a fine tenor quality who, if he had desired to, could have had a career in opera.

However, Columbia was willing to pay the popular operetta artists higher wages than Mr. King could afford. Columbia had Molly Picon and Lebedoff. To offset Columbia's wage advantage I hired Ludwig Satz, a character comedian. He was really great and sold well. In the Italian catalogue we issued popular hits that came from the Piedmont city in Italy. They selected the best songs by competition every year. The Neapolitan songs were the most popular, and often we would have Caruso sing one of the winning songs worthy of his great voice.

Of course, we also had the singers of the vaudeville houses. There was a group of actors who made comedy dialogues about their priests. It is odd, but Catholics, like the Jews, do not condemn poking fun at religion, provided that it is not offensive. It was necessary to have these sketches translated into English, so that we would not be criticized by the church. These records were very popular with the Italians. Italians and Jews, despite their strong beliefs, seem to enjoy poking a bit of humor into their religion. I cannot remember German or Swedish Protestants ever doing that.

Outside of the Hebrew cantor records, the Jewish artists (in Yiddish tongue) often spoke of God as if He were their Father and they had intimate and personal touch with Him.

There were two common themes in Jewish comedy records. One was their fun with various Yiddish dialects—the German, Austrian, Lithuanian and Russian Jews. The German Jew was characterized as pompous, the Austrian (Kalitzenaner) as naive, the Lithuanian (Litvak) for his lisp. However, the Russian (really Ukranian) spoke the popular and accepted dialect. The Scholom Aleichem stories were highly appreciated. When Scholom Aleichem met Mark Twain, Aleichem said, "I am the Mark Twain of the Jews," and Mark Twain replied, "I am the Scholom Aleichem of the Americans."

I found the Italian artists easy to contract. The Jews had their method. They would request the price, and then say, "I'll think it over and see you tomorrow and give you my answer." The next day they would say that they had been to another company that had offered them a higher price. I would then offer them a higher figure, and again they would ask for another day to decide, and again they would go through the same routine. This went on until they finally accepted a price.

The Scandinavian artists were entirely different. Once you liked their work, they accepted a fair offer and, no matter what the competition offered them, they remained faithful to you. However, if, after a while, you told them their sales were slipping, they would say, "I guess my clientele is tired of me. I'll quit recording and go back to my old job."

The Greek artists invariably offered me money or presents after recording. I had lots of trouble refusing what I considered a bribe. They absolutely refused my "no," and finally I had Mr. Calvin Child, our head executive, and a very distinguished-looking man, tell them that it was against the rules for me to accept any gifts. Their interpretation of this was that I did not think them worthy or important enough to accept their money.

The German records were my most difficult problem: It was the competition of the fine Odeon records made in and imported from Germany. They had a wonderful artist in the tenor Richard Tauber, who was a combination of John McCormack, Al Jolson and Bing Crosby. He sang opera, popular songs and operetta hits. Once I tried McCormack on a splendid German song, and he did a fine job, but he was too expensive for our German Department, and he was too busy to worry about my problem.

I decided to let Odeon have Tauber exclusively—he was too much competition and was in a class by himself. I turned to comic records and visited the German Yorktown Cafes between East 80th and 86th Streets and formed comedy teams that sold well.

Another artist that was very popular with our German buyers was Marek Weber's orchestra—a fine group that played both popular and semi-classical compositions. I formed a few novelty combinations: a Schrammel orchestra consisting of strings, zither and accordions, and, also, an International Quartet of xylophone, clarinet, accordion and bass. These records were listed in many national catalogues. An attractive piece, like the *Cuckoo Waltz*, with translated titles, sold in German, Polish, Swedish and Italian catalogues. Sometimes, the dealers would sell them to their domestic customers—the Domestic Department was meant for the American-speaking people.

THE VICTOR SALON ORCHESTRA

However, the most successful combination I formed [and conducted] was from my strings, piano, flute, drums and some added novelty instruments. It was finally called the Victor Salon Orchestra [1924]. Its success was due to the enriched and improved sound of added recording horns, using regular violins, violas, cellos and string bass, instead of using a tuba and special arrangements.

This was the time of mechanical recording and, instead of violinists using their own violins, they played on a Stroh instrument (built like a skeleton violin) with an attached horn.[2] It had an unnatural tone. Compared with the greatly improved electrical recordings of today, it sounded very primitive. So, with my determination to get a better sound and have my musicians use their own instruments, I experimented, and I was fortunate enough to have, in my New York studio, an engineer who worked with me, despite the objection of the head recording engineers, the four Sooy brothers.

Up to this time a large horn was used to record the whole orchestra, with the violinists and other string players using Stroh string instruments and with a tuba playing the bass part. By experimenting with horns for each instrument, the improved sound of the Victor Salon Orchestra created a popular demand. The result was a mellow and more natural string sound. The improvement brought requests from the Domestic Department, and we recorded ballads and popular numbers. So great was the demand for my new orchestra that for three years I recorded over a hundred titles a year and the Company listed a two-sided record in a special weekly issue. My name was put on the label for the first time, and my reputation grew tremendously.

I began using the big hits like Berlin, Romberg and Kern melodies, plus semi-classical numbers. I extended the repertoire with Mexican and South American tunes like *Estrellita, Cielito Lindo* and *Ay, Ay, Ay*. The Chauve Souris (Russian) troupe's coming to America brought *Dark Eyes* and the *Parade of the Wooden Soldiers*. Before each issue there was a standing order of a half million records.

Paul Whiteman and his orchestra were engaged after we heard him in Atlantic City. Hickman was contracted by the Columbia Phonograph Company, but for some reason did not click. Whiteman became our number one seller.

Paul Whiteman offered me $400 a week as an arranger and player. That was five times more than the Victor was paying me—it was a great temptation. My wife and I talked it over, and decided that my goal was not to get immersed in the dance field.

Paul Whiteman helped me a good deal, whether he knew it or not. Two years after his initial proposal, he offered me a guarantee of $25,000 a year as a unit under his management—again I stuck to the Victor job. Two years after that, he offered me a guarantee of $35,000, when I was fighting for $17,500 at the Victor.

This time I signed up with him and asked him how he could offer me $35,000, when the Victor would only give me $15,000. He said, "Don't worry—I can get you more money at Victor, and I'll have you on radio. You will be tops in that field." I then asked him for the contract and tore it up—Paul was surprised at my action but did not become angry. I explained my reaction: "If you can get it, so can I."

Later on I found the reason for his last offer, and also the reason why Mr. Eddie King had approved of my signing with Whiteman. But that's a long story [not in the autobiography; perhaps because King was going to leave Victor] and better told in a later chapter.

THE FOREIGN DEPARTMENT

Back to the Foreign Department. It was often difficult to separate the Czech dialects. Nearly every artist claimed that he could sing Jugoslav, Moravian, Serbian and Czecho-Slavic dialects, but I doubted their ability to satisfy the natives, who could detect the flaws in their pronunciation. The Slavs near Hungary were apt to absorb part of their dialect from their contact with the Hungarian language.

Mr. Eddie King would become annoyed by the dealer's complaints. He would say, "Why can't they have a language like English?" and I would reply, "Well, would you have John McCormack sing a Cockney song or Jolson sing an Irish song?"

King said, "Well, it is all English at least."

We could record dances like the polka with a clarinet and an accordion, if the melody was catchy, and place the recording in a different nationality catalogue with a translated title. Sometimes I played polka on the clarinet during my first five years with the company.

By 1920 I was conductor and manager of the Foreign Department. By 1922, besides the Foreign and Export Departments, I was arranger for the domestic catalogue. I arranged some Neapolitan records for Caruso and, finally, conducted a date for him. Unfortunately, he died before I entered the Red Seal (operatic) Department.

THE *Prisoner's Song*

I became involved in two new departments: Country Records and the Race (Negro) Orchestra. The Okeh Record Company issued a great seller. It was a hillbilly tune called *Wreck of the Old '97* [1924]. The Victor had neglected the country records and the Race Orchestra. Now, with the tremendous hit of the Okeh record, our dealers, who were mostly exclusive Victor, clamored for a catalogue to counteract the Okeh and the other smaller companies.

The Victor was slow in satisfying the demand, but finally I was approached to record the *Wreck of the Old '97*. Since the Okeh record had been issued about eight months before, I was worried about our chances to come out well enough to compete. I picked a singer, Vernon Dalhart, a Southerner, and asked him to learn the requested number. However, I did not want to depend entirely on the eight-month-old hit. I asked all of the Broadway publishers to find a suitable potential hit for the B side of the record. I received about thirty songs, but they all had the Broadway flavor, and my experience with the folk melodies of many nationalities convinced me that they would not do.

In the meantime pressure was growing from our dealers; our Camden sales force demanded a quick release; and Vernon Dalhart needed money and the [recording] date. I called Dalhart in and said, "You are from the South. Don't you know any good tune that would sell on its own merits? I really must find the proper tune."

Dalhart answered, "I have a cousin living with me now, and he is always humming a tune he calls the *Prisoner's Song*."

I said, "Come tomorrow and sing it to me." He came the next day, and his first remark was, "The lyric is good but the melody is bad."

I said, "Sing it." After about four bars I said, "You are right; it is a very poor melody. Now, just recite the lyric—do not sing," and as he recited the lyric I composed the melody for the *Prisoner's Song*, one of the greatest selling songs (records) ever issued.

Two days later the date for recording was set. I had asked Lou Raderman, my concertmaster, to try my melody on the viola one day before the recording. I wanted the viola, instead of the recording violin, to get a mournful sound. I felt that I had a hit.

Ronnie asked, *"How can you tell or know a hit?"*

I answered, "It is true, it is almost impossible to predict a hit, but there are times when a 'natural' is heard, and one can be confident of the results almost immediately."

The moment we finished the *Prisoner's Song*, Dalhart remarked, "The Victor is lucky. They get a fine melody and a lyric free"—meaning that his lyric was public domain and my melody belonged to the company through the terms of my contract.

The record became one of the all-time greatest sellers, and for months we could not supply enough records to the dealers. After the record had been out for six months, Mr. Bernstein of Shapiro-Bernstein Publishing Company came to the Victor claiming royalties. Of course, I protested. I knew that I had composed the melody. As for the lyric, Dalhart claimed that his cousin wrote it, reversing his original statement that it was a public domain lyric song by prisoners for many years, or a folk poem. Mr. Eddie King got into the fracas, and, instead of protecting the Victor or me, came to me and said, "Nat, since the Victor, according to your contract, owns all your compositions, let us agree to pay Bernstein royalty for the lyric only, and not pay for the music."

In the meantime Bernstein offered me my full royalty and credit on the sheet music, provided that the Victor would pay royalty on both the melody and lyric. I refused, saying that it was up to the Victor to decide, since the melody belonged to them. Why Mr. King, my superior, did not insist at least on control of the right to own the melody copyright, I never understood—the record sold by this time three million copies. But I was out of the credit while Dalhart recorded the *Prisoner's Song* for many other companies.

The story came out that Dalhart hardly paid any royalty to his cousin [Guy Massey], who died one year later. This record, with the two melodies, *Wreck of the Old '97* and the *Prisoner's Song* began a famous lawsuit. Someone claimed that the *Wreck of the Old '97* was not a folk tune, but composed by someone living in the South. I believe that a settlement was finally worked out. I was really angry at the Victor and Mr. King for not protecting my composition.[3]

THE YEARS 1920 THROUGH 1924

Here are some of the items that my expanding work got me into. As I said before, I was brought to the Victor Company to assist Mr. King in the

Foreign Department. I orchestrated and conducted. As Mr. King advanced, I then took charge of the catalogue. After that I became musical director of the Export Department. I formed the Victor Salon Orchestra.

There was the *Prisoner's Song* [1924], my West Virginia trip [1925; see chapter 4] collecting sixty-four hillbilly tunes, and the time I spent in the Harlem section of New York City to start the Race Record Catalogue. About 1922 I was called up at 4 a.m. to catch the 7 a.m. train to Philadelphia. Mr. Joe Pasternack, our Red Seal conductor, had a nervous breakdown, and I was selected to take his place.

So by 1924 [or 1925] I was mixed up with the following catalogues: Foreign, Export, Domestic, Hillbilly, Race and Red Seal. I probably had ten different orchestras under different names. Even my name was changed at times, so that our record customers would not become saturated by one name conducting so many different types of orchestras.

The reason for my recapitulating the above is to show how far I had advanced: from a staff conductor to a featured artist.

My salary had increased from $50 per week to $250 per week. Knowing my value and also remembering Paul Whiteman's offers, I wanted to have my contract changed. There was also resentment that I had not received the royalty due for the popular *Prisoner's Song*.

Since 1924–1925 was the turning point of my career, I will hold this period for later on. I want to elaborate on some items of the 1920 to 1924 years.

CAMDEN

My Red Seal period of conducting brought me into the company of some of the greatest artists in the world: John McCormack, Galli-Curci, De Luca, Rothier, Rosa Ponselle, Martinelli, Farrar and many others. Then there were the Victor Symphony records that used the Philadelphia Orchestra and the New York Philharmonic Orchestra. The Victor Symphony orchestra records were sold at lower prices than the records recorded under the names mentioned above, although we conducted the same orchestras as Stokowski or Mengelberg or Toscanini.

When I arrived in Camden to take Pasternack's place, I was told to record Tchaikovksy's *1812 Overture*. My orchestra was the Philadelphia Symphony. I noticed that my idea of many horns and the string players using their own violins, instead of skeleton Stroh violins, had been adopted.

Since there were so many little horns used, it was impossible to have the conductor stand on the same level as the orchestra. In order to see my baton, the players playing next to their horns had to look up, and I was placed on a podium near the ceiling.

It was very uncomfortable in that position, and I had to bend forward to see the men and for them to see me. I never checked on the remark made to me that the *1812 Overture* had never been recorded, due to the limitation of the mechanical sound method and the massive sound of the many chimes necessary for the composition, plus the pounding of the bass drums to denote the sound of cannons.

The date lasted from 10 a.m. to 1 p.m. In the afternoon I conducted Galli-Curci, Martinelli, De Luca and Rothier in the *Rigoletto Quartet* and some other operatic arias. Having little sleep and conducting the morning session in an uncomfortable position, I was really tired out.

I went back to my Philadelphia Hotel, had dinner, and then went to bed. My next date was the following morning at 10 a.m. I awoke at 8 a.m., ready to take a shower, have breakfast, and then get to the Camden studio—but I could not move. The awkward position of the morning recording threw my back out of center. I lay there helpless—unable to move. I tried for over a half hour and finally managed to kick a table near my bed and knocked it down with the telephone that had been on it.

Pretty soon someone was sent to my room, and I asked for a doctor or an osteopath to straighten me out. Luckily there was an osteopath clinic near there, and I was helped enough to painfully get out of my bed. I got into a cab and arrived at the studio in time to continue my orchestra recording. In about three days I had recovered completely, but it was a frightful experience.

From then on I was the Red Seal Conductor. Later on Mr. King told me that they had a meeting to decide who would take Pasternack's place. Leopold Stokowski and Walter Damrosch were considered. It was Mr. King who claimed that he changed their minds. I had worked closely with him, and he knew that I had played in symphony orchestras and in opera houses. Why he did not choose Rosario Bourdon, assistant to Pasternack, I never could understand. I guess Eddie King really did sell them Nathaniel Shilkret. Mr. King was tough on salaries, but very loyal to those who worked under him. Now I was busy conducting at New York and Camden. I still had the Foreign, Domestic, Export, Hillbilly and Race Departments.

RACE DEPARTMENT

I must relate my experience to start the Race Catalogue. This was before Duke Ellington and other Negro bands. To bring a band to our studios meant traveling through Harlem during the wee hours of the morning and staying with them until the 10 a.m. recording time. If you left them on their own, you would find yourself with a band with a few missing men.

We were at the studio at 10 a.m. Of course, both the band and I had no sleep. For a while they argued about the pronunciation of the instrument cymbal. Some pronounced the "y" as a short "i" and some as a long "i." It was a lively give and take, and I stopped it before it got out of hand by giving them the proper pronunciation.

There were two saxophonists: one a six-foot-three Negro who played quite a few instruments strapped to his shoulder, and next to him was a lithe five-foot-two Jamaican Negro. The little fellow kept bawling out the big fellow. This was the period of mechanical recording, and in order to register a solo passage, the player had to get up and walk to the recording horn.

The little fellow, the more intelligent of the two, did his best to instruct the slow-thinking big fellow when to walk to the horn for his solo. We started recording, and when we came to the spot where the big fellow had to get up, he received a few not very gentle nudges from the little fellow. The big fellow, with a blank look, wondered why he was being poked. Getting no response from the big fellow, the little saxophonist jumped up and ran to the percussion section and picked up a big tympani stick and then, with all his strength, hit the big fellow on top of his head. [The end of a tympani stick is made of cotton.] Down went the big fellow, with all of his hanging instruments.

I stopped the music, walked over to the small man, and asked him why he hit the big man. He said, "He is dumb. He does not understand."

"You could have hurt him." I said.

The reply was, "You can't hurt his head, it is too thick. Besides he spoilt the record." I explained that spoiling a record is nothing to get excited about—it was inexpensive. And so we went ahead and finished the date.

The Hungarian Gypsy Orchestra dates generally started with almost a fist fight—so I thought. I tried to get them started, but their heated conversation was not easily stopped. Finally I asked one of the men what they were arguing about so vigorously. He said nothing important. They were discussing whether or not it will rain. What a lot of energy wasted!

THE JOHNSONS

By 1924 Eldridge Johnson had a nervous breakdown, and his son came to the Victor Company to learn the recording business. He was a very young and shy lad. He seemed to take a liking to me and frequented my office.

Two projects for which Mr. Johnson, senior, had very little use were introduced at that time. The first was radio. We went on the air and broadcast with Galli-Curci, John McCormack and my Victor Salon Orchestra. The second was electrical recording. Johnson senior was sure that radio was just a fad, and the electrical recordings preferred by the younger officials were looked upon by the older officials with suspicion. Nevertheless, with Columbia accepting both developments, Victor was forced into the two—radio and electrical recordings.

The young Johnson said that if I remained with the Victor Company indefinitely, he would put away one quarter of a million dollars in stock for me. Within a few months after making that statement, the Victor was sold [1926] to Wall Street firms, and I never saw young Johnson again.

THE SHAPE OF A PHONOGRAPH

Up to 1924, Mr. Eldridge Johnson was head of the Victor Talking Machine Company.[4] There were two committees: the Executive Committee and the Artist and Repertoire (A&R) Committee. Mr. Calvin Child was on both committees. He did not personally attend the A&R meetings. Mr. Harry MacDonough was chairman of our A&R Committee and reported our decisions to Mr. Child. The A&R group consisted of MacDonough, King, myself, Wielage (in charge of distribution), Porter (liaison for the business and recordings), and Davis (assistant to Child for the Red Seal stars). Later on Mr. Cairns was added.

For some time the contention was the curved or flat-top phonograph. We realized the fact that women did not want the curved top, but Mr. Johnson insisted that a phonograph must have its distinctive furniture, and a flat-top was not a phonograph. This cost us the loss of a great deal of machine sales. Finally, Johnson grudgingly gave in and allowed a flat-top phonograph to be built [1925].

BORRAH MINNEVITCH

The Bruno Company of New York was the Victor's largest distributor. One of the officials of the Bruno Company was Mr. Hauser. He was a fanatic about harmonicas. He had devoted years to propagating the Ger-

man Hohner Harmonica. Finally he asked me to feature the instrument for
recordings. He claimed that we have never brought out a good record of
the harmonica.

He introduced Borrah Minnevitch, a featured vaudevillian and an extremely great harmonica performer. Borrah was an erratic fellow and had
a great sense of humor. I appointed the recording date at our Camden
studio. It was in the early 1920s—a few weeks after Enrico Caruso's death.
We were still recording by the mechanical method.

We started at 10:00 a.m. with Minnevitch and added the guitar player
Roy Smeck, who was even wackier than Minnevitch. There was one great
problem. Minnevitch played by ear, and he never played a number the
same way twice. We struggled from 10:00 a.m. to 1:00 p.m. Then we
took one hour for lunch and returned at 2:00 p.m. We tried again, and by
4:15 we still had not recorded one side of a record. We just could not get
Minnevitch to remember his routine.

By then we were ready to strangle Minnevitch. We were on the eighth
floor, and we were all worrying about getting back to New York for our
broadcasts.[5] As we were directing our insults at Borrah and ready to throw
him out of the window, he turned to us and said, "What is the matter with
you fellows? Didn't Caruso make mistakes?"

Before the boys began to mangle him for his sacrilegious remark, I asked
them to give it one more try. In the few remaining minutes we succeeded
in playing two acceptable three-minute records.

What came out of the harmonica date was my request to Mr. Hauser of
Bruno Company to have the manufacturers build different size and registers
for group players. That set up bands all over the world.

ROY SMECK

I noticed Roy Smeck had a knack of getting unusual effects with his various
guitars. I engaged him to join us for one of my Victor Salon Orchestra
recordings. Lou Raderman, my concertmaster, kept putting his hand in his
pocket, taking out pieces of candy, and eating continuously. After a while
Smeck asked Lou for a piece of candy. At first Lou said, "Don't bother me,"
just to tease him. Then Lou gave him a piece. After that Smeck started
to put his hand in Lou's pocket, eating his candies quickly, until the paper
bag was emptied.

The next day we were recording again. Lou started to eat candy, and
Smeck started to help him. The trouble was that Lou had exchanged the
original bag with Ex-Lax tablets [a laxative]. For about an hour and a half

Smeck kept eating the laxatives. Just as we were ready to record our third number, Smeck suddenly jumped up and cried, "I have been poisoned!" and ran out of the room and straight to the bathroom.

Outside of Lou Raderman, none of us knew why Smeck was taken ill. We went into the men's room. Smeck had closed the partition, still crying, "I have been poisoned; I'm dying!" He sat there for about twenty minutes, and by this time Lou had told us that the candy Smeck ate was a laxative. I asked one of our officials to say he was a doctor and would examine Roy.

After the bogus doctor examined Smeck, he assured him that he was in no danger. We did finish the four numbers despite the complaints from Roy. For a long time Roy Smeck was sure that Lou Raderman hated him and wanted to poison him.

GIOVANNI MARTINELLI

In our A&R Committee, Mr. Davis, a cultured and refined gentleman with a mild and shy manner, was told by our rougher individuals to speak to the great Martinelli and reduce his $25,000 a year guarantee to $15,000. This was a complete surprise and shock to Davis. His duties were to assist Mr. Child and to keep the great artists happy. He had, by his excellent manners, endeared himself to them and, in fact, was considered a friend of the artists. Asking Martinelli to accept a reduction in his guarantee was too much to expect from Mr. Davis, after their many years of friendship.

However, as I said, some of us were firm and some were downright harsh. They claimed that Martinelli's records were not selling enough to warrant a guarantee. I sympathized with Davis, but no doubt the contract had been discussed with our executive board and then handed to us to carry their verdict through.

Davis had to transact the order and met Martinelli. Davis came back the next week and told us Martinelli was very unhappy about the proposed cut and wanted time to think it over. He took some time in deciding, and during that period the great Enrico Caruso died. That put a new slant on the matter—with Caruso gone, Martinelli became the number one attraction of the Metropolitan Opera House. Davis was summoned and told that he should get in touch with Martinelli immediately and offer him his $25,000 guarantee. As you can imagine, Martinelli refused to sign, and he received an additional $10,000 for a total of $35,000.

MARTINELLI AND THE BIG HORSE

I received a phone call. I asked, "Hello, who is this?"

"Martinelli."

"Yes, Mr. Martinelli, what can I do for you? This is Shilkret."

He said, "Please, maestro, have my orchestration in F for the *Big 'orse* song," and he rang off. I couldn't understand why he would want to sing the popular comic ditty *Horses, Horses, Horses*. It was very popular at the time, but Martinelli singing this was ridiculous. I asked one of our Italian singers to speak to Martinelli and get things straight.

Martinelli was contacted, and I was told that what he had pronounced as "big horse" was really the ballad *Because* (*Because I Love You*).

RUDOLFO CARUSO

After Caruso died there was a flux of German, French, Italian, and other national Caruso's. Some bragged that they had greater volume than Caruso, but we never considered using any of them. One day a young Italian singer came in and claimed that he was Caruso's son from his first marriage. His name was Rudolfo Caruso. He was quite a voluble talker, and he claimed to have a better voice than his father. Rudolfo said that the great Caruso was jealous of him and gave him no encouragement.

Knowing what a wonderful personality Caruso had, I took little stock in his [son's] bragging. He had a fair voice, but it was not good enough to be considered for recording. He threatened to tell the whole world about his father. He managed to get some bookings, but after some time he was never heard from again.

MIGUEL FLETA

I must talk about a tenor who came from [Spain and performed in] Mexico. He was sent to New York [1924] by his government to appear at the Met and to record for Victor. His name was Miguel Fleta. I recorded with him, and I thought that he had the voice nearest to Caruso. Besides his splendid singing of operatic arias, he was an outstanding interpreter of folk songs. Since I looked for material for our Export Department, I was intensely interested in his great rendition of *Ay, Ay, Ay, Estrellita* and other South of the Border melodies. I imitated his excellent style and used it for my Victor Salon records.

Fleta was quite a character, and, in the end, ruined his career. He was to sing *Rigoletto* at the Met one night. He arrived in time and then announced that he wanted to sing another opera—*La Traviata*. With the stage set for *Rigoletto*, the opera house was in a panic. He was impossible to reason with, and after a long period of altercation, they finally made the change to the *La Traviata* scenery.

While the change was being made, Fleta slipped out of the building and disappeared. This, of course, created a scandal. As for the Victor, he was booked to do a broadcast one night, and when he did not show up fifteen minutes before the concert we were obliged to call Mr. De Luca, the baritone, to substitute for Fleta and broadcast without a rehearsal.

His antics boomeranged: His government paid $25,000 for damages, and he was sent back to his country. I never heard of him again. In fact, he was ostracized in his own country and never recovered his position.

EVA GAUTHIER

The French catalogue sold poorly in the United States, but better in Canada. One of the outstanding and remarkable young singers was Eva Gauthier. She was a French Canadian who had married a wealthy financier from Belgium. She spoke perfect French and English, and she recorded many French folk songs for us. She gave quite a few recitals, and her appearance was striking. She had bright black eyes and black hair, parted in the middle and combed flat on each side.

In her recitals she sang classical music and added George Gershwin tunes. The musicians, she and I did a Stravinsky program of her works at Aeolian Hall. Her gowns, which she created and sewed by herself, were the talk of the town.

Her husband admired her immensely but insisted upon her giving up her concert career—she refused. For a long time her recitals created tremendous excitement. She was praised by critics for her splendid voice, her daring repertoire, and her champion struggle to introduce new music. But it was her remarkable gowns that were admired by the women. Her success lasted for some time, but, as she influenced other recitalists to follow her novel repertoire, competition grew. After a few years her attendance fell off, and she found out that crusading does not lead to a career that lasts for a lifetime.

However, she loved music very much, and, rather than give it up, she became a dress designer. She went on and on until she became ill. She managed to survive by doing secretarial work for one of the societies for singers—I believe AGMA.

Recently I heard of her death. It was a tragic ending for this woman who was a music pioneer. There is a movement to revive her memory in the form of an Eva Gauthier Foundation. No one deserves this tribute more.

AL JOLSON

One sunny afternoon Al Jolson, Bourne of the Berlin Music company, my son Arthur, then eight years old, and I went to the New York Giants baseball game. I had informed my son that Al Jolson was a funny man who would make him [my son] laugh a good deal. We arrived at the ballpark, and, of course, Jolson became the center of attraction.

Al Jolson was an enthusiastic baseball fan, and all through the game loudly commented on various situations. The spectators enjoyed his remarks. At a crucial moment the Giants could have won the game with one hit. With the people tense and quiet, the third strike came, and the Giants had lost their chance. Jolson started to sing the Hebrew prayer for the dead, and the crowd reacted, there being quite a few people who knew the prayer.

When the game was over and Jolson was going to his car, I said, "Arthur, thank Mr. Jolson for the good time we had and taking us to the game."

Arthur looked at Jolson and said, "Thank you for the game, but you did not make me laugh—you were not funny." Despite his quick wit Jolson could not answer that. He just stared at Arthur and went his way. As Art Linkletter often says, "Children say the funniest things" in their naive and uncompromising manner.

CONCERTMASTERS AND NEW CONDUCTORS

Ronnie: *"Was Lou Raderman your only first violinist?"*

I answered, "I had many concertmasters, but Lou was a unique violinist and stayed with me for many years. As you know, I had more than one type of orchestra. My use of Lou came in an unorthodox way.

"First of all you must know that when someone is playing as one of the musicians and then becomes a conductor, there exists a peculiar situation.

You cannot just get up and expect full cooperation from the men, because during your playing time with them you have a different relationship with them. Some that were friendly are now jealous of your new position. It is hard for them to accept you as a leader. Also, you must gain their respect. Any criticism can be misconstrued as personal.

"They watch your conducting, and, knowing that you are a bit nervous, will interject their own thoughts: some wanting to help you and others trying to put you in your place. They all expect to remain in the orchestra whether you think them capable or not. It takes patience and time to do your best and not disrupt a set orchestra. Besides, during your first chance to conduct, you have to iron out your own faults—as a player you are relaxed and detect mistakes easily, but it is different in your new position.

When one stands in front of an orchestra, the sound is different from what one hears as a player. Besides your quick ear and your talent, it takes experience. The old cliché that no one is a hero in his own town is true."

During the mechanical recordings a violinist had to have a big and solid tone to record well. David Mendoza was my first violinist, and he filled the job well. When he became a conductor at the Capitol Theatre, he quit and suggested that I engage Eugene Ormandy. He was a fine violinist, and he played one date, but his tone was not robust enough for our type of mechanical recording. Mendoza then recommended a man who had a very good reputation as a player. He had been the finest concertmaster with the finest symphony orchestra, but he was reputed to be temperamental and had been almost impossible for many famous conductors to work with. His name was Gregory Skolnik.

I told Mendoza that Skolnik would look for trouble, and, since I was rather new as a conductor, it might be best to forget him. David insisted and said that Skolnik had reformed and learned his lesson. In fact, he was financially in trouble, and, on account of his reputation, conductors did not want to hire him.

I gave in and hired him to play all the concert dates at the Victor. The price for concert dates at that time was $15 for a three-hour session. The price for dance dates was the same, but it had become the standard practice to pay $25 for a three-hour session, because of the style and the improvisation expected from the novel players. Having heard Lou Raderman play with my brother Jack Shilkret's orchestra at the Little Club, I was excited by Lou's natural and beautiful tone. He was engaged for my dance and novelty dates.

After the first number of a Lucrezia Bori date, Skolnik said in a rather pompous manner, "Mr. Shilkret, I want to talk to you."

I said, "Fine, but after the date."

He said, "No, it must be now." Again I told him after the date. We had just finished our second number when he insisted with more vigor that he must talk to me. Knowing I was dealing with a troublemaker, I decided to hear what he had to say. He began, "Mr. Shilkret, you are cheating the company you are working for." I asked in what way. He replied, "You are paying me $15 for a date, and you are paying a much inferior violinist $25 a date—that is cheating the Victor Company."

Well, in my mind, I figured here is my first encounter with trouble as a conductor. How to settle this and how to keep my dignity? I finally looked at him and said, "Will you answer the question I will ask you?"

He said, "Yes."

I then asked him, "Who is the better violinist, you or Lou Raderman?"

He said, "I won't insult my intelligence to answer that ridiculous question."

I then remarked, "I'll answer it for you: Lou Raderman today is a better violinist than you."

That upset him, and he jumped up, grabbed his violin, and walked out of the room. And that is how Lou Raderman became my concertmaster for my concert and dance orchestra. It turned out that Lou was the perfect man for the job, and he was also a wonderfully gifted player. He had studied with a fine teacher, and his natural and gifted talents made up for the briefness of his encounter as a studying violinist.

Many of the violinists I engaged had studied for years to become soloists. Some had gone to Europe, studying with the finest teachers, but they acknowledged Lou's wonderful playing. They would argue about his fingering, even his phrasing, but they had to admit that despite their knowledge and many years of hard study, they could not outperform Lou.

When studied violinists would ask Lou to try their fingering, as it was the proper way, Lou would shrug his shoulders and then play a difficult passage flawlessly, in his own way, and they could not find any fault with his results. Their opinion was that Lou Raderman was exceptional. After all, the great composers like Schoenberg and Heitor Villa-Lobos claimed that they were practically self-taught. His violin playing elicited the praise of many artists: Elman, Heifetz, Rachmoninoff, John McCormack, Harold Bauer and many others.

Lou and I had plenty of battles, but, knowing his value, I worked with him. Lou did not take himself seriously in the beginning and preferred to play as the mood dictated. As I see it now, perhaps he was too young to understand; perhaps he depended upon his natural talents; perhaps he was afraid to think too hard about that which came naturally; or perhaps he just needed more experience. Well, today, in his early sixties, he has learned a lot and he is still one of the top violinists in Hollywood. He had a wonderful tone, perfect technique, and a clear pitch. His work with the Victor Salon Orchestra had the quality that made these recordings so popular. He had a happy disposition and always was ready for a laugh.

He would work steadily for about two years and then leave for about two years. He followed this pattern. In addition to Lou, I had some of the finest concertmasters play for me: Piastro, Kortalasky and, especially, Jascha Zayde. For a time I had Zayde take over the first chair in classical programs, and Lou never complained. He and Zayde respected each other. Zayde, also a young man before coming to America, had been concertmaster with the famous Russian composer Glazunov for five years.

ARTURO TOSCANINI

As a rule I never supervised symphony conductors while they recorded. Being a conductor, I thought they might consider my suggestions as criticism. One day, in my early days at the Victor, Mr. King came to my room and asked me to go into the recording room.

"Who is recording?" I asked.

He replied, "Arturo Toscanini and the La Scala Opera House Orchestra." I entered the recording room and spoke to the recording engineer—this was still in the time of mechanical recording.

The engineer, Charlie Maisch, said, "He drops down to such a pianissimo sound that all I get is a scratch sound of the needle, and no music."

I entered the room where Toscanini and the men were rehearsing. The maestro greeted me and then started to conduct the fourth movement of Brahms' *First Symphony*. I listened for about one minute and then stopped him. He looked at me inquiringly, as if to ask why I stopped him. I said, "You are dropping the volume too low. We cannot record any sound of it."

He started again, and after about two minutes I stopped him again. I said, "Too soft, too pianissimo."

He said, "I can only play as the composer wanted it played—if I am not recording it properly, that is your affair. I must play my music properly."

He started again, and this time I let him play almost to the end and stopped him again. By this time he was furious, and he started to tell me what was on his mind. I tried to follow his rapid Italian and interjected some of my own opinions. He then said, "Why don't you speak Italian?"

I answered, "Why don't you speak English? You have been in America long enough." With that I walked out of the room.

A week later Toscanini heard his records, picked them up, and smashed them against the wall, and he did not record again for a long time. When he did record again, it was with the improved electrical recording.

By the way, I was not impressed with the La Scala orchestra. Maybe in those days I was used to the American orchestras influenced by the broad lines and fullness of German conductors. Even Toscanini changed his interpretation from his *Ninth Beethoven Symphony* performed with the Metropolitan Opera Orchestra in comparison with the New York Philharmonic later on. He was always great, but conducting symphony music steadily broadened his style. I had another experience with Toscanini later, but that belongs to my radio years.

Mengelberg, the great Dutch conductor, had conducted the New York Philharmonic for three years, and, near the end of his contract, allowed Toscanini to go on a three-week tour. When the orchestra returned, Mengelberg made a very indiscreet remark at a rehearsal. He said, "It took me three years to develop a great sound with the orchestra, and in three weeks my work has been destroyed."

The men, knowing that Mengelberg was leaving and Toscanini was taking his place, heard this remark with great displeasure. Besides, their experiences with Toscanini were good, and their admiration for him was great. From then on Mengelberg lost the friendship of the musicians. For his last recording date he was to do the *Tannhäuser Overture* one morning from 9 a.m. to twelve noon. It was 11 a.m. when Mr. King came into my room and asked me to go into the recording studio and try to get Mengelberg to record.

"Why," I said, "it is 11 a.m., and he has been here for two hours. What's wrong?"

"Well, he has lectured and talked for two hours, and, when I ask him to record, he excuses himself, goes into our private ladies' room, and eats apples."

I asked, "Why apples?" and King answered, "He is on an apple diet for his health. See if you can do something to have him record and finish by noon."

I walked into the recording room, and Mengelberg greeted me with, "Good morning, Mr. Shilkret. I have been lecturing and pointing to my discovery of a middle melodic line of Richard Wagner's *Tannhäuser Overture*. It is a very interesting discovery." I could see the men were not interested, and, considering that they had played the overture hundreds of times with many great conductors, I could not blame them for their feelings.

I said to Mengelberg, "That is really a wonderful discovery. Why don't you come tomorrow morning and record your rehearsal for us?"

"Why," he said, "maestro, it is not possible. They are leaving tomorrow for a tour with Toscanini."

I said. "That is alright—you don't need an orchestra."

I wondered if he would become angry at my remark, but instead he smiled and said, "Dat's very good, very funny!" He then turned to the orchestra and said, "Gentlemen, let us record." Of course, my remark put the men in stitches. Anyway, my idea won, and Mengelberg finished the overture by noon.

MORTON GOULD

Morton Gould, as a very young boy, often came to my rehearsals and recordings. He showed great talent as a composer and a pianist as a mere boy. His father was always with him, and he talked about his son Morton with the same gusto as the Hollywood studio press agents used. And Morton Gould lived up to his father's flattering words. He has become one of the most successful conductors and composers in America.

PAUL WHITEMAN, ROXY AND ELECTRICAL RECORDING

Although the original Dixieland Jazz Band was recorded for the Race Department, it was not a Negro band. It consisted of five white musicians who were top jazz players who had learned their lessons by listening to Negro musicians. It started a new trend in popular music.

It was about 1924 when Mr. Rothafel, known as Roxy, asked me to form an orchestra similar to Paul Whiteman's band. He said that I would receive $1200 a week, and that was more than I received at my Victor job, and I could combine that with my recording. There was a good reason for rejecting his offer. I told Roxy that Paul Whiteman's orchestra was not just a matter of hiring good jazz and novelty musicians. Paul had carefully selected men for years and rehearsed them to get splendid results. As he traveled a good deal, he met novel instrumentalists and singers.

Roxy insisted, and I said I was not exaggerating the difficulties. Then he said, "Nat, do me a favor. Erno Rapee (his conductor) is going over a score written by Harling. It is written for an eight piece jazz band and our large movie symphony orchestra. It is wonderful, and I am performing it in two weeks. It will take the place of the classical piece we usually use to open our show."

I went into the room, and there were Rapee and Harling at the piano. Harling, a good composer of classical music, had imbibed too much liquor, and for a while I could decide little about the merits of the piece as a novel composition. Finally I realized that it was neither a good jazz piece nor a good classical number. I went back to Roxy and said, "The composition, as far as I can tell, is not very good, and knowing that you are trying to introduce some new American work—something sensational—I say don't do it." Roxy was terribly annoyed at me, but I stuck to my opinion.

The Harling composition was played for one week and was not the sensational success predicted by Roxy and Rapee. It was never played again. On the other hand, Paul Whiteman commissioned George Gershwin to write a number for his Aeolian Hall concert, and Gershwin came up with the sensational *Rhapsody in Blue*.

Victor Herbert wrote a suite for Whiteman for the same concert. It was a splendid suite, but it could be played by any orchestra. It did not have the flavor of the American idiom.

I was connected with the Paul Whiteman recordings, and often, when Paul was busy or annoyed by his boys, he would ask me to record for him. In fact, when the *Rhapsody* was recorded again for electrical recordings, I recorded and George Gershwin was piano soloist.

There was a good reason for my substituting for Paul. After the great success of the *Rhapsody* at Aeolian Hall, Paul played the number on his road trip. The audience, now wanting to hear the Whiteman band do their special dance arrangements, was not enthusiastic about the *Rhapsody*.

Whiteman believed in the *Rhapsody*'s ultimate recognition and kept on playing it. To make people like it, he made cuts and, to create more excitement, he even accelerated the tempos. As it happened in time, every audience requested George Gershwin's *Rhapsody*—it became a classic.

When we went into electrical recording, it was done at the Liederkranz Hall. This was a German Club, and, when the Victor started electrical recording, our old studios were too small. From my acquaintance with the German Department, I came across Liederkranz Hall. They needed money, and we needed their hall. It turned out to be the finest recording studio we ever worked in.

Well, it was a large hall, and our engineers, not having had the time to experiment with the new method, tried various ways to position the orchestra and the piano. When electrical recording began, there were no soundproof studios. The new method was extremely sensitive and picked up outside noises: the policeman's traffic whistle, kids' yelling, boat whistles, automobile horns, etc. We had the policemen attempting to keep the streets quiet, but there were noises that they could not control.

So when Paul came to record the *Rhapsody in Blue* with Gershwin, he had two strikes against him. First of all, the changes in tempos he made during his road trip had become a habit with him, whereas Gershwin, the soloist and composer, heard the music as he had conceived it. However, the greatest obstacle was the position the recording engineers insisted upon. To get the proper results, they placed the piano one hundred feet from the orchestra and the conductor two hundred feet from the orchestra.

With these problems, Paul and George would not get together. Paul finally said, "Nat, take over." Since I had recorded at the hall for about two months, I was able to control the orchestra and the piano. Soon after that, our engineers rectified the problem of separating the orchestra from the piano and the conductor. Today the seating of an orchestra during a recording is practically like it is at a concert hall.

Electrical recording required a good deal of experimenting before we could control it. A questionnaire was handed to the two committees, asking our opinion of electrical recordings. The older men were against it, and the younger men were for it, even though it was still in a crude stage. As I remarked before, Johnson was reluctant, but he signed with the Western Electric Company.

It was just before the summer of 1924 [actually 1925]—one of the hottest summers—that two rooms in our Camden studio were prepared. We were to record electrically enough masters to start our dealers selling the Victrola and the new type records. It was a tremendous task. We would have to exchange all of the old phonograph machines and all of the old catalogues (records), so that our dealers could stay in business. That meant a demonstration record for publicity and approval of our dealers. It also required enough electrical records for the dealers to sell.

As for recordings, we started with our Metropolitan Opera stars, our solo instrumentalist artists like Kreisler, Heifetz, Elman and well-known pianists. My Victor Salon Orchestra also recorded. Our great problem was the lack of soundproof studios. Poor Miss Ponselle sang a difficult aria seventeen times during one of the hottest days of the year. We finally succeeded on the seventeenth take. This went on for the whole summer.

I also recall our Victor Salon recording of the popular novelty *Nola*. It was a very tricky arrangement, and we recorded it over twenty times, but we could not get a satisfactory master, again on account of the outside noise.

Somehow we did manage, by working day and night, to assemble a fair list of new electrical recordings. Now, how were we to sell the new machines and records to the dealers? We had to take back their old stock and replace it with the new. It was a great expense.

I was asked to record the demonstration record. I was told to spend as much time as necessary, but, above all, sell the idea.

The Columbia Company and the Victor Company were competing and ready to show off between nine hundred and five thousand voices. I was to prepare a demonstration record to supersede these huge choirs.

The time element was important, and so I went through my library to find a number that would show the possibilities of electrical recording. I was asked to give samples of solo instruments from the lowest to the highest notes, a large choir, a string ensemble, a brass band, solo voices, a male quartet, female trios, a mixed quartet, a piccolo, trumpets, dance orchestras, percussion, etc.

I found no printed composition that would fill the demand. It was too late to orchestrate a double-faced record of ten minutes. I decided to compose a fitting number and quickly wrote the *Victor March*. Instead of an arrangement, I had three hundred copies made of my piano sketch, with a few indications for the large group ready to record.

I had engaged a symphony orchestra, a band, a dance orchestra, a vocal quartet, a choir and soloists. I gave instructions as to many changes I wanted to get as many effects as possible. All they each had was a piano vocal sketch, and with their great skill and wonderful experience we recorded the number.

The demonstration turned out to satisfy the dealers and the company. It became the theme song for our Victor broadcasts for over three years. Quite a few years later, Irving Berlin's *God Bless America* came out, and it was similar to my *Victor March*. It was learned that Irving Berlin had written the melody of *God Bless America* in 1917 or 1918 for the troops in a show, and it was not used—it was put aside for the future. Of course I believed him. Berlin is a genius with melodies and lyrics—he did not need to plagiarize.

NOTES

1. Correcting for inflation to the year 2000, this amounts to a drop in annual earnings from $130,000 to $45,000.

2. Gracyk [2000] describes the Stroh violin "which had a specially attached diaphragm and horn (patented in 1899, the device was invented by John Matthias Augustus Stroh and manufactured by his son Charles)."

3. Malone [1968] describes the *Prisoner's Song* as "the biggest selling record in Victor's pre-electric recording history, it approached the six-million mark." Nat and his son Arthur fought unsuccessfully for Nat's composer's rights until the 1950s. Some authors acknowledge Nat Shilkret's role as composer: Malone [1968] writes, "Nathaniel Shilkret, the Victor Company's staff accompanist, added a few words to the song and thought up a melody."

4. Johnson retired in December 1926 when the banking houses Speyer and Company and J. and W. Seligman and Company bought all shares, a majority of which belonged to Johnson. See, for example, Gelatt [1955] for the history of Victor and Johnson's dominant role in its development.

5. Caruso died in 1921, and commercial radio broadcasts began in 1923.

If the Minnevich recording session was really a few weeks after Caruso's death, the reason for needing to be back in New York City could not have been to begin a broadcast.

CHAPTER 4

RADIO AND RECORDING

The Victor Company will endeavor to secure engagements for the services of Mr. Shilkret, in conducting orchestras in places where by means of electrical devices the performances of said orchestras, at the time they are given, may be rendered audible outside of the place of performance (otherwise known as radio broadcasting), on terms which are mutually agreeable to all parties.

—1928 Shilkret–Victor Contract for Employment

METEORIC GROWTH

With my expanded duties and my record ideas clicking, I felt that I should not only figure as a staff conductor, but also as a featured artist. At this time [1925] my salary was $250 a week, with exclusive service. Mr. Harry MacDonough was the chairman of our A&R Committee. He had once started as a popular singer. He was an intelligent man with a good education, and he was able to get full cooperation from our committee.

I decided to ask him for a raise of $100 per week, exclusive for recordings, but if I composed anything it was my property and not the Victor's. He agreed to my request for ownership of my compositions but made a curious statement, so unlike him, about my salary: He said, "I'll raise you $50 a week and no more, over my dead body."

Some time later he explained the remark. He was only receiving $300 a week and, since he was my superior, felt that he would not condone my receiving a higher salary than he. We finally agreed upon a settlement of a $50 raise with the privilege of earning $50 more on the outside, but not recording for any other firm.

With my appearances on a few radio broadcasts and my publicity on Broadway, I contacted N. W. Ayer and Son agency and offered my services for a radio program at $50 for myself and reimbursement of the cost of the orchestra. I did not receive anything for arrangements and copying expense.

They came up with a sponsor, Hire's Root Beer. The complete cost of the program amounted to $335. There was no charge for the air time. This was practically the beginning period of radio. After a few weeks Hire's complained that the costly program did not really help their sales. However, they stayed on for twenty-six weeks. I was called in by the agency, and I was sure that this would end my radio career. Instead they offered me four new sponsors at $500 each—a total of $2000. Of course I accepted.

With my signed contract I went to Mr. MacDonough's office and showed him the contract. He immediately okayed the $50 extra, and not over his dead body. Whiteman's offer of $35,000 a year guarantee had not been out of line. Paul had predicted that he could easily earn that sum for me.

My radio career was meteoric. For years I had from six to fifteen sponsored broadcasts a week. I can hardly remember all my sponsors: General Motors (twice), Eveready, Mobil Oil, Esso [now Exxon], Salada (with James Melton), the Smith Brothers' team (Hillpot and Lambert), Maxwell House Coffee, Hall of Fame, General Electric, Eastman Kodak, Victor Talking Machine, the Pennsylvania Railroad, bankers (the Bankers' Hour), and many others. About the only cigarette hour I never broadcast for was Lucky Strike. This was because they had a rule that no orchestra conductor or artist could appear on their program if they had any connection within six months with another cigarette hour. I never had a six-month period without a cigarette hour!

My radio programs ran into the thousands during the next ten years. In the meantime, Wall Street firms had purchased [1926] the Victor Company. They did not interfere with our A&R Committee. We went along as usual, except that Mr. MacDonough was [had been in 1923] elevated to the executive committee.

Before I get into my radio career I want to put down some other items.

THE STRAND THEATRE

Although I seldom had time to accept outside engagements, I did get into a movie house, the Strand Theatre [1927]. I was given the same marquee lights as Charlie Chaplin. I engaged fifty-four men in the pit. It was a moving pit, and for our feature we were raised to the level of the stage. We played our arrangement, and then came a few acts that we worked with.

I was getting into trouble with everyone because I had to conduct four performances a day at the theater. Then there was the preparation for the next week's show. My Victor artists and my recording work could not be neglected. I also had my radio—I had four sponsors. It was just impossible to do justice to everyone.

Mr. Plunkit was the manager of the theater, Mr. Dreyfus stage designer, and Jack Green assistant to Dreyfus. Green was a splendid pianist and once was in the Pinto New York Boys' Orchestra. I was getting more and more interested in the theater.

Somehow I kept things going together for five weeks. By this time we had added a Russian Ballet as a regular part of our show. In my orchestra I had Fud Livingston as arranger, and he was terrific. I had not been able to engage any of the men working for me at the Victor or my radio station. They were earning too much to play at a movie house.

I looked for a concertmaster, and was introduced to a young violinist [Zayde] recently from Russia. He had been concertmaster for five years with the composer Glazunov. To protect his family, he had decided to leave Russia and come to America.

He had not much luck in America. He had only been offered an engagement with a small traveling orchestra at a low salary. He wanted to meet me and play for me. To my surprise, he was a wonderful soloist. I engaged him immediately at $350 a week as concertmaster.

THE LAST STRAW

One time I signed the Victor Salon Orchestra for an appearance at Bristol, Connecticut, and this turned out to be unfortunate. It was Thursday, and the concert went off well. I acted as Master of Ceremonies, and I found myself talking to an audience for the first time in my life, and I enjoyed the experience.

By 11 p.m. we were ready to leave for New York. The men were all booked for rehearsals for their work or to record in some studio the next morning. I was to get to the Strand Theatre for the Friday morning rehearsal and get ready for the first show where the critics of the papers would get their write-up for the evening papers.

After a quick bite we started for New York. Lou Raderman was driving and Milton Rettenberg was sitting in the back seat. We traveled for about an hour and Milton started to pick on Lou. He repeatedly told Lou that he was driving north, opposite the direction to New York. Lou wouldn't listen to Milton and kept on traveling. By 5 a.m. Lou was convinced that Milton was right. By this time we were far north. We had to turn around and go south.

We finally got to the Harlem Bridge about one hour after our dates. We were driving very fast when we were stopped by a traffic officer. He asked Lou Raderman for his license. Instead Lou took out a badge (a police badge given to him for a performance at police affairs) and showed it to the policeman. The officer looked at the badge and threw it into the river and then ordered Lou to drive on. This was a real blow to Lou—it had saved him many traffic tickets. He was really shaken up!

By the time we got to the Strand Theatre the rehearsal was practically over. Leo Erdody, my assistant, had gone through the rehearsal. I announced that I would conduct the show, even if I had missed the rehearsal. Erdody would sit near me and let me know the routine and the cues of our routine, and I would get on without a mishap.

Behind me I could hear Mr. Plunkit and Mr. Green arguing. Plunkit was against my conducting the important Friday afternoon performance because a mishap would give the show a bad review. Green excitedly told Plunkit if he spoke to me I would quit. I conducted the afternoon performance and everything came off well. I was terribly tired because, with all my work, I had not slept a wink in four days. Then came the second afternoon show, and, since the manager, the stage director and the electrical stage hand had disappeared after the first show and left the care of the second show to their assistants, the mishaps began.

As I started my overture, my part of the pit went down instead of up to the stage level, and the rest of the orchestra went up. I found myself in the dark with about six orchestra men, a harpist and Erdody. Coming from a bright room, I was now in absolute darkness. Not having slept in four days, I was too tired to stand; I sat down and I immediately fell asleep.

This was the last straw. I quit at the end of the week. I had been at the theater six weeks, and it proved too much of a strain. I had quit in time. I was in trouble with my radio sponsors and the Victor artists. I must have been a glutton for punishment to even have attempted such a schedule. Sometimes one learns from experience in a hard way.

SIR LOUIS STERLING

It was the coming of Louis Sterling (now Sir Sterling) that changed everything. He was born on the East Side of New York, migrated to England,
and, by his courage, hard work and great personality, became head of the
Columbia British Phonograph Company.[1] Being a very generous and kind
man, he was instrumental in accomplishing many projects for the needy.
This brought him knighthood, and to notify his East Side friends he printed
a card that read

SIR LOUIS STERLING
From Orchard Street to Buckingham Palace.

His objective in coming to the United States was to bolster up the
American Columbia Company. They were financially in a bad state. Sterling bought controlling interest in the company for $2,500,000 (thanks to a
loan from J. P. Morgan). He also signed up for electrical recording a few
weeks ahead of Victor.

His next move was to gather all the information possible that would
help his company. From what we heard, he figured that the Victor Company
would suffer a damaging blow if he could entice Paul Whiteman and his
orchestra, Mr. Harry MacDonough and Mr. Eddie King to sign up with the
Columbia Company.

It so happened that Whiteman at that time needed money for some
reason. Sterling gave him $100,000 in advance and he left the Victor Com-
pany [1928]. With Paul Whiteman, MacDonough [in 1925] and King [in
1926] leaving Victor, it left a gap in the Victor staff, and I was promoted
to being in charge of recording.

I was elevated to top man in recording and given a new contract for
$2000 a week. This lasted for seven years. My radio contracts were keeping
me terribly busy, and, in fact, my radio remuneration was much greater
than my Victor contract. As Caruso said ten years earlier, it is feast or
famine for an artist.

Mr. Walter Clark and Mr. Cliff Cairns were brought in. My experience gave me great importance. With my many broadcasts and the Victor
catalogues I was sought after by many artists. I kept at least two hundred
musicians busy steadily. The man who engages talent is in a strong position, but the responsibility is great. Later I will tell you more as to the
results. Now I am reminded of some other happenings during the time of
our Wall Street owners.

EDDIE KING

As I remarked before, the Wall Street bankers did not interfere with our running of the company. There was one exception. They sent an efficiency expert to our New York office. Mr. King was still with us when a man who looked like a Confederate colonel announced that the Wall Street Bankers had sent him to report his findings as an efficiency expert and that he could be of some help to us.

After he left, Mr. King, who had an explosive temper, came to my room and said, "What do you think that damn fool asked me? He asked me how many people are employed in our New York office. I told him six. Then he said get rid of one of them; you can do with five men. I asked him 'who did he suggest?' and he said take your pick—Shilkret or Scott. I then lost my temper and told him to get out of my office." Scott was our handyman. I then asked Mr. King, "How could he come to the conclusion to fire either the handyman or the head musician? How did it come about?"

"Well, he first asked me the names of the men employed. Then he asked me their positions, and I answered 'assistants of mine.'"

I wondered, "Why did you use the term assistant for everyone? How could he understand the difference between the handyman and me?"

After Mr. King's second wife died he remained a bachelor for a long time. He was the last man we would have suspected to have been interested in a medium, but, to our utter astonishment, he announced that through a medium he wanted to contact and speak to his second wife. We thought he was joking, but he was in dead earnest. Not only was he serious, but he engaged a medium for an evening in our studio and he invited Mr. Mac-Donough, Mr. Higgins, Mr. Cairns and me for the séance.

As we sat in a circle the medium (a woman) called on the spirit of Caruso to sing for us. We heard a voice, not very good, singing an aria. Then he called upon Mrs. King to contact him. At that moment I stuck Mr. King with a pin, and he jumped up and exclaimed, "She just touched me," and he started to speak to her. Her answers to Mr. King were extremely vague, and finally the séance was over. We tried to tell him that the medium was a fake, but he was absolutely convinced that his wife had been in touch with him, as he said, "Why I felt her touch." Of course I never told him that it was the touch of my pin that he felt.

I must relate one incident that happened later. Sometime in 1928 the efficiency expert went to Wielage, who was in charge of record pressings at Camden and asked for the number of records of all titles sold in the last three years. This included classic and popular records. He came up with the brilliant idea that if a record, no matter how important the artist, did not sell a certain amount in the last three years it should be destroyed.

As a result many masters of our greatest names were destroyed, while the new popular records passed the test. In other words, a popular tune with a life of perhaps three months was preserved, while many of the greatest artists' records from 1900 to 1925 were lost forever. It was a tragic and devastating loss for music. When we realized what we had done, we just groaned and hung our heads in shame.

I want to tell you an amusing story about Mr. King. For some time the popular dance records were undergoing changes of style. The Chicago bands were popular, but they were being challenged by New Orleans, New York and Hollywood, and we were receiving complaints from our traveling agents concerning our popular records. Mr. King fumed over their complaints. He would argue with our agents, and it was getting on his nerves. For weeks he would complain to MacDonough, Mr. Cairns and me, saying that there would have to be a showdown.

We traveled to Camden every Monday for a committee meeting. One day, on our two-hour trip, he announced that this was the day he would settle his troubles once and for all. We tried to warn him, but he would not listen.

The meeting started, and for the first time Mr. King sat in his place, not saying a word. His face was clouded, and he appeared restless. We were discussing some item, when all of a sudden King brought his fist down on the table with a resounding thump, stood up, and, in a trembling voice, said, "Gentlemen, I have had a change of life!"

Well, you can imagine the effect of that remark. We all started to ask him how did it feel, etc. King tried to stop us and explain what he meant, but it was no use. We kidded him unmercifully, and he never made his point, which was that unless we stopped the agents from picking on him he would quit. He did not quit, and we did not stop our agents' complaints.

Mr. Eddie King, my superior at Victor, had been a pretty good drummer in his early days. He had a cymbal that he was fond of, and, when he was engaged by the Victor as a manager, he brought the cymbal with him. As he supervised the many dance orchestras' recordings, he always held the cymbal in his hands, ready to strike it at spots at which he thought it would help.

The cymbal got on the nerves of all of us, and so we would bang it as hard as possible, just for our satisfaction. After a while it started chipping, piece by piece. Poor King would complain that other drummers did not know how to hit a cymbal properly.

Even with the cymbal half broken, he still held on to it while we watched it, hoping it would break apart. Finally it was reduced to such a mess that he threw it out, much to the relief of everyone.

Mr. King was not a man who wasted money. If a singer booked for a recording date was unable to perform, there was always a lady substitute to sing with the orchestra. Otherwise the musicians would have to be paid, even though they did not perform. Madame Schneider was an elderly Jugoslav woman who came in daily, always sitting and knitting away, ready to substitute. She carried her orchestrations with her, ready to sing at a moment's notice. King made her a permanent fixture. She was a folk singer—not too good—but reliable and cheap.

HILLBILLY SONGS

After starting the Hillbilly catalogue with the *Prisoner's Song*, we (Victor) received a letter from a man [C. B. Obaugh] who claimed that he had one hundred hillbilly tunes for sale. I was sent down to meet him and offer him payment for same.

On a cold December day in 1925 I arrived at Staunton, Virginia, about 7 p.m. I looked around the station but saw no one. It was fairly dark, and I wondered why the man was not there to meet me. It was a lonely place for a stranger. I waited for almost fifteen minutes when I spied a man coming toward me.

It was the man who had written to us. He claimed that on account of his auto giving him trouble he was late. We started for his home, and he told me that it was his wife who knew the tunes and that she would play them on an organ—which turned out to be a mouth organ (harmonica).

Arriving at his home, I met his wife, a woman who said that she was thirty-five years old and looked over fifty. I sat down with my music paper and a pencil. The wife pulled her harmonica from her pocket and the husband sat at his typewriter, ready to put down the lyrics. We worked until 3 a.m.—seven hours and not one complete number was accomplished. When she played a tune she did not know the lyrics; when she remembered the lyrics she could not recall the melody. At 3 a.m. I called a halt.

I went to bed cold and disappointed. My room was in the attic three flights up. The only heat I had was a hot iron bar placed at my feet. It was too cold to undress. I took off my shoes and slept with my clothes on, plus my overcoat. About 3:30 a.m. the man came to my room and suggested that a trip to his folks 150 miles away in West Virginia would bring results. The village was 150 miles away from a railroad, and there were quite a few folks who were known as folk singers; in particular, a young lady and an old fiddler.

My time was limited. This was Tuesday, and by Friday I was to begin my Strand Theatre engagement.[2] He claimed that we could arrive at his folks by Wednesday late afternoon and get back in time to catch the

Thursday afternoon train for New York.

In order to accomplish this, we would have to leave early and travel through bad roads and hills. He explained that the roads were slippery and during winter weather had some dangerous spots; however, the greatest danger was my blue suit—I might be taken for a government officer looking for moonshiners. I told him that I was ready to take my chances. Coming all the way from New York and returning empty handed would put me in an awkward position.

It seemed to me that I had slept a few minutes, when suddenly a light appeared in the pitch dark and I heard voices coming from outside. A few minutes later he appeared and said breakfast was ready. It was exactly 5:30 a.m. I went downstairs into the dining room next to the kitchen and found, to my surprise, their ten children and an old pappy, all staring at me. I had worked with the couple for over seven hours and had not heard one word from the children.

The food came, and the smell of the grease turned my stomach. They started to eat, but I could not get enough courage to taste a bite. The children all watched me, and I was embarrassed. I picked up a fork and toyed with the greasy food and finally said I was not hungry.

We started on our trip in his dilapidated car in pitch darkness. In a nearby town he stopped for gas, and I walked into a general store and bought some crackers and American cheese. On our way through the hills and dales we visited a few homes trying to gather some tunes, but the people were all too shy to respond. The old folks were hard to speak to; the middle-aged ones couldn't remember; and the young ones hardly knew any tunes.

We rode on, and I was entertained at various places where calamity had occurred and, for each terrible story, a song had been written. Many folk songs came out of these tragedies. It was getting to be about 3 p.m., and still no folk song. Finally, we came near the vicinity of the old fiddler. In order to reach his cabin we would have to get out of the car and walk across a snowy mountain. By the way, my deal was $20 for each complete tune—music and lyric.

Fortunately, we were saved the walk over the mountain, as my guide recognized the old fiddler walking toward us, holding on to the reins of his horse.

For ten minutes the old fiddler eyed us suspiciously, without uttering a word or showing any sign that he knew the man I was with. Finally, the man reminded him that he had played at his wedding. That brought a response from the fiddler, and, instead of talking about tunes, he insisted upon doing some tricks with his horse. However, we got to music, and he pulled out a harmonica and played some tunes. He even tried to sell me *Yankee Doodle*. Like many fiddlers, he knew tunes, but no lyrics.

By this time we had trouble getting rid of him, and I was really in the dumps. I suggested that we go on and invite as many folks as we meet to a party at his folks' home. The attraction: a man who could write down any tune they sang and would play it back immediately on a pedal organ. Many homes had a pump organ, probably sold to them by some fast-talking peddler. They were pretty wheezy in sound, but good enough to be heard and appreciated. We arrived at his folks' home about 6 p.m., and we had dinner. To my surprise, the food was excellent, and the chicken tasted like paradise to me, since I had hardly eaten anything but cheese and crackers for a day.

After dinner I took a walk, and there, about two hundred feet from me, I encountered a small bear. Can you imagine my feelings, being a slicker from a city? Not knowing what to do, I just stood there looking at the bear. I tried not to show fear, and, luckily for me, he finally went away.

About 7 p.m. people started to arrive, and some refreshments were served. I sat down at the organ and started to get the folks in a proper mood. With drinks and food and a lot of dancing, the middle-aged folks started to supply me with melodies and lyrics. With the true comradeship that music produces, everyone got into the spirit.

I tried hard to get a consensus of opinion, since there were heated arguments about what was the proper tune or the proper lyric. By 3 a.m. I had collected fifty-two tunes and twelve dance tunes.

There was one great disappointment. The young lady who knew more tunes than anyone did not appear. It seemed that during the previous summer she had been going out with some young fellow from the city, and he left after the summer season. It was an unwritten law of the rural people that no one else could take his place, and with the cold weather and snow on the ground she refused to come to our party. I have always regretted her absence. If it had not been for the Friday opening of my Strand Theatre engagement, I would have gone to her home. With fifty-two tunes at $20 apiece, my friend would be richer by $1040. For an itinerant peddler that was like a fortune.

Of course, I was dreadfully tired by 3 a.m. My feet ached from all the pumping on the organ. Again I went to bed with a hot iron, but I had not reckoned on my friend; $20 a tune made him avaricious, and for an hour he and his friends tramped up to my room, trying to sell me more melodies. By 4:15 a.m. I threatened to use my hot iron (shaped like a baseball bat) if they woke me again.

We drove back to his home in Virginia, and he tried to sell me more tunes before I boarded the train.

I believe that folk songs were originally composed by talented minstrels or some gifted singers without technical musical knowledge, but with melodic and poetic inspiration. They sang, and their melodies were picked up by other people. The music and the lyric traveled through many villages, cities and countries, changed and polished by hundreds, and finally coming to us as a gem. Sometimes the gem came in different shapes, but, to our delight, a natural gem.

Over thirty of the tunes were recorded by various singers: Frank Crumit, Johnny Marvin, Frank Luther and Carson. I had collected some tunes with various versions. With my experience in the Foreign Department, I had gone through hundreds of folk songs. I picked the version that was the most natural sounding.

RALPH PEER

Now that the Hillbilly and Race records had been launched by Victor, I brought in Ralph Peer to help us, by having him travel with a recording engineer to go South and record local singers.[3] He was paid $80 a week and expenses. He took several trips, and the next year he asked for a raise.

I okayed the raise of $80 to $160 per week. Mr. Walter Clark met Peer, who sold Clark an idea. No raise, but a royalty of one cent per record side that he would divide with the artist. Mr. Clark was not too experienced in the record business and, since the royalty figure was two cents per side, thought it advantageous for the Victor Company to accept the offer. When I heard of this I was stunned. No one on the musical staff had been offered royalty for his arrangements or compositions, and here was a man collecting royalties with other men's compositions!

Peer went ahead and recorded hundreds of tunes. In fact, so many that his royalties were becoming large payments. He also extended his recordings to the Export Department. He added Mexico and South America to his territory. It came to a point where the Victor Company wanted to make new arrangements. Peer, always a soft speaker, but shrewd, sold the company the idea of Victor financing a publishing company, making him president, and dividing the profits.

For years he recorded and printed the material gathered. By this time he had a substantial catalogue, but he was careful not to sell his music. A huge printing sum was expended, with the loss so great that the Victor Company decided to sever the relationship.

During that period[4] there was a new demand for Mexican and South American hits. Also during that period, ASCAP (the American Society of Composers and Publishers) broke with the radio broadcasting companies, and BMI (Broadcast Music Incorporated) was formed to control ASCAP.

By this time the Peer Music Company received a large offer from BMI.

Peer retained his ASCAP affiliations for part of his catalogue, and accepted the BMI offer. With his efficient manipulations, his firm was now valued at 20 million dollars. Not a bad finish from an $80 weekly earning.

RUDOLPH VALENTINO

When Rudolph Valentino died [1926] I composed a tango called *Fate* (*Valentino Tango*) and had Shapiro and Bernstein's publishing firm print it in sheet form. I recorded the tango, and it sold well. It seemed that Bernstein made a deal with International Music Inc. to sell the music to Mexican and South American firms. I was not informed of this, and imagine my surprise when I saw fifty-four editions printed South of the Border, some with my name as composer and some with other composers named.

I received royalties from Shapiro-Bernstein, but as usual no royalty from International (Ralph Peer). Mr. Peer professed great friendship for me, but that did not entitle me to any royalty.

MORAN AND MACK

In addition to the Red Seal and Black records, we had a Blue label; the difference: 10 percent royalties for the Red Seal artists and 5 percent for the Blue Seal artists. The Blue label artists were far above the average performers, but did not have as good a reputation as the leading operatic stars. It would take pages to mention all the well-known artists in our many colored labels. Once a year, the fine Blue Seal artists spent one week in a group to record the popular Broadway operettas. Later on it became popular to use original Broadway casts. Green and Purple labels were also used.

For a while we went in for comic records of vaudeville headliners. This started when I attended a Revue that featured Moran and Mack (the Two Black Crows) in a sketch. I invited them to try recording.[5] After picking the best of their material, we were ready to make a deal.

We had never paid any royalties for comic records, and, when Moran and Mack asked for a 5 percent royalty, our executive committee turned them down. I was furious and presented my arguments to our A&R Committee, knowing that the Two Black Crows would sell sensationally. Well, we were given an okay to engage them at a 5 percent royalty. I called the comedians, and by this time they had contacted Columbia Company, who offered them a 10 percent royalty agreement.

We could have had them on the 10 percent terms, but this time we were definitely refused. As I predicted, the Two Black Crows Columbia record was a sensational seller, and the material used was exactly what I had worked out with Moran and Mack.

This started a search for comic artists. Fanny Brice and many other top vaudevillians were signed up. The Victor Company had learned its lesson, and 10 percent royalties became standard.

I remember one phrase from the Fanny Brice sketches—it was not what she said that was so funny, but rather it was the inflection of her voice. She said she was in a delicatessen store, and just then a stick-up man came in and ordered everyone to hold their hands up high. Someone in the sketch asked, "What did you do then?"

Brice replied, "What could I do, with my hands in the pickle barrel?"

GENE AUSTIN

One day at the Victor I was asked to listen to a "pop" tune called *When My Sugar Walks Down the Street*. It was a popular melody published by the Mills Music Company.[6] Jack Mills brought a rather young stocky fellow to demonstrate the tune. As the young fellow sang the song, I was pleasantly surprised by his voice and style. I asked him his name, and he said Gene Austin. I okayed the acceptance of the song, and then told Austin that I wanted him to record his voice. Gene said in surprise, "I auditioned for Victor twice, and I was turned down."

That was news to me, and then I told Gene, "I am giving the song to Aileen Stanley and to you for a duet." I called Aileen, a lovely lady and a popular artist, and told her that, if she agreed, I would like her to okay the duet—Gene Austin's name would not appear on the label. She was gracious and said, if I wanted it that way, she would go along with my idea. The duet was recorded [1925].

Three days later I received a call from our Camden office, inquiring about who the singer was in the Aileen Stanley recording. I asked why they wanted to know. They replied, "Sign him up at once."

"Why the hurry?" I asked, "You turned him down twice."

So Gene Austin, unknown and struggling, was signed. My usual contract with new popular artists was $200 a side for one year and an option for one-cent royalty after the first year. Gene Austin's rise came after his third release. He jumped from an occasional $50 a week artist to a $4000 per week artist, due to his record releases. After his year was up we signed his option.

By this time he was receiving all kinds of nightclub and theater engagements. His records were selling at a tremendous rate. I picked four numbers for him, and one of the numbers was *My Blue Heaven*, composed by Walter Donaldson.

Success went to Austin's head, and he started drinking. The morning he recorded *My Blue Heaven* he came in feeling somewhat high, but knocked off four numbers in two hours. The two records sold over a million copies within a short time. He earned $40,000 on his first royalty recorded date.

I collaborated on a song *Look Down That Lonesome Road*. It became a standard and was included in the Universal film of *Show Boat*, sung [on Bb17551, recorded in 1929] by Paul Robeson. [The voice in the film is that of Jules Bledsoe.] Filming *Show Boat* and not using Jerome Kern's marvelous songs was practically asinine.

Here was what happened: Billy Rose was musical supervisor of the film, and he influenced the producer, Carl Laemmle, Jr., saying, "Why use the old songs?" He was referring to one of the greatest scores of all times: *Ol' Man River*, *Make-Believe*, etc., saying people were tired of these songs.

That was how *Lonesome Road* was introduced in the *Show Boat* film. Gene Austin's record became a great favorite. For thirty years the song has been recorded by every popular singer and dance orchestra: Bing Crosby, Frank Sinatra, Tommy Dorsey, and many other artists.

GEORGE OLSEN

I started to feature Fred Waring, whom I regarded as a man of original ideas. I tried to engage Guy Lombardo, but Mr. King's first act was to sign him for Columbia. Just then Jack Robbins, a music publisher, asked me to listen to a small combination headed by a drummer, George Olsen. I went down to the nightclub where he was playing, and I thought his band had possibilities. The band did not impress me as much as his trio of singers shoving a small piano around the tables.

George did a few records with me, conducting without creating too much of a stir. At the third recording date I chose Jerome Kern's *Who* for him. As I listened to the arrangement, I was not satisfied with the first chorus, which was played out of tune by his saxophone section. I asked Olsen to allow me to change it to his singing trio. George said, "Do they know the number?"

I answered, "Sure, I heard them sing it to me and my wife when we were at your club."

The record turned out to be one of our best sellers. In fact, George Olsen's band became a favorite, and it changed a $600 a week band to a $4000 a week attraction. As for Whiteman's large band, I managed to keep up this style with my own dance recordings. Of course, we had quite a few other bands—especially from Chicago which, for popular music, was leading the rest of the nation at that time.

MISCHA ELMAN

At the Victor we were waiting for Mischa Elman. This had been his first tour not accompanied by his father. Senior Elman was with us, and while we were waiting I got a crazy idea. Old man Elman always considered his son's talent to be superior to that of Jascha Heifetz. It was an old story with him.

I went up to him and said, "You know that Mischa recorded a few records for us while on tour." I added, "Please don't tell him. He wants to surprise you!"

Elman senior said, "I won't say a word to him. Please, let me hear the records."

I telephoned our receptionist and told her to let us know when Mischa Elman arrived. Then I picked up a few records and played them for the old man Elman. What he did not know was that he was listening to new recordings of Heifetz. As he listened he grew more and more enthusiastic and remarked, "Isn't it wonderful. It is good-bye Heifetz. The tone, the technique ... Heifetz will never be able to beat my Mischa." Pretty soon our receptionist telephoned that Mischa had arrived.

We beat a fast retreat and watched behind a pillar. Mischa came in, and they greeted each other in the Russian fashion. A few minutes later, the father said, "You have a secret, isn't it so?"

"What are you talking about?" asked Mischa.

The father: "I know; you can't fool me."

Mischa said, "Stop talking riddles. Tell me what you know."

The old man smiled and forgot his promise to us. He said, "I just heard the records you made while on your tour." Mischa then asked his father to play the records. The old man, in his excitement, said, "It is good-bye Heifetz. These are the greatest records you ever played."

Mischa was suspicious and went over to the Victrola. He heard about one minute of it and then threw the record on the floor. He turned to his father and said, "You fool, these are Heifetz' records." I kept away from Mischa for some time.

PAUL WHITEMAN

Paul Whiteman, despite his great success, had peculiar misgivings before he left the Victor. He told me one day that both of our names, his and mine, were too long for the public. He claimed that names like Lopez, Ben Bernie, and Ted Lewis were shorter and easily remembered. I did not agree with him. In fact, he insisted upon Lopez and Bernie not being engaged by the Victor Company.

The Masons gave a dinner in honor of Paul, and my Victor Salon Orchestra was engaged to entertain the guests. Evidently, Paul was impressed by the sound of our strings. The next week he added a fairly large string section to his saxophones and brass. It was a fine ensemble.

I would sometimes hear that Paul had a great band, but that he was only a fair conductor. That is not true. I consider Paul Whiteman a splendid conductor. Whether he would have made a good or ordinary symphonic conductor is not relevant.

He had started out as a symphonic violinist or viola player in San Francisco. He formed a dance band, with Ferde Grofé arranging. Up to this time dance bands, more or less, played from printed notes and added some improved ideas according to their ability.

Paul was a good enough musician to realize that fine arrangements would bring class to the music. In dance organizations it is the leader who picks outstanding instrumentalists and brings out the style, color and unusual effects, blending them into a perfect ensemble. He does not rehearse the band for perfect technique. He is looking for novelty and beauty. It is not correct or academic beating that makes a novelty band a success; it is the imaginative leader who creates the outstanding sound, by his sensitive ear and his striving for unusual effects, never stopping until he gets results that distinguish him from the less-determined conductors.

I just mention a few of the men Whiteman brought forth: Ross Gorman, Henry Busse, Siegrist, Grofé, Hazlett, Venuti, the Rhythm Boys with Bing Crosby, Morton Downey and many other talents. Whiteman had the idea of commissioning George Gershwin to write the *Rhapsody in Blue*. For me Whiteman was a fine conductor and a fine musician.

With his expanding orchestra, he tried to form an American orchestra, combining his dance novelty band with the symphonic orchestra. He spent a fortune arranging classical music for this combination. He had men like Deutsch and Floridia arranging Wagner, Liszt and other classical composers. He did not get very far with the idea. The dance or popular audience did not accept it, and the people who liked the accepted symphonic classics played as the composers had conceived their ideas were not impressed.

Leaving the Victor was not a smart move for Whiteman. At Victor he had built up a vast audience for his dance band. They appreciated his adding of strings to the novelty band. However, the Columbia record buyers went for smaller dance bands, for Ted Lewis and for less complicated combinations. Whiteman was too symphonic for their taste. His Columbia records were not as successful commercially as they had been with Victor, whose buyers were more sophisticated and able to appreciate Whiteman's style.

For a long time he did not mind his men drinking and, in general, their jokes. After a few years he grew tired of both their drinking and their tomfoolery. The newer, younger men in his band called him "Pops," and he had to correct them, telling them to call him "Mr. Whiteman." He had been generous with his salaries. His men were the highest paid musicians. When the price was $15 for a three-hour date he paid his men $25 for each master. Since four masters were recorded each session, his men received $100, instead of $15, plus their regular salary.

At a certain period, many of his top men left him, probably because he could not keep up the high salaries. As a result, I got to use the Dorsey brothers, Ferde Grofé, Busse, Challis and Satterfield (two arrangers), and others in my recordings and broadcasts.

While he was recording his last sessions at the Victor I asked him why he had changed to the Columbia Company. He told me that I could record as well as he with my popular orchestra. I did not believe him. I thought the main reason was that Sterling's offer of $100,000 came at a time Paul needed cash. In answer to Paul's comment I said, "You should have spoken to me. I would not have recorded another dance number." He did not answer me.[7]

When Paul Whiteman left the Victor, our officials were really worried. Becoming the head conductor and manager, I came to the conclusion that, instead of trying to follow Whiteman's style, I would concentrate on smaller compact dance orchestras.

In later years, after touring, Whiteman finally became an executive with a TV and radio station. I had been offered the job, but turned it down.

AUDITIONS

During the Wall Street ownership we had auditions for new talent. A lady came in and sang for us. After she finished we gave our secret sign for the engineer not to record her, just let her sing. This would be followed up with a form note that we were not interested in considering her for our catalogue. A week later we received a call from one of the Wall Street brokers, saying that he and the lady who made an audition for us would come down to hear her audition record. We had to confess that we had not recorded her because we did not think enough of her voice to make a record. He was furious and gave orders that from now on we must inform the artist of the truth. If we decided not to record any singer we must tell them our reason.

Well, we tried that, and it became a hardship. Instead of hearing many contestants, we were just about able to hear four in a six-hour session. A lady came in for a test. She was well dressed and pretty sure of herself. When she was through with her rendition we told her that we would not record her. She demanded angrily to know why. We told her that we did not consider her rendition good enough to be recorded. She insisted that we must give her our reason for refusing her. We said that her diction was poor. She flared up with, "That is ridiculous. I have proof that critics have written articles of my perfect diction." As we pointed out other faults she grew incensed, and there was no way to get rid of her. Having had more experiences like this, we finally told our Wall Street banker that, if we are to go through more time wasting, we will refuse to audition any new talent. The order was rescinded.

I remember one amusing incident. A young violinist came in for an audition. I told him that we could not use him because we had Kreisler, Elman and Heifetz and no room for another violinist. He said, "I know that, but I would record for the Black Label, and my records would be sold for a lower price." Again I told him that we could not use him. He then said, "Who are you to tell me that I am not good enough to record? You are really not a musician."

I did not tell him who I was. I asked, "Who did you expect to audition you?"

He answered, "Nat Shilkret."

Again I did not inform him who I was. I asked him who his teacher was.

He answered, "Mr. Maximilian Pilzer."

I said, "Just wait a minute." I called for someone to go into the recording room and whispered in his ear to bring Mr. Pilzer out. When the young fellow saw his teacher come out, he picked up his violin case and started walking out. Before he got to the door, I informed him that I was Nat Shilkret.

QUIRKS AND TIDBITS

Ronnie asked for some unusual stories, and sometimes I did not tell him funny stories, but would relate what I called "quirks"—peculiar quirks of people in the business—and "tidbits"—anonymous quirks and complaints:

John Charles Thomas, a splendid baritone soloist, claimed that when in doubt and undecided, he flipped a coin.

Sam Feinsmith, a good legitimate clarinet and saxophone player, insisted that he could play jazz as well as Artie Shaw, Jimmy Dorsey or Benny Goodman. He was really a square.

The Victor Executive Committee decided that radio was just a fad and would disappear after a short time.

Eldridge Johnson's quirk that a phonograph top must be curved—it cost the Victor a good deal of sale losses until he finally gave in to a flat top.

Mischa Elman's jealousy of Heifetz, when there was room enough for success for both of them.

De Pachmann, a great pianist, decided in his declining years to have a piano built to further his technique. He was celebrated for his marvelous technique on a standard piano. He recorded with his curved piano, but he made many errors.

Claude Debussy's whole tone scale was a sensational success. A young composer told me that Debussy had invented seventy-two different scales. It did not help his composing.

Walter Damrosch asked Barrère, the famous flutist, what he would do when he became too old to play. Barrère: "I'll become a conductor."

Toscanini to Labate, an oboe player: "How can you afford to play so bad?"

Labate replied, "With my $50,000 in the bank."

A wrestling match is on TV, and Toscanini watches and yells imprecations at the villain as vehemently as if the orchestra were playing wrong notes to spite him. Pablo Picasso also watches wrestling with great enthusiasm.

The Victor used Nat Shilkret for my popular records and Nathaniel Shilkret for my classical releases.

Johnny Green for years used Johnny. Now he has changed it to John Green. I like Johnny; it fits his character.

Listening to a group of players discuss the most difficult instrument: Violin! No, piano; no, trumpet; no, cello; etc.

I heard the following remark by a successful publisher of popular music: "Why are composers and lyric writers always beefing about us? All they give us is a ruled paper and a lot of black dots—we make the hits for them. Without us there would be no hits."

Temperamental opera stars to Arturo Toscanini: "Maestro, you must recognize me as a star and follow my interpretation."

Toscanini's reply: "Madame, I recognize only one kind of star, and that is in heaven."

July 4th and New Year's Eve are the busiest days of the year. A cellist, in order to find work, became a saxophone player, but without the necessary jazz style—in other words, a real square. It was almost closing time at the union headquarters, and still no offers. A contractor having trouble filling his quota and seeing a saxophone case asked him if he was busy on the Eve. "No," was the reply.

"Are you hot—can you play jazz?"

The poor fellow was so annoyed that he replied, "Don't ask me. Ask my wife!"

I know a young conductor who was engaged as a guest in an important symphonic orchestra. To impress his importance he deliberately changed a note in the first horn part. The piece was an established standard work. At the first rehearsal he made his prepared speech: "Gentlemen, I cannot understand why so many distinguished conductors have not discovered the false note in the horn part. Please, first horn player, correct your $F\#$ to F natural."

The first horn player said, "I did not play $F\#$. I know this composition by heart and never looked at the music."

A poor conductor's remark: "The musicians are in a plot to ruin me."

A male harpist claimed that the conductor criticized him continuously because he was in love with a female harpist.

After the 1929 market crash, musicians and many others claimed they lost fabulous amounts: With 10 percent margin, $10,000 on margin became a $100,000 loss.

Musicians in the pit: Watch them at the last number, packing before the last note and rushing madly to get out of the theater—then talking for an hour on the street.

Here is a story that went the rounds: A very young man went to a Philadelphia concert, with Leopold Stokowski conducting, and became obsessed with the idea of joining the orchestra. He bought a violin and started to study. His determination was so great that he diligently worked for eight years and then went to Europe for two years.

Finally, he applied for an audition and was accepted and seated in the second violin section. A week went by and Mr. Stokowski asked him for an interview. The Maestro asked him, "Do you enjoy your work with the orchestra?"

The answer, "Oh, yes, I love it."

Stokowski continued, "Do you like playing for me?"

The answer, "It has been my life's ambition."

"Well then, why do you make such awful faces and such contortions while you play? Do you dislike my interpretations?"

"No, Maestro, I simply dislike music!"

This is a silly story but was repeated often.

THE FIRST YEARS OF BROADCASTING

In my first year of broadcasting I worked for Hire's Root Beer, Maxwell House Coffee, Eastman Kodak, Eveready Batteries and Smith Brothers Cough Drops. The Maxwell Coffee program started with Miss Cornelia Otis Skinner, with her inimitable sketches, Crooks, who was a tenor, Rex Schepp, who was a banjo player who knew our sponsor, and my orchestra. When we started the show, the value of the coffee company was twenty-two million dollars. We stayed with them for some time. While we were still broadcasting, Maxwell Coffee was sold for forty-four million dollars to General Foods.

For a while we tried to answer letters about musical questions. Someone asked what were rehearsals for and, in order to answer honestly, I got an idea. I decided that Lou Raderman would be the guinea pig. I told him that he would play a solo the next week. "What shall I play?" he asked. I told him I'd let him know.

A few days before the broadcast he came into my office. I expected John McCormack to come any moment to discuss his new recordings, and I told Lou to get lost. But he insisted on seeing the solo number. To get rid of him I sang one note and repeated it in a fast temp, tuka, tuka, tuka, tuka, and said that is your solo. Lou asked, "What kind of solo is that?"

At the rehearsal Lou again asked to know the solo. I told him he would see it tonight at the broadcast. He was so angry that he got up, saying he would not play a solo without a rehearsal. I informed the announcer that I was trying to show the value of a rehearsal. Lou would play [probably 1929] a solo that had been written, called *Plantation Dance*. Lou would not see the music until I handed it to him when he was announced. The next week he would perform it again, but this time rehearsed and studied.

Lou finally gave in and played it without ever seeing the music. He did a very good job reading the number. The next week he did a wonderful job, showing the difference between playing a composition read and a playing a composition practiced and rehearsed.

Another question was: "Did a man ever play a bass solo?" Of course I heard a bass solo played very well, but I did not look around for a bass soloist, and besides I was not fond of the clumsy instrument for a solo. I decided to put humor into the broadcast.

There was a Russian named Ziporkin who had pestered me to let him play a solo. He claimed to be the greatest bass soloist in the world. He would stop me any time we met and repeat his request. He was annoying and persistent. This went on for a long time. Imagine his surprise when, in our next meeting, I informed him that I had put him on for a solo the next week. What he did not know was that I had spoken to McNamee, the announcer, to follow [speak along with] the music and get some humor out of it. Ziporkin came to the broadcast all dressed up. We had built a platform six feet high, and, as he got ready, we tied a string to his peg, without him knowing it.

McNamee listened, and his theme was an elephant dancing a dainty Gavotte for the King and then climbing the stairs to the throne, performed by the great bass soloist Ziporkin. We started in a gavotte tempo with the well-known *Gavotte* by Gossec, and as we went along I increased the tempo, and, by the time we got two thirds through the piece, we were at a furious pace. Just then we pulled the string, and the bass moved about two feet. Poor Ziporkin, in the sudden shift, lost his bow and finished the gavotte pizzicato. I had increased the tempo gradually, and so Ziporkin was hardly aware of the change. With perspiration dripping down his face, his clutching the clumsy instrument, and his effort to pizzicato his way through the solo, he was really a sight.

We finally finished with McNamee reciting how the elephant fell down the stairs, and with plenty of orchestral effects to help the illusion. Of course, the men of the orchestra were in stitches, while I kept a straight face. Ziporkin, in all the excitement, never realized the joke. No doubt his friends later on related what McNamee had announced. I was never bothered by Ziporkin after that.

MRS. BUSHMAN

In my first connection with the General Motors Broadcast, General Motors went on the air and appointed a Mrs. Bushman as supervisor and impresario. It is difficult for me to fathom her idea of programming. Evidently, she must have received a huge budget. She contracted the New York Philharmonic Symphony Orchestra, with Mengelberg conducting, Pat Conway's band, Edwin Franko Goldman's band, my orchestra, a huge mixed chorus, the Reveler Quartet and a few solo artists.

With this array of talent in the room, she asked the various groups to perform. At the first rehearsal she asked the New York Philharmonic to play a number, and then I played. By the time the rehearsal was through, I did forty-five minutes and the Symphony Orchestra fifteen minutes. The same thing happened with Conway and Goldman: I always received the bulk of the time. This went on for quite a few weeks. I was embarrassed, especially for Mr. Mengelberg.

I knew that sooner or later she would be in trouble on account of the waste and the expense. So one day I spoke to her. I said, "Mrs. Bushman, you practically engaged enough talent for five sponsors. I have a year's contract, but I will not insist on the fulfillment. If you are in trouble with the sponsor, you can terminate my services immediately."

She answered, "It is true. I am in lots of trouble," and she thanked me. Soon after that she was forced to endeavor to cancel her many contracts. Some artists and organizations insisted on their contract terms; others made easier terms. I tore up my contract.

One band leader insisted upon full settlement, and so, for the rest of the year, he and his band of forty-five men were paid weekly, but they had to come in and sit around for two-hour rehearsals and one-hour performance time.

AGENTS

I had one agent for just two programs. Radio was growing by leaps and bounds, and my broadcast programs came from telephone calls or from the radio station directly. The agent asked me to give a radio concert at Madison Square Garden. He combined two sponsors and gave me an order to engage a few Metropolitan stars and the Metropolitan Opera Chorus.

The agent's living habits got him into trouble, and he absconded with my fees. I also had to pay $25,000 to my artists and musicians. I never sued him, but from then on, I was wary of agents, unless they were from legitimate companies, like Ayer and Son, Benton and Bowles, J. Walter Thompson, etc. In New York and Hollywood, practically all contracts are made through agents.

The Eveready Programs

The Eveready Battery Company, a subsidiary of Union Carbide, was a sponsor for many years. It was supervised by Mr. Furness, and the work was done with my help and the help of two young men, Douglas Coulter and Gordon Whyte, two highly cultured men. They were omnivorous readers and were interested in literature, art and music. In fact, in everything old or up-to-date.

The program had two seasons. Winter programs were of the highest order, and the Summer program ranged from the banal to original Broadway operettas. We had our weekly meetings at which we discussed coming programs with heated pros and cons. Mr. Furness would listen calmly and finally decide the issues.

Our Winter program discussions were generally violent, with Doug, Gordon and myself hurling insults and accusations against each other. I would listen to their criticism of my work, generally on the lack of interest of my musicians, and I would come back by finding fault with their script.

One meeting stands out clearly. We were meeting one Saturday morning, deciding on the Winter format. The meeting started at 9 a.m., and by 10 a.m. we were loudly giving our opinions without restraint. Just then there was a timid knock at the door, and we paid no attention to it. About fifteen minutes later there was another timid knock, but, when we opened the door, no one was there.

This went on practically every fifteen minutes. Meanwhile, we were demanding and proposing all kinds of ideas. There was no limit placed on the program. It was an institutional program, and, since four hundred million batteries were sold monthly, we did not pay attention to ratings. We were yelling, "*I want* this" and "*I want* that" at each other.

By 11:45 a.m. we were tired and hungry and thoroughly exasperated. We had finally decided that we would start our operatic program with the entire Metropolitan Opera House Ensemble for the first week and then broadcast *La Scala* in Italian, French, German, Russian, English, and so on.

Meanwhile, I was thinking about similar meetings, and so I decided to ridicule their pompous proposals. I practically out-yelled them with my "*I want*," and insisted we get in touch with the greatest novelty of all: Engage Gabriel and his horn and a host of singing Angels, and that is what "*I want*."

As they looked at me in amazement, there were a few knocks at the door. This time we jumped quickly and ran to the door. We opened the door, and there was an old Irish lady with a mop and pail, looking frightened and pale. We asked her what she wanted, and, in a quivering voice, she replied, "All *I want*, gentlemen, is the spittoons. It is very late and Saturday. All *I want* is the spittoons."

That, of course, broke up the meeting. By then, when one of us spoke the words "*I want*," we added the spittoons. As usual, it ended up with my orchestra and some other attractions added on for the following Winter program.

However, I must add, the Eveready Winter Program was by far the finest series of broadcasts. We did *Tristan and Isolde*, with story and music, Shakespeare plays, the Commander Byrd's *Skyward* book and numerous classics. My tone-poem, *Skyward* was composed and played for Byrd, and it was recorded by Victor. Not finding anything suitable for the program in print, I started *Skyward* at 6 p.m. and, by midnight, finished the score. With six copyists writing the orchestral parts, we were ready for the 6 p.m. rehearsal, despite the wet manuscript music papers. The composition followed the story (Byrd and three flyers), and Byrd seemed especially moved by our performance.

While I was at RKO Studio [1935–1937], a young lady came up to me and greeted me with a kiss. She said, "Don't you remember me? I often sat on your lap." It was Betty Furness, daughter of Mr. Furness, who had been the Eveready Hour supervisor. At that time Betty was a child.

At one concert we programmed Brahms' *Requiem*, with Bodanzky conducting. I was asked to write an introductory fanfare to introduce the work. I gave it to Bodanzky, and he asked me to conduct it. He claimed that, unless he had time to study the music, he would feel uncomfortable that he would not render it properly. I could only wonder at his timidity about reading a common time fanfare of a few bars.

For one of our Summer programs we decided on engaging successful Broadway writers and introduced thirteen original musical shows—I wrote one. We had our hands full trying to come up with new ideas weekly, but we got through pretty well.

I remember a harrowing broadcast. It was a musical play broken into three acts. We got through the first act and the introduction of the next act. The announcer picked up the third act instead of the second act. Hearing him announce the third-act musical number, I switched into the number mentioned. This threw our story out of line, and for the rest of the hour we had to rewrite the script and change the order of the musical numbers.

With a white sheet, which I always had ready, I wrote in large type all the changes. My experienced musicians, always alert, followed my writing, and we finished the broadcast without a mistake.

This reminds me of the few times during our first broadcasts when the light bulbs blew out. It happened during the middle of Gershwin's *Rhapsody in Blue*. We carried on, and with the help of candles secured, we finished the work without any mishap. It is surprising how many compositions can be memorized by an orchestra that has played together for a number of years.

ALOIS HAVRILLA

Havrilla, who eventually became a well-known announcer, started with WEAF at the time when radio broadcasts were signed off the air by an announcer. Since he had two shows to sign off the air within four or five seconds, he had to stop each show and then rush into another studio (close by) and announce them off the air. One day he came into my Eveready Hour, walked up to me, and, while I was conducting, asked, "What hour is this?" I thought he was kidding, and so I pushed him aside. He then turned to Lou Raderman and asked him the same question, while Lou was fiddling away. Lou laughed at him and told him to go to hell. He was sure Havrilla was trying to kid him. Poor Havrilla had forgotten the name of our program and was trying to get an answer. He went from one musician to another and received nothing but rebuffs.

He stood in the middle of the room, helpless. The engineer stopped the sound, and Havrilla, seeing that we were off the air for a moment, yelled, "Please, what is the name of the sponsor?" At last we understood his dilemma, and we all yelled, "the Eveready Hour." He finally announced the cutoff, but he must have been late for his second studio.

A CONDUCTOR WHO COULD NOT READ MUSIC

As I mentioned before, Douglas Coulter and Gordon Whyte of the Eveready Hour were highly astute and knowledgeable. Gordon prided himself on his musical know-how, despite the fact that he was self-taught. We often played Debussy or Wagner as musical background. I would conduct and Gordon would stand near me humming the melody and moving his hands as if he were conducting.

He claimed he could read a score, and sometimes I thought that he could really do it. So one day, as I was rehearsing Wagner's *Siegfried Idyls*, I turned to him and asked him to take the baton because I had to leave for a few minutes. I pointed to the bar we were at and left. Gordon was delighted; he started conducting, and got along pretty well. He turned the pages of the score, as if he were capable of reading and following the score. I got back a few minutes later and asked him what bar he was on. He pointed, and he was about ten pages ahead of the orchestra. Actually, Gordon memorized music by listening to records. He could not read a note of music.

MRS. CURTIS

Ronnie, I must tell you about my experience with a society lady. She was Mrs. Curtis, wife of a prominent banker. One day a handsome young man about twenty-eight years old walked into my office and wanted to engage my orchestra for a social affair. I refused, saying that with my Victor work and radio broadcasts it was impossible to find the time. He said no one refuses Mrs. Curtis. I told him that I could get Whiteman and his orchestra, but he said that Mrs. Curtis did not want anyone but me.

He insisted, despite my telling him that my orchestra men were too busy to do outside engagements and that they were very expensive. He would not take no for an answer, even when I told him that I would not play for a dance or conduct while people ate—I only played as a concert orchestra. He agreed to my conditions, and when I named a price that was pretty stiff, he said money was no object. I finally agreed.

Two Steinway grands were hired, and we arrived at a mansion situated on the North Shore of Long Island. The party was in the garden. A stage had been erected, and the place was beautifully lighted.

Just as we started, it began to rain heavily, and in a few minutes the house was crowded with guests and my orchestra. I let Lou Raderman take over, and I went over to speak to Mr. Curtis. I asked him if he liked these parties, and he replied, "Not much, but my wife enjoys them, and so I let her have her way!"

I noticed that the guests were handing many champagne bottles to my boys. Since the situation had become quite informal, I did not mind. The guests were very near the band, and they kept requesting their favorite tunes. After a while, I was asked to take over and play *Rhapsody in Blue*. With the brass players there was little to fear, since they were generally used to liquor. Tommy Dorsey and Del Staigers were in that group. However, I wondered about the rest of the orchestra. Giving them liquor so freely was a risk.

As I was conducting, I noticed Irving Cohen, the oboe player, who could not hold his liquor, with a stony look in his eyes. He did not seem to move his fingers, just blowing a monotone repeatedly. I simply could not get his eye, and his loud tone was getting to sound silly. I suddenly got an idea to turn a ridiculous situation into a comic one. I decided to stop the orchestra and let Irving keep on blowing. His eyes were dilated, his cheeks puffed out, and his face practically blue. He kept on tut, tut, tut, tut, while the guests watched him, getting a great laugh out of the funny sounds. Oblivious of anything, Cohen kept this up for at least a minute, while the guests and orchestral men roared. Suddenly Irving stopped, opened his eyes, and then slid right off his seat. This got the greatest laugh of all.

The party came off well, and we enjoyed it as a change from our busy routine. However, I refused to do any more outside dates. I received a few requests from the Long Island set, but my excuse was that I had promised Mrs. Curtis to be exclusive for her.

OSCAR LEVANT

My acquaintance with Oscar Levant is more or less superficial. Although I saw a good deal of George Gershwin, I never saw them together, despite the fact that they were friends. Evidently we missed each other.

Oscar came to me one day when he was a freelance pianist and asked me to find a place for him in my orchestra. Knowing that he was a fine pianist, I instructed my two pianists, my brother and my first pianist Milton Rettenberg, to use Oscar Levant when they were busy.

At first Milton, who had given up his practice as a lawyer to be a musician, refused. It seemed that they did not like each other. However, I insisted, and Milton said, "Okay, we do not speak to each other, but I'll make up with him."

The next day Milton came up to me and announced that he would rather quit than hire Oscar. I asked him what made him change his mind, and he said, "That so and so Levant! I met him and greeted him and he looked at me and said, 'So you are condescending.'"

A few years later I was head of the musical department at RKO Studio in Hollywood. I was stopping at the Wiltshire Hotel, and I met Oscar. He was living in Irving Berlin's suite. Again he asked me for a job, and I hardly knew what to say. The only possible opening was a rehearsal pianist at the studio, and that kind of a position would be too menial for him. Oscar then asked me to go to Berlin's suite. He sat down at the piano and began playing various excerpts from classical music—piano pieces, symphonic work, etc., and, by chance, I named each one, despite the fact that, at times, his harmonics were his own. After a while, he said, "You know too much for a successful leader."

Oscar said, "Let's have some fun." We went across to the Brown Derby restaurant. Oscar chain smoked and drank coffee incessantly, and he kept looking for someone, in fact anyone, willing to be asked questions, so that he could take personal satisfaction in showing their ignorance.

Soon, in came Peter Lorre, and Oscar called him over. Then started the bombardment. Question after question followed, and I felt that Oscar was going too far. I was embarrassed, and when the actor left, I told Levant that I had another engagement and left.

After that Oscar Levant became famous on the *Information Please* program. His wit and fine talent as a pianist made him a celebrity. We were both on the Magic Key (RCA) broadcast. He was to play three Debussy piano solos, while I conducted the orchestra and vocalist.

I went through my numbers and, in order to time the program, asked Oscar to play his solo numbers for me, so that I would know his timing. He said, "I'll play them, but you go out of the room."

I asked, "Why?"

He got up and walked away and said, "Because I'm a lousy pianist," and I answered, "I know you are a lousy pianist, but play for me."

Levant turned around quickly and said, "I don't like to hear that," and walked out of the room. Of course, I was just trying to be an Oscar Levant wit, but evidently Oscar could not take the dirt he dished out continuously.

As it happened, I took a chance that his three numbers would be close to my timing, and the concert ended on the dot. After that I just remembered that we were both on the George Gershwin Memorial Concert at the Hollywood Bowl [a year or two before the Magic Key Broadcasts]. He played the Gershwin *Piano Concerto*, and I conducted the *American in Paris*. We heard each other, but did not meet.

Oscar Levant told me a story. He was studying composition with Arnold Schoenberg, and he had written a composition and brought it to the master for criticism. Schoenberg looked over the music for a while. Suddenly music was heard coming from a marching band in the street. Schoenberg directed Oscar to the window and asked, "Where are they going?"

Oscar replied, "I don't know."

Schoenberg then handed Levant his manuscript and quietly said, "There is your answer."

SYMPHONIC ORCHESTRAS

There was a period in the late 1920s and the early 1930s when American artists were sought, and it was a period when I spent a good deal of time at the Metropolitan Opera House. I had four subscriptions a week and could walk in at any time, because of friendship with Earl Lewis. He was a wonderful chap and a great booster for young American talent.

He could tell almost to a penny, by the artists booked and the name of the opera, what the opera would sell. Not only was I interested in the opera for my Victor records, but also for my broadcast soloists. During Earl Lewis's stay at the opera, Gladys Swarthout, Richard Crooks, Helen Jepson, Grace Moore, Marion Talley and many others were introduced. Later there were James Melton, Lawrence Tibbett, Rose Bampton and Risë Stevens. There was a rehearsal room on the second floor, and Pelletier prepared them for their opera roles.

It was about this time, due to newspaper articles, that American symphony conductors had increased opportunities. Arthur Judson was the leading person for choosing symphony conductors.[8] He chose three conductors from radio: Eugene Ormandy, David Mendoza and me.

Ormandy was given a trial, starting at the Stadium Summer Concerts of the New York Philharmonic Orchestra and immediately showed great talent. He became conductor at Minneapolis. As for Mendoza, I have heard so many conflicting stories that I'll pass over this and say nothing happened.

As for myself, I met Mr. Judson, and he asked me if I had any ambition to become a symphony conductor. I replied, "Yes, definitely."

He then asked, "Do you have an agent?"

I said, "No."

He said, "Well, I'll be your agent and receive 20 percent." I agreed to that. He followed up with, "What did you earn last year?"

I did not think it was any of his business, but I replied, "$400,000, not counting my royalties from my compositions."[9]

He said, "I am not interested in your composition royalties, but I would receive 20 percent of your $400,000 for your conducting, or $80,000."

Of course, I refused—I had built up my earnings through hard struggle, and I could not have an outsider horn in on something that he had not produced. Sometimes I wonder if I was right in refusing.

However, I never had the terrific urge, as I have heard many other conductors remark, of having the thrill of controlling one hundred musicians. I like conducting, but it is not a passion with me. I can understand composing becoming a passion, but conducting is an interesting job which you do to get results—that's all.

I always liked to conduct without too much fuss or ostentation. I never had any trouble getting the respect or results in my many years of conducting. I was fairly strict, but never abusive. My men and I were together ten hours or more a day, and the tension, the hard work and an informal atmosphere made our relationship friendly.

I did get offers to conduct symphonic orchestras, including the Boston Pops, but that came when they were nonunion. I conducted the Robin Hood Dell concerts in Philadelphia for one summer [1935]. That turned out to be lots of hard work. They paid the soloists very little money and did very poor financially. I was earning enough on the outside, and I returned my fee, so that the money would flow back to the orchestra players. I also received offers from Detroit, but I was too busy at that time.

This reminds me of Fabien Sevitzky, who once asked me, "How can such a fine musician like you be satisfied conducting records and radio? Why don't you become a symphonic conductor?"

I asked, "What do you earn a year?" He did not answer, but I knew: $15,000 or $20,000. I told him, "I earned over $400,000 last year."

He looked at me and meekly said, "I understand."

Fabien Sevitzky conducted [later, in 1943] my *Serenade Rhapsodic*, which I wrote for my friend Rex Schepp, a banjo soloist. Schepp is quite a buoyant character. He started out as a top vaudevillian act, played in my Maxwell program, and then, with a fine sense of business, bought a few radio and TV broadcasting companies. Well, while I was in Indianapolis, Sevitzky invited my wife and me to his rehearsal and then for dinner at his home.

At the rehearsal he seemed to pick on the first clarinetist a great deal. At one passage he made the man repeat a phrase at least fifty times. Sevitzky continued to find fault no matter how the clarinetist played it. I didn't know the man, but I felt sorry for him.

I knew that Sevitzky was not doing this for my benefit. I felt that he was trying to belittle the man in front of the whole orchestra. At dinnertime I asked him, "Mr. Sevitzky, what was this all about—the fuss with the first clarinetist?"

His explanation was that, during the summer layoff, the man accepted a circus job. He asked, "Don't you think I was right?"

I said, "No. I think you were unfair and cruel to insult him that way," and I added, "What can a fine musician earn in Indianapolis during the slow summer season? After all, he has a family to support. Your season is only twenty-five or thirty weeks at the most. Why did you not take him with you, since you were conducting in a South American city?"

He said, "I could not do that."

Except for that incident, I found Sevitzky to be a very fine man and a very good conductor.

One thing I never liked about symphonic engagements (and which is typical of most symphonies) is the difficulty in raising funds, which often requires kowtowing to the governing committees concerning their ideas about programming. The conductor gets mixed up in all that, and his earnings are not too good. Of course, there are exceptions.

My experience in radio probably spoilt me. The fees were enormous, and the sponsors would leave the programming to you when they had faith in you and were satisfied with your results. Radio and recording was, for me, the American way, in contrast to the European method. I read letters by Beethoven, Mozart and others. When I thought of the insults that they had to suffer, I became sad and then furious.

Walter Damrosch had the General Electric program, and I substituted for him for twenty-six weeks. When I took over, I had a fairly large symphonic orchestra and enjoyed playing classical music. I remember one incident. We were performing the first movement of Brahms *First Symphony*. It was the last number on the program, and, as we were beginning, Milton Cross, the announcer, came over to me and whispered, "Nat, I'm very sorry, but I miscounted the time. You are two minutes over." I began shuffling my score, and found a suitable cut. I always had a large white piece of cardboard handy. I called my brother Jack, who had no piano part for the number, and had him mark the cut on the cardboard and hold it up for the boys to see. We finished on time.

THE DORSEY BROTHERS

Both Tommy and Jimmy were part of my orchestra at one time. Tommy was an extrovert, Jimmy an introvert. Jimmy, in his quiet manner, drank as much as Tommy. Jimmy played his part with great seriousness. Tommy was full of fun and laughter.

When I conducted the classical General Electric Hour, I had a first trombonist from the New York Philharmonic with me. When he left for the winter season, I asked Tommy to take his place. Tommy refused, saying that he could not read the various clefs used in classical music. I asked him to sit with the Philharmonic player for a couple of broadcasts.

The Philharmonic trombonist said that Dorsey, with his fine tone and natural talent, could become a first-rate symphonic first trombonist. Tommy remained and did a splendid job. Whether he learned to read the tenor and alto clefs or wrote them over in his own way, I really do not remember. However, I had to write his trombone concerto in just the bass and treble clefs.

THE ARTIST AND REPERTOIRE COMMITTEE

Ronnie, you asked me if it is important for an A&R man to be a musician. It all depends on upon what buyers you are trying to sell and what department you are in. To the first question I would say "no," because I have seen Jack Kapp of Decca making a success, not as a musician, but as a businessman with an idea plus an instinct for engaging the right man at the right time.

When the record business was at a low ebb, he cut the price of records from seventy-five cents to thirty-five cents. Then he made a deal with Bing Crosby and worked out a stock participation with him because he didn't have the money to pay him cash. He took advantage of the record lull and brought in the best bands in the country, which were only available because the two major record companies were doing very little recording; and I must repeat that he lowered prices sharply during depression time.

Sometimes it takes a businessman to bolster the record sales, but do not get the impression that a musician is not important. I would say Mitch Miller has done a fine job in the popular field, and he is a good musician.

I won't talk in detail about my accomplishments, but I'll say this much: I sure had a variety of departments as manager and conductor. You can call me an up-to-date A&R man. I looked for talent in the Foreign, Export, Hillbilly, Race, Dance, Semi-classical and Red Seal Departments.

One of the difficult things to do is pick tunes for the popular records, especially if you are also a recording artist. There are vocal groups and dance bands all trying to get hits. No matter what numbers you assign to the artists, they will blame you if some other artist happens to record what becomes a hit.

Let me give you a typical example. I heard a new tune demonstrated: *Ain't She Sweet* by Yellen and Ager. I thought it had great possibilities. I offered it to four of our contracted dance leaders, and they all turned it down. Rather than be late on the release, I brought it home, orchestrated it, and recorded it with my own dance band [1927]. It was a big seller. For weeks I was accused of picking the best numbers for myself, and by the very leaders who were lukewarm to the merits of *Ain't She Sweet!*

Often you are faced with difficult decisions. You pick a number you are sure will be a hit, and you have competition from other recording companies. You feel pretty certain that the other companies will put it out with their top artist. Pretty soon one of your fair-selling singers asks you for the number. He may complain that he is not selling as well as your top artists because he does not get the hits. Well, you are on the spot. Of course, you'll pick your most popular artist for that number. That creates bad feelings, but, after all, it is important that your releases of successful songs be ahead of your competition.

It is not so difficult to pick the material for concert or opera artists, although even in that field there are some clashes.

There was a man who was never satisfied with the numbers assigned to him. He would wire that he and his band would leave one week for recording, writing, "Please let me have the best tunes available." I refer to Jean Goldkette.

I would send him a few songs. He would come to New York and wanted guarantees that the numbers picked for him would become hits. Of course, no one can be sure of that, but I would do my best to assure him that I picked top tunes for him.

He would then go from one publisher to another and ask them what will be their hits. Naturally, they overvalued their material. He would also listen to song writers. The result was that he would appear the next day and tell me that he wanted to change some of my assigned numbers.

Knowing Jean, I would say, "Okay, I'll let you pick some of the tunes you especially like." This would upset him, because, after listening to so many publishers, songwriters and pluggers, he could not make up his mind. This went on for a few days, and, by this time, he was so muddled that he finally picked the numbers I had given him originally.

Jean was really a fine concert pianist who drifted into a dance band by some strange fluke. He had one of the best dance bands in the country. It included the two Dorsey brothers, Bill Challis as arranger, and a few other top men. I conducted the band while Goldkette sat in a chair in back of the room listening. When the band did not do their best or kind of horsed around, he would almost be in tears. He was a very soft-spoken and gentle man—very sensitive, and one could not help liking him.

He listened to everyone and found it difficult to make up his own mind. As much as I liked him, his wavering mind made it an ordeal to finish his recording dates.

My impression of Kate Smith, hearing her at a musical comedy, was not good. I thought her voice was rough, almost like shouting. Mr. King, my superior at Victor, liked her. I gave in to him and said nothing at the committee meeting. I was wrong, and Mr. King was right. She became a star and one of our Victor best sellers. It was my faux pas. One can be wrong as an A&R man at times—but not too often and keep his job.

JEANNINE I DREAM OF LILAC TIME

In 1928 the Victor was still in the hands of the Wall Street brokers, but David Sarnoff[10] was often attending our committee meetings. He just listened to us and never suggested anything. In 1929 Victor became RCA Victor Division.

During 1928 I was asked by the Victor Company to score a short picture, a one-reeler, as a demonstration for a picture studio, to show how records could be synchronized with the movie industry. I received a film showing Mozart, Beethoven and Haydn in heaven playing cards. Then the scene fades to an organ grinder in a street of Vienna, and the front of the organ shows the same picture as in heaven. I chose the popular song *Wien du Stadt meine Traume* (Vienna, City of My Dreams) as my theme. It blended well with the film, and the Victor received a contract covering practically all major studios.

Since most of the best musicians were busy day and evening in New York, picture synchronizing was booked in Camden from midnight to 4 or 5 a.m. It was a busy and hectic period.

We engaged large orchestras and did numerous pictures for MGM-Paramount and Warner Brothers. This went on for some time, until the Jolson story. From then on, Hollywood became the place for picture recording.

One of my first scorings was for a film called *Lilac Time* [1928], and it starred Gary Cooper and Colleen Moore. I was more interested in the theme song than in scoring the picture. In fact, all I wrote was my song *Jeannine*. I developed it in many moods and let a composer-musician fill the rest of the film with printed music. This was a time when publishers printed lots of mood music.

Young Johnson was still with the Victor, although Wall Street had bought us up. Mr. Walter Clark and I contacted Warner Brothers. (I believe another company, First National, was interested in the picture.)

The picture was considered important financially, and we were ushered into a room of one of the executives. He looked and acted like Hearst's cartoons of a Tammany Boss I was assigned to do the score, and this executive glared at me and said, "I have twenty songs for the picture, but there is one number written by a lady, a friend of mine, that you must use as the theme. It is called *Lilac Time*."

I disliked his attitude, and I told Mr. Johnson and Mr. Clark that, if I did not write the theme, I would not do the picture. That started quite an argument, but finally when Mr. Johnson told him the Victor Company always relied on my judgment, he gave in and said, "Alright, but I expect a hit song like *Ramona*, and the name of your theme must be *Lilac Time*." I refused to accept his title and asked to see the film. I would then consult my lyric writer for the title.

Since *Ramona* had been a Feist publisher song, I expected to submit my composition to them and use Wolfie Gilbert as lyricist. There were about thirty men in the screen room, and about five minutes into the picture

Colleen Moore is looking up at the sky, waiting for Cooper, a flyer during World War I, to arrive.

She is anxiously awaiting his arrival, and she bends her head from right to left. This movement gave me my theme. As you know, a projection room is dark except for the beam from the projector. All I had was a Melachrino cigarette box, mostly covered by fine print. However, I put the box in the light beam, which obliterated the picture.

There were cries of "get out of the light, sit down," etc.—and that was how *Jeannine* was written. I met Wolfie Gilbert at Feist, and he wrote the lyric. We decided on *Jeannine I Dream of Lilac Time* as the title.

Wolfie complained, with apology, that the verse was not up to my standard, and I said, "Who ever listens to a verse? The chorus is important." Gilbert was an old-timer in the popular field, and he showed me my error. He said that every part of a hit song was important. I rewrote the verse, and I was glad for his criticism.

At that time Feist had two waltz hits, *Ramona* and *In a Little Spanish Town*. As a rule, one waltz hit was considered enough for a popular publisher to work on. Now, a third waltz had been added, and the executives and pluggers were scared.

However, they could not refuse to accept a song from Nat Shilkret, who was influential at the Victor. As it happened, the three waltzes all became smashing hits—*Jeannine* sold almost two million sheet copies. It was recorded at the Victor by John McCormack, Gene Austin, Jesse Crawford, my Salon orchestra and other dance bands and vocalists.

Besides receiving a fee for scoring the film, my royalties amounted to $75,000. It still earns money for me, but *Lonesome Road*, written in 1926, has passed the *Jeannine* song by now. Today composers receive their compensation through recordings and broadcast—also movies.

FATS WALLER

After recording and arranging the Victor Salon Orchestra, I decided one time, for the sake of variety, to record without arrangements. I would hire top players like Lou Raderman, Tommy Dorsey, Sannella, Rettenberg, and Kress (a guitarist), all of whom had good ideas, and, with just scratch ideas, rehearse for hours on each tune. I encouraged them to suggest ideas, and I was satisfied if, in six hours, we recorded just two selections, rather than the usual eight records.

We had worked on the tune *Chloe* [1928] without much success. It was getting late, and we had to catch the 5 p.m. train to New York for our radio dates. It was about fifteen minutes before quitting when I said, "Boys, let us try it once more—if I'm not satisfied, we'll stop." We began our last attempt, and then we heard an organ playing with us, and it sounded great. We walked over to the organ, and there was Fats Waller, with a jug of gin. I quickly asked him to join us and use his marvelous ideas, and we finished in time. Later he recorded a few more records with us, and the name of the combination was Rhyth-Melodists.

For some reason we did not record many tunes with the Rhyth-Melodists, but for many years I received calls about Fats Waller and his connection with the group.

WOOLCOTT AND THE BARRYMORES

John Barrymore was scheduled [1928] to do a record of "To be or not to be." I had engaged his own conductor to play the date, since I had no experience with John Barrymore. I wanted to know what musical background music he played for John. I received very little help from the conductor. All he said was that Barrymore was hard to please and that he expected lots of trouble. I then decided to play the slow and beautiful movement of Borodin's string quartet. My boys played a few bars for Barrymore, and he accepted the music immediately.

I met Ethel Barrymore through Alexander Woolcott, a brilliant writer and a radio personality. He had commented on my Stephen Foster album in one of his books. I cannot recall his exact words, but in essence he wrote, "I can think of nothing more pleasurable or exhilarating than walking on the Atlantic boardwalk on a cool spring day or listening to the Stephen Foster album played by Shilkret's orchestra and singers."

He brought me to a couple of Ethel Barrymore's parties. Sitting on the floor with a drink in her hands, she listened with seeming pleasure and enthusiasm to the music in the Foster album. What a great artist she was, and with a wonderful personality.

One morning I met Woolcott at his hotel, and evidently he had just awakened to my ring. He ordered some fruit juice and asked if I would join him. I ordered orange juice. Woolcott said, "Oh no, make it half orange juice and half grapefruit juice—never drink orange juice alone."

He then proposed lunch at the Algonquin Hotel, the place where I generally ate. He and I got there, and then he said let us join the round table. That was the famous "Round Table" where the finest writers and wits met each day for lunch. I sat through the lunch and listened to the most erudite, sharp, and often biting comments I ever heard. It was exciting, but once was enough for me.

An American in Paris

George Gershwin came into my office at the Victor and said, "I am going to Paris tomorrow, and when I return I'll have a composition for you to record." Upon his return, Walter Damrosch performed the *American in Paris* at his weekly concert [December 13, 1928]. George called me and gave me a list of instrumentalists needed to record *American in Paris* the next day. He would bring the score and parts. What he forgot was to mention a celesta player.

The next morning Gershwin was at the recording studio, and we started to play the manuscript. As we ran over the number, George kept suggesting this and that for about fifteen minutes. I finally turned to him and said, "George, please get lost for about one hour. This is a new work for me and the orchestra. Let us get acquainted with the score. I'll understand you, but not until then." George went off, but I was sure that he stayed in the hall, where I could not see him.

When he returned, I said, "George, you forgot to let me know that a celesta player was needed."

He was sorry and said, "I'll play the celesta."

We recorded the *American in Paris*, but George was so excited that, in one place, he did not play the celesta.[11] When we finished, Gershwin said, "Nat, I'll never hear it played better."

I immediately offered him $2500 for the privilege of broadcasting the number for two of my air concerts. George, after the first playing, said, "Why, that is better than the record." After the next performance he came out with, "Nat, I thought that you would never surpass the second performance, but you really did it this time."

I said, "Maybe we were not so good the first time."

This reminds me of a Victor broadcasting story. We were on the air for a very long period. For each performance the Victor would send out notices to all our dealers with a place for comments. We received lots of weekly mail with the usual complimentary remarks. One night we were taken off the air for some reason, and the next few days we received the same complimentary letters.

PRIZES FOR COMPOSERS

About 1927 or 1928, Columbia and the Victor offered prizes for composers. The Columbia competition did not have any restrictions on the composers. The Victor, with two prizes, accepted only American composers. Columbia, celebrating the Schubert Centennial, at first wanted a finishing movement for Schubert's unfinished symphony, but changed their requirement to a symphony composition as an apotheosis of the lyrical genius of Schubert. Prominent musicians were picked as judges. A three-movement symphony by a forty-year-old Swedish composer, Kurt Atterberg, was awarded the prize. After its first London performance, the well-known musical critic Ernest Newman suggested that the work was reminiscent of other works. Newman claimed that Atterberg fitted his music to satisfy the jurists, and that he had taken different works of quite a few composers and fitted them together.

In fact, Atterberg was not really a composer, but a critic, and admitted that Newman was correct. He had really piecemealed the various composers' works and formed a three-movement symphony.

The Victor offered two prizes: one for a symphonic work of at least twenty minutes length, and one for a semi-light American work of seven or eight minutes. The symphonic prize was $25,000, and the lighter work $10,000. The opinion of the jurists of the five works considered for the symphonic prize was that not one of them deserved the whole $25,000. They divided the money equally among the five pieces. Russell Bennett won three prizes, and Louis Gruenberg and Aaron Copland won one prize each.

For the lighter work, our jury consisted of Roxy, myself and a third party whom I cannot recall. We found two compositions worthy of the prize. I chose Thomas Griselle's *Nocturne and March*, and Roxy was keen on Rube Bloom's *Song of the Bayou*. Again Roxy and I were on opposite sides. I won on a technical point. I had played Bloom's *Song of the Bayou* on a broadcast once, and that meant it was ruled out. I was sure that my choice was correct, although Bloom's piece was more commercial.

The composer Griselle had studied with Nadia Boulanger, the woman teacher in Paris who had produced such marvelous development in America's finest composers. She was a remarkable woman and a fine pianist.

ALBUMS

I proposed recording an album of well-known composers, consisting of five double-faced twelve-inch records. I had trouble convincing our A&R Committee. Their objections, as they put it, were, "We have enough trouble selling one record at a time, so why try to sell five records in an album?" I insisted for about one year, and finally, with the help of Mr. King, the other A&R men gave me permission to do a Victor Herbert album. Probably they grew tired of listening to me and thought that one trial would stop me.

The Victor Herbert album was issued [1928], and it was such a great success that it was followed up with a Stephen Foster album, a Franz Schubert album, featuring John McCormack, the Revelers, and my Victor Salon Orchestra, an Ethelbert Nevin album, a Rudolf Friml album, and a second Herbert album.

JOSIAH KIRBY LILLY

The Stephen Foster album grew into quite a grand project because of the interest shown in it by the well-known pharmacist Josiah Kirby Lilly. After the Foster album was issued, I received a few letters from Mr. Lilly stating that, since his youth, he loved Stephen Foster's melodies, and my album gave him great pleasure. Later on I received more letters from him, and this developed his interest so much that he contracted ten musicologists to gather much Foster sheet music, both in this country and in England.

In Foster's time composers had their music printed by various music publishers, and, besides that, minstrel shows bought melodies. There were many editions of similar compositions due to pirating of many publishers. In two years the compilation of Foster melodies was practically complete. In Indianapolis Mr. Lilly erected a small building dedicated to Foster.

He put all the gathered music together, came up with a Foster album, and distributed it to all our public libraries. It was beautifully done, and it was a real contribution to a famous composer. Lilly also eliminated many false rumors about Stephen Foster in the album preface. Lilly's final gift was a building erected in the Pittsburgh University at a tremendous cost; it is called Stephen Foster Hall.

I met Mr. Lilly in Indianapolis. He was a hale and hearty man over eighty years old. When I called him, he invited me to his home and thanked me for revitalizing his interest in Foster. I said that it was too bad that he had not lived during the time of Franz Schubert or Mozart—he would have sponsored them, prolonged their lives, and brought happiness to them. He was pleased by my remark.

He also said that he had commissioned a symphonic composer to write a symphony or a tone-poem based on Foster's tunes. His judgment was that the original compositions, in their simple form, satisfied him more than arrangements, no matter how good—not even your wonderful arrangements, he added. I asked him what he spent on his Stephen Foster project, and he said, "$2,000,000. I used some of the most popular artists in radio: Vaughn de Leath, Frank Crumit, Gladys Rice, and the Revelers." James Melton, the top tenor of the Revelers, started his climbing career when I picked him to sing Foster's *Jeannie With The Light Brown Hair*. His rendition was superb. From then on Melton not only stayed with the Revelers, but became a soloist in his own right.

JOHN MCCORMACK

During the Franz Schubert recording, featuring John McCormack, the Revelers, and my orchestra, we took a brief rest between recordings. McCormack was ready to continue, and when he noticed the two tenors Lewis James and James Melton were not listening, he cried, "Listen tenors," and James, in his young brazen manner said, "You're a tenor too."

"No," said McCormack, "I'm a man with a high voice." After the recording, John McCormack presented me with a gold cigarette case with the following words inscribed:

> *To Nat Shilkret*
> *a token of friendship and gratitude for his*
> *splendid cooperation in making my records.*
> *His friend*
> *John McCormack*
> *Dec. 7th, 1928.*

For some reason, John McCormack and Victor Herbert were not friendly toward each other. Whenever I mentioned Herbert's name and called him an Irish composer, John would say, "Herbert is not the great Irish composer—Sir Stanford is the real Irish genius." McCormack sent me Charles Villiers Stanford's *Irish Rhapsody, #4* score, written in 1914 in Europe. I never asked, but I believe their differences were political views.

RUDOLF FRIML

After my first Victor Herbert album, I asked Rudolf Friml if he would play the first two sides of the Friml album. For the first side, he just sat down and played one of his popular numbers, and for four and a half minutes he extemporized effortlessly, without a mistake. For the second side, I gave him the theme and asked him to use it for four and a half minutes. Again he did it perfectly, with no hesitation. The rest of the eight numbers were played and sung by our contracted artists and my musicians.

REGINALD DE KOVEN

Looking for a composer for a new album, I telephoned Mrs. Reginald De Koven in her palatial mansion on Park Avenue. She invited me to visit her. I arrived, and, in her most regal manner, she brought me to the library room. She went to a special case and carefully opened it. Since I did not know too much of De Koven's music, I asked her if I could examine the volume she had in her hands. She refused and said, "No one can desecrate his music by touching it." I then said that all I wanted to do was study it—she still refused. Actually, outside of De Koven's operetta *Robin Hood*, I did not have a high opinion of his music that I had studied at the 42nd Street Library.

I bid the lady good-bye and was glad to get out of her mansion. I went back to the library at 42nd Street and Fifth Avenue—I still was not convinced that a De Koven album would be interesting. I decided to forget the idea.

NOTES

1. From Gelatt [1955], pp. 210–211: Due to financial difficulties, Columbia sold its British branch in 1922 to a group of people which included Sterling, then Columbia's European General Manager.

2. Correspondence from Obaugh and his audacious son document the Staunton trip, down to the very detail of the cheese-and-crackers lunch, described later in the section, as being in December 1925. A Strand Theatre program (shown in the archival edition of this work) establishes 1927 as the year of the Strand Theatre engagement. Either Nat had an earlier Strand Theatre engagement to which he was referring, or, we think more likely, he had some other obligation requiring him to return to New York on Friday from Staunton.

3. Peer was already a hillbilly talent scout. For example, Malone

[1968] writes, "In the spring of 1920, Ralph Peer, recording director of Okeh Records, recorded a Negro blues singer, Mamie Smith. This recording generated a boom for blues music and launched Okeh into a ranking position as a record company. ... Ralph Peer then was sent into the South to ferret out folk performers wherever they might be found." Peer came to Victor about 1926.

Mixing history with gossip, we note that Peer later divorced his first wife Anita to marry his younger secretary. Anita Peer, out of spite, sold the publishing rights to part of his catalogue to Nat's son Arthur.

4. "That period" evidently is from 1926, when Peer joined Victor, to 1940 when BMI began operating.

5. Rust [1973] lists a Victor test recording of Moran and Mack made January 11, 1927.

6. Crawford [1992] notes on pp. 101–102, that Irving and Jack Mills founded Mills Music in 1919 and quotes Sanjek, from *American Popular Music and its Business: The First Four Hundred Years*: "[Irving Mills] made more recordings than all other studio supervisors combined."

7. Many writers attribute Whiteman's leaving Victor partly to being jealous of Nat Shilkret. For example, Sudhalter and Evans [1974] write, "The reasons for the shift appear to be rooted in rivalry with Nat Shilkret over who recorded what material. Whiteman had for years assumed first crack at whatever songs he wanted, and the fact that Shilkret was more and more often recording many of the same selections, thus undermining what Whiteman saw as his personal market, angered the 'King of Jazz.'"

8. Crawford [1992] describes Judson as the well-connected head of an American management firm and quotes Hart, from *Orpheus of the New World*: "All agree that from 1915 to 1956, at least, Arthur Judson exercised a power and influence in the symphony and concert affairs of this country without equal then or at any other time." Werner Janssen tells, in his unpublished autobiography, of unintentionally bypassing Judson and later being forced to pay Judson a commission on all of his (Janssen's) performance fees, without getting a single booking from Judson in return.

9. Corrected for inflation, $400,000 in 1930 is equivalent to about $4,000,000 in the year 2000.

10. David Sarnoff (1891–1971) was the first to recognize the commercial importance of radio and was a leader in the early commercial development of radio as general manager of RCA in 1921. He formed NBC in 1926 and became president of RCA in 1930. Sarnoff was also the first to develop television commercially.

11. Jablonski and Stewart [1973] note an error on the record label of this recording: "The first recording of this work, made in February 1929, was performed by the RCA Victor Symphony Orchestra with Nathaniel Shilkret (RCA Victor LPT-29; coupled with the 1927 'Whiteman'

Rhapsody). This is a thoroughly delightful performance, the first complete recording of a Gershwin work and one in which he—as well as the famous taxi horns he brought from Paris—participated. GG [Gershwin] may be heard contributing a few bars on the celesta in a brief transitional passage about halfway through. For years the label stated that he was at the piano, which must have mystified many. The recording is one well worth having."

CHAPTER 5

SOUND MOVIES AND RCA

The year 1929 was one of great change. RCA had bought Victor. The great stock market crash ushered in an economic downturn that saw record sales decline by 94 percent. Listening to radio was free, so radio thrived, and so did the radio career of Nathaniel Shilkret. The rapid transition from silent movies to movies with synchronized sound was nearly complete.

In 1929, the Victor Company was doing well, and then in October the stock market crashed. On November 1, 1929, Thomas Edison discontinued records and phonographs. Henceforth, the company would concentrate on radios and dictating machines. Edison at that time was eighty-two years old.

By 1930 RCA, despite the assurances about radio and phonograph joining together on equal terms, was essentially interested in an extensive plant and a well-organized system of distributors and dealers for selling radio sets.

On September 19, 1930, RCA sponsored a ceremony in Camden, adding humiliation to injury, dedicating Camden as "Radio Center of the World." The advertising budget for records was drastically cut, and contracts with Red Seal artists were allowed to lapse. There were just a few of us left—John McCormack, Jascha Heifetz, Lily Pons and I, the only conductor. I had a contract until 1935. In 1930, RCA issued what was advertised as "the book of Enrico Caruso's recordings."

David Sarnoff was evident at this period. He was a brilliant speaker and a man of great ability. However, he had little faith in records. Many of our staff were fired. It was heartbreaking to see men who had worked for the Victor Company nearly all their life finding themselves out of work at age fifty.[1]

Word came to me that I would take orders from three NBC men who were artist managers and had no idea of the recording business. It was a ridiculous situation for me and for them. For six months there were no records made.

One day I received a request from one of the managers, Mr. Schad, to record a ballad made popular by the Roxy gang. He wanted John McCormack and me to record it. I received the ballad, but I thought it was a poor composition and hesitated to show it to McCormack.

Two days later I got a phone call, asking me not to record the number with John McCormack. I asked why and was told that he would come to my office and explain the reason. Mr. Schad met me and told me that, since McCormack's contract was for $150,000 a year and mine $100,000, he would have to charge for six months of our services, for a total of $125,000. That was the accounting method used for radio artists. He suggested that I pick a singer and a conductor other than McCormack and myself. He also said that NBC added 20 percent for their artist managerial department. Since this was his first venture in recording, he was reluctant to show such a heavy expenditure in his initial trial.

Well, James Melton and some conductor recorded the ballad. When Mr. Sarnoff heard about the silly affair, he left word that both McCormack and I engage a symphony orchestra and record one week of anything we desired. In other words, it was a classical jam session.

What a wonderful time we had. John McCormack was probably the greatest lieder singer living. We feasted on Schubert, Schumann, Hugo Wolf, Mozart and Wagner. The old Victor routine of sending masters to my New York office had been changed. I did not hear any of the records. Luckily, John McCormack had some of the records sent to him for approval.

Quite a few years passed, and John McCormack died [1946]. By this time RCA Victor was recording and wanted to issue a McCormack album. I was called by Lilly McCormack and asked if I had any of her husband's records done at our classical jam session. RCA could only find a few masters. I told her that for the first time during my long Victor recording, I did not receive the master copies due to the confusion in the Victor to RCA Victor transfer. Our reliable Victor personnel were being replaced, and the new company had not started to function in an orderly fashion.

Finally, some records were traced to the well-known musical critic Ernest Newman in London. Newman was an admirer of John McCormack, and John often gave him new records. I received quite a few calls for McCormack records, but I could not help them. In 1952, I went to a music shop and found a new album issued with some of the numbers recorded. I guess enough masters were found to fill an album. I never found out if another album was issued.

MARION TALLEY

Miss Marion Talley came from Kansas and had a lovely voice. She was a coloratura by practice and not by nature. She had many enthusiastic admirers, and she was sponsored by her state to come to New York and sing an audition for the Metropolitan Opera House powers.

Out came a girl in pigtails, singing beautifully. She sang as a soprano. Everyone was full of praise, but she was too young for just soprano roles. They decided to send her to Europe to study voice and operatic roles, not as a soprano, but as a coloraturist. She came back two or three years later, recorded for the Victor Company, sang at the Met, and went on a concert tour.

At last, Kansas had turned a sweet, everyday American average girl into a great star. During her success, she was engaged by RCA Victor to sing at a broadcast concert in the Walt Whitman Hotel in Camden, with my Victor Salon Orchestra and McNamee as sponsor.

The occasion was the opening of the Camden plant exclusively to manufacture radio sets for RCA Victor and other sellers. It meant the hiring of 30,000 men. The governor, the Philadelphia mayor and other dignitaries and the tycoons of the radio business were there.

When my orchestra and I arrived at about 7 p.m., I met Miss Talley and her ever-present mother. They had been there since early afternoon, all dressed up and ready for a concert appearance. Mrs. Talley was sweet and patient.

It was announced that the concert and broadcast would not start at 7 p.m. because many important people had not arrived. Miss Talley smiled and said it was alright. Later on, I found out that she and her mother had not eaten a thing for hours. Then dinner started, and by 9 p.m. the hall was so filled with smoke that it was decided to have the after-dinner speeches first, and at 10 p.m. sharp the broadcast concert would start. Miss Talley still smiled and showed no rancor or temperament.

However, McNamee, the announcer, and my flutist, MacDermott [possibly E. McDiarmid], had different ideas. They both had worked hard all day, and, faced with a three-hour wait, their idea of relaxing was to hire a room in the hotel and start drinking.

When I finally assembled my boys at about 9:45 p.m., I noticed the two Macs were missing. I was told what room they were in. I went in and found McNamee on the bed and MacDermott on the floor—both were intoxicated. Perhaps I should say extra high, because both were able to take plenty and somehow get along. With some assistance we managed to get them downstairs.

Of course, I was not responsible for McNamee, but MacDermott was in my orchestra, and the coloratura numbers without a flutist were almost impossible to perform. Here was one of the most important concerts of my career. I was not only playing for the people in the room, but also for millions of listeners, and I was faced with an announcer who could hardly stand up and a stewed flutist who had to play duets with Miss Talley.

I thought fast and went to see Miss Talley. I told her that my flutist had eaten something bad, and, if he was unable to play his part, some other instrument would have to fill in. She was very sympathetic and said she understood. I worried about the whiskey aroma of both of the men, but I had to take that chance.

I had warned the boys near MacDermott not to let him stand up, but to keep him seated. (As a rule, an instrumentalist playing a solo stands up near the mike.) I don't know how we got through the concert, but we managed. A few times MacDermott was prevented from getting up. The concert went off quite well. Even McNamee struggled through without any major mistakes.

After the last note had been sung and McNamee was ready to sign off, the boys forgot all about MacDermott. Miss Talley was taking bows and extended her hand to MacDermott to share in the applause. Mac got up and then fell flat on his face. I signaled the boys to get MacDermott up to his room.

By this time I figured Miss Talley had discovered the real cause of MacDermott's condition. She grabbed my arm and insisted upon seeing the poor flutist who had played the concert, despite his illness. She mentioned how brave he was, etc., and I said that a doctor had been sent for and that he was resting comfortably.

She handed a bouquet of flowers to me to give to MacDermott with her good wishes and compliments. I went up to the room, and found McNamee and MacDermott asleep, side by side, on the bed. I put the bouquet of flowers between them.

THE THEREMIN

In 1927 Professor Leon Theremin demonstrated an apparatus called the

Theremin. It was an electric instrument employing oscillation, that is, the combining of two electric currents of different frequencies. In 1929, the Victor Company placed the Theremin on the market. To feature the instrument, I had a fine violinist practice the thing, and I also had one in my home. This instrument, when set, would react to any movement near it.

McNamee, the announcer, with his exciting voice, could sell water for champagne. He gave a flattering and elaborate testimonial about the heavenly and ethereal tones of the Theremin.

The violinist started to manipulate the instrument with a beautiful soft melody. McNamee walked over to the player, and, as his body contacted the electrical vibrations of the instrument, it started the worst noise I ever heard. McNamee was startled and started jumping up and down, thinking that he had stepped on a wire. The howling became more violent as he jumped around. We finally got him away, but by that time the demonstration was ruined. The best manipulators of the Theremin were the cellists. Cellos were similar in range to the electric instrument.

THE CONGRESSIONAL MUSIC
LIBRARY CONCERT

I was requested by Carl Engel to give a concert at the Washington, D.C., Congressional Music Library hall [1929]. It was the first program ever to be performed that was not in classical music. We, that is my orchestra and I, were asked to show the development of American music in the lighter form.

Many distinguished notables were in the audience, including Mrs. Hoover. There were arrangements of *St. Louis Blues* by Handy, the Victor Company prize winner of semi-classic, of *Nocturne* and *March* by Thomas Griselle, of *Rhapsody in Blue*, of my *Negro Spiritual Paraphrase*, and arrangements of other American composers.

It was a daring attempt for Carl Engel to introduce American music outside of the classical repertoire in the august chambers of the Congressional concerts. It was a bold decision for a distinguished musicologist to make. Evidently he was convinced that the popular composers of America were important enough to receive the attention of the concert audience. I believe that the program was successful, and, as Mr. Engel told me, that there were many complimentary remarks and no complaints.

Anne Shilkret

At one time, Mrs. Shilkret would receive all the proceeds, and then pay all the boys. However, her social life increased, and often she was a week or two late in making out the checks. Going over her mail, she found a two-year-old check for a concert we played at the Congressional Library.

It was a government check for $4500. She had paid the musicians, but had never put the check in our account. After a brief talk, we decided to cash the check, hoping it would be honored. By Jove, it was. After that I engaged a secretary to take care of my business—Mrs. Shilkret never forgave me for doing this to her.

Rudy Vallée

At a committee meeting Rudy Vallée's name came up. Rudy had just started in radio, and I was anxious for us to engage him. There was some objection to the quality of his band, and I said that he could use my orchestra. It was his popularity with women, who liked his voice, that was important.

Rudy was given a contract, but he rejected my offer to build up his band. He said that, since the radio audiences had heard him and his band, it would not be honest to substitute other men. He was the only band leader who would not have me conduct his band. Well, he surely made good and had quite a career.

At one time, when he was at Yale, he asked me if I would recommend him as leader and singer for a Mexican and South American trip using one of my band titles, the International Orchestra, which was a popular orchestra in our Export Department.

I had received a few offers to tour with the International Orchestra. I wrote and offered them Rudy Vallée as leader and singer of my orchestra. The offer was not accepted; they wanted me personally to lead the tour. By the way, Rudy told me that he could speak Spanish.

Church Chimes

At one period the Victor Company was experimenting with church chimes. The idea was to be able, through amplification (electrically) to build church chimes cheaper.

I was sent to three places to hear the result of our work on church bells: first, at a place four blocks away, on a bridge; second, one-half mile away; and, third, one mile away. I reported that I heard the chimes, but found that the overtones were not correct. The RCA Victor Company was greatly disappointed with my report. Leopold Stokowski had also heard the chimes. The company decided to give a testimonial to the engineer who had come up with the idea.

Since my report was negative, I was not asked to speak at the dinner. Stokowski was a guest, and he was chosen to give his approval. Leopold was a very able speaker, and his speech lasted for some time. He spoke of beautiful bells, beautiful music, the church and the stirring choirs—a most sentimental mish-mash of practically nothing that pertained to the church chimes. He was congratulated on his address, and the company insisted that I had made an error in failing to enthusiastically embrace their experiment. Actually Stokowski never mentioned the church chimes in his speech. I did get some satisfaction out of the affair. The church chimes did not revolutionize the bell industry. I doubt if they ever sold the idea to any congregation.

THE VIBRAPHONE

In the quest for new sounds, I asked my drummer, Joe Green, to speak to his brother George, who was a wonderful xylophone artist and an inventor. I wanted vibrating steel bells with a foot pedal, so that the vibration could be controlled. I used the results of his work for the first time with my Salon Orchestra, and the new sound received many complimentary notices. I offered the Victor Company exclusive rights for three years, but they would not okay my request. The vibraphone had become a popular orchestra and solo instrument, and now we find it in dance and concert orchestras. Lionel Hampton was often used at MGM for vibraphone solos. Now he had made the instrument his career.

MY SINGING DUET WITH LAWRENCE TIBBETT

I had a recording date to conduct Lawrence Tibbett for the Victor at Liederkranz Hall, on 58th Street, between Lexington and Park Avenues. The date was for 2 p.m. At 11 a.m. I was at the dentist to have a tooth pulled. The dentist's office was about six blocks away from the Victor studio.

When my tooth was pulled, I walked east to the Liederkranz Hall. I felt a little dizzy and sat on the stone stairs at the entrance. I figured it was about 12 noon, and I thought I had a two-hour wait for the 2:00 p.m. date. As I sat, a violinist came along hurriedly and asked, "Is the date off? It is 2:30 p.m., and I am late."

I walked to the recording room and apologized for being late. We started to record Rossini's *Largo al Factotum* from the *Barber of Seville* [1930]. When he (Tibbett) came to the "Figaro, Figaro" lyric, I started to sing a duet with him.

Tibbett stopped and wondered if I found something wrong with his singing. I looked a bit dazed and sat down on a chair. My brother played trumpet, and he was a doctor. He came over and asked me what happened to me—singing and laughing at the same time. I told him that I had taken gas at the dentist over three hours ago. He smelled my mouth and said, "You were given laughing gas, and you received the effects a few hours later." After a few minutes I was ready to conduct. I finished the date, and that is how I came to sing a duet with Tibbett.

GENE AUTRY

Gene Autry came to New York to get started as a cowboy singer. He had auditioned for the Victor Company and had been turned down. He came into my office and said, "I might as well quit and go home." He told me that the Victor had turned him down.

I told him not to be discouraged. I said, "I was at the committee session when we voted against a contract for you, not because we did not like your voice, but because we had recently made deals with two similar singers. We could not find a spot for you at this time."

Gene went on and became a very popular star. My wife and I visited him in Hollywood, and he did quite a few tricks with his favorite horse in back of his house.

Ronnie, the young trumpeter, asked, *"Do artists you helped appreciate it when they become well known and are successful?"*

I said, "I do not know, and I do not expect praise. As far as Gene Autry, I often heard him say that, if not for Nathaniel Shilkret, he would have quit trying to make singing his career." One time, when he was a great success, I had written a song in his style, and I asked him to favor me by doing the song. He was polite, but he never sang the song.

RUSS COLUMBO

Russ Columbo recorded for the Victor. I conducted his numbers [1931], and he attained lots of popularity. Con Conrad, writer of the *Continental*, was with him at all dates. Conrad treated Columbo like a child. He would cry out, "Sing like this! Watch Shilkret! Do as you're told!", etc. He was Russ Columbo's Svengali, and I am not exaggerating!

WILLIAM HARTMAN WOODIN

During the Depression Franklin D. Roosevelt selected William Hartman Woodin as Secretary of the Treasury. Mr. Woodin was a quiet man who looked like anything but a financial wizard. He had one hobby. He loved to compose music of the salon type. He would hum the melody and have a musician write a piano version. I was chosen to record about twelve numbers of his.[2] He listened to his new compositions with the glee of a child who received new toys.

CARUSO POSTHUMOUSLY

Caruso records, after his death and the coming of electrical recording, started an effort to build the sound of his mechanical records to fit the new Victrola. It was necessary to get a fuller tone in his voice and dub a new orchestra over the old thin orchestral sound. (Dubbing simply means recording one or more tracks, and then combining the new recordings with the original master and, finally, making a composite track.) Eight old records were tried. After numerous unsuccessful tries I was asked to try my hand at it [1932]. I engaged thirty-five men from the Philadelphia orchestra and used the church studio.

It was important to synchronize with the old recordings, whether or not I agreed with the previous interpretation. The music must fit exactly, or we would end up with two orchestras conflicting. Today musicians are familiar with earphones. They have learned to hear a sound track and match what they hear, just like movie actors and TV performers move their lips to synchronize to a sound track sung by another singer. But in the early days musicians, and especially symphonic players, refused to use earphones. It was up to the conductor to follow the old track.

Added to the above, the outside noises crept into the sensitive micro-phones of the electrical recordings, since these recordings were done before soundproof rooms were built.

It was a torturous six-hour session, but at last eight records were com-pleted. I had no desire to hear the accepted masters, and it was not until a few [one or two] years later when I was in Stockholm, Sweden [1933], that I heard a Caruso record and said to the dealer, "That is Caruso, but how did you get such a solid sound by the orchestra?"

The record dealer brought the record to me and said, "Your name is on the label as the conductor." It was one of the records done in the Camden church studio.

Ronnie asked, *"How did you conduct solo passages?"*

"With my fingers for each new note. The player followed my finger movements. Had he used an earphone, he would not have to watch my fingers."

BIX BEIDERBECKE

I was asked to do a radio program [Camel Pleasure Hour, 1930] by N. W. Ayer and Son agency, but their radio time interfered with one of my other sponsors. Then I was asked to put a great orchestra together, with Charles Previn to conduct under my supervision. The best players were engaged, and one of the men was Bix Beiderbecke. I chose Bill Challis, a friend of Bix, as arranger, and asked Challis to watch Bix.

Any record with Bix playing his extemporaneous chorus was a sure success. But Bix was not reliable, and I had my doubts about hiring him. Challis promised to keep an eye on him and said that Bix had reformed.

Well, Bix was a phenomenal trumpeter. He had an unusual style and a wonderful tone. He appeared in the first two shows. On the third show, we had to look for him at some saloon. He appeared late for the fourth and fifth show and disappeared before the sixth show. He was a genius in the jazz field, but he was cursed with alcoholism. The funny thing was that he could not hold his liquor. There was a film made of Bix Beiderbecke's life. He died on August 6, 1931, at the age of twenty-eight. Bix composed *In a Mist, Flashes, Candle Lights,* and *In the Dark.* Bill Challis wrote the piano solo from Bix's playing.

Brokenshire, the announcer with the persuasive golden voice, was with us all during the Chesterfield Hour. He was almost as elusive as Bix Bei-derbecke. He had to be watched in saloons, and he often announced feeling high. Later in his life he took the cure and became well known for his craftsmanship with tools. He had his own program on TV.

RED NICHOLS

Red Nichols recorded for the Victor and other record companies. He also played with other leaders as a trumpeter. I used Nichols in my recordings. He was a quiet, sober young man and different from the general run of jazz men in the late 1920s. He had a fine combination called Red Nichols and His Five Pennies. He led the little band and played along with them. He had lots of style and many fine ideas, and his records sold well. His great sacrifice for his child has been turned into a movie.

It is men like Nichols, Johnny Mercer, Hoagy Carmichael and a host of other musicians in the popular field who exemplify the fact that, to be great in popular or jazz music, one does not have to drink to excess, smoke marijuana or live a riotous life. In the 1920s and 1930s, drinking was considered smart for a jazz man. Today it is considered a weakness, not a sign of talent or a necessity to get into the mood.

I remember Red Nichols' recording session with pleasure. He came to the date well prepared and finely rehearsed—no fuss, no excitement, yet with a sincere and tense feeling to do a good job, and he accomplished this with grace.

HENRY BUSSE

Henry Busse was another of the quiet jazz men—a superb trumpeter with a beautiful tone, especially with his thin tone mute. Henry talked with an accent, and his little mustache fitted his rather round face and jovial smile. He worked for Paul Whiteman for a long time, and I believe their difference came on account of money. Henry left Paul and wanted to start his own band. Paul objected to the Victor Company taking on Busse, but I used him in my band for a while and then gave him the chance to record for Victor with his own band. This opportunity started Busse, and he became a successful band leader until his untimely death.

ARTISTS

During the Victor broadcasts, I was given $10,000 a week for artists. I cut that down to $7500 and still found enough money to commission young American composers to write semi-classical pieces for my orchestra.

The Victor broadcasts were a panorama of practically all great artists in both the popular and classical fields, and also included theater greats. I'll just mention some in each category: in the popular field, Chic Sales, Helen Kane, Rudy Vallée, the Revelers, Frank Crumit, Johnny Marvin, Gene Austin and Stoopnagle; in the classical field, John McCormack, Galli-Curci, Rosa Ponselle, Chaliapin, Crooks, Lily Pons, Elman, Mary Garden, Elizabeth Rethberg, Gigli, Harold Bauer, Lucrezia Bori, Schumann-Heink, Tito Schipa, Marion Talley, Jeritza, Tibbett, Casals, Heifetz, Segovia, Geraldine Farrar, Martinelli and De Luca; and, from the theater, Judith Anderson, [Cornelia] Otis Skinner, Basil Rathbone, Alice Brady, Dennis King, Eva Le Galliene, Fay Bainter, and Henry Hull. We also did Opera Nights and Stainer's *Crucifixion* with a large choir.

One night we invited the widows, Mrs. Edward MacDowell and Mrs. Ethelbert Nevin. I had done a Nevin album. When I asked Mrs. Nevin what her children thought of their father's compositions, she told me that they were hardly interested; perhaps unenthusiastic would be better than hardly interested.

Nevin's music was a delight to record. As the Reverend Campbell remarked at Nevin's funeral, "When his music gave delight to his friends, it gave real delight to him." His music today is relegated to light classic repertoire. When Mrs. Nevin was invited to our Victor broadcast she was an old lady, yet she showed that in her younger days she must have been beautiful. MacDowell and Nevin were a year apart, with MacDowell born in 1861 and Nevin born in 1862. MacDowell appreciated Nevin's talent—his fresh and spontaneous lilting melodies.

Nevin's compositions became known throughout the world. He was probably the most popular composer for years. His *Mighty Lak' a Rose*, the *Rosary*, and *Narcissus* became international favorites. He should have become immensely rich with his works, but during his life, publishers were the only source of revenue.

Today, with TV, radio and records, plus ASCAP, Nevin would be recompensed properly. Mrs. Nevin rendered her greatest service to publishers and composers in 1909, the year Congress was considering a new copyright bill. Up to that time phonograph records and player-piano rolls, that sold in the millions, never paid any royalties for their music.

There was a good deal of opposition, but the new copyright law was finally signed by Theodore Roosevelt. John Philip Sousa, Irving Berlin and other well-known composers and authors fought for these important laws. Sousa describes Mrs. Nevin's efforts in the copy of his memoirs which he autographed for her: "To Mrs. Ethelbert Nevin who through her unaided effort made Congress see the justice of the composer's claim to his property, and in consequence of the Copyright Act of 1909." This happened eight years after Nevin's death.

Despite her advanced age, I found Mrs. Nevin a vivacious and sparkling lady. She seemed very happy, listening to our performance of her husband's works. This was in 1929 or 1930.

Mrs. Edward MacDowell realized the dream of her husband. They had discovered Petersboro, a town in New Hampshire, and bought an eighty-acre farm and built a log cabin there. It was MacDowell's house of dreams, where he wrote his *Fireside Tales* and *New England Idylls*. He often thought of an artist colony at Petersboro. Mrs. MacDowell made the fulfillment of his idea her life work.

Her concert tours, playing his music, were made for the distinct purpose of raising funds to maintain the colony at Petersboro.[3] Today it is the summer refuge of artists, composers, poets and writers who come to work in the spot that MacDowell wrote his last two sonatas, his *Sea Pieces* and his later miniatures.

Ernest Hutscheson, head of the Juilliard School of Music [beginning 1937], was the soloist and played MacDowell's *Piano Concerto*. Mrs. Mac-Dowell was a delightful guest, and her address was inspiring. Both Mrs. Shilkret and I were invited to the beautiful estate at Petersboro, where we stayed for about two weeks.

Unfortunately I never got to record a MacDowell album. I cannot remember why, unless it was the time RCA (Radio Corporation of America) acquired the Victor Company, and recordings were stopped for some period. Of course, I did record separate MacDowell numbers often.

It is not easy to appraise MacDowell fairly, in his relation to American music or to music of the world. Often he is compared to Edvard Grieg. He caught the moods of the forest, the fields and the ocean. His musical speech was his own. When American music is mentioned, his name comes forward as one of our foremost composers. Today his piano music is often played—his four sonatas, the *Tragica, Opus 45*, the *Eroica, Opus 59*, the *Norse, Opus 57*, and the *Keltic, Opus 59*, exemplify his genius.

Tito Schipa, as Don Ottavio in Mozart's opera, was considered one of the greatest triumphs, due to his wonderful bel canto voice. We had rehearsed the aria *Il Mio Tesoro* (To My Beloved) in the afternoon. On account of time, he was to sing one verse, and the orchestration was so marked. The orchestration we used was not to my liking, and so I had my librarian get the score and parts from Mapelson's Metropolitan Library. The new parts were distributed to the orchestra. I learned a lesson: Never conduct a new score without a quick rehearsal to check the music.

In the evening we started the aria, and Schipa sang the first verse divinely. As he backed off from the mike he heard the orchestra play the introduction to the second verse. In his excitement, he made a quick turn around and hit a piercing, sharp note of surprise. Then he went to the mike and sang the second verse. Of course, he was startled.

From then on, even when an artist like John Charles Thomas would say, "Nat, we don't have to rehearse this aria," I would say, "You don't have to sing with us, but I'll quickly rehearse the music to make sure the parts are correct."

Pablo Casals broadcast with us a few times. He is one of the greatest cellists, and, on his first appearance, he asked me if he could address the string section. Naturally, I agreed. He spoke to my string players, asking them not to force their tones, because, as he said, "You can get as much sound by playing naturally as by forcing the tone." He demonstrated this by playing a few passages for them.

They were greatly impressed by his short demonstration, and it was wonderful for me to conduct the orchestra, which blended so well with Casals' matchless tone quality.

Feodor Chaliapin was another story. He was nervous and explosive, and at a rehearsal for his broadcast never stood still. He would walk back and forth, wave his hands and talk in a loud and boisterous manner. Mrs. Bertha Brainard, who was in charge of the station, came to me and asked, "Is he angry?"

I said, "No, he's always like that."

We were rehearsing a Russian folk song, *Down the Street*, one of his favorite numbers. He had sung it many times with a piano at recitals. It was the story of a drunken peasant walking on the road. Near the end the tempo increased so much that I asked him if he would not accelerate to such a furious tempo, since an orchestra is not just a lone pianist. Especially the bass passages needed some leeway.

He understood and said he would remember at the concert. Everything went fine until near the end. In his excitement, he left out two bars, and when I noticed this, I immediately gave the orchestra a two-bar cut. When the concert was over he apologized for his mistake, gave a me a real Russian hug, and thanked me for my quick recovery of his error.

At one recording session, he was doing a number with his pianist, who had been his accompanist for years. Suddenly he stopped singing, ran over to the piano, kicked the chair of the pianist, crumpled the music in his huge hands, and threw it under the piano. The pianist just stood there looking at Chaliapin. A few minutes later Chaliapin got on his knees, picked up the music, handed it to the pianist, apologized, and kissed him on both cheeks.

The next try turned out to his satisfaction.

Chaliapin was one of the greatest artists of all times, and the hundreds of stories about his temperament could fill books.

Jeritza was so different—she was absolutely uninhibited at rehearsals. I did a Wagnerian program with her when she decided to do Wagnerian opera roles. We were rehearsing, and she was sitting on the floor, partly relaxing and clowning. Just then Mrs. Bertha Brainhard walked into the room to meet Jeritza.

Jeritza never liked strangers at her rehearsals, and, in polite German, asked, "Who is this Dame?" "Dame" in German is absolutely a proper and polite word, but Miss Brainhard, a lovely and charming lady, knew only the unfavorable English connotation of the word.

She drew herself up and said, "I will not stand for anyone calling me a dame," and stalked out of the room. When I informed Jeritza of Miss Brainhard's importance, she asked me to speak for her and explain the difference between the German "Dame" and the American "dame." Miss Brainhard, one of the sweetest ladies I ever knew, would not relax or forgive her.

A curious discovery concerning Jeritza: I was conducting an aria, and, when her entrance came, she did not respond. I stopped the orchestra and asked her why she missed her entrance, and she said, "You did not give me the cue."

I said, "It was not necessary, since you were reading your notes," and she replied, "I was looking at the text—I cannot read music."

Well, you could have knocked me over with a feather. Here was a great international singer who had memorized over a hundred roles, both operas and operettas—yet she could not read music. Of course, I have heard of many popular artists who cannot read music (Bing Crosby is one), but an opera star! Well, Ezio Pinza did not read music.

Helen Morgan, star of Jerome Kern's *Show Boat*, came to our Victor studio to record. She was extremely nervous. Mr. Baravalle, who conducted the *Show Boat* production, was with her, and he tried to pacify her. I asked her if she would feel safer with Baravalle conducting for her records, but Baravalle insisted upon my conducting. Helen finally sang her four songs, and the result was splendid.

Mischa Elman was booked for a Victor broadcast to play a Tchaikovsky concerto. He was to start the concert. I was all dressed up in evening clothes because it was a broadcast with a participating audience. As I was ready to leave my home, Mrs. Shilkret asked me to take our wire-haired terrier, called Rex, for a short walk in Central Park. I told her that I had very little time because of my Victor broadcast, but Anne [Mrs. Shilkret], who always worried about the dog, pleaded that he had not been out for some time, and so I said, "Okay, for a few minutes."

It was a cold day, and the snow was piled up fairly high. When I got to the park, I untied his leash and let him romp around. After about two minutes I whistled for him, but he grew playful and, as I tried to fasten his leash, he ran away again and again. Time was getting too close for comfort. I couldn't leave him loose, and I couldn't hang around without missing my broadcast. Yet, knowing Mrs. Shilkret's attachment to her pet dog, I just stood in the snow wondering what to do.

Just then a man (who turned out to be the chorus master of NBC) called Rex, and he held him for me. I grabbed Rex and asked our doorman to bring him to our apartment. I jumped into a taxicab and told the driver to get to NBC in a hurry. When we got to 59th Street and Columbus Circle we skidded. Luckily the cab straightened out, and I arrived at the broadcast about in time to give the downbeat.

One of my sponsors was a music lover who collected Stradivarius violins. He had two violins, a viola and a cello. He asked me to have my string quartet play these four instruments at one of my concerts. I hesitated to take a chance with such expensive instruments, but he assured me that they were insured.

We received the instruments, and, at first, my boys did not like their sound. I asked them to use them for a while. They did so and fell in love with the sound. They found that the difference between their very good instruments and Stradivarius instruments was in the bowing. They had to use less force, and the tones carried farther than with their own instruments.

I selected Hugo Wolf's *Italian Serenade* and had them rehearse for a few months. When they finished the number, Harold Bauer, the great pianist who was soloist for the program, remarked that it was the finest string quartet he had ever heard. This time the boys were reluctant to give up these precious Strads. The players were Lou Raderman, Jascha Zayde, and the two Borodkins.

THE SMITH BROTHERS PROGRAM

The Smith Brothers program was changed from using two male singers and a small orchestra to using Miss Rose Bampton and a twenty-eight piece semi-pop orchestra. It was an orchestra studded with players like Artie Shaw, Chester Hazlett, Tommy and Jimmy Dorsey, Lou Raderman, Charlie Margulis, and Manny Klein, all joined by Miss Rose Bampton's luscious and beautiful voice. She was used in both classical and popular

Broadway songs, with orchestral arrangements in rich color. Miss Bampton sang in pure tone and fine diction. She did not cater to the "pop" song style. The orchestra supplied the needed touch for a splendid program. George Marek, now head of RCA Victor Division, was in charge of the program.

ARTIE SHAW

It was unusual to find Artie Shaw playing first saxophone while Jimmy Dorsey played the clarinet. Later Shaw featured the clarinet, while Dorsey favored the saxophone.

Artie, being the first saxophonist, was the most ardent player for perfection. While the boys were given five minutes rest, Shaw would gather his saxophone group to practice and iron out any phrasing flaws. As a saxophonist, he had one of the finest tone qualities. As a clarinetist, he had more style than tone.

Near the end of the session he quit, saying that he had two reasons: one, he wanted to write (books) and, two, he was paying a large percentage of his earnings for some car accident that happened a few years ago.

AYLESWORTH

Aylesworth was a fine and pleasant man who developed radio to a peak success. When he became president of NBC, he walked into one of my concerts while we were playing Beethoven's *Fifth Symphony*, first movement. He listened for a moment, and then for a while danced a fox-trot with his wife. To his untutored ear it sounded like a popular tune.

THE UNION

In 1930, the musicians in New York City began feeling the effect of synchronized picture scores—gone were the large live orchestras in movie houses. It was also depression days, and there were fewer social affairs. Outside of a few Broadway musicals, the dramatic shows were not using an orchestra. There were fewer records made.

A few rabble rousers stirred up the musicians and proposed that all work must be divided, whether or not the men were capable. They proposed that every orchestra must have one third of it members from the men out of work. This would have meant that every leader who had built up a special orchestra must employ, for each engagement, one third with men supplied by the union.

This alarmed the men who had employment based on their ability, and a general meeting was called. In a crowded assembly hall there were many speeches, and the commotion was great, and the result was awful confusion. Finally, it was decided that eight musicians of the unemployed would form a committee and add as chairman one man who they could trust to find some relief. That man had to be someone who was in a position to understand their situation and also be able to help them.

Walter Damrosch was named but turned down. Many names were mentioned and turned down. My name came up, and I was chosen. With my heavy schedule, I didn't know if I could find the time. It came to the point that I had to engage other conductors to take my place at rehearsals. It was not only time consuming, but also very expensive, because the eight men could never agree on any suggestions.

I also noticed that seven out of eight members were only interested in helping themselves, not their fellow musicians. Some of their ideas were so ridiculous that I (as head of the committee) would not allow them to propose the ideas to the general assembly. One day they acted very vague and secretive. They claimed that they had an idea so great, so stupendous, that all the musicians' worries were over. They had gone ahead and invited the musicians' National Committee to come from St. Louis to New York to hear their idea.

They simply would not tell me what they would discuss with our National Board, and so I went to the meeting with them. Of all stupid and nonsensical schemes, this was by far the worst. They proposed that the American Federation of Musicians form a corporation and buy up all the radio stations, all recording companies, all ballrooms in the country, and all movie houses in the United States, and then distribute musicians on jobs.

Here I was, in an embarrassing position. A party to an asinine proposition that was simply impossible. I did not try to stop them, knowing that the St. Louis committee would puncture their balloon.

The president of the national union asked how they could finance such a scheme. Their answer was to sell stock at $10 a share. They were asked, "Do you have any idea what buying all radio stations would cost, or buying all recording companies, moving picture theaters, theatrical buildings and all the ballrooms in the nation?"

Also, how would it help the elder musicians? They replied stupidly that these musicians could take the place of the hat check girls, etc. Of course, the idea was laughed at and turned down. What finally happened was that the New York musicians' union gave seven of the men jobs as detectives, overseeing that the union laws were obeyed. Only one of the eight men offered had refused to accept the job.

About this time Roxy (Rothafel) came up with an idea, and he spoke to me about it. His proposal: Let him announce Sunday morning concerts from 11 a.m. to 12 noon with 250 musicians and soloists. He would furnish 125 men in his theater, and the theater would supply 125 men who would receive the union price. Since I was in close touch with my Victor artists, I was supposed to speak to the artists and have them perform without fee, as a gesture to needy musicians.

I told Roxy that as far as I was concerned, I was willing, but on one condition. "What is that?" he asked.

"I want a guarantee, so that if there is any deficit, that the union will not lose any money."

Roxy hit the ceiling! "How can it lose? We'll make a fortune, and 125 musicians and the union will make lots of money."

Again I said, "I insist upon a guarantee."

Roxy was quite a flamboyant character. He threw a sumptuous party, invited Mr. Aylesworth of NBC, and proposed broadcasting the concerts and having Mr. Aylesworth guarantee any losses. Aylesworth could not make up his mind. We were very friendly, and he asked my advice. I told him that I was only interested in protecting the musicians, and so I could not honestly represent two sides. Later Mrs. Aylesworth spoke to me and said, "Nat, I am afraid my husband is partly convinced by Roxy, but I feel that he is taking too much of a risk, and it may hurt him." I could not advise her any more than I could her husband. Mr. Aylesworth finally decided to guarantee the concerts.

Now came the time to put the first concert together. Erno Rapee, Roxy's impetuous conductor, got into the act. He insisted that Arturo Toscanini or Leopold Stokowski conduct, and that I also get one of the great stars from the Metropolitan Opera House.

I tried my best to have Beniamino Gigli as the first soloist, but he refused, saying that he did not want to sing in a movie theater, and besides the prices of $2 and $1 were lower than his recital seats, and that would hurt his reputation. As for Toscanini and Stokowski, I knew that they would not appear.

And so, for the first concert, Mr. Aylesworth was given the task of furnishing the artists. He came up with Walter Damrosch (who was under contract with NBC) and, as soloist, Mme. Schumann-Heink.

That infuriated Mr. Rapee. The idea of having Walter Damrosch, and not him, was too much for him. If Toscanini and Stokowski were unavailable, then he thought he should have been asked to conduct. I then proposed that we should have different conductors each week, so that he would not be burdened with a weekly program.

Rapee, in his usual excited manner, then said, "Over my dead body will I allow anyone else to conduct but myself."

I said, "Fine, you do all the conducting."

For the first concert I managed to buy and sell five hundred tickets. The profit was $2000. Later on I learned that Roxy and Rapee spent $2000 on pictures of each conducting the orchestra. Now came the second, third and fourth concerts, and receipts were less and less. By this time Rapee was calling me up and, in his excited voice, saying, "You are letting us down. I am doing all the work," etc. "Why don't you conduct the next concert?"

I replied, "Okay. Over your dead body. Isn't that what you said?"

He said, "Never mind what I said. You'll get a great pleasure conducting 250 men. It is a splendid thrill!"

This went on for the fifth, sixth and seventh week, and by this time he was calling me daily and using his favorite S.O.B. phrase, but I kept on saying, "Over your dead body."

Roxy went on a tour with his Gang, and Rapee was left with the concerts. By the ninth concert Aylesworth was really in trouble. It had cost NBC a good deal of money, and he stopped the concerts. I was lucky that I had insisted upon a guarantee! I believe that the loss would have cost the union over $50,000 without the guarantee.

ERNO RAPEE

I do not wish to belittle Erno Rapee—he was a fine conductor and musician and wrote three successful theme songs (*Diane*, *Charmaine*, and *Angela Mia*). However, he was ambitious and excitable. There was one trait I liked about him: When he wanted to horn in on your program, he minced no words. He would declare without any restraint, "I'll get your job." I preferred that to the way of some men who flatter you and then, in their sly and underhanded way, knife you in the back. It is easier to deal with a man who lets you know what he will do.

We unfortunately had one more clash—no, two more. The first when he called me up one day and asked me to come over to the Roxy theater. He brought up the radio programs and proposed that we (radio conductors) form an exclusive club and do our best to keep any outsiders from getting on the air. There were about seven or eight men who were doing most of the radio programs. I refused, asking what would have happened to me if, at the beginning of my radio career, there was such a club?

Young conductors must get their chance. Then I really upset him. I asked, "Have you any radio program?" He said no. I then said, "Then you would not be eligible for the club!"

The second clash involved the Mobil Hour. This happened a few years later. David White, the young man in charge of the Mobil Oil Hour broadcast, called me up and said, "Mr. Rapee, who is our conductor, is leaving us to take a position in a Hollywood studio. Would you care to take over the hour?" I accepted. I was to start in two weeks.

Mr. White was kind, intelligent and most gracious, always ready to help any artist. After signing a contract, he asked me if I would mind going on the air for Rapee's last concert and saying a few words. I then asked what he would have me say to Rapee, and he told me that I would receive my script. He also said that Rapee would write the script. Knowing my friend Rapee, I said, "That is fine, but please let me have the script as soon as possible." I called Mr. White a few times, and he made the excuse that Rapee was very busy, and, as soon as he received it, he would let me know.

I appeared in the last performance, and still no script. As I sat in the NBC studio listening to the broadcast, the orchestra started the last number, and I was still waiting for the script. Just then I was handed two sheets. I quickly glanced at the first paragraph and realized that Rapee's script contained a few sentences I could not condone.

I was introduced at the mike with Erno Rapee facing me. As he greeted me I dropped his script on the floor and started ad-libbing, and, not finding my words in the script, he became confused and started to speak in his native tongue, Hungarian. I quickly interrupted him and said, "Thank you Mr. Rapee, and I, likewise, wish you the best of luck," and that was the end of the broadcast.

Rapee was beside himself, and, as soon as he recovered, started his usual tirade at me for not sticking to the script. I answered, "If you thought I would read such a phrase as 'I hope I can attain the level of your standard' and more like that, you must be crazy."

And so I started the Mobil Oil Hour [in January 1930], Wednesday, 9 p.m. to 10 p.m. I retained the soloists that had been popularized by the Roxy programs, Gladys Rice and D. Stanbury, but added guest artists like Emilio de Gogorza, Percy Grainger, Allan Jones, Lindbergh, Fritzi Scheff, George Gershwin and other attractions.

It was a very pleasant hour with my forty-five piece orchestra, and David White was a wonderful supervisor.

FERDE GROFÉ

Ferde Grofé left Paul Whiteman about the time Henry Busse, the trumpeter, did. I believe Paul, who was the soul of generosity in salaries, did try at this period to keep his expenses down. Taking a cut in salary is not popular, and so Ferde, top arranger for Whiteman for many years, was out of a job.

I put Ferde under contract to arrange one number a week for the Mobil Oil Hour at $200 an arrangement. He started to compose, and came up with the *Mississippi Suite* and the *Grand Canyon Suite*, both favorites in records and concerts.

JAMES MELTON

James Melton, tenor, was a soloist for the Mobil Oil Hour. A few times he wanted to sing Lehár's popular *Du Bist Mein Herz Allein*, and I refused him because he could not show me the publisher's permission. Melton was never easy to handle. He decided to talk to the president of Mobil Oil and complain that I would not let him sing his favorite number.

The president promised to talk to me. Also, the legal department at NBC declared that Melton could sing the number. I spoke to the president, and he said, "I met Franz Lehár in Europe, and he said that I could have any of his songs done on my broadcasts." With my Victor Company experience, I knew that the permission must come from the publisher and not the composer. Well, James Melton sang the number for quite a few radio broadcasts.

A friend of mine, Mr. Paul Heinecke, had slowly gathered deals from many publishers all over the world, and he took notes about performances of music he controlled in the United States. When he gathered enough evidence of radio music performed without permission, he asked $250 from each radio station that aired the numbers he controlled. Melton, for singing his favorite number, was sued for $250,000. With that money, together with the money from other illegal uses of his music, Heinecke started SESAC Company[4] [in 1931], and he became powerful, like ASCAP and BMI.

WILLIAM PALEY AND THE
CHESTERFIELD HOUR

About six months into the [second season of the] Mobil Hour, I received
word through my pianist Milton Rettenberg that William Paley, president
of CBS, wanted to meet me.

Paley, like Sarnoff, had a dynamic personality. He asked me if I was an
exclusive NBC artist. I told him that NBC (through RCA) had taken over
my Victor contract and that I was an exclusive Victor recording artist, but
I was freelance in radio. I added that, up to this time, I had broadcast
for NBC, but I was getting tired of my NBC sponsors changing to CBS.
It meant engaging other conductors to do my sponsor's broadcast when a
show shifted from one network to another.

I had to make a quick decision, and I decided to tell Mr. Paley that, if he
wanted my services, I would be willing to do what he required. His answer
was, "I want you to audition for the Chesterfield Cigarette Company. I
have tried to sell them most of the top orchestras for over a year but have
been unsuccessful. I will pay for the audition."

I engaged my orchestra, and, before we finished our first number, I was
stopped. I was surprised and wondered what had happened. I was ushered
into Mr. Paley's office and met Mr. Carmichael of the Chesterfield firm
and was offered a contract for six fifteen-minute shows per week, with a
twenty-six week contract. I accepted.

The format of the program was my orchestra and a baritone soloist,
Mr. Gray. He was really a movie star artist with a nice voice, but a limited
repertoire.

Mr. Aylesworth, who had been a friend of mine, objected to my appearance on the rival network and tried to take me off of my NBC hours.
However, my sponsors refused, and I did not lose one of my NBC hours.

There was one hitch: My Mobil Hour on Wednesday finished at
10:00 p.m., and my Chesterfield program started at 10:00 p.m. Since NBC
was on 55th Street and 5th Avenue and CBS was on 52nd Street and
Madison Avenue, it was arranged for me to leave NBC just as the closing
theme started—about three minutes before 10:00, have an elevator waiting
to bring me down, jump in a cab with police escorts, drive four blocks to
CBS, ride up in a waiting elevator, and then start conducting the Chesterfield Hour about 10:01.

This worked out fairly well until the seventh program. By this time I
had met many of the field men of the Chesterfield. They complained that
the broadcast with a large orchestra and a rather ordinary baritone was
not listened to with enthusiasm by the college boys. Since that was the
audience they were trying to entice, the program did not help them.

By this time I was not satisfied with the setup, and I went to Mr. Paley and asked him to accept my resignation. He asked what the reason was, and I told him that the program was poor, and I believed a change should be made.

He told me that I was wrong and that the Chesterfield people were very well pleased with the program. We argued for quite a while, and finally I said, "Mr. Paley, please let me talk to Mr. Carmichael. I'll say that it is your idea, and let us find out what he'll say." Mr. Paley gave me the okay.

I met Mr. Carmichael, and he listened. When I was through, he picked up a letter written by his son at Pennsylvania University and asked me to read it. The letter stated, just as I had pointed out to Mr. Paley, that the college boys did not like the program.

I suggested that he engage Lombardo's orchestra and try to secure three different artists for two nights each. My recommendations included Bing Crosby, Ruth Etting and the Mills Brothers. He agreed on the artists, but insisted that I stay on with my orchestra. I then suggested cutting my orchestra from forty-five to twenty-eight in order to do the popular numbers more effectively.

When I went back to Mr. Paley, he became anxious to make the change immediately. I told him that, since I was changing most of my orchestra, I would have to get permission from the musicians' union on the notice period. Mr. Paley said to make it two weeks. I will pay the men for two more weeks, and they do not have to appear.

I spoke to the men, but they wanted to think it over. With Mr. Paley urging me to hurry and the boys not willing to come to a decision, I told the orchestra men to take it up with the union representatives. Unfortunately, the union officials had just been swept into their positions by one of these political campaigners who promised everything. The first thing that came up was that the former officials had put in a $75 per week price for one hour of rehearsal and a fifteen-minute broadcast for six nights per week.

Since the new officials (called the Yellow Ticket) were anxious to please the musicians, they claimed that they had to get four weeks' notice. However, that was not all. After the third broadcast, the Chesterfield supervisor had complained that five of the brass section came in late and, if any changes were necessary, that they could not be told of the changes. I therefore told the boys that they must get to our 10:00 p.m. broadcast by 9:55 p.m.—not to rehearse, but to learn of any changes in the program.

And so the notice became a secondary issue. With the Yellow Ticket officials trying to impress the musicians, officials decided that, since the men appeared five minutes before 10:00 p.m., that constituted a rehearsal; and they contended that five minutes, whether we rehearsed or not, must be paid at the rate of $6 per hour for a thirteen-week period.

That meant about $25,000. Since I could not expect CBS or Chesterfield to shoulder this bill (although I'm sure they would have done so at my request), I argued that none of the men received less than $125, which was $50 more than the union required, and that quite a few received $200 ($125 above the union requirement).

The New York union board voted against me, and so I appealed to our National Board. Not only did I win my appeal, but, from then on, all musicians had to allow a five-minute period before a broadcast, both for instructions and their readiness to start the hour on time.

It was the first, and only, time I had any trouble with my orchestra men. Considering the many years of good friendship and good comradeship, plus the many favors I had given them, I was really hurt. Of course, as soon as I received the reversal of the decision from the National Board, many of the men claimed that they were not to blame—that they were prodded and shamed by the usual cries of "chicken," etc.

I did not get Bing Crosby or the Mills Brothers. They had just signed with other sponsors for their first broadcasts. CBS finally secured Ruth Etting, the Boswell Sisters and the Street Singer. The announcer was the soft- and silvery-tongued Norman Brokenshire. He was very good, but he was not reliable. He was picked up at bars and often brought in at the last minute, a wee bit high.

The twenty-eight piece orchestra was carefully put together and had quite a few players who became top dance band leaders. It was a compact semi-classical dance combination that played wonderfully. The Boswell sisters were superb; Ruth Etting was great; and the Street Singer, Arthur Tracy—well, if you liked him, he was fine. I did not feel that he belonged in the group.

At a Chesterfield Hour, we were honored by a visit of the great Italian composer Ottorino Respighi. After the broadcast he asked the brass and saxophone players to stay. Between 10:15 p.m. and 3:00 a.m. the boys played all the American style in various passages. It showed the interest European composers were finding in our American musicians. In the orchestra I had Tommy and Jimmy Dorsey, Margulis, Hazlett, Artie Shaw, Manny Klein—all top players. Respighi looked like a distinguished Beethoven.

Sometime I'll tell you of the unusual happenings. For now, I'll say that Mr. Paley gave me quite a few new broadcasts and, after a year, insisted upon an exclusive contract. I refused, and so I left the Chesterfield after more than one year of broadcasting.

The difference between CBS and NBC was that, although NBC wanted me as head of their station on a fixed salary, they never insisted, while CBS did. I had gone through that experience with the Victor. I could get at least the same remuneration from one sponsor as I could from a fixed NBC or CBS salary. By this time, I was on the air fifteen times a week—again, Caruso's "feast or famine" came to my mind.

SAM FEINSMITH

We were on the Chesterfield Hour [1932] for some time, and one of the saxophone players, Feinsmith, was the only man who was not in the class of the players like Artie Shaw, Hazlett and Jimmy Dorsey. However, he was a good musician and played many instruments; he was very handy, but he was a square. One day he came to me and complained that he never was given a chance to play a jazz solo. I thought he was really in earnest. He bothered me for some time, saying that he wanted to show that he was able to play jazz as well as anyone.

His insistence annoyed me, and I wondered how I could show him up. He came to me and asked, "Nat, can I be excused for the last twenty minutes of Saturday's rehearsal?"

I said, "You would want to go when I put you on for a solo?"

He said, "Then rehearse my jazz solo first."

At the rehearsal he wanted to try his solo, but I told him that the arrangement was not ready. At last, he had to leave, and I told him not to worry—the number was *Coming 'Round the Mountain*, and all he had to do was to jazz around the melody between the Boswell sisters' singing.

From the beginning of the broadcast Sam kept looking on the pages of the last number, *Coming 'Round the Mountain*. We had put impossible passages in his part, and his face was a puzzle.

Well, we got to the last number. What he did not know was that we had rehearsed the number, and I had assigned Sam's solos to various members of the orchestra. As he came up to do his solo, I reached for his instrument and whispered, "the wrong instrument." This happened seven times, since the number had a short chorus.

By the seventh chorus, he had not played a note. He was loaded with instruments by this time, and, just as he got near the mike, one of the violin players put out his foot, and down went poor Sam, with all his clarinets and saxophones.

By this time the Boswell sisters were singing and crying, rather than laughing. The orchestra members, being in on the joke, were really laughing into a roar. The number finished, and the Boswell sisters came to my platform, and Connie said, "Please don't do that again; we could hardly sing." The orchestra men filed out of the room quickly, and there I was in the room, with Sam on the floor.

He looked at me and said, "Why did the boys get out so fast. Was it a joke on me?"

I looked at him and said, "Don't ask me to let you off early. You spoilt the whole song."

For weeks he went from one man to another, asking if it had all been a hoax on him. He never found out, but he stopped asking for a jazz solo.

I used to kid Sam about his clarinet playing, just to tease him. Since I had played clarinet for many years, he would ask me to try his new clarinets. I would say after I played, "So you think you're good."

About fifteen years later I met him on Sixth Avenue, near the NBC building. He greeted me with, "Hello, Nyat." I asked him what he had been doing, and he said, "I have been playing with Fritz Reiner, and I have improved immensely. When I was with you, I thought I was good, but really I was lousy."

I returned with, "Sam, I always said you were a lousy clarinet player, but you didn't believe me." Of course, I was kidding, but Sam took it seriously.

He turned around and said, "The same old Nyat," and disappeared.

RUTH ETTING

Twice a week Ruth Etting appeared on the Chesterfield Hour. She had a fine fresh style and a resonant vibrant voice, and she used it with great skill in popular music. She had a quiet way of working, but one could sense a feeling of uneasiness, even when she smiled.

Her appearance at rehearsals was dramatic—not due to her, but due to her husband. For reasons unknown to any of us, he was called "Colonel." He was of small stature and had a lame foot, and I guess that was the reason "Gimp" was added to the title "Colonel": Colonel Gimp [Martin "Moe the Gimp" Snyder]. He was short, dark and looked like the proverbial tough Chicago gangster, and, to cap it all, he acted mysteriously tough. He hovered around Miss Etting like a Svengali. He was her manager, her protector, and her chief advisor for picking and interpreting songs.

We would start our rehearsals with an orchestral number that would last about one half hour. Then we would wait for Colonel Gimp and Miss Etting to arrive. Dead silence ... and then we would hear the thump! thump! thump! of the Colonel's feet. The door would be opened, and Miss Etting would walk in with a cheery "Good morning."

Then Colonel Gimp would enter, his face severe and threatening, as if to say, "Well, anyone looking for a fight?" Then he would come over to me and whisper, "Got any trouble with the plumbers?" He always called the saxophone players plumbers.

I would say, "No, Colonel, everything is in fine shape."

"Good," he answered. "Tell me if anyone is looking for trouble."

After that Miss Etting and her pianist would start her song with only herself and her pianist for the verse, and then the orchestra would join in the chorus. This was the part of the rehearsal that was taxing on our nerves.

Gimp would stop Ruth, go over to the pianist, glare at him, call him awful names, and insist that he was playing wrong. The poor pianist was a shy fellow, and often he paled at Gimp's remarks, much to Miss Etting's and our embarrassment. Gimp's anger sometimes frightened us, and we surely thought that he would strangle the pianist before the season was over.

One morning he centered his attention on Miss Etting's singing. Maybe he was trying to show his authority, or maybe they had quarreled at breakfast. Anyway he came out of the control room, thump! thump! thump!, and walked over to Ruth and, in a soft, quivering voice filled with anger and emotion, spoke close to her ear. We could not hear what he said, but, when I looked at Miss Etting's arm, I noticed that he had pinched her so hard that her arm was black and blue. I felt sorry for her, and my heart went out to her. After a few minutes we resumed the rehearsal.

Whenever Gimp was in the room, there was nervous tension. Rumors were that he had once been associated with Chicago gangsters, and then he met Ruth Etting. He fell deeply in love with her, and through sheer bravado and threats, gave her the chance she needed to show her talent. There was no doubt of his sincerity in his mad love for this beautiful girl. Slowly, with the Colonel as her manager, she climbed the ladder of success, until she was one of the highest-paid popular singers in the country.

As she rose to her position and absorbed the dignity and culture of other artists, she could not help noticing that the Colonel remained the same crude character, belligerent, jealous and coarse. Her loyalty for his help (or was it fear?) kept them together for a long time, but the tension was too great, and finally this marriage ended in tragedy. Ruth fell in love with another man—a pianist and a coach. Gimp shot him, but only wounded him. She divorced Gimp, and then the Colonel went to prison [1938].

About a year after the shooting, Colonel Gimp (out on parole) was standing outside of the Brown Derby restaurant on Vine Street, Hollywood, looking tired, and his face had a haunted look. Lou Raderman, who had been my concertmaster on the Chesterfield Hour, knew the Colonel. In fact, Lou often laughed at Gimp's remarks, and the Colonel would try to scare Lou by glaring at him. The Colonel came to me once and, in his mysterious voice, declared that he would rub out that guy with the saw (meaning the bow).

When Lou saw Colonel Gimp in his forlorn condition, Lou's soft heart melted. He walked up to the Colonel and said, "Hello, Colonel." Gimp looked at him, recognized Lou, and returned his greetings. Lou invited the

Colonel to join him. They entered the restaurant, and, during the meal, Lou told me that the rough and tough Gimp cried like a baby and said, "Lou, you are the first person in weeks who said hello to me."

I met Miss Etting a few years later, and she looked fine. For a while she sang around a bit. Whether she is active now is something I do not know. As for the Colonel, I have not heard anything about him since Lou Raderman told me the story.

MORE BROADCAST STORIES

On Sundays I did five programs. One was General Motors. This was supervised by Mr. Henry Souvaine. The format: my sixty-five piece symphony orchestra, a guest conductor, and guest artists.

The guest conductors invited were heads of the symphonic orchestras throughout the United States and Canada. We had Reiner, Ormandy, Toscanini, Bruno Walter and many others. The instrumentalists were Horowitz, Elman, Heifetz, Rosa Ponselle, John Charles Thomas, Lily Pons and a host of great ones too numerous to mention.

I was on this concert broadcast for two years. I would conduct one to three numbers and conduct for the soloists. The guest conductor would be introduced, and I would hand him my baton (if he used one).

Naturally, unusual things happened. I remember the night Ormandy was guest conductor. Evidently, he came to the concert a few minutes early, and, when he saw the music stand with scores on it, he ordered a stage hand to remove the stand and music, because he conducted his numbers by heart.

Imagine my surprise when I came out for my first number—no stand or music. With my five broadcasts on Sunday, it would have been impossible for me to memorize fifty or sixty numbers, besides various cues and script. Somehow I got through my first number and then went backstage to find my stand. It was nowhere in sight, and so for the rest of the program I managed to conduct by memory. What I wanted to know was whether the beginning of each number started with an upbeat or a downbeat. I had my concertmaster point with his finger, up or down. Once I heard the first few bars, I managed to conduct the whole piece. The accompaniment of the vocalist was the greatest strain.

Then there was the Toscanini concert. We tried to secure his appearance and finally succeeded. As his fee he was given a $17,500 car that he presented to his son-in-law and daughter, Mr. and Mrs. Horowitz.

Toscanini would not use my orchestra, and insisted upon eighty-five men of his New York Philharmonic—we gave in on that. We suggested

Horowitz as the soloist, but he thought it would be too much of a family affair and asked for the singer Lotte Lehmann.

He came to the rehearsal while Mrs. Toscanini, a group of General Motors officials, Milton Cross, who was the announcer, Souvaine and I listened in the monitor room. I did not conduct at this concert.

After Lotte Lehmann rehearsed her *Fidelio* aria, she came to me and said, "Mr. Shilkret, this is the first time I ever sang for Maestro Toscanini. Will you please ask him to conduct the aria a little slower?"

I looked at her and exclaimed, "You want me to tell Toscanini that? Do you want him to bolt out of the room?" Then I said, "If the Maestro conducted a trifle fast, he had a good reason. You will not have to worry. He'll follow you at the concert." ... and he did!

When the rehearsal was over, and before Toscanini came in, I warned Milton Cross that the Maestro would probably conduct a bit faster when he had an audience. I told Cross to be ready for about two more minutes of announcing.

That almost started a riot. Mrs. Toscanini said that he never changes his tempos, etc. I let it go at that. Then Toscanini walked in and asked how the orchestra sounded. Everyone raved about the sound and said it would be the greatest concert ever performed over the air.

He turned to me and asked, "How was it Shilkret?"

I answered back, "Not good."

There was consternation on everyone's face—they were sure that the Maestro would refuse to conduct the broadcast. Toscanini then started to shout in Italian, calling them liars and flatterers and ordered them out of the room.

He walked over to me and put his arm around my shoulders. He asked me what was wrong in a very quiet voice. I told him that studio H-8 had a peculiar acoustical problem, and I had many experiences in that room. I suggested that we get a porter to rearrange the seats and the stands of the orchestra. The Maestro said, "Never mind the porter—let us go to the stage, and you tell me where each stand and chair should be placed." And so, for almost an hour, the Maestro placed the seats as I directed.

The concert came off magnificently—except for one slight hitch: Milton Cross had to ad-lib for two minutes—Toscanini had beaten his rehearsal time by two minutes.

There was one concert that was really heart rendering, and that was the Willem van Hoogstraten and Vladimir Horowitz performance. Horowitz was angry that he did not appear with his father-in-law, Toscanini, and, when he was told that van Hoogstraten would conduct him in Chopin's *Concerto*, he really blew his top.

He said, "That so and so, I'll not play with him." What could I do? Van Hoogstraten had called me that morning and wanted to speak with

Horowitz. But Horowitz would not meet him. Evidently they had some misunderstanding before.

So Horowitz finally came to the rehearsal and turned his back on van Hoogstraten. They began, and the conductor, after a few passages, stopped the orchestra and asked Horowitz nervously if the tempo was alright. Horowitz, without turning around, made an impatient wave of his hand and practically told the conductor to shut up and not bother him.

Then came the concert. As I walked into the room, I noticed that a one-foot-high platform had been added to the stage. I asked the porter why this had been done, and he said that Mr. van Hoogstraten had ordered it, so that he could get closer to the soloist.

They started the concerto, and van Hoogstraten, in order to get nearer to the pianist, got in front of the open top of the piano, therefore, blocking the flutist's view of his baton. As I sat in the monitoring booth, I heard the flutist come in one bar too soon. Horowitz and the orchestra noticed it immediately and jumped the bar. Van Hoogstraten, being too near the pianist, noticed it too late, and, in his nervousness, tried to make up the lost bar.

I knew that they (the orchestra) would not pay attention to the conductor and would go along with Horowitz. Of course, things straightened out in the next eight bars, but I could see the looks Horowitz threw at the poor conductor. Finally they finished, and the audience applauded. Souvaine tried to have the conductor and the soloist acknowledge the applause, but Horowitz, at first, refused. Then he was practically pushed out behind van Hoogstraten. As they walked out Horowitz kept pounding the conductor's back, yelling faker, charletan, etc.

It was a sad, yet comical, sight. Van Hoogstraten, about six feet, four inches—and Horowitz, about five feet, five inches, beating the big man. I tried to see van Hoogstraten after the broadcast, but he disappeared quickly. I felt sorry for him. It was the extra one-foot platform that prevented him from cueing the flutist who could not see him. Also, being too near the vibration of the piano, he could not hear the flutist's mistake.

I must tell you about Rosa Ponselle and the Artur Bodanzky concert. Bodanzky was a guest conductor. He rehearsed the orchestra, and I rehearsed my number and Miss Ponselle for her aria from the opera *Norma*. After the rehearsal some officials thought that, since both artists were Metropolitan Opera House stars, Bodanzky should conduct Miss Ponselle.

Bodanzky gave many excuses. He did not care to conduct it, and, besides, he did not know the *Norma* aria. Finally, we prevailed upon him to do it. He asked for a rehearsal, and so we tried to get them together.

Ponselle wanted an afternoon rehearsal because she did not like to sing too early. Bodanzky insisted upon a morning rehearsal so that he could rest the afternoon before the concert, which was from 6 p.m. to 7 p.m.

Ponselle won out, and the rehearsal was booked for 5 p.m., one hour before the concert. I got to the rehearsal at 5 p.m., and there was Bodanzky, very much upset, but no Ponselle. I went over the aria with Bodanzky. By the way, there was a large chorus with the aria.

It was 5:30 p.m., and no Ponselle. It became a tug of war to keep Bodanzky from walking out. About 5:35 p.m. Miss Ponselle was seen slowly walking up the aisle. By this time the audience was being seated. Ponselle got on the stage, and Bodanzky started the rehearsal without greeting Miss Ponselle. They finished the rehearsal two minutes before the concert started.

This story has a postscript which I will relate later.

I had another concert broadcast that went over big. The name was Hall of Fame—sponsored by some cosmetics company [actually Lysol, in 1934]. Attached to the program was an obnoxious Mrs. Sponsor, a second wife who had been secretary and had married the wealthy boss.

What annoyed me was her attitude toward some of the great artists. She thought and acted as if she were an impresario bestowing gifts on them. She would come to rehearsals, meet the artists, and try to impress upon them that she was a benefactor of the arts. Of course, she was ignorant of music.

One day the Victor Company asked me to use Mischa Elman. They had guaranteed four broadcasts at $5000 for each and had only used him three times. They offered, for $1500, to let me use him for the Hall of Fame program. I went to Mrs. Sponsor and suggested Elman as soloist. She showed me a picture of Heifetz and asked me to engage him. Naturally, I said that I would be glad to talk to his manager. His price was $6000 for one broadcast, and she okayed the sum.

She was not too sure about Mischa Elman, but I convinced her that a concert without him playing the violin concerto of Tchaikovsky would be unthinkable. Elman was engaged.

When I asked Mischa Elman to play Tchaikovsky's violin concerto, he told me that he had done it too often lately and preferred to play the Bruch concerto. I could not tell him what I had told Mrs. Sponsor, and so I insisted upon Tchaikovsky. He was adamant and would not give in.

And so I had to make excuses to Mrs. Sponsor. Personally, I did not think she knew the difference between Bruch and *Yankee Doodle*. I explained to her that he had played the Tchaikovsky concerto with the Bruch arrangement. She looked puzzled, but fortunately did not pursue the subject.

I was so annoyed by the spot Elman put me in, that I had Zayde, my concertmaster, play the Tchaikovsky concerto on another program. He did a marvelous performance, and I asked Mischa what he thought of his rendition. He just said, "It was alright."

Another time, Lucrezia Bori was the soloist, and her fee was small compared to others, $1000. This gracious lady, this wonderful artist, was treated without dignity by Mrs. Sponsor. Actually she was always catering to male artists, especially the good-looking and younger men.

John Charles Thomas, one of the best baritones, put Mrs. Sponsor in her place when he heard of her treatment of Mme. Bori. He was a handsome man, and Mrs. Sponsor played up to him. At the rehearsal she sat near us and Thomas, as usual, would say, "Nat, we do not have to rehearse that." This went on all through the rest of the program. He was ready to depart when Mrs. Sponsor walked up to the stage and asked him to please sing one number especially for her. He made a short reply: "Okay, come to our broadcast at 8 p.m., and I'll sing for you," and then walked out on her.

After a year of using concert and operatic artists, Mrs. Sponsor asked for movie stars. Katharine Hepburn was engaged and insisted upon doing parts of *Romeo and Juliet*. This was before her great Shakespearean roles. Aylesworth, who seemed to know her well, told her to use parts of her successful films, but she would not change her mind. He was pretty rough with her, but to no avail. Evidently, he was right, because the radio critics gave her some awful reviews. To her credit and determination, a few years later she did Shakespearean roles to great acclaim.

Mrs. Sponsor called me to say that she had met Mme. Alda and had promised her a date on the Hall of Fame. She asked me to call Mme. Alda, who was living at the Waldorf-Astoria Hotel. I called her and made a date.

I could never forget my first contact with her during my early Victor years. Sitting in my office, I received a phone call, and the voice said, "You tell Mr. Child that, if I do not get the following songs for my next recording, I'll raise hell. He has been giving Alma Gluck the best numbers; no wonder she is a top seller," etc. I asked who she was, and she said Mme. Alda.

At that time she was Mrs. Gatti-Casazza,[5] and she was really using her weight around the Metropolitan Opera House. In many ways, she was a remarkable woman and a fine artist, but really quite rough if she did not like anyone.

I arrived at the Waldorf perhaps five minutes late and called her at her penthouse suite. She answered and said in an angry voice, "Why the hell do you have to call me—come right up." I entered her suite, and the first thing she said was, "Why do you hate me?"

I replied, "I do not know what you are talking about."

She said, "Yes you do! You have never engaged me, and you have avoided recording for me."

She may have been partly right, but I did not answer her. Then she said, "I am in a hurry. Don't you know that I broadcast from here daily? You can hear the orchestra in the other room."

I told her that I really did not know of her broadcasting, and, besides, if she is late I'll leave, that all I wanted to get was her suggestions for our Hall of Fame program. She said, "Let us go over *Ave Maria*, the Gounod-Bach version." I sat down at the piano, and she began walking excitedly up and down and singing the melody rather fast. She stopped and said, "faster." I replied that the original Bach prelude should not be hurried, despite the slow melody of Gounod. She looked at me and then said, "Let's forget all this. Come and have a drink with me. I want to speak to you about Rosa Ponselle and Bodanzky."

We went to the bar, and she poured out a drink. She then turned to me and said, "Tell me about why Ponselle slapped Bodanzky at the Victor broadcast." I told her that, wherever she got her information, it was absolutely false. She did not believe me.

Then came the rehearsal, and, as she came into my orchestra, the boys tittered. She had become quite heavy, and she had put on a short dress, not flattering her fairly heavy legs. She took a look at the men and pointed to the clarinet player, Chafferilli, who knew her well from the Metropolitan Opera. She pointed at him and said, "Take that clown out of the orchestra, and also the man next to him." That was Possell, husband of the well-known soprano Helen Jepson.

I winked at the two men, and they went out, but stayed in back, playing their parts by memory. The rehearsal started, with Mrs. Sponsor sitting in the first row. I realized that Alda was up to her old tricks to get even for my neglect of her.

We were doing an aria from Puccini's opera, *La Boheme*. She did as I expected. She stopped me three times, and in a sugary voice said, "Mr. Shilkret, you know I learned this opera with the composer Puccini, and sang the Mimi role with Toscanini," etc.

I looked at her and said, "Puccini is dead and Toscanini is not here. Shall we rehearse or shall I substitute you for another soprano?"

If she thought that Mrs. Sponsor would make any difference to me, she was mistaken. Instead of growing angry, she smiled, and the rest of the rehearsal went over smoothly. At the concert she looked fine and sang divinely. That is the last time I saw her.

THE UNION AND TRANSCRIPTIONS

In 1930, when I got mixed up with eight rabble-rousers at the union, I tried to warn the National Musicians' Committee about the use of records to take the place of live musicians. I told them that I had been loaned out by the Victor for experiments, and that it was their aim to use records for radio and commercials.

The committee made the same mistake regarding radio that Mr. Johnson had in 1924. They declared that nothing would take the place of live musicians. They would not listen to me. I wanted them to not allow recordings without making some deal whereby the union controlled the records.

In a short time my warning to our International union board came true: Musicians were now competing with their own records. I did quite a few transcriptions with a few companies. Since I could not fight them, I joined them. However, I believe I was the only musician who insisted upon a yearly royalty of x dollars as long as my name was in their catalogue list.

NBC was against using records instead of live announcing. Columbia started to make transcriptions that included commercials. I tried to convince RCA Victor to follow suit. Sarnoff did not agree, and so I formed a company with two other men and called it Shilkington Transcriptions—a combination of our three names. We had one sponsor (I believe Bond Bread [actually, Freihofer, 1930–1931]), and, in two months, we were $5000 ahead. When Sarnoff heard about it, he declared that he did not want another company using the RCA Victor facilities. He dissolved our Shilkington Company and started a transcription company which he called Thesaurus.

Nothing was done about transcriptions for many years. By then records had replaced most of the live musicians in America. Transcription companies sprang up overnight. By 1942, Petrillo stopped recording. It was too late. A year later Petrillo made an agreement for musicians to participate in the earnings, but the damage had been done.

There are practically no radio orchestras, and very few TV shows, using live musicians now. After all, records are cheap, and live musicians are very expensive. Music may be important to TV and radio shows, but the musicians are getting very little out of it.

Europe is even getting much of the picture recording done at one half or one third of the cost in the United States. The future picture is not too bright for live musicians.

LAST TWO ENCOUNTERS WITH ERNO RAPEE

I want to relate my last two experiences with Erno Rapee. As I said before, he left the Mobil Oil Hour for a studio engagement in Hollywood. He stayed one year and then returned to New York. The day he arrived, he called me up.

He informed me that now that he was back, he was ready to take over the Mobil Oil Hour. As he said, "After all, you were substituting for me."

I asked him where he got the idea that I was his substitute. I was engaged because he left the hour. However, I said, "If they want you back, I won't stand in your way."

I spoke to Dave White, and he told me that I was wanted and that Rapee would not be accepted. I received many calls from Rapee. I told him that I never accepted a radio hour unless the conductor on the hour gave me permission, but Rapee's philosophy was "dog eat dog." I then said, "Okay Erno, if you can get the Mobil Oil Hour back, all the more power to you. Do what you wish. I'll stay on while the powers want me." Well, he never got back to me.

Finally, he did succeed on the General Motors Hour. I had it for two years. Henry Souvaine came to me at the beginning of the third year and said, "Nat, it hurts me to tell you that I have been asked to use Erno Rapee. I just feel terrible to tell you this." Somehow, he got to the wife of one of the important executives at General Motors. He sold her the idea that my having many sponsors was not in the interest of General Motors. They could have his exclusive services, etc. Evidently the lady fell for his argument.

Henry added, "You have done a swell job, but I must bow to their wishes. However, I'll continue to pay you your fee as long as I have charge of the program." I told Souvaine that would not be necessary. I wouldn't take any money unless I rendered service. I thanked him. Well, Rapee finally succeeded. The hour lasted just one more season.

SHORT STORIES

Rosa Ponselle: I was a great admirer of Rosa Ponselle's voice. Her vocal range in her low, middle and high notes was perfect. Her decision to end her career at the pinnacle of her artistic height was regrettable to me.

Just before a rehearsal Mrs. Shilkret and I must have surprised Miss Ponselle. She was standing up with her head tilted, evidently gargling. I went to introduce Miss Ponselle to Mrs. Shilkret. Miss Ponselle, without a moment's hesitation, spit out, with a healthy flow, whatever she was gargling. She walked over to my wife and gave her a hearty hand shake.

Alfred Wallenstein: Alfred Wallenstein, cellist and conductor, was a Toscanini favorite. While he was still a cellist with the New York Philharmonic Orchestra, Bruno Walter was invited as a guest conductor by Arturo Toscanini. Wallenstein hardly looked at Walter, and even went so far as looking out at the audience and nodding and smiling at his friends in the first few rows.

Bruno Walter was respected by all musicians, and he got results without undue temperament. He was annoyed at Wallenstein's behavior, but, being a great conductor, he refrained from reprimanding him before the whole orchestra. He used a more subtle method.

He approached Wallenstein and asked, "What would you like to do after you quit playing cello?"

Wallenstein answered, "I would then want to conduct."

Bruno Walter remarked, "That is a very commendable ambition. Would you mind if I gave you a piece of advice?"

"Of course not," replied Wallenstein.

"Well here it is:" said Walter, "Never engage a Wallenstein."

Jerry Wald: Before Jerry Wald, Hollywood producer, left New York, he was a very young, brazen radio critic, or rather a columnist for the *Graphic* newspaper. He did more mudslinging than criticizing. His column was read by many artists with fear. He was the scourge of the radio business. He went out of his way to print semi-slanderous news about anyone. For some time he got away with it.

Once he picked on the songwriter Lew Brown, a man with a fiery temper. He said that Brown was galavanting with some pretty blond singer. Brown had his troubles with his wife, and, after a separation, they were at the point of making up their differences. Then Jerry Wald's column came out, and Brown's wife read it, and that was the end of that romance.

He (Wald) had picked on the wrong man. Brown caught Wald eating at a restaurant and gave him a real working over. Finally, he pointed his finger at Wald and said, "Get out of town or I'll do this to you whenever I meet up with you." Jerry Wald left New York, grew up wisely (?), and became one of Hollywood's best producers.

Mr. Hill: At a broadcast (I forget the name of the sponsors), we were on the last program of our season, and all the artists who had been featured were put together to do their best number. The producer, a highly emotional fellow, was seated in one of the listening booths. Next to him, in another booth, was the composer Jerome Kern.

In the studio, George Gershwin was at the piano, ready to play his *Rhapsody in Blue*. The announcer, Mr. Hill, started to read his script, but, by his carelessness, he had dropped a sheet and was reading page 7 instead of page 6. Since Hill had not announced Gershwin's number, I could not go ahead.

Here is Jerome Kern's description of what happened the next few minutes: He heard an anguished cry from producer Sanford—Kern rushed into the next booth and saw Sanford yelling incoherently and flailing his arms wildly, and then the poor fellow fainted. Somehow, after seeing Sanford through the window, I gave the start for the *Rhapsody in Blue*. Knowing

Sanford's temperament, even for slight slips, I figured that he would not recover for a while. My going into the *Rhapsody* gave Hill a chance to recover page 6 and announce Gershwin during our playing.

A Packard broadcast: At the Packard auto broadcast, I had two great lady artists: Geraldine Farrar and Mary Garden. The same week, I recorded Gloria Swanson and Irene Dunne—what a beautiful ensemble of lovely ladies.

The Manville Hour: One of the craziest hours—I mean fifteen-minute program—was the Manville Hour. The features were the columnist Floyd Gibbons[6] and a sixteen-piece brass band. Floyd, the fastest talker in the world, announced the news. Between his announcements we played the fastest and loudest band numbers you ever heard. It must have been a maddening fifteen minutes for listeners. Whoever came up with the idea must now be in a mental institution. I forgot to mention that Floyd Gibbons had one patched eye and was louder than Winchell.

The Eastman Kodak Hour: The Eastman Kodak Company was a pleasant hour. The soloist was a pretty young lady. Her name was Countess Albani. Other guest artists included Paul Robeson, Cornelia Otis Skinner, and Nick Lucas.

Sir Thomas Beecham, son of the Beecham of Beecham pills: He came to America as a guest conductor for the New York Philharmonic Society. Beecham was a famous conductor and a man who stood for no nonsense from anyone. He was also somewhat eccentric. As he raised his baton to rehearse the orchestra, he was startled by a sizzling noise. Looking at the floor, he discovered that the orchestra men had scattered thousands of Beecham pills on the floor. This infuriated him, and for the next few minutes they received a lecture in Sir Beecham's most tense and cryptic manner. They never crossed him again.

Toscanini: Toscanini was relaxing at his home and turned on his radio set. An orchestra was playing a symphony by Beethoven, and, since he had not tuned in at the beginning, he did not hear the announcement. As the orchestra went on, he started to severely criticize the tempo, the style, etc. He kept that up with great gusto all through the work. When the symphony was finished, the announcer said, "And this was the New York Philharmonic Symphony Orchestra, conducted by the great conductor, Arturo Toscanini."

GRACE MOORE

Grace Moore, the lovely soprano, played the role of the typical prima donna after her successful movie, *One Night of Love* [1934] was released and she became a celebrity.

Before that Grace Moore came up the hard way. However, good looks and her pleasing voice helped her tremendously. In her start she was featured in Irving Berlin's *Music Box Revue*. As a result of her singing the songs of the shows, the Victor recognized her value.

After her European studies, Grace Moore auditioned at the Metropolitan Opera, and, like all newcomers, she hung around the opera house waiting for her chance.

Some time later the Columbia studio in Hollywood gave her the chance to star in a picture that had a girl singer who made good. No one in the studio paid much attention when making the picture. It was a filler, to be sold with better pictures. In fact, one hour before the preview, one of the smart aleck officials of the company declared it a "stinkeroo." Well, the picture turned out to be a smash hit, and, of course, the smart aleck took the credit for discovering Grace Moore's potential.

Grace was very sweet to people she liked, but to those she disliked she was mean and catty. One either loved her or hated her. Up to a certain time she was easy to work with. However, in one program I really had it out with her. It was on a broadcast. The format of the program was to feature a well-known artist, playing the big hits of their career. I was engaged on a flat money basis: so much for my services and the orchestra, and the overtime paid by me.

Grace Moore arrived looking as beautiful as ever, smiling and good natured. Then she read her script, and there ensued an argument, with the producers and writers working feverishly to make the changes Grace insisted upon. That lasted two hours. After that we started rehearsing.

We were broadcasting from a room that, from my experience, had middle register notes that produced a woof sound. I generally thinned out the notes in the middle register. We were rehearsing two songs from one of her Broadway shows, and she had brought the original scores from the theater. I thinned the orchestration, but Miss Moore complained that the changes in the orchestration did not give her enough support.

I let the men play the official notes, checked the sound in the engineers' room and found I was right. To avoid more loss of time, I finished the numbers to Miss Moore's satisfaction. However, I instructed the boys to play my changes at the broadcast.

Grace's time wasting left me with just a short time to rehearse her aria from the opera *Louise–Depuis le Jour* (Ever Since the Day). Grace had a fine voice, but for some reason never was a thorough musician. There are many artists with wonderful voices and good memories who depend on their intuition to get by. No matter how hard they study, they lack the patience to really know their part thoroughly. Grace was that type. We had taken so much time on the two simple operetta songs that we had very little time for the aria.

After I ran over the *Louise* aria, I said to Grace, "You did it badly, and we must go over it again."

She flared up and said, "I have to have fifteen minutes to rest before the broadcast."

I replied, "I won't conduct you if you refuse to go over the aria again."

The producers were in a panic, and seven minutes went by with the sponsor and the producers trying to get us together. Finally, she did rehearse the aria again. I pointed out her errors, and helped her come in at the proper time. The show went off well, and everyone was exhausted, but happy.

Going over to Miss Moore, I asked her, "Grace, why all these temperamental outbursts today? You never acted like that before."

She smiled and said, "For years I took it from everyone, and I was very easy to get along with; but I got no thanks for making it easy. Now, I make a fuss, give them hell, and everyone sits up and takes notice of me."

Then I said, "So this was all premeditated, and I paid for the fun." Grace laughed that off. Despite it all, I liked Miss Moore very much. She was outspoken and nasty to some people, but completely sincere and lovable to the people she trusted. Her devotion to her husband was touching. She adored him, and he loved the ground she walked on.

BILL BACHER

Bill Bacher started as a dentist, but had a secret ambition to write. He sent a story to a magazine, and it was accepted. He immediately quit his dental practice and decided to find a place for himself in the radio field.

He was given a chance at the Benton and Bowles Advertising Agency. When I met him he was working on a few radio shows as producer and writer. Bill looked like an anemic Harpo Marx. His most successful broadcast was the Showboat Hour.

Palmolive-Colgate decided to do a series of operettas [1934], and sometimes operas featured the opera star Gladys Swarthout and the baritone Mr. Webb. The dialogue was spoken by actors whose voices matched the singers' voices. I believe Agnes Moorehead spoke the dialogue for Miss

Swarthout.

Bacher was producing and writing four shows a week and was overworked, but he loved the excitement. I had a large orchestra of fifty men, and I would get my script bit by bit at the last moment.

The night before the rehearsal I would be at my office with three arrangers, eight copyists and a duplicating machine for the string section. As the script came in, I would compose the music to fit the script all through the night, from 10 p.m. to 8 a.m. The orchestral parts would be ready for the 10 a.m. rehearsal, still half dry. Sometimes, after we received the script and finished it, Bacher would change his mind, and we were obliged to do a new routine.

Benton and Bowles were fine gentlemen, smart and efficient, but they were never in accord with each other on the program. About every two months they would alternate working on the program. No matter what Mr. Benton decided upon two months ago, Mr. Bowles would cancel it, and vice versa. They were both smart and good showmen, but neither liked the other's ideas.

Bill Bacher was an excitable fellow, and he was loyal to everyone who worked for him. He seemed never satisfied, and he loved to rehearse and rehearse until he was satisfied.

He had one fault, and he was very sensitive about it: He liked comic bits in his script, but, alas, he was not a natural comedy writer. There he would be, standing up, going through a comedy scene, and laughing to his heart's content. Then he would take a look around him, and, if everyone else was laughing as heartily as he, he was satisfied. But if they didn't laugh enough, he would get mad and repeat the scene again and again.

One day he asked me to fire four or five boys in the orchestra, especially the most talented one, Lou Raderman, my concertmaster. He would glare at Lou because Lou never laughed. Lou, knowing Bill's tendencies, had schemed with a few men near him never to laugh at Bill's comedy scenes.

Bill said, "Nat, I cannot stand some of your fiddle players. They have no sense of humor, and when I see their deadpan faces after a funny situation, I get sore and discouraged." I thought Bill was kidding, but he was really serious. Luckily he did not know that Lou was deliberately trying to get a rise out of him.

Repeating the comedy spots became expensive, taking an undue amount of rehearsal time. I finally laid down the law and told Lou to cut the deadpan routine out. He went the other way, and, from then on, they laughed and roared at every joke. I knew that Bill was a pretty smart fellow, and he would get wise to the tomfoolery. This time I was even firmer and cut the nonsense out.

It is difficult for orchestra men not to become tired and bored, sitting for hours and rehearsing generally simple music on commercial shows over

William Shilkret with sons Jack (left) and
Harry. Photo courtesy of Neil Warner.

Jack Shilkret (left) and Harry Shilkret,
ca. 1904. Photo courtesy of Neil Warner.

A page from the April 6, 1902, *New York Herald* describing the Boys' Symphony Orchestra of New York, conducted by Alfred F. Pinto. Clarinet soloist Nathaniel Shilkret is pictured in the upper right corner with the caption "Nathan Schildkraut, a Nine Year Old Star." He was actually twelve years old when the article appeared.

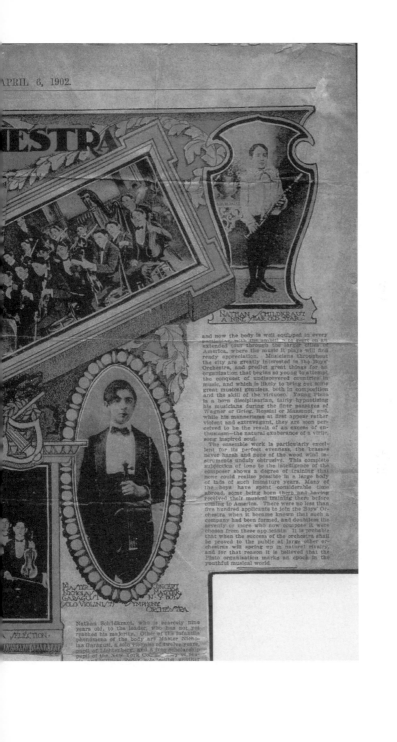

ESTRA

NATHAN SCHILDKRAUT
A NINE YEAR OLD STAR.

MASTER NICHOLAV GARAGUSI SOLO VIOLINIST

CONCERT MASTER OF BOYS SYMPHONIC ORCHESTRA

SELECTION

and now the body is well equipped in every particular, with the ambition to go on an extended tour through the larger cities of America, where the music it plays will find ready appreciation. Musicians throughout the city are greatly interested in the Boys' Orchestra, and predict great things for an organization that begins so young to attempt the conquest of undiscovered countries in music, and which is likely to bring out some great musical geniuses, both in composition and the skill of the virtuoso. Young Pinto is a born disciplinarian, fairly hypnotizing his musicians during the finer passages of Wagner or Grieg, Rossini or Massenet, and, while his mannerisms at first appear rather violent and extravagant, they are soon perceived to be the result of an excess of enthusiasm—the natural exuberance of a virile, song inspired soul.

The ensemble work is particularly excellent for its perfect evenness, the brasses never harsh and none of the wood wind instruments unduly obtrusive. This complete subjection of tone to the intelligence of the composer shows a degree of training that none could realize possible in a large body of lads of such immature years. Many of the boys have spent considerable time abroad, some being born there and having received their musical training there before coming to America. There were no less than five hundred applicants to join the Boys' Orchestra when it became known that such a company had been formed, and doubtless the seventy or more who now compose it were chosen from these applicants. It is probable that when the success of the orchestra shall be proved to the public at large other orchestras will spring up in natural rivalry, and for that reason it is believed that the Pinto organisation marks an epoch in the youthful musical world.

Nathan Schildkraut, who is scarcely nine years old, is the leader, who has not yet reached his majority. Other of the infantile phenomena of the body are Master Nicholas Garagusi, a solo violinist of twelve years, pupil of Lichtenberg, and a free scholarship pupil of the New York Con...

Nat Shilkret.

Jack Shilkret, 1923.

Lou Raderman, one of Nat's concertmasters.

Eugène Ysaÿe, the world's
leading violinist during his life.

Cantor Rosenblatt,
a Victor recording artist.

Henri Leon Leroy, 1913, clarinetist;
brought, together with bassoonist
Auguste Mesnard, oboist Marcel
Tabuteau and flutist Georges Barrère,
from Paris to the United States by
Walter Damrosch in 1905 to play in the
New York Symphony Orchestra. He
was a fellow orchestra member and
clarinet teacher of Nathaniel Shilkret.

Maxwell House Coffee Hour Orchestra includes Lou Raderman (violin, second from left), William Schade (flute on right), Auguste Mesnard (bassoon), Harry Shilkret (trumpet on right), Joe Green (xylophone), and Jack Shilkret (piano). Announcer Milton Cross is standing on the right.

Unidentified Shilkret Orchestra includes brothers Jack (piano, sitting among the violinists), and Harry (trumpet on right), Joe Green (drums), Lou Raderman (violin on left) and Pete Eisenberg and Benny Posner (two other violins).

Nat Shilkret with Mrs. Ethelbert Nevin at a Victor memorial broadcast of
Nevin's music.

Left to right: Arthur, Anne, Nat Shilkret, ca. 1928.

Arthur Shilkret, 1931.

A SIX-STAR MOBILOIL RADIO CONCERT

MOBILOIL'S 155TH AIR SHOW FEBRUARY 3RD

The world famous baton of Edwin Franko Goldman, Guest Conductor, band master par excellence, will lend further distinction to this gala Anniversary by leading the Mobiloil Orchestra in its Concert, broadcast over the 53 stations of the Mobiloil Network—nation wide from Maine to Texas, from Florida to Oregon. 11,-000,000 families — yourself, the dealers, their friends and customers—are invited to tune in.

9:30 P.M. E.S.T. WEDNESDAY "THE BIG NIGHT ON THE AIR"

Nathaniel Shilkret, conducting radio's premier orchestra —50 pieces—Gladys Rice, Douglas Stanbury and John Holbrook. And as guest instrumental soloist, Del Staigers, and his golden trumpet. Superb entertainment—a six-star, all-star cast—celebrating the Third Anniversary of one of radio's Big-Night-On-The-Air headliner shows.

THE BIG THIRD BIRTHDAY PROGRAM

1 Another Candle in Your Birthday Cake
   (special arr.) . . . . DeRose
   Augmented Orch.—Shilkret and Goldman conducting
2 Dream Lover from "Love Parade" . Schertzinger
   Miss Rice and Orchestra
3 Onward, Upward . . . . Goldman
   Orchestra—Goldman conducting
4 Yesterthoughts . . . . Herbert
   String Choir and Orchestra—Shilkret conducting
5 I Love a Parade . . . . Arlen
   Mr. Stanbury and Orchestra

6 a. On the Mall . . . . Goldman
      Orchestra—Goldman conducting
   b. Carnival of Venice . . . . . arr. Staigers
      Del Staigers, Cornetist, and Orchestra
7 a. Some Sweet Day . . . . Shilkret
      Jeanine, I Dream of Lilac Time
      Have You Forgotten?
      Entire Ensemble
   b. My Heaven of Love . . . . . . Goldman
      Encore by Entire Ensemble
8 Triumphal March from "Aida". . . . . Verdi
   Augmented Orchestra—Goldman conducting

From the Third Anniversary Mobiloil Broadcast flyer, which contains the complete program schedule for the February 3 and February 10, 1932 broadcasts and, in a reproduced news clipping, describes a portion of the December 16, 1931 broadcast.

NATHANIEL SHILKRET
And His Famous Recording Orchestra
Lead the Parade of Talent

NATHANIEL SHILKRET and his music are known and loved everywhere. At 16, assistant to Walter Damrosch; at 24, retained by Victor Company to develop a new style of orchestral scoring, and today one of America's foremost composer-conductors, he devotes his full talent to "Song and Story" in the interests of American banking.

HEAR THE BEAUTIFUL THEME SONG, "Dancing in a Dream." This beautiful waltz, written by Nathaniel Shilkret, has never before been played over the air. Mr. Shilkret's orchestra, above, are giving this new composition its world premiere on "Song and Story." You will hear it at the beginning and end of each program.

MR. SHILKRET, taking time off from his position as musical director for RKO-Radio Pictures, has supervised and conducted the musical portions of "Song and Story." He has injected into the series a degree of enthusiasm, musical excellence and sheer entertainment such as we believe have never before been built into a bank radio program. Mr. Shilkret's highly competent orchestra, under his amazing baton, unite to bring you the type of music that has enchanted millions of listeners on the Camel Cigarette Program — the General Motors Program — the Standard Oil Program.

Music of Popular Appeal Chosen

SOME of the musical selections used are illustrated on this page. Other melodies with broad appeal which are included in this series are "Bambalina," "The Toy Trumpet," "Dark Eyes," "Moonlight and Roses," "The World is Waiting for the Sunrise," "The Merry Widow," "The Grand Canyon Suite," "Old Black Joe," "Plantation Dance," and many others, all presented in sparkling and original arrangements.

Musical Copyright Fees Are Paid by the A. B. A.

As YOU may know, music is copyrighted and each time it is played on the radio a fee must be paid to the copyright owners. Some tunes cost 50¢ each, some 25¢ each, while some are in the "public domain," and are free. However, in selecting the music for this series the very best — and hence the most expensive — melodies have been selected. As a matter of fact, *the musical copyright fee for the series of thirteen programs is over $14.* You need not be concerned with this charge, however, as it will be paid automatically by the Association and is fully covered by the subscription price you pay for the series.

Advertising brochure for the *Song and Story* transcriptions recorded in 1938.

Front table, left to right: Ronald Modell, Nat Shilkret and Joseph Amato, the percussionist used in *Paris '90* in Portland, Oregon, in January 1953. The photo was taken at Amato's Supper Club. Photo courtesy of Ronald Modell.

Taken on the set of *Shall We Dance*; from left to right, seated: stars Fred
Astaire and Ginger Rogers, composer George Gershwin; standing: dance
director Hermes Pan, film director Mark Sandrich, lyricist Ira Gershwin,
music director Nat Shilkret.

Nat with George Gershwin.

Barbara Shilkret, shown with gown designer Baroness de Strasser, modeling a gown in *American Weekly* in 1939.

Arthur and Barbara Shilkret and their children Niel and Joan, ca. 1954.

and over again. TV shows are really worse than radio, because they repeat and repeat the numbers for the voices, lights, dress rehearsals, etc.

During the last few shows there was friction between Bill and Benton and Bowles Company. I was in the room and could not understand why Bill became so disturbed. But Bill was eccentric and would not take even slight criticism lightly. He quit at an impulse, so it seemed to me, and despite all the effort made to have him change his mind, he left.

About two months later, I received a call from Bill. He had set up a producing office on the strength of his fine shows. He had received $500 a week working on four shows. He told me that he had signed for a new show for Esso at $600 a broadcast. He asked if I would take care of the music, and I accepted.

Before I get into the new show, I want to mention that one of the singers of the chorus in the Palmolive-Colgate program was Risë Stevens. We quickly were attracted by her fine voice. We would try to use her in the duets with Miss Swarthout. Later she went to Europe, returned to America, and became an operatic star with the Metropolitan Opera House.

Well, the format of the Esso show was based on a Broadway operetta called *O'Flynn*, a swashbuckling Irish hero. The composer was a Mr. Hauser, and the original production had about eight songs. Bill Bacher said he needed four new songs each week, and, since Hauser could not deliver so many new tunes, he asked me to compose them.

Knowing Bill's love of rehearsals, I asked for a fairly high figure, $4900 per week, for my services, the orchestra and the chorus. He paid the soloists.

I was happy for Bacher's sake, and, now that he had only one show a week, I received my script in plenty of time. I believe we had about twelve or more hours of rehearsals in two days. Before the first show, with our rehearsal over, we went out for a bite, and, about one hour before the broadcast, we sat in our dressing room going over the last minute details.

Mr. Hackett of MCA was in charge of the show, and just then he received a call from the Esso people, who said that they wanted to add about thirty seconds to their prepared commercial to introduce a new product. Mr. Hackett promised to leave room and asked Bill Bacher to make a thirty-second cut in the show to find time for an added commercial.

Bill looked at him and said, "Like hell I will. Every word I wrote, and every music note in the show is important, and I'll not change anything. You call Esso up, and tell them so." Hackett looked at me, and I looked at Bill. Knowing Bill as I did, I knew he would put up a fight.

Hackett said, "I can't tell the sponsor that. MCA does not do business like that. It is their show, and I won't tell them that."

Bacher answered, "If you won't tell them that, then I'll tell it to them."

Hackett said, "No you won't. MCA is responsible, and I am here to see that they get what they ask for. After all, it is only a thirty-second cut."

Bill put on his coat and said, "Then I'm going home," and started for the door. Hackett and I were stunned, and I was really sore at Bill. As he came to the door, he turned to me and said, "Nat, you don't think I am unreasonable, do you?"

Well, I let loose and called Bill every name under the sun and ended up with, "I not only think you are unreasonable, I think you are crazy."

Bill looked at me, walked back slowly to the room, and then, as if he were making a great sacrifice, said, "Alright, if you feel that way, what should we do? The show is rehearsed exactly to fit the allotted time."

I replied, "That's easy; let's sing one chorus less of one tune." I mentioned the melody, and that is the way it was settled.

After the show Bill asked me to handle all of his future shows and become a partner in his new production company. I said, "Bill you are too temperamental for me. Engage me when you want to, but I do not want any partnership with you." We always got along well and remained friends for years.

But, to continue, we had done three or four shows one afternoon. While I was rehearsing another show at Radio City, I was told that Bill had collapsed in another studio and was in great pain and was calling for me.

I left my room and went to see Bill. He was terribly sick; I believe it was an ulcer pain. Bill, in a weak voice, asked me to take care of the Esso program and see his assistant, called the "old stager."—I forget his real name [Henry Neely]. Bill was taken to the hospital and operated on.

I went on with the show, with the help of the old stager, and after the third show Bill asked for me. I went to the hospital, and the nurse said that Mr. Bacher was a very sick man, but I could see him for a little while. I found Bill as pale as a ghost. With his covers up to his neck, all I could see was his wild hair, his big eyes and his face, as white as chalk. Going over to him, I said, "How are you, Bill?"

He said, "Never mind that; how did the show go last night?"

I replied, "Well."

He asked, "What do you mean 'well'?"

I shrugged my shoulders, but did not say anything. Bill then asked, "Well, tell me; I want your honest opinion."

I replied, "Do you really want me to truthfully tell you?"

Bill answered, "Of course," and looked belligerently at me.

Maybe it was perverse humor or maybe it was his attitude that affected me, but I told him, half in jest and half in earnest, "Bill, you know that I want you to get well, but I am hoping that they keep you here for a good while to rest."

Bill asked, "Why?" I believe I stunned him.

I answered, "Well, you did the show with twelve or fourteen hours of rehearsal. The old stager and I did each show in four hours of rehearsing, and I came out $1800 ahead on each show more than I did with you."

Bill nearly had a fit and almost passed out. He started screaming, and the nurse came in and ordered me to leave. I don't think that Bill ever got over that speech of mine. I guess it wasn't funny then, but I laugh every time I think about it.

PIETRO FLORIDIA

Ferde Grofé and I studied with Pietro Floridia. Mr. Floridia had me study Johann Sebastian Bach—well-tempered clavichord preludes and fugues— for two years. He would also have me write four-bar and eight-bar themes every week. I wrote one hundred to two hundred different harmonies. For orchestration, he would pick parts from acts from Carl Maria von Weber and Wagner operas. I would use a piano vocal score and then orchestrate it and compare my orchestration to the original. Floridia would then criticize my score and show me my weak spots. He did not want me to imitate the original, but to use my own ideas. When my orchestration was good, he did not hesitate to say that it was nearly as good as the original.

Mr. Floridia told me about his experience. He claimed that he translated Wagner operas from German to Italian. He spoke of his first opera, *Pauletta*, that won a prize of $10,000. He was a very young man then, and he admitted that he became slightly inflated with his success. When Ricordi (the great publishing house of Italy) asked him to do another opera, he demanded an exorbitant price. They told him that they would give it to a new and talented composer if he refused their offer. He turned them down.

The newcomer was Giacomo Puccini, and the opera, *La Boheme*. I asked Floridia, are you a friend of Arturo Toscanini? "No," he said. "Of course, we know each other, but he will not speak to me, or even look at me. He claims that I have the 'evil eye'—an Italian superstition."

At one period in his last few years, I had Floridia stop working commercially and guaranteed him the money he needed, so that he could teach. We met once a week, despite my busy schedule, and we just discussed building a classic library for radio and recording of the masters like Bach, Chopin, Schumann and Debussy.

When he died, he left a letter for me to finish the last twenty minutes of his final opera. The text was in Italian.

ROGERS

One of the strangest requests was to score two short movie reels for a young man, Rogers, whose father was one of John Rockefeller's partners. He had engaged the famous Weber and Fields team to appear in his movies. Young Rogers and his wife had rented, in the middle of New York City, an apartment without furniture except for a few chairs and a small table. They had thirty dogs running around the rooms. He claimed that he and his wife loved dogs.

Well, we finally got down to business as he drank champagne continuously—bottle after bottle was emptied. The conversation went on for at least two hours, and finally Weber spoke up. "Look, we have been arguing about the difference of $25 for some time, and yet you have drunk over $200 worth of champagne. It makes no sense. Why, and what is your reason?"

Rogers replied, "Well, you see, when I asked my father to enter the movie field, he told me that he would let me have a certain amount and no more. However, he would not cut my allowance for my usual expenses. That is why I cannot run over the stipulated amount for my movie adventure." We finally made two pictures. The young fellow's mind ran in two categories: liquor and women. The pictures were never released.

SIR THOMAS LIPTON

Mr. Aylesworth asked me to do an audition for Sir Thomas Lipton.[7] He was a very distinguished looking man, and, when we finished, I was introduced to him. I asked him if he enjoyed our effort, and he replied, "Oh, yes it is a very fine day." I then asked him if he was pleased with the announcer, Mr. McNamee, and he said, "I will leave for England tomorrow." Of course, I realized that we had been playing for one hour and that he had not heard us, because he was practically deaf.

JAENECKE

One of the greatest horn players was Jaenecke. The horn is a difficult instrument, and the player must have fine nerve control. I used him often, and, from his quiet manner, no one would ever have thought of his ever getting nervous.

Arturo Toscanini had great respect for him and asked him to play Mozart's *Horn Concerto*. Jaenecke agreed, and then came the day of the concert. To Toscanini's surprise and dismay, Jaenecke became so nervous that he refused to get on the stage. It practically stopped his career. He never recovered.

FREDERICK FRADKIN

One of the finest violin soloists and concertmasters was Freddy Fradkin, and, despite his fine playing, he was a comic character. Rather, he liked to play jokes.

He had been concertmaster for the great Boston Symphony Orchestra for some time. One morning he was asked by one of the ladies' social clubs if he would give a short recital for the prominent ladies of Boston. He called his pianist and told him to be at the club for a short recital.

He selected Saint-Saëns' *Introduction* and *Rondo Capriccioso*, Opus 28, for his first number. He had played it dozens of times, and so they did not have to rehearse it. He finished the rather short introduction and then looked at the audience. There he saw the great French composer Saint-Saëns sitting in the first row. He started the *Rondo* part, and his mind went blank. He played the first phrase. When he repeated the phrase for the fourth time, the pianist thumped the next phrase, and then Fred's mind and memory recovered, and he finished the piece.

The ladies brought Saint-Saëns to Fred Fradkin, and they said to the great master, "Have you ever heard it played like that?"

Saint-Saëns, in the most polite and wonderful manner said, "No, I never heard it played like that before."

Poor Fred; this awful episode bothered him for years.

About six years later he was in France and took the trouble to find Saint-Saëns. He referred to what happened in Boston, but Saint-Saëns, as polite as ever, told him that he did not remember the episode.

Another story I heard about him was not so funny. After he left the Boston orchestra, he was engaged to play at movie houses when they were still using large orchestras. He received $500 extra whenever he played solos. There was an old violinist who idolized Fred. The old man, for some strange reason, had an expensive Stradivarius violin. The only one he allowed to play the violin was Fradkin when he played his solos.

He would keep the violin case near him, and it would be opened for Fred. One day Fred was to play his solo. The old man walked up to the stage and gave Fradkin the Stradivarius. Fred played his solo and then walked into the pit and handed the old man his instrument. As the old man was ready to take the instrument, Fred purposely dropped the violin real hard to the floor—the violin broke into pieces.

This had an unfortunate result on the old man, and he fainted. In fact he almost died. Of course, this was all Fred's idea of a joke. He had substituted the Stradivarius with a cheap violin.

Fradkin had earned lots of money with his brilliant mastery of playing, but he was a restless man. At one time he opened a restaurant that failed. He went back to music and played radio dates in the violin section. He never lost his sense of humor and his flair for playing jokes. Every conductor had great respect for his ability, despite the fact that he kept the violinists near him in stitches and often disturbed the behavior of the orchestra. I lost sight of him when I went to Hollywood.

TWO VIOLINISTS

While I was at rehearsal, a young man, about thirty years old, dressed in an old fur coat, asked me for a position. He claimed he was the greatest violinist in the world. I asked him to play for me, and he astonished me with his tremendous technique. What I did not like was his lack of control in tempo and style. However, I thought he should be given a chance, and I put him on the fourth stand of my first violin section. He was far from a disciplined orchestra man, and the man next to him complained that, in fast passages, he would show off and play faster than was proper. I knew that, and so I spoke to him.

He had another idiosyncrasy. When we would take a five-minute rest, he would walk over to the mike and play some of the most difficult violin passages, much to the annoyance of the other violinists.

One evening he came in dressed in evening clothes, plus a high hat. I asked him why the attire. He said, "I have been invited to give a recital by a very important music lover. It may be my chance to become a great soloist." The next day he bragged about the effect his virtuosity had made on his fashionable audience. One of the violinists overheard him, and told me that he was dreaming. He had seen him walking in the street one hour after the broadcast, with his fur coat, high hat and violin case.

I had to let him go. He was not manageable as an orchestra man, despite his phenomenal technique. I lost sight of him.

In contrast, I heard a player called "the Phantom Violinist." He was fortunate to have a brother and brother-in-law who were top leaders in radio, recording and theater.[8] He was a severe critic of other players, and that brought up the question, "had anyone ever heard him play alone?"

Generally, before a rehearsal or a concert, violinists walk around, getting their fingers in shape. The phantom violinist never practiced. His brother-in-law finally became annoyed by his continuous fault-finding of other violinists and decided to teach him a lesson.

He stopped the orchestra at a difficult passage for the violinists and said, "Gentlemen, I want each violinist to play this passage alone." He went from one player to another, asking them to perform the passage. When it came to his brother-in-law, there was a pause. The phantom violinist got up and walked out of the room.

The rumor went around that no one ever heard him play, and the man who sat next to him said, "Why, he never played so that I could hear him. He would go through the motions, but he never touched the strings to the bow." That, of course, was an exaggeration, but from then on he was called "the Phantom Violinist!"

ORCHESTRAL MEN'S ANTICS

I must tell you of some of the antics of various busy orchestras. Paul Whiteman's orchestra introduced the hot foot. This would sometimes infuriate Paul, but, as I said, it is hard to keep men from having their fun when they are terribly busy. My boys favored goosing.

One of the popular tricks that opera musicians will play on a newcomer to deflate his ego is this. A young and inexperienced violinist will join an orchestra of old-timers. Being a bit of a show-off, he will try to impress the established violinists what a great talent he is. His mannerisms annoy the players near him.

Then they get together and pick a spot in the opera where there is some difficulty for anyone who has not played the opera to be able to count the bars. During recitatives, the orchestra, to accentuate the dramatic music, will often have a very loud chord (secco). The violin players, knowing the music by heart, pick up their arms and then make a quick downward motion, as if they are to play a loud and vigorous chord. Instead they keep their bows an inch above the strings.

The young fellow watching them thinks that it is the time for the loud chord and plays the strong chord with gusto. You can imagine the result. The conductor, the audience and the artists hear a scratchy lone violin chord. The orchestra musicians break out in a roar of laughter, and the conductor glares at the poor fellow. He is really deflated.

One of the silly activities of the brass section was the spit ball. They were so clever at annoying men in front of them that it was difficult to catch them at it.

Another stupid trick on a violin player is to put a strong-smelling piece of cheese under his nose, at the end of the violin near his chinrest. Men are often no different than boys in their desire for fun.

QUIRKS AND TIDBITS

Fritz Kreisler: "I select #3 record as the master. I know it is not as flawless as #2, but the expression and phrasing is better."

Three angry people at a musical show—Drummer: "The conductor is glaring at me and wants more drum. The lady near me is complaining that I'm too loud. What the hell am I supposed to do?"

Bad conductor: "Please follow me!"
Concertmaster: "Get us mad enough and we will!"

To a prima donna: "Madame, you acted your role in the love duet with more expression and feeling than usual—any reason?"

"Sure. That stinking tenor is on a garlic diet, and I kept turning away from him. If he doesn't change his diet, I'll eat limburger cheese."

Disgruntled musician: "That b------ is a sadist and an egomaniac."
The conductor: "Why do my men torture me?"

Violinist: "I'll sit on any chair in the violin section, but only on the right. I won't turn pages." (The man on the left has to turn pages.)

TWO MORE VIOLINISTS

This reminds me of two violinists. They sat together on a stand. The man on the right was a little fellow with a quick temper, quick reflexes, and a good memory. The player on the left, who turned the pages, a little slow and very large.

As the music came near the end of the page, the little man on the right read the last line at a glance and wanted the big fellow to turn the page sooner. To make him hurry, he would often hit him with his bow. This went on for a long time, and the big fellow never complained. In fact, it became a routine. But one day the big fellow was in a bad mood, and when the little fellow hit him with the bow, the big boy hit him back. That surprised the little fellow, and he thought it was just an accident. Again he hit the big fellow, but much harder. Now he realized that the big fellow had deliberately hit him, because the page still was not turned. This started a fight, with both of them getting into a duel with bows. The conductor thought they had gone crazy. After the last number, the big fellow picked up the little fellow and shook him a bit. At the next performance they were separated.

JASCHA HEIFETZ

Every great violinist has been named as the artist who walked into the NBC elevator and been told he cannot ride in the elevator with a violin case. When he says he is Elman, or Heifetz or Menuhin, he is told, "I don't care if you're Dave Rubinoff, you must take the musician's elevator."

This reminds me of Jascha Heifetz. I engaged him for a solo on the Hall of Fame program [1934]. I suggested that he play the *Zigeunerweisen* (Gypsy Airs). He said, "That is too difficult to do with an orchestra. It takes too much rehearsal time."

I was so surprised that I said, "Are you kidding?"

Evidently, he resented my tone, and he said, "I'll do it, but remember what I told you."

At the rehearsal he played the piece and purposely exaggerated the Gypsy style of the melodies. I let him have his fun for about two minutes, and then I stopped the orchestra. I looked at him and said, "Mr. Heifetz, you can play it backwards and I'll follow you." He laughed, and then we started again and played it through without a stop.

A story often told—Heifetz to Dr. Einstein, when they were playing chamber music and the famous doctor lost his place: "Can't you count 1,2,3,4?"

GREGOR PIATIGORSKY

I heard an amusing story from one of my Russian copyists. It was about the great Russian cellist, Gregor Piatigorsky. In his early days, in order to get along, he played with Russian cafe orchestras (gypsy style) and was acquainted with their music. When he became a famous concert artist, he would often visit Russian restaurants and meet musicians he once knew.

He was in New York in the early 1930s and went to one of the Russian places. There was an orchestra playing, and, when they got through the number, the cellist left his seat. Piatigorsky walked over to the leader, an old acquaintance, and, as a lark, asked if he would mind if he took the missing cellist's place.

He sat down and played along with the orchestra. The cellist came along during the number and watched Piatigorsky play. He walked over to the great cellist and asked, "Have you just arrived in America? You are a very good player."

Piatigorsky said, "Yes, I'm new in this country."

The cellist then told him, "You'll never make a living playing cello in America—now all cellists are taking up the saxophone. Take my advice and become a saxophonist." When he was told that he had just advised the great cellist Piatigorsky to become a jazz saxophonist, well, he was terribly embarrassed. Of course, the great artist got a real kick out of the experience.

UNPERFORMED WORK

The only two composers that I paid even though I did not perform their works were Johnny Green and Joseph Schillinger. Johnny Green (about in his early twenties) wrote a rather nice suite for Paul Whiteman. I thought he would write a light semi-classic, or rather semi-popular, number for me. Instead, in his pretentious manner, he came up with a piano concerto. We rehearsed it twice, and after the second rehearsal he got up from the piano and said, "It's pretty bad." I agreed with him.

As for Joseph Schillinger, he was a composer, a lecturer, a teacher, and an outstanding mathematician. He attracted many students, and his system of musical composition became well known. He offered me a symphony—I believe it was called the *North Russian Symphony* [1930]. I rehearsed about one hour each time for weeks. It was ultra-modern, and, I thought, mechanical. It was taking too much of a chance to perform it over the air. His rehearsals cost me a good deal of money. He was paid his commission fee, but it was not performed.

NAHAN FRANKO

Nahan Franko was a character—a fine violinist and conductor with the profile and hair of Johann Strauss, Jr. In fact, he had portrayed Strauss in a movie. For years he played concertmaster at the Metropolitan Opera House, and he conducted the Sunday night concerts. He was in charge of the orchestra. At one point there was some discrepancy in handling the payroll, and he was asked to resign.

That was a blow to him, but he was not a man to give up easily. In fact, he became a society leader and also toured with his own orchestra. I played for him (on the piano) at the McAlpin Hotel at 34th Street and Broadway. He would hide behind the pillars and watch his men. If he thought they were careless in their performance, he would approach the orchestra platform and fire the culprits. He was strong, and, if he was given an argument, he would grab the musician by the back of the neck and throw him out.

At one affair in a palatial home on Park Avenue, he went to the kitchen and demanded a meal for his musicians. The chef threatened him with a large knife, but he did not scare Nahan Franko. Franko grabbed the chef's hand, and he gave in.

When Nahan Franko grew older and things changed, he would come to NBC and ask me to hire him. He was not in want, but he loved to be around music. I had no place for him, but I spoke to Cesare Sodero, the NBC operatic conductor. I asked Sodero to please have Franko play in his operatic series. Sodero said, "I wouldn't mind, but he is a troublemaker—I know him." Finally, I fixed it for Nahan, and he was put in the violin section.

A week later I met Sodero and asked him how Franko was behaving, and Sodero said, "Oh, I had to get rid of him. Do you know what he did in the first broadcast? He deliberately turned his chair around, so that his back faced me. During the performance he played the opera by memory and kept bowing to his friends in the audience. He was impossible."

When Franko died, his nephew Edwin Franko Goldman, whose character was just the opposite of his uncle, took care of his estate (as far as his library). I bought all his scores and classic orchestrations. I was practically offered many autographed letters, pictures, etc. of the greatest musicians of the last fifty years almost free. I am not a collector and turned the offer down. My son Arthur is an avid collector, almost down to match folders. We often speak of the rare collection, and I get a lecture from him.

IRA ARNSTEIN

There was a man named Arnstein. He was a Russian immigrant, and he paraded as a pupil of the great composer and pianist Anton Rubinstein. He tried to look and act like Rubinstein, with long hair, a high hat, and a fur coat. He called himself Professor Arnstein. At his first concert on the East Side of New York, he announced that he would introduce his new work, an oratorio. What he really played was a Rubinstein oratorio.

He finally got into another racket: suing other composers for plagiarizing his music. He had written one piano salon piece that sold fairly well. From then on, he sued almost every other composer who wrote a hit. He was an extrovert, and even when his lawyer represented him, he would hardly let the lawyer talk. Some publishers, rather than go to court, preferred to settle his nuisance case for $200 or $300. This encouraged Arnstein, and after a few years, he paraded up and down Fifth Avenue at Radio City with placards reading "unfair to genius."

Finally he sued ASCAP, BMI, NBC, CBS, Irving Berlin, Feist, Shilkret, Kern and a host of other well-known composers and firms. This happened at the time ASCAP was having trouble with the radio networks.[9] There were at least sixty people in the court room, and Arnstein was in his glory.

After four days at court, Judge Hand asked Arnstein, "Do you really think that all people steal your ideas and are against you?"

"Yes," said Arnstein.

The judge then asked, "Am I against you?"

Arnold replied, "Yes, you're are against me, and you have been bribed by all these people."

That was the end of the trial. From then on, the court, after many years of experience with him, forbade him to sue unless he would pay the court cost. Of course, he was not able to accomplish that. Despite his many years of suing, he was really poor.

JAMES FITZPATRICK

I scored many travelogs for James Fitzpatrick. He was financed at the start by a man named Bristol. Then he sold stock to Hugo Riesenfeld, and then to Nat Finston, my brother-in-law, and finally I bought into his company. Bristol received nothing when the pictures seemed not to catch on. Riesenfeld received no money, just some films. Finston received half of his investment, while I settled for the amount of my investment.

By this time Fitzpatrick connected with MGM Studio and was helped enough to go into color pictures. They were successful, and James owned his company completely. He married a wealthy widow, his first attempt as a husband, and things went on smoothly except that his wife insisted upon accompanying him on his trips. That annoyed him, and she criticized his pictures, which wounded his ego.

This wound up with Fitzpatrick allowing her to pick a cameraman and letting her make some films. A quarrel started when James' wife claimed that the reason for his ordinary results was his penny pinching. He claimed that was the reason for his success. She countered by claiming that if he spent more money, his pictures would have more value and make more money. His wife produced some travelogs, and they were very good.

Fitzpatrick became jealous of his wife's connections with the cameraman. It resulted in a divorce. When I was talking to James about marriage and its heartaches, he remarked, "If I ever married again, I would insist upon my wife's staying home and having at least six children," and that happened in his second marriage to a very sweet girl.

ALFRED LANDON

I received my honorary doctor's degree of music at the Bethany College, Kansas [1934]. They had rehearsed their orchestra so that I could conduct it the night before the degree ceremony. I wired that I would not be able to come for the orchestra concert, and so they postponed it to the day of the degree ceremony. With me for a degree was Alfred Landon, two-term governor of Kansas and later the Republican nominee for president, running against the Democratic candidate F. D. Roosevelt.

It was a very hot day—107 degrees in the shade—and, as we were getting ready for our speeches, the governor, as nervous as I, said, "I really don't know what to say. They want me to talk about Indians."

I said, "I am lucky. If I run out of talk, I can introduce my first conducting number."

ALFRED WALLENSTEIN

Alfred Wallenstein, a cellist with the New York Philharmonic, came to me and told me that Toscanini liked my conducting of broadcasts. I did not believe him, but, after all, it might be true. He then asked if I could help him earn some money.

I told him that I could not offer him a playing job, since he had one with the best symphony. I suggested a novel combination of four cellos, some strings, woodwind, harpsichord, celesta and a percussion man. Mr. Floridia and I would write some novel arrangements for the combination, and it would be different than other set orchestras. Wallenstein would be the first cellist, and it would be known as the Wallenstein Ensemble.

A few days later he came in to me and told me that he was acquainted with an old lady, the wife of a dairy company president. She wanted her husband to sponsor a broadcast series. Wallenstein had mentioned me as conductor. The dairy company bought one radio hour at NBC, and the first broadcast was two weeks away. He asked my price, and I said $1000 per broadcast. They would pay for the orchestra, arrangements and copyists, and Wallenstein would receive 10 percent of my fee; he agreed.

The next day I received a call from Douglas Coulter of the N. W. Ayer and Son advertising agency. He was an old friend of mine. He said, "Nat, I never thought you would ever do anything like this."

I asked, "What are you talking about?"

He said, "Well, Nat, I really didn't believe it. Do you know Wallenstein?"

I answered, "Yes."

He said, "Well, we have a dairy account. They are a big account, and we booked them for an hour show with Charlie Previn as conductor.

"A Mrs. Sponsor told us that Previn would not do. She heard from Wallenstein that Previn was a fake and a clown, and so she wants Shilkret to be engaged as the leader of her husband's broadcast."

Naturally, I explained that I had nothing to do about that, and, under the circumstances, I would not consider accepting the hour.

Doug said, "Don't do that; we may lose the account. You accept the show and go through with the broadcast as if I never spoke to you. I'll see that Previn understands the mix up."

I conducted the broadcast, with Richard Crooks as soloist. After the concert, Mr. and Mrs. Sponsor, Wallenstein, Crooks and I went across 55th Street and Fifth Avenue and had some coffee at Childs restaurant. During our coffee, Mrs. Sponsor (a gabby old woman) spoke about her husband's greatness, and claimed that, because of his shrewdness during the 1929 stock crash, he kept $23 million of assets intact and saved his company. For his brilliance, she said, he should be nominated for the highest office of the United States—the presidency! We listened to this drivel, while the husband said nothing—probably embarrassed by her.

Then she questioned Wallenstein (who sat next to her) about artists, conductors, etc. Wallenstein berated every conductor mentioned, while I interjected praises for their merits, until I got on Wallenstein's nerves. He whispered, "What are you trying to do, have me lose the account?"

The next day Wallenstein came into my office and said, "Nat, there is lots of opposition to me at N. W. Ayer's. They said that they can engage you without interference."

I said, "Wally, I won't accept the broadcast without you, since it was you who came to me first. Therefore, why not agree and promise that both of us will not accept the broadcast without the other?" Both of us agreed.

About two weeks later Wallenstein came and said, "Nat, the dairy show is starting a thirteen-week series very soon"—and then he hesitated. He finally said, "Well, I hope you don't become angry with me."

I asked, "Why?"

"Well, I have charge of the hour, but I have engaged another conductor, Barzin (an excellent musician)." Actually, it was not Barzin, but Wallenstein, who became the conductor.

I said, "On account of my promise to you, I told the Ayer agency that I would not accept the broadcast without you. But why did you break your promise?"

He looked down and said, "Money. I will earn much more money by engaging Barzin."

I sat looking at him for some time and then quietly told him, "Wally, I don't know what your dealings have been in the past, but as far as I am concerned, get out of my office and don't come around again."

A couple of years passed, and Wallenstein became musical director of WOR. Being a good musician and a talented artist, he did well at WOR. As a conductor, he adopted the stern method of his idol, Toscanini, and made life miserable for his orchestra men.

Some of my men played for him, and they finally came to me with complaints. Wally had announced that anyone working for me would be fired. They asked me what to do. I promised to handle the situation. I called Wally at WOR and said, "Wally, this is Nat Shilkret. I hear that you object to any of your men working for me. Is that correct?"

He said, "Yes," and then I told him, "Wally, after I get through talking to you, I am calling up the musicians' union headquarters and putting in a complaint that you are preventing musicians from earning money. You realize that you will receive a heavy fine and, perhaps, be thrown out or suspended?"

Wally hesitated for a while; then he said, "Nat, this is all foolish. Let us forget the past and become friends again. I'll rescind the order to my musicians." We had lunch, conversed a while, and then he requested that I come to WOR and do a concert of my compositions. I accepted.

The next time we met, he was conductor of the Los Angeles Symphony. I enjoyed the concert and thought that he did a good job. I went backstage to congratulate him. By this time he acted like a great maestro. With many people in the room, he shook my hand and looked the other way. This was the first and last time I ever went backstage to offer my good wishes. The business of going to an artist after a concert to say the same cliché, "how marvelous you are," is like the requests of autograph hounds.

What can you say to an artist who just got through a grueling concert but "you're wonderful," etc. The artist probably dislikes the whole act, but, as is often said, "If people and autograph seekers stop coming, then you are really losing your popularity." Whether they like it or not, they are stuck with it.

NOTES

1. The situation was no brighter for the music business than for the musicians. Sudhalter [1999], on p. 666, says, "This was the Depression, after all, and recording had been among the hardest-hit of all businesses. There was little enough money around, [and] Americans by the millions seemed to be saying: why spend it for records when you could stay home and hear all the music you wanted on the radio, and at no cost?" Malone [1968] (see also Gelatt [1955]) quantifies this: "In the year 1932 only six million records were sold, a striking contrast to the 104 million records that had been sold in 1927."

2. The September 1931 issue of the *Phonograph Monthly Review* describes some of these recordings: " ... special releases include ... a set of eight ten-inch discs by the Victor Salon Orchestra under Shilkret. ... Shilkret and the Victor Salon Orchestra devote themselves to the compositions of William F. [sic] Woodin, who has displaced Ambassador Dawes as the premier American businessman-composer. The pieces run in typical salon channels: Gypsy Love Song, Pensee Sentimentale, Temple Dance, Cradle Song, Souvenir de Montmarte [sic], etc., etc., facile enough but of scant originality or distinction. Shilkret, as usual, makes the most of the music."

3. The MacDowell Colony was established at about the time of Edward MacDowell's death in 1908.

4. SESAC originally stood for the Society of European Stage Authors and Composers, but was changed, so as to retain the initials, to Selected Editions of Standard American Catalogues when Hitler's influence made normal business relations with Europe impossible; currently the organization says SESAC is the entire name of the organization; see Meyer [1958] for further information.

5. Giulio Gatti-Casazza was general director of the Metropolitan Opera Association from 1908 to 1933. The Metropolitan Opera Association is the most important U.S. opera company.

6. Biographical sketches of Gibbons in DeLong [1996] and Dunning [1998] show the newscaster to be even wilder than the Manville show described here.

7. Sir Thomas Lipton (1850–1931) built the Lipton Tea Company.

8. A guess, based on our knowledge of the family, is that the Phantom Violinist was Arthur Finston, and his well-known brother and brother-in-law were Nat Finston and Nat Shilkret, respectively.

9. Correspondence and legal papers in the Nathaniel Shilkret Archives indicate that Arnstein initiated at least three lengthy legal battles against Nat, waged between 1929 and 1939. In one of these Nat had to pay personally the legal bills, which totalled over $2500 (equivalent to approximately $30,000 corrected for inflation to the year 2000).

CHAPTER 6

MOTION PICTURES

While an employee of Victor in New York, Nathaniel Shilkret conducted or wrote music for more than thirty motion pictures. He worked on both feature films and one- and two-reelers for studios that included First National, MGM, Columbia, Universal and United Artists. On November 18, 1935, he commenced duties in Hollywood as head of the music department and musical director for RKO.

The year 1935 found me a bit tired of radio and the new status of RCA as owner of the Victor Company. Within a year after RCA had acquired the Victor, they completely disrupted the record business. We were introduced to quite a few newly appointed Victor presidents. They were given testimonial dinners in their honor, and we knew that they would be dismissed almost immediately.

Besides, I had really no vacation [prior to the trip described below] for over twenty years, except for two weeks in Havana [ca. 1923] to study their dance rhythms. I had done over six thousand sponsored programs and thirty-six thousand records, besides movies and concerts, all of which resulted in a working schedule of nearly twenty-one hours a day and, consequently, very little sleep.

[In 1933] I left four sponsored shows on radio and was allowed a sabbatical leave from the Victor. My European trip was to be two months vacation, but it lasted three months. With me were Mrs. Shilkret, my son Arthur, and Sydney Finston, who was my wife's younger brother and

Arthur's friend. It was mostly a guided tour. I enjoyed it, but I felt that, if I ever got to Europe again, I would stay in various places for a long time, in order to acquaint myself with the natives.

Seeing a lot of buildings, museums and churches grows tiresome when spending little time in various cities. It seemed that between Mrs. Shilkret's acquisitions and my son's stamp collections, we were on a buying spree.

When we got back to New York, I finished my Victor contract, and then Mrs. Shilkret and I decided to go to Hollywood, where our family lived, and then we decided to go to Hawaii, Lake Banff in Canada and, finally, back to New York.

When Mrs. Shilkret and I were ready to leave for Hawaii, I was asked to say a few words on radio. While riding to the radio station, I got an idea of writing a song, rather than making a speech. I wrote a song called *Farewell Malihini*. It did not become a hit, but it sold well enough to pay for my trip and more.

The last president of RCA Victor became the head of the RKO Hollywood studio and asked me to join him as musical director of the studio. I went along with him. With that position, I was also to record for the Hollywood Hotel radio show, with Bill Bacher, and the Camel Cigarette Hour.

I was warned by my friends in New York that I would not like Hollywood. However, my mind was made up for a change, and so I arrived in Hollywood about September 1935.

The first thing I noticed was that Hollywood musically was still a small city compared to the active New York. Of course, they had their symphony orchestra, concerts, etc., but the music they were interested in was moving picture music. Each movie score was criticized, and competition was keen. The idea at that period was not to write music of artistic value, but compose effective music scores, that is, effective commercially. Some directors or producers were more musically critical than others and spent time talking with the composer; others considered music a necessary nuisance, and an expensive one at that.

As for musicians, they were mostly a jealous, competitive crowd. In large studios, composers used every trick to get assignments for the "A" pictures and grumbled when they were assigned to "B" pictures. The "A" pictures had the big name stars, a larger budget and often better stories than the "B" pictures, which were considered "fill-in's." When, on a rare occasion, a "B" movie became successful, it was called a "sleeper."

When I arrived at the RKO studio, I found that the other composers and conductors acted according to their nature. Coming from New York, where I had my own orchestra, my own radio hours and almost complete control of recording artists, I found it strange to cater to the whims of my associates, directors, producers and others.

MAX STEINER

One man, Max Steiner,[1] had been a successful scorer at the studio, and he resented my being head man. I tried hard to please him, and I raised his salary, but his pride was hurt, and he continually talked about the injustice of studio heads.

We became friends a few years after he left the studio, and he apologized for his petty attitude and lack of consideration for my feelings when we first met. Knowing him as I did from experience, I laughed the whole thing off. I knew that if a similar situation came up any time, he would act the same.

I would not say that all composers are that envious in Hollywood, but at least 75 percent are exactly so. Some are not open about it, but the knife is always there. The Los Angeles union officials objected to my coming to Hollywood and being head of a studio and having two broadcasts and a recording contract. This attitude of the union was based on complaints from their members who were scared by the great influx of newcomers, especially from New York.

And so I could not start my Hollywood Hotel radio program. As for the Camel broadcast, they let me keep that, but one hour before our concert, they told me that eleven of the thirty-three musicians could not play. I asked them why, and they answered, "These eleven men, although members of the Los Angeles union, originally came from New York." That was the limit, and I wanted to walk out of the studio.

I was threatened that, unless I used the men they picked to replace the New York men, they would cancel my visiting or transfer privileges, and I would not be able to stay at the RKO studio.

Here I was, up against a situation I had never thought possible. I was forced to go along with their order. The Camel program consisted of my orchestra, guest stars and the Benny Goodman trio.

One of our artists was the famous prima donna, Galli-Curci. I knew her from my Victor recording days. She was probably the greatest coloratura singer of all times. In her last Victor broadcasting, she was ill with a goiter growth. As she sang, she crossed herself a few times, seemingly suffering, and then she retired.

Her visit to my Camel show was her try for a comeback. She sang fairly well, but her high notes were gone. She knew that she was not the great artist of bygone days. I conducted and heard her in both of her performances after retirement.

Max Steiner told me some experiences. One was about a picture called *Symphony*. The young producer asked him who was the greatest symphonic composer. Steiner said Beethoven. The producer told Steiner to engage him to write the music for the film.

Steiner told about a time when an official of RKO asked him if he would score an important picture in three or four days. Max told him, "I just scored and conducted a picture. I am tired and need some rest." He was told that it was imperative for this picture to be shown within a few days, because the Wall Street tycoons were coming to finance the next year's budget, and a good deal would depend upon their viewing this picture.

Max refused for some time, but finally the idea that he would be the savior of the studio flattered his ego. Max then asked how he could finish the picture in time if he had to go home for food and sleep. The executive said, "Max, we'll have a bed put next to your office, a maid to clean up, a cook and service. You do not have to leave the studio," and so Max worked Thursday night, all day Friday, Saturday and Sunday. He had arrangers and copyists working with him.

By Monday morning, he left his office and walked outside. The sun was shining brightly. His eyes were glassy, and he walked in a daze. Besides, he had very poor eyes. As he slowly walked for about a block, he met the executive.

The executive greeted him with, "For heaven sakes, Max, you look terrible."

Max couldn't believe his ears. He sputtered, "But, but, but you implored me to finish the picture. I scored it with about five hours sleep since Thursday."

The executive said, "Oh, Max, I'm sorry. I forgot to tell you that we decided not to show the picture."

Max claimed that he was so tired and angry that he fainted and fell down.

SAM BRISKIN

Back to the RKO studio. For four months things went along nicely. Then a new president (or manager) came to the studio—Mr. Sam Briskin. He had been brought in from Columbia studio and was known as a strict budget expert, a man who could cut financial corners. He had very little recognition as a producer from an artistic viewpoint.

The second day after he took over, he asked me to see him. Without even a friendly start, or even an introduction, he said, "Nat, you know that I am head of the studio."

I said, "I know."

He continued, "Whenever I sign your weekly check, I see red!"

I answered, "Why? Do you want to pay me more?"

He said, "You know what I mean."

As a matter of fact, I did know, because I knew Lou Silvers, his Columbia musical director, and he told me Briskin's salary (probably the lowest ever paid by any studio). Lou had worked many years for him and made good.

I then said, "What do you consider a fair salary for a musical director?"

Briskin answered, "$250 per week."

I asked, "What would you pay a top director?"

He said, "$300 per week."

"What would you pay Toscanini?"

He said, "$350 per week."

"Well," I said, "now would you like to hear what I would pay you?"

"No," said Briskin, "I am not paid by you."

"Well," I said, "I am not paid by you. We are both hired by the same studio, and whether or not you want to hear it, I'll tell you my opinion of your salary.

"In New York you received $35 per week as an accountant. You were working for my accountant, and he said you were not even a certified public accountant. That is what I would pay you—$35 per week. Since you put me in the same salary class as Toscanini, I would receive ten times more than you."

He looked at me for a while, and then said, "Well, Nat, no use to our getting off to a bad start, so let's forget the whole conversation."

I said, "Okay with me, but remember, I also have the privilege to do two radio broadcasts a week and some Victor recordings."

He asked, "Will it interfere with your studio work?"

I said, "No, I'll arrange rehearsals and recording around my studio schedule," and we left it at that.

The first thing Briskin did was to fire Max Steiner,[2] cut out my arrangers and the steady studio orchestra. I was left with one scorer, Mr. Roy Webb.[3]

After my discussion with Briskin, he called me up, and, in a very sweet voice, asked me if I could see him. I was in his room, and he said, "I just received a telephone call from Roach's studio, and he asked if he could use your services to put a few finishing touches to Laurel and Hardy's *Bohemian Girl* picture. You did score the film in New York; isn't that so?"

"Well, I really did not score the film." I was asked to record (on film) most of the arias from Balfe's opera, the *Bohemian Girl*, and I engaged Lawrence Tibbett and a chorus and recorded about twenty numbers plus some original comic bits. Mr. Roach would put the pieces together in Los Angeles (really Culver City).

Briskin asked, "What did he pay you?" I received $5000 for my services for three sessions. That was the last I heard from Roach. Briskin then said, "Well, that is what I'll charge him for your services."

I walked to the door and said, "Mrs. Shilkret can buy a fur coat for $2500. The studio can keep the other $2500."

Briskin brought his closed fist down on the table and said, "Your contract with us gives us the right to hire you without giving you anything but your salary." I said I was overworked in the studio, and I deserved some consideration if I was to work all day at RKO and then spend nights at Roach's. Briskin said, "Read your contract." I then asked if I could read my contract. He said alright, but when he called the legal office on the lot, he was told that it was in Los Angeles, fourteen miles away.

I sat down and said, "I'll wait"—and much to his annoyance, I sat in his room listening to his blustering voice, his dates and his placing bets. He asked me if I had anything else to do, and I answered, "I'll wait."

Finally, the contract arrived. He handed me the contract and said, "Read it."

Instead of reading the contract I walked to Briskin's desk and said, "Send the contract to Mr. Roach. I have to sleep at night," and I walked out.

I called Roach and told him about my talk with Briskin. Evidently he didn't like Briskin, and he called him some four-letter names. I then told Roach that I would help him without any pay, but I told him that Briskin's price was too high, and, besides, I would not have my studio receive all the money as long as I am completing my work for them. Roach called Briskin and told him to forget the whole thing. Luckily for me, although Briskin was head of the RKO studio, he had no jurisdiction over Pandro Berman's[4] production on the "A" pictures. So for about a year, I had very little connection with him. What Briskin did accomplish was to leave me with only one assistant, Mr. Webb. Whenever we needed an orchestra or arranger, I had to hire the best men available.

RKO PICTURES

My first picture was with John Ford on a film called *Mary of Scotland*. Katharine Hepburn was Mary, and she was a wonderful actress. Working with John Ford was a pleasurable experience. During his directing, he would chew at a handkerchief continuously—just a habit, I guess. He was in full command, always kind and considerate with all his actors and crew.

My next film was *Winterset*. Burgess Meredith and Margo had the leading roles. My score received special mention, although *Anthony Adverse*, scored by Korngold, received the Oscar trophy. After all, the latter was an expensive picture with a great story and a tremendous cast.

There were other films, and they came in fast and furious. Between Webb and myself, we probably did fifty pictures a year. I recall the Fred Astaire and Ginger Rogers musical; Lily Pons; Martini; and *The Toast of New York*, with Edward Arnold, Cary Grant and Frances Farmer.

During Nino Martini's debut at RKO [*Music for Madame*, 1937], he complained about his leading lady, Joan Fontaine. She was on her first picture, and she was very young, very slim, beautiful and full of spirit. Martini said, "How can I show my ability as a screen lover with such a child?"

I said, "Nino, you were not picked for your acting; you were picked for your fine voice."

The producer of two of Lily Pons' films was Jesse Lasky. With Lily Pons there were four actors—I should say three comedians and one actor—Oakie, Auer, Jenks and Gene Raymond. The movie *That Girl from Paris* has a simple story. Lily Pons, an operatic singer, is in love with the leader, Gene Raymond, of a four-piece dance band. The jazz band is having trouble getting along, and while they are traveling in a ship, with just enough money to pay for their trip, they discover Lily Pons as a stowaway. They have to hide her.

To find a place for her, Oakie decided to give this great opera star a haze. They worked her over, and Lily thought that this was a necessary rehearsal, done to help the comedy scene. As I watched the four handling Miss Pons very roughly, I grew concerned for her health (she was to sing the next day). I called Mr. Lasky and asked him to stop the exaggerated hazing. By the time the quartet got through with their so-called fun, Miss Pons could hardly stand or sit down. Anyway, their rehearsal was stopped.

With Miss Pons was André Kostelanetz. They were not married yet. Kostelanetz came to the studio weekly. He flew to New York for his broadcasts. Lily was a person dominated by habit. When she came to our recording room, she had to have the same engineer, the same booth, the same chair, etc., that she had used in a picture studio a year ago.

Evidently, Kostelanetz had become a habit. He made all her decisions and controlled her movements completely. At one operatic recording, he picked on her incessantly, and she burst into tears and cried, "Who do you think you are, Toscanini?" I was astonished at that time, because Lily Pons had attained the height of an international star and celebrity, while André was just coming up as a radio conductor. I had known Kostelanetz as a mild man, but now he was throwing his weight around.

In the film, the story comes to a point where the four jazz musicians get an engagement at a nightclub with a German proprietor. He wants to change his place into a hot spot. Lily, trying to stay near her lover, Raymond, asks for a job as entertainer. The proprietor insists that she must sing jazz, although she is in character as an opera singer.

The actual band that played was Jimmy Dorsey's orchestra. Gene Raymond was fingering the saxophone (the playing was done by Jimmy Dorsey), and Gene was so meticulous that he practiced the sax for many hours each day, so that he could match Jimmy's fingers.

Now we had to find a number that would sound jazzy and still be suitable for Miss Pons. Kostelanetz insisted upon okaying our choice. Fud Livingston, the arranger, and I picked a few numbers. After three arrangements, André, coming weekends, would look at the results and find some fault with the number or the arrangement.

As Kosty and Fud were at the piano going over one arrangement, Kosty pointed to one spot and said, "Change this phrase."

By this time Fud had enough and said, "If you know so much, you fix it."

Kosty got up and, in a very haughty spirit, grabbed Miss Pons and walked out of the room.

The next day Kosty was back in New York. I got a new idea: Why not have the proprietor ask Lily if she can sing the blues?—and Lily would respond, "Yes, I can sing the *Blues Danube*." She was engaged to sing in the nightclub with the jazz band. Before Kosty came back we recorded an arrangement of the *Blue Danube*, with Lily singing an almost straight rendition, with some florid trimmings and the band jazzing it up. It turned out splendidly, and without Kosty's opinion. It became the feature of the picture.

For the operatic arias, Kostelanetz really put on a show. He did a very unorthodox thing. Maybe his contract for his services was paid by the time taken for his conducting. I remember one of his aria recordings, *Une Voce Poca Fa* (I Hear a Little Voice), from the *Barber of Seville*.

He ordered an orchestral rehearsal for a full day (an unheard of procedure). Then Miss Pons came in the next day and recorded at least twelve takes of the same aria. It should have taken one or two hours to get a satisfactory recording. It took them over thirty-six hours. And that went on for every operatic recording.

Now came the time for picking the best rendition, with Miss Pons, Kostelanetz, her singing coach, and myself. We started listening. This took days because Kosty would pick one phrase of one take, a note from this phrase, and, after about forty changes, the film was pasted together. Well, we finally finished that picture and another one.

The RKO studio had started the team of Fred Astaire and Ginger Rogers. They were a smash hit. In Irving Berlin's picture, *Top Hat*, he received $200,000 in cash, plus a percentage of the picture's gross earnings.

I did not conduct this film because it was done before I joined the studio.

The next Astaire-Rogers musical was written by Jerome Kern; it was *Swing Time*. He received $75,000 in cash. Berman was the producer; Mark Sandrich, the director; and Hermes Pan, the choreographer. Kern was greatly respected, and no wonder. He had written many of the greatest songs for America and the world.

He had an idea for his play. He wanted to start the picture with a vaudeville act, and with their high opinion of him, they let him use the studio for one week, and then he left. His one week was never used in the final finished version. I believe the vaudeville sketch cost the studio about $100,000. He wrote a fine score with the following hits: *The Way You Look Tonight, Bojangles of Harlem, Waltz in Swingtime, A Fine Romance,* and *Pick Yourself Up.*

After the Kern musical, George Gershwin was assigned to write the next Fred Astaire and Ginger Rogers picture. For some unknown reason, there was a lack of confidence in George's ability to write a popular song. The opera *Porgy and Bess* had taken a good deal to compose, and George had not written any Broadway musicals for a period. They thought that he had gone high-brow. He received $50,000 for his services.

There was no title, and only a bare idea for Fred Astaire to be a classic Russian ballet dancer and Ginger Rogers to be a well-known American popular dancer. They meet—they quarrel—they separate—and, finally, they get together.

In back of the minds responsible, it would all evolve around a ballet, something like Gershwin's *American in Paris.* George arrived and played the ballet he had written. We listened—then silence. Either it sounded different from what they expected, or they could not connect the music with their flimsy idea of a story. My thought was that it sounded a bit like Cuban or Mexican music.

George also had a few songs that would be introduced in the picture. Pandro Berman, the producer, seemed pleased with them, and so was I. I do not remember Astaire's or Sandrich's opinions. Anyway, there was not great enthusiasm expressed, that is, as far as I can remember.

They started the shooting without, as I said, much of a story. The script was worked on daily, somehow working in the boy meets girl, a spot for a romantic love song, a few spots for dance songs, the ballet in the third part, and the gadget to get them together.

By the time we got to the ballet, some of the numbers were changed. I remember that, after filming and recording the first part of the ballet, Mr. Berman, the producer, came back from a vacation. When he heard the ballet he said, "I don't hear the main hit song. That must be in the ballet." Since we had filmed the first part to George's rather lively 3/8 tempo, I had to record the hit song, which was in rather slow fox-trot tempo, to fit the lively steps of the ballet. Somehow, I did it so it looked okay.

There was another song used in the ballet, and Fred Astaire, Mark Sandrich and I had an informal meeting with Gershwin. We were seated on the floor of the studio. Astaire started and said, "George, I do not like the song you wrote for the last part of the ballet. In fact, it stinks." (I do not remember the exact word, but it was an emphatic expression.) Sandrich, the director, backed him up.

I was hoping that George would take offense, but, instead, he quietly said, "I like the song, but you don't have to accept it. I can find use for it in my next Goldwyn picture. Do you have an idea of what you want?"

Fred said, "Yes. Call it 'Shall We Dance.'"

George asked, "Is it a question?"

"No. It is the title of the picture."

George said, "Nat, come to my home at twelve midnight. My brother Ira and I will write it tonight."

I received the song, and we recorded it to Astaire's steps. We had a preview, and then there was one more change. The middle part of the ballet—remember the ballet was the solution of the whole story. We decided to do the middle part music over.

George by this time was working at the Goldwyn studio, and I was busy doing a ballet on my picture *The Toast of New York*, using my hit song *The First Time I Saw You* for the producer, Mr. Ed Small. Fred was anxious to finish the picture *Shall We Dance*, and so he decided to write the song himself. He had Miss Rogers, Sandrich and himself at a meeting, and gave the arranger, Fud Livingston, a theme and rhyme, and had him arrange it. Unfortunately, Fud Livingston, although a wonderful arranger, was not a composer. Besides, he was a heavy drinker, and I guess, in his difficulty to make anything out of Astaire's sketch, began drinking.

The next morning I started to conduct Fud's arrangement. I was pretty sore that Fred had gone ahead without George Gershwin and me giving the approval of music in a score of Gershwin. As I tried the music, I found it impossible to make any sense of it. I tried it in every way—with our symphonic orchestra and Jimmy Dorsey's band (hired to put rhythm to the music), then with Dorsey's band alone—but to no avail. Fred insisted that we try again and again, because he was anxious to take a trip to England to visit with his sister. By noon, I stopped the session for lunch.

We were back at 1 p.m. for another try. I tried my best, but the music was, in my opinion, not good enough for a Gershwin score. I finally called the date off. There was lots of commotion over my refusal to go ahead. It gave Sam Briskin the chance to complain that seventy-five men had been called without results. It cost $10 an hour for six hours, which amounts to $4500, plus studio time. I was sore at Fred Astaire's taking it on himself to compose for Gershwin, angry at Berman's changing the first part of the ballet, sore at their attitude toward Gershwin—in fact, just plain disgusted with all of them.

We had a meeting at which I expressed my opinion, and then I said, "Let me have George, Russell Bennett and myself meet tonight. We'll have the music right by tomorrow morning," and that is what we did.

Briskin tried to make a big deal out of it, and I told him if we had not fired the arrangers under contract, this would not have happened. He threatened not to sign my option. I told him the studio would get rid of him before my contract was through. He said, "I've got a long contract."

I told him, "I know your contract. Your option comes one week before mine, and, besides, you are not getting the salary you claim, by 50 percent."

And that is what happened. He did not sign my option, but he was through one week before I left. I had the pleasure of telling him so before he was released.

I was asked to do the next Fred Astaire picture. I told Briskin that I would see my agent. My agent asked me how many pictures I was scoring. I said four or five. He said, according to your contract, they can only have you do as many as will not interfere with your health or sleep. You are working too hard.

When I told Briskin my agent's instruction, he almost had a fit. My agent handled Briskin after that, despite Briskin's threats to cancel my contract or not sign my option. By this time I would not work under him at double my salary.

Briskin had a henchman, Rogell, who had the reputation of being tricky and tough—especially on money matters. Rogell asked me if I wanted to keep Roy Webb, my only scorer, on the lot. I said, "by all means."

Rogell said, "You know his salary is $250 a week and his option calls for a $50 raise. Do you approve?"

I said, "Yes. He deserves the raise."

For about a week Webb avoided me, and I wondered why. He was such a quiet and mild-mannered man. I thought, why the change? I spoke to him and asked, "Webb, why are you avoiding me?"

He replied, "You know very well."

I answered, "But I don't know."

"Well," he said, "Rogell told me that you wanted to get rid of me and that you were jealous of me, and that you asked him to fire me."

I said, "And you believe that?"

"I did."

I asked what happened.

"Well, Mr. Rogell said that, despite you, he would engage me if I allowed him to cut $50 out of my present salary and accept $200 per week." Webb agreed, and so he signed for less salary than he was receiving.

I spoke to Rogell, and his typical remark for his kind was, "What are you complaining about? You wanted him, and you've got him; and the studio is saving $100 a week." What a slimy bunch!

The Informer [1935] was a low-budget film that made good. With John Ford as its gifted director and with Victor McLaglen and the Irish Abbey Theater actors, it was quite successful. Max Steiner's score was effective. [McLaglen, in fact, won an Academy Award for the role.]

Before Sam Briskin came to the RKO studio, Ford had been asked to direct another Irish picture, *The Plough and the Stars* [1936], which used many of the same actors as *The Informer*.

When John Ford finished *The Plough and the Stars*, he took a vacation on his boat. At this time Briskin came into the studio as head. I was in the screen room when Briskin reviewed the picture.

He listened and watched the film and made notes. By the time he was through, he had cut and changed so many parts that the picture became a mess, story-wise. He claimed that he could not understand the Irish actors, and he cut out most of the important dialogue.

Since Briskin was mostly a businessman and not an artistic person, he was hardly the man to review a picture. Since he had respect for John Ford's great ability, he wanted some reply concerning his changes, and so he sent Ford a terribly long telegram, about forty pages, telling him, in detail, all of his changes. The telegram was, I believe, very expensive. It took time to find John Ford on his boat. Finally, he was located, and here was his reply to Sam Briskin's almost book-size telegram: "Tut, tut–J.F."

As for Fred Astaire, he is a great performer, as a dancer, singer and actor. As far as his dances, he is easy to work with and follow. He knows what he wants, and, in a few words and a few steps, gives you a perfect description. But he is a moaner, never satisfied with his work. He rehearses endlessly, and poor Ginger Rogers was worn to a frazzle. Her mother, a very smart lady, told me that she would not allow Ginger to dance in another picture with Fred. Ginger was quite thin at the time; she had lost fourteen pounds in her last picture.

And no wonder—I recall a difficult dance of over five minutes. Fred had her do forty-nine takes of it, and then, in his persuasive way, asked her to do a fiftieth take. That meant perhaps three days of continuous dancing.

Let me explain how a dance is done. It all looks so easy watching the screen, but it is an endless amount of work. First, the choreography is worked out with the music, scenery and steps. A musical number is selected. The dancers have a rehearsal pianist. As the ideas evolve, the pianist plays rhythms or tunes to follow the choreography. The arranger sets it together, often rewriting the music to fit the choreography. That done, the musical conductor rehearses it with the dancer or dancers.[5]

For Fred Astaire, he would give the tempo. Generally he asked for what he thought would be the proper tempo, and then record again, a little faster because he thought (correctly), after watching the dance on the screen, that it looked slow. As I said before, Fred was so sure of his dancing that we would get results quickly.

Now comes the photography of the dance without sound. The record selected is played over a loud speaker and is repeated as many times as needed. The producer, the director and the artists dancing will repeat the dance until they are satisfied. Now we have the music and the choreography. Next comes the sound of the feet, which is dubbed.

Ginger Rogers' feet sounds were done by Hermes Pan, the Greek choreographer—probably as good a dancer as Fred. It was a thrill to watch Fred and Pan go through dance after dance and never miss a tap or foot sound, no matter how intricate it was. It was really phenomenal. Then, if the dialogue or extra sounds were necessary, that was also dubbed. By the time the scene was ready to be put on one track, they might have to impose on the final and finished track six or more tracks.

There was one more headache, and that was Sandrich and Fred making up their minds whether the tap sound should satisfy the ears or the eyes.

That was a lulu! I was in the cutting room with a young cutter, George Marsh. He had just married that afternoon and promised his wife that he would meet her about 8 p.m. for dinner.

Since wives are not allowed in the studio, George asked his wife to stand near the window of his cutting room. By 9 p.m. he was still there, almost ready to leave. In walked Sandrich. He looked at the dance and said, "George, my eyes are following the dance, and it does not fit."

George said, "Fred wants the taps to follow the dance and the music."

Sandrich said, "Never mind what Fred said. I want my eyes to see the dance follow the music."

Poor George told his wife to wait for a while. He was almost ready to leave by 11:30 p.m., when Fred Astaire walked in, took a look at the film, and ordered George to change it back. Since Fred and Sandrich both wanted their way, they had poor George so confused that, after a while, it took him an hour to find a track. Finally, he told his newly wedded wife to go home and wait for him. I stayed with George until 9 a.m., and we finally decided to do what Fred Astaire wanted.

There was one number called *Slap That Bass* that Sandrich went haywire over. He wanted the slap and sound of machinery used, starting with one sound of metal, followed with numerous other sounds of machinery, and finally mixed up with a deep colored voice and a large chorus.

The idea was colossal, but it needed lots of work and experiment. Three sound men were sent out to various factories, and they all came back with all kinds of factory sounds—hundreds of them, but when we tried to fit them to the picture, we failed, and we went back to our sound effects in the studio library.

As I said before, Fred Astaire is a great artist and a perfectionist. It is wonderful working with him, but it is a tiring job—sometimes nerve-racking. Yet he is a perfect gentleman, speaks quietly, and does not get rattled or nervous with anyone but himself.

Let me go back to George Gershwin. After we finished the picture *Shall We Dance*, we gave a concert for the RKO distributors. George complained that he was having composer's stomach trouble, and I kidded him about his eating habits.

A few days later he was at the Goldwyn studio. I heard that he had fainted. I had received a phone call from him to see him. Before a date was made, he was at the hospital, and then I heard that he had died. It was a terrible shock. I have often wondered what he wanted to see me about.

As for Ed Small's *The Toast of New York*, with Frances Farmer and Edward Arnold, it portrayed the character of the Baron Robber, James Fisk, and his love for Josie Mansfield, played by Frances Farmer. The big ballet scene was a costly spectacle, but it was cut out in the final showing. Small had engaged a lyric writer, Wrubel, and a composer to write a love song for Miss Farmer to sing. He had paid $1000 for it, but Miss Farmer did not like the song. I watched the proceedings for a while, and then decided to write a song, in case Miss Farmer refused to sing the $1000 song. It finally happened, and then I showed them my song, *The First Time I Saw You*. She liked it immediately.

Small hated to eliminate the original song, but since I was on the staff, he did not have to pay me. Small insisted that Wrubel do the lyric. Wrubel, at first, insisted that the first song was better, but Miss Farmer won out. When my song became a hit, Wrubel admitted that it was better than the original. Small became so enthusiastic about my song that he wanted all incidental songs printed. I tried to tell him that they only fitted the picture and had no value as hit songs. Three other pieces were printed, but they had no popular appeal.

ALAN MOWBRAY

In a Nino Martini picture [*Music for Madame*] Alan Mowbray had to conduct quite a bit of the *Tannhäuser* overture by Richard Wagner. Not to be criticized for his portrayal, he asked me to show him the proper way to lead the symphonic orchestra. He worked hard at it and did a good job. In fact, an excellent job. This was 1937. When I was in Hollywood, I met Mowbray again—this was 1964, twenty-seven years later. We were at the actors club, and he asked me to come to a room on the second floor. There was a small upright piano that he had donated to the club, with hundreds of autographs scratched on the piano. He asked me to find my name. I found it, and above my name I had written the Pilgrim's theme of the *Tannhäuser* overture. He then sang the opening and conducted the music as I had taught him. He still remembered. He was so pleased when I complimented him on his conducting.

JEANETTE MACDONALD AND NELSON EDDY

While in Hollywood from 1935 to 1938, I recorded for the RCA Victor. The duet dates for Miss Jeanette MacDonald and Nelson Eddy were far from their picture portrayals. Miss MacDonald disliked Eddy thoroughly. She complained that the arrangements always started with Nelson Eddy's voice, and that her part was not outstanding enough. Also, when singing together, she would manage to get ahead of him to practically hide his voice.

She complained to me and blamed the studio manager for the arrangements. Actually, it was my idea that a baritone voice at the beginning of the record would make a better sale.

The studio manager came to me and asked that her voice should start some of the numbers. Nelson was very nice about it. After all, she was a great star. I will say that many of their duets were not recorded in a very romantic atmosphere.

LEOPOLD STOKOWSKI

A story was related to me by two reliable men. It concerned a hoax played on Leopold Stokowski. A musician in Hollywood was a contractor for symphony conductors. He also liked to be a host for some well-known personalities.

He invited Stokowski to one of his barbecues, and, as an attraction, hired a very pretty prostitute for $20 to sit next to the famous conductor and entertain him fully. She was told to say as little as possible and to listen to Stokowski and simply use a few clichés such as "it is wonderful" and "I enjoy your concerts."

Stokowski was vastly pleased by her attention, since she listened to him without talking too much. So for over an hour he waxed enthusiastic about music. Evidently, she was clever enough to impress Stokowski, and he told the contractor that the beautiful lady was not only lovely, but highly intelligent.

When the meal was over and the group was standing around, the lady went over to the contractor and said, "Here is the $20, I can't take him."

My Music Library

When I began radio broadcasting, I had a modest library, consisting mostly of my own arrangements. When my programs had attracted many sponsors, I decided to build up my library. For a long time the networks did not have much of a library. In my fifteen or more years of radio broadcasting, I spent $965,000 on arrangements and printed classical music. Sheet music of popular numbers were gladly given to conductors by publishers because they received money for use of their copyrights on the air.

However, popular music had to be orchestrated and arranged in a novel style. This meant an outlay for arrangements and copying. For my operas and operettas series, I bought three thousand vocal scores at Schirmer; for opera and symphony dates, many classical symphonies. I had Mr. John McCormack and Chaliapin buy lots of music from Europe. Since my sponsors paid for the music, I used it on their programs. I did not overspend on my own. I remember putting in a bid to buy up all music, score and parts of a defunct German opera house. Luckily, I did not get the deal.

It meant that I had two librarians and a copyist to take care of torn parts, careless handling of the musicians, and torn pages due to much neglect. When I signed up with RKO to become their musical director in 1935, I stipulated that they must ship my whole library from New York to Hollywood and find room for my music. It cost them $3500 to do this.

While at RKO, I decided to come to New York for a two-week vacation around Christmas. In New York I was asked to conduct a classical program by NBC. Not having my library, I had to rent about eight numbers from the NBC and other libraries: a concerto, an overture, two operatic numbers, and four concert pieces. By this time, NBC had bought Walter Damrosch's library for $25,000. Damrosch was under contract with NBC. Also, Mr. Mapleson, the czar librarian of the Metropolitan Opera House, had passed away, and his son started a rental library. My rental fee for the eight numbers was nominal.

That finished my complete library aspirations. It was past the days when music was hard to rent. I decided to get rid of most of my library. It had become an expensive hobby. I donated a few thousand printed orchestrations to the schools of Hartford, got rid of many original orchestrations, and sold some vocal, opera and operetta scores.

Finally, I packed some unusual and important musical text books and asked my son to deliver them to the New York Library at 42nd Street. My son Arthur stopped me from giving everything away. He packed all my music and stored it away in cartons. Well, what he will do with all this I do not know, and, really, I do not care. Sometimes, I feel sorry for having disposed of my vocal opera scores, but I have enough miniature scores of the classics to keep me busy for as long as I live.

NOTES

1. Max Steiner, born the year before Nat Shilkret, was also a child prodigy. He graduated from Vienna's Imperial Academy of Music at age thirteen and wrote an opera at age fourteen. He scored over two hundred motion pictures, which earned him three Academy Awards and fifteen more nominations. His pictures include the original 1933 *King Kong*, *Gone With the Wind*, *Treasure of the Sierra Madre* and the *Informer*, discussed later in the autobiography.

2. The account in Karlin [1994] is amusing, even if slightly at odds with the account given here: "Max Steiner had worked for RKO-Radio for about five years, during which time he had scored 111 pictures for them. When he asked for a salary increase in 1936, he was told that the studio would make a decision over the weekend. They did—and replaced Steiner with Nathaniel Shilkret as general music director. Steiner read about it in Monday's *Variety*."

3. Roy Webb, a founding member of ASCAP, came to RKO in 1933 as Steiner's assistant. From then through 1958 Webb scored many films.

4. After having several positions at RKO, Berman produced films for RKO from 1931 to 1940. He produced many more pictures for MGM from 1940 to 1970.

5. Croce [1972] comments on Nat Shilkret and his role in this process: "Another old friend of the Gershwins was Nathaniel Shilkret, music director of RKO. Shilkret had conducted the radio première of 'An American in Paris' and had recorded it for RCA Victor. Like Max Steiner before and Victor Baravalle after him, Shilkret conducted but did not himself compose or orchestrate the music heard in the Astaire-Rogers films. The music director delegated these assignments to groups of arrangers, sometimes sketching out themes that he wanted developed in the main titles and underscoring."

CHAPTER 7

RETURN TO NEW YORK

Mr. Shilkret ... in August, 1938, became ill. ... Mr. Shilkret not only suffered physical pain, but had dizzy spells which affected his remembering musical scores. ... An examination showed ... that he had suffered a loss of approximately sixty or seventy per cent of his blood. ... On April 20, 1940 he underwent a very serious operation and had about 60 blood transfusions and was advised by his doctor not to work for at least a year. However, he disregarded his doctor's orders and went to Chicago to perform on the Carnation program in the latter part of July, during August and into, perhaps, the first week of September, 1940. This amount of work was too strenuous for him and he suffered a slight relapse and is still under the doctor's care.

—**J. Everett Blum, narrating,** *June 10, 1941;*

testimony, N.Y. Board of Tax Appeals, Docket 103773

In March 1938 I left for New York and started the Ruppert Knickerbocker Beer Hour. The men who had been my steady orchestra members until 1935 were scattered. Certain men, like Jimmy Dorsey, Tommy Dorsey, Artie Shaw, and Benny Goodman, had formed their own bands. Wilbur Bradley took Tommy Dorsey's place. Mr. Ruppert was ill in the hospital, and I dedicated my *Christmas Overture* to him.

THE GERSHWIN AND HERBERT ALBUMS

In [1938 and] 1939 I started to make transcriptions and some Victor records. I was asked to do eight albums, and, since I was anxious to build up another fine orchestra, I asked for $20,000 for the eight albums. The Victor manager said that he did not believe he could secure that sum. He asked if I would consider $1000 a broadcast with the NBC orchestra and, while on the air (for the Magic Key Hour), they would record me at the Victor studio which was two miles away from the NBC studio.

I made an agreement to do, for the first two albums, a Gershwin memorial and a Victor Herbert album at $1000 per broadcast, a royalty of 10 percent of the retail price ($7.50 per Red Seal album) and $400 for copying bills.

With only two hours of rehearsal, I went through ten new arrangements of four and one half minutes each side, for five double-faced records. I did not hear any playback to criticize the balance. If any mistakes occurred in our broadcast, then they would stay as played for the final masters. The NBC orchestra was fair. The soloists were Jane Froman, Felix Knight and Sonny Schuyler and the NBC Chorus. Two men, an oboe player and a harp player, were removed eight minutes before the end, because the NBC contractor had forgotten they were engaged for a Toscanini rehearsal.

I was angry at that, and so, for the Victor Herbert album, I refused to use the NBC orchestra, and insisted upon having two separate sessions—one for the broadcast and a second session an hour later for recording.

I offered James Melton the tenor part for the Herbert album, but he demanded what I thought was too high a price. I had heard the Roxy program and was quite pleased with their tenor, Jan Peerce. I got in touch with Peerce, and he was glad to record—probably his first recording.

Most of the men I engaged were from the Metropolitan Opera and the New York Philharmonic Symphony. The sopranos were Anne Jameson and Gladys Rice. Thomas L. Thomas, baritone with the Victor mixed chorus, was a soloist also. Two of the women of the chorus said, "Mr. Peerce doesn't seem to use much voice."

And I answered, "You're wrong. Listen to him in a few minutes."

I went over to Jan and asked, "Why are you crooning instead of letting your voice out?"

Peerce said, "Isn't that the way to sing popular music?"

I said, "Evidently, you never heard Victor Herbert's favorite tenor, Paul Althouse. Paul had a tremendous solid voice. Please sing with your natural splendid voice. It is ideal for Herbert's music."

And let it out he did. His rich and luscious voice was perfect for the album. At one time, he asked me to let him hold a high B-flat until I thought he had held it long enough and then give the sign to cut off. We came to the spot, and as he held the high note he closed his eyes and did not see my cutoff. Just when he was getting blue in the face, he opened his eyes, and I quickly gave the sign to cut off.

When we finished the record, he asked why I had not given the sign sooner. I said, "I did, but you closed your eyes and did not see me." Jan Peerce became a leading tenor at the Met. He is still one of the great operatic tenors.

The Gershwin and Herbert albums sold pretty well in the first year. I received $5000 in royalties. My son Arthur printed a small brochure and sent it out to the Victor dealers the second year, and over ten years I received more than $250,000. I had offered my services for eight albums for $20,000—they paid me over a quarter of a million dollars for just two albums!

PAUL ROBESON

I recorded *Ballad for Americans* with Paul Robeson and the American People's Chorus, with Earl Robinson as choirmaster and composer [February 1940]. Paul Robeson did a magnificent job. He was a man with a deep bass voice, but his tones were so vibrant and brilliant that he sounded like a robust baritone. Actually, he sang most of his songs about two tones lower than other bass singers. It was too bad that he became disillusioned about the United States. He was a great man, and he could not help resenting the unfair attitude against his race.

A SERIOUS ILLNESS

After that I didn't make any more albums because I became ill. During 1939 and 1940 I really suffered. I could not sleep, and I was in pain. I did a few small albums for the Victor: Tchaikovsky, Sibelius, Lehár and Ziegfeld hits.[1]

I lost weight and blood. I passed out a few times while conducting. I had to do a Tchaikovsky album, and I was arranging it, but by midnight I was terribly tired. I called Morton Gould to help me. He said that he was busy but he would send his assistant, Phil Lang. He came, and at 3 a.m. he quit. I finished my arrangement at 8 a.m.

After the recording that morning, I went back to my hotel and slept until noon. I got up for breakfast and walked from 59th Street to 57th Street and Seventh Avenue, opposite Carnegie Hall. I met a few men of the Philharmonic orchestra. I had lost so much blood and weight that they asked, "Don't you feel well?"

I answered, "No worse than you feel after a Stravinsky rehearsal." They left, and in a few minutes I felt ill, as if I would faint. I sat down and passed out.

When I opened my eyes an officer was smelling my breath, and I was told that I had passed out for thirty-five minutes. A crowd gathered, and a man came forward and identified me. He leaned down and, in dialect English, whispered, "Can you fix me for a position with your orchestra? Please tell your contractor about me. My name is (I forgot his name)." I was in no state to remember anything.

An ambulance came and the attendant was told to take me to the office of my brother, Dr. Harry Shilkret. Harry immediately had me taken to the French Hospital. For over one year, I had gone from one doctor to another, for one test after another, but they did not solve my trouble. At the hospital I was given continuous blood transfusions. It was not until the twentieth day that they discovered the trouble. I was told it was an ulcer, but later, after the operation, they said it was cancer.[2]

After the long operation, performed by the marvelous surgeon, Dr. Wright, I was asked to take a pill in order to sleep. I was very weak, but I refused it. I do not think that I ever take more than one soda mint a year, and then I never swallow it. And that goes for aspirin or any other pill.

After three months, I left the hospital with an open side [colostomy]. I went to Chicago to conduct two broadcasts, an operetta show at WGN and the NBC Carnation Milk program.

DINAH SHORE

When I arrived in Chicago for the WGN operetta series with Bill Bacher, he told me that Petrillo had thrown me out of the musicians' union. I asked why, and he said it was because I did not ask Petrillo's permission to engage him [Bacher]. I said, "Should I go back to New York?"

He said, "No." In his confident way, he announced, "I'll fix it," and he did. Petrillo told Bacher that he did it just to show who was boss in Chicago. Some sense of humor.

Before going to the hospital I had started a big dance band. This was 1939 when I was very ill. I had Bill Challis and some others make the

arrangements, and we rehearsed for about two months. We selected the
best possible men, and then I told Bill that the band was pretty good, but
not entirely satisfactory, however. I wanted to look for a good girl vocalist.

I called the NBC and CBS agencies and asked them to pick a vocalist
for my band. CBS came up with no one worth considering. NBC had quite
a few girls. One girl was featured by them. She was a French girl who sang
popular American music. I considered that a bit phony, although she had
a good voice.

I listened to about twelve girls that afternoon, but I did not select one.
Finally, I asked, "Haven't you anyone else?"

The agent said, "Yes, there is one more girl, but she is new."

A young lady who had stood apart from the other girls came up. I
heard her sing about half a chorus, and I exclaimed, "That's it! She is
wonderful. What is her name?"

"Her name is Dinah Shore."

Before I could make connections with NBC, I was taken to the hospital.
When I came out three months later Dinah had become well known; and
later she was a great star. The rehearsals with my band had been costly,
but after my illness I lost interest.

About July or August 1940, I was in Chicago for a dinner with Bill
Bacher, and I invited Dinah Shore with us for dinner. Bill, as usual, carried
on a lively conversation while Dinah, very young then, sat quietly, hardly
saying anything. Then, without reason, Bill came out with a remark so
silly that I wondered how he could think that way. He remarked, "Dinah,
you are a fine singer, but you are sure dumb." Dinah was dumbfounded,
and I was so angry I could have slapped him.

I often wondered what Bill thought of his remark after she became a
great star and had her own show. I never forgot his words, but, knowing
Bill, I was sure that it just came out without any malice. Sometimes a
person says things without thinking.

BENNY GOODMAN, TOMMY DORSEY AND HARRY RICHMAN

While in Chicago, I went to visit Benny Goodman between his shows. Since
I had been a clarinet player, we discussed the instrument. I had only heard
him play jazz music, but I discovered that he was a first-class classical
clarinet player, with a fine symphonic tone and lots of technique. As we
know, he has played chamber music with many prominent quartets.

I also visited Tommy Dorsey after his late show. He had five shows that day, and he was very tired. I suggested that we have a quick bite and then retire. What happened—we landed at the Chez Paree club, featuring Harry Richman. When Harry saw us, he came over and said, "Do you want me to get my orchestra leader really sore and see him walk out on me?" This was far from what we wanted, but he was too excited to wait for our answer.

He was announced and started his number. After a few bars he stopped the orchestra and told the leader that he was too loud. Then he stopped him again and said he was too soft—again, you are too fast, and then you are too slow, and by this time the leader became really angry and walked out.

After his act he came over and told us that he was joining the air force as a pilot, he had stopped drinking, etc. We took it all in, not believing him much. He seemed too old to be accepted as a flyer.

We stayed until 3 or 4 a.m., and then Richman invited us to go out to some joint and have a drink. We came to a striptease place, and Harry invited all the girls to sit with us. Evidently, he forgot about being off the wagon and started drinking one glass after another. I counted seventeen drinks, and he insisted that everyone empty their drinks. Since I had just come from the hospital, I did not drink on account of my condition, but Richman was too far gone to listen. Finally, after a few jibes at me, I asked him, "Do you really want me to empty all these cups?"

He said, "Yes."

I then said, "Fine." I got up, grabbed the table cover and pulled it, and all the glasses fell to the floor.

Richman looked at me and asked, "Who is drunk now?"

Now came the time to settle up. I whispered to Tommy that this was a clip joint and the bill will be a few hundred dollars, asking, "How much money do you have?" He said he had about $150 and I said I had about $100. Tommy came back with, "Richman is known to forget his debts." We were relieved, because Harry settled the bill.

By this time we were really tired and wondered how to get rid of Richman. Tommy said he wanted to go to his hotel to get something. We stopped and we (Tommy and I) got out. Tommy went to his room, while I walked to my hotel. I wondered how long Harry Richman waited for us!

THE BEVERLY HILLS HOTEL

After seventeen weeks, I could not control my draining side and decided to take a long vacation. I went to the Beverly Hills Hotel in Beverly Hills,

California.

I wrote many compositions, but I did not conduct. It was a beautiful hotel, and I stayed there over a year. In the meantime, my son went into the music publishing business, and I contributed to it. With the beautiful weather, the swimming pool, Nat Finston and his lovely daughters, I felt fine. Of course, I missed Mrs. Shilkret, but she never liked Hollywood. She was a dyed-in-the-wool New Yorker.

What became a bore was listening to some characters around the pool. One man, Jan Kiepura, came around, and I had watched his egotistical behavior twice, once at the Paramount studio and then at the Hollywood Bowl concert.

I went to a recording session at the Paramount studio, and Kiepura was singing a song by a fine composer, Erich Wolfgang Korngold. For no good reason that I could discover, Kiepura was complaining about everything and everybody, especially Korngold.

Finally, he turned away in the middle of a song and said, "Is this the way to treat a greater tenor than Caruso?" I could have murdered him. Besides, I did not think his voice was good.

At the Hollywood Bowl concert, with his wife, Marta Eggerth, he was very rude to her. At the end of the concert, he let her take a bow for about two seconds, and then he shoved her away, took the stage alone and stayed there, and ignored her entirely.

One day at the pool, he walked in, all dressed up, and started to tell us how great he was. He was introduced to me, and, in a supercilious way, asked, "Are you a musician?"

I answered, "I was conductor and manager for the Victor Talking Machine Company for many years, and I had the pleasure of turning you down for our Red Seal Department."

That and similar bores made me think of getting back into the harness again.

NOTES

1. The Lehár album (*Viennese Gayeties*) and the *Ziegfeld Follies Hits* album were made in 1940 after Nat's April 20th surgery. The light classical albums *Robin Hood* and *Hansel and Gretel*, made for children, and the album *I Hear America Singing* were also made in late 1940.

2. Nat Shilkret's son Arthur said that he (Arthur) was informed before the surgery that his father had cancer and told after the surgery that the cancer had spread and Nat had only two years to live.

CHAPTER 8

MGM AND RKO-PATHÉ

Yesterday I spoke to Louis K. Sidney, who is one of the top men at Metro, Rufus LeMaire, and Al Lichtman, and they all like the idea of your joining them very, very much. . . .

This is the exact setup, Nat, in reference to your status in Hollywood. . . . As you know, Forbestein at Warners, Previn at Universal, Lipstone at Paramount, and Newman at Fox are in solid. Since it would be most difficult for us to secure the jobs of any of the above men for you, there are only four other studios open, three of which, Republic, Columbia and RKO, would be out of the question. I know that you would not enjoy working under any of the men mentioned above, so I really think MGM is by far the best setup for you.

In reference to the conversation with Nat Finston, I do believe that $500.00 for the first year, $600.00 for the second year and two years at $750.00, plus the privilege of a broadcast and recording dates, is about the best we could do for you.

—Ray Stark, The Salkow Agency,
letter to Nathaniel Shilkret, September 26, 1942

I mentioned that I might start working again. I returned to New York in the beginning of 1942. I did some transcriptions and started the series called *This Is America* for RKO-Pathé. During the third day, I received a telegram from MGM—would I care to come to Hollywood and sign with the studio as a scorer for pictures? I accepted.

Before I left the city, Mr. Paley of CBS called me. He inquired about the Columbia recording catalogue: Would I recommend him acquiring the company? I told him that I had been interested in buying it and had approached our Victor distributor, Bruno, to buy it with me. They were not interested.

The price for the Columbia Company was a very cheap bargain, and after my talk with Mr. Paley, he purchased it for a higher price—$700,000. It was still a bargain.

Dr. Wright examined me, and said that my side wound was ready to be closed—the operation had been successful.

My MGM duties were simple enough. I was to conduct my own scores and also conduct for any other composer. The MGM studio was much larger than the one at RKO, and, therefore, there were more intrigues. Despite my refusal to enter into any of the cliques, it was impossible to avoid them. My brother-in-law, Nathaniel Finston, head of the music department, and I had to listen to a good deal of gossip from his friends and his foes.

Despite the rumors, Nat had very little to do with my getting the job. My agent was Ray Stark, and he sold me to one of the producers who told Finston to engage me.

For two years I did mostly conducting and a few minor pictures. At the end of the year, Johnny Green and I did a two-reeler, and it was the only picture that received an Oscar award for music.[1] It was then that the ice was broken.

A little later, Nat Finston left the studio. I quit with him, as a friendly gesture. Four days later I was called up and engaged again. With my brother-in-law off the lot, everyone became friendly, and I enjoyed my next few years at MGM.

LOUIS GRUENBERG

One funny thing happened, and I hope that the splendid musician I am going to write about will not be offended. I have great respect for him as a man and a composer—a musician of big standing. This is not a typical Hollywood story.

I was assigned to conduct a picture, the *American Romance* [1944], produced and directed by King Vidor, with music composed by Louis Gruenberg. King Vidor, a successful producer of many fine pictures, has described his MGM experience in his autobiography.

I'll tell you about the musical score. King Vidor brought Louis Gruenberg in as a musical composer for the *American Romance*. For a producer to ignore the large musical staff of MGM was a bit daring, since Nathaniel Finston, head of that department, considered his MGM composers to be tops. But, after all, the producer has the first and last say. Therefore, Gruenberg was engaged at a stipulated salary per week.

Often the composer is brought in shortly before the picture is finished. Vidor insisted that Gruenberg start from the beginning of the shooting date, so that he would get the mood of the story and not be hurried. Vidor was anxious for a great symphonic score.

As Mr. Gruenberg followed the daily takes, he composed tons of music for a full symphony orchestra of eighty or ninety men. Being a sincere and earnest worker, he put his body and soul into his work. Needless to say, Mr. Finston was annoyed at Vidor and Gruenberg, because he had to add Gruenberg's salary to his already bulging budget, while three or four of his own staff who were competent to score the picture just sat around.

The picture progressed slowly, and Gruenberg was on the payroll for eight months, and the picture was not finished. There was friction, of course, but King Vidor insisted that Gruenberg must stay on.

It was in the tenth month that I was brought in to conduct the *American Romance*, and so Gruenberg asked to see me. As a staff musical composer, I worked on pictures daily, and, although I worked diligently on every picture, the work became routine. I would look at a finished picture, study and analyze it for musical effects, then go through it, and, after a week of recording, would forget the whole thing as another job done.

Not so with Mr. Gruenberg. This film that he had lived with for almost a year was sacred to him. At our first meeting, he told me, in a voice shaking with emotion, that he had selected me as conductor. He asked, "Have you seen the picture?"

I said, "Not yet."

"Have you looked at the music?"

I answered, "Just a few pages at the library."

And then came the astonishing questions while we walked through the immense MGM lot. "How is your health? Do you sleep well? What do you eat?", etc. Naturally, I thought Gruenberg's solicitous inquiries about my health unique. In fact, I went to Mr. Finston and asked, "What I am getting into?" We had quite a laugh over the thing, and I found that Finston was more than annoyed at the whole affair.

He said, Mr. Gruenberg's bill, just for his service, was up to $30,000, not counting the reams of copying written by the library staff. Finston said that Gruenberg had written twice as much as needed, because at least 50 percent of the picture would be cut out for the final showing.

This complaint was, from experience, justified. Finston claimed that a composer should not write his music until the picture is complete and all the cuts have been made. As for Gruenberg, he was acting under King

Vidor's orders, so it was not his fault if many scenes were changed and cut.

Well, finally the day for recording came, despite the fact that the last reel was still being worked on. The day before the recording (and by this time I was familiar with the music) I received a phone call from Mr. Gruenberg, asking, "Will I go to sleep and be ready for the early morning date? Was I feeling well?", etc. I assured him that I was in tip-top shape, etc.

That evening Nat Finston asked me to join the boys for a poker game. I said, "Okay, but I have a 9 a.m. date for the important *American Romance*."

He said, "I know that. You quit whenever you want to," and so I was at the poker game at 9 p.m.

At midnight I was winning $1400. I threw in my chips and said I must leave. Of course, the players objected, and so I volunteered to quit without taking my winnings. "Oh, no!" They wouldn't think of that—I must continue, and so time dragged on, and the more I tried to lose, the more the money came in.

By 5 a.m. I was still a large winner, and I wanted to get a few hours sleep. "No, you can't quit," they said. This went on until 8:15 a.m., and then the game broke up. I got to the recording studio by 8:45 a.m., with no breakfast and no sleep. Gruenberg was there, pacing up and down and worried that I might be late. Again he inquired about my sleep, my health, etc. I told him that I had a fine night's sleep, and that I was feeling great and ready for a hard day's work. (What a liar!)

At 9:00 a.m. sharp we started with ninety men, and the music sounded vibrant and exciting. By 10:30 a.m., the main title was finished, and Gruenberg was in seventh heaven. After living with the picture for almost one year, he was hearing his music. This is a thrill that every composer dreams of, and only a composer knows the pleasure and joy to be gotten from it.

We sailed along nicely for about a week, and then we struck a snag. At first King Vidor would compliment Mr. Gruenberg often, but when he heard the romantic theme, he was not pleased and thought that it did not have the feeling of the picture. As we progressed, King Vidor came to me with his complaints. I was torn between my great respect for Gruenberg's ability and my desire to satisfy Vidor.

Things became worse as we went on. A good deal of the music became distorted, because cuts had changed the original timing of the scenes. Many places that Mr. Gruenberg had been told would be scenic, had dialogue, because the cuts changed the timing. Even the romantic scene had been rewritten in a hurry.

Well, it seemed a mess, and I felt sorry for Mr. Gruenberg, after all his hard work. First of all, the friction between Finston and Gruenberg was causing strain to the breaking point. By this time, even Mr. Vidor was not protecting him, and I was in the middle.

The day before Mr. Gruenberg's contract was over we were in the part next to the last reel. I was driving him to his home. He turned to me and said, "Nat, I wish I was anything but a musician. Here is a whole year gone to waste."

I said, "Mr. Gruenberg, don't feel too bad about it. After all, they changed so much of the picture. It wasn't your fault."

"It isn't only the picture. Look, I wrote a grand march in another picture, and there were requests for it, and today I received a check from the publishers—$4.65. Isn't it terrible?"

I don't know what got into me, but, I am ashamed to say, that at times tragedy brings out the fool in me. Stopping the car, I brought out of my wallet a $2000 check by the same publisher (won in the poker game the night before the recording of *American Romance*).

Mr. Gruenberg's eyes popped out, and he asked, "What composition brought that sum?"

"Oh," I said, "just a little work."

"What, a little work? Was it a popular tune?"

"Oh no," I said, "a little chamber work."

He exclaimed, "A chamber work? Why, that is impossible!"

I said, "Well, here is a check to prove it."

His answer: "Nat, I can't understand it. I just can't understand it!"

By this time I felt I had gone far enough, and I tried to make him understand that the publisher had lost it in a poker game. Believe it or not, Gruenberg had not listened to me. He kept muttering, "I don't understand it. I cannot understand it!"

I will go into only a little further detail on the saga of *American Romance*, because it is almost "an American Tragedy," what with the old script and the new finish that necessitated some new shooting. I finished the picture without Mr. Gruenberg.

Mr. Vidor and Mr. Gruenberg had started with the finest intentions to produce a great American saga of the steel industry, but it all came to grief in the cutting room. My own belief is that the original story had been written as a combination of a documentary and a love story with great pictorial scenes and fine music. It would have come out as an artistic picture, but not a financial success.

The powers in the studio may want great pictures, but money is also important. They prevailed on King Vidor to make many changes. The mining and making of steel is very interesting, but the love interest must be strong.

The story was about a poor foreign immigrant coming to America looking for an opportunity. He has no money and walks all the way from New York to the middle of the United States, in the mining district (Masaba Mines). His great desire for knowledge and hard work in the land of free enterprise fulfills his dream. The original love interest was there, but not exaggerated. Well, the higher powers insisted that the romance be developed and made important. The result was a tampered with story, and the end of an epic.

As an addition to the story, an airplane plant was introduced into the story to show the now powerful immigrant helping his adopted nation by producing airplanes to contribute to our war effort.

Gruenberg sent in his last work. He must have been in a dismal state of mind. The piano sketch was orchestrated. I looked it over and decided that Mr. Vidor would find it too static. Not having time to write another composition, I got an idea to play the composition twice as fast as written and repeat the number. King Vidor thought it fit the scene wonderfully. At last, the picture was finished. I was glad that Mr. Gruenberg was not around to hear my interpretation.

RUDOLF FRIML'S STORIES

On June 14, 1944, in Hollywood, I had dinner with Rudolf Friml, and we went to Sarney, where his son Billie Friml played piano. The purpose was to form a publishing firm to be called Friml-Shilkret-Donaldson and Gus Kahn. It never came to any head. However, Friml told me a couple of very interesting stories, which I relate now.

Emma Trentini was an Italian soprano who sang beautifully and was very temperamental. In 1912 she performed Victor Herbert's operetta *Naughty Marietta*. After the success of *Naughty Marietta*, Herbert was asked to write another operetta for Trentini. When Herbert saw Trentini, he spoke of conducting the opening night.

Trentini said that she would not sing if he conducted. This angered Herbert, and he said, "I'll be damned if I write another note for that little ---!" This put Oscar Hammerstein, I (the producer), and Otto Harbach (the author) on the spot, and so they looked around for another composer.

Schirmer, a publisher, suggested a new young composer—a Czech, Rudolf Friml. A meeting of all of them was arranged. Rudolf Friml's appearance did not inspire confidence in Hammerstein or Harbach, but they were willing to listen. They asked Friml many questions about his experience, ability, etc.

Well, Friml told them that he had an opening chorus, a set of tunes and more tunes ready. Truthfully, he had written nothing, but, as always, his improvisation was wonderful. He sat down and improvised one tune after another for a supposed operetta.

They listened, fascinated by his piano playing. However, when they told him that the dramatic music would take a seasoned composer to write (they mentioned Frank Tours), Friml, with confidence and nerve of youth, said, "No. I do all the music or nothing."

And so he received the commission to write *Firefly*. After finishing the score, he was brought to see Trentini. He came to her hotel with Hammerstein and Harbach. Friml entered her room, and he saw a little figure of a woman, with hair all over her face, combing her hair. Friml was amazed. All the time he had thought that Trentini was Tetrazzini, the famous coloraturist, a very buxom woman, and he quickly turned to Schirmer and asked, "Is this Tetrazzini?"

"No, you damn fool, this is Emma Trentini, not Tetrazzini."

"Well," replied Friml, "don't tell her that I speak English. I have no desire to meet her."

Friml then played one number after another from his *Firefly* score on the piano. Trentini kept combing her hair to the rhythm of his melodies. When he was through, she looked at Friml and just uttered one word to them, pointing at Friml, "Dumb!"

On the opening night Friml overslept and missed the first act. As it happened, Trentini never sang at rehearsals, always worried about saving her voice, and, therefore, Friml had not really heard her sing. Friml arrived at the theater just when the curtain came down at the end of the first act and the applause was terrific.

Finally, Trentini sang an encore and Friml was thrilled by her voice. When he went backstage, he knocked at her door to congratulate her, but she wouldn't open the door.

And so Friml got his opportunity because a temperamental soprano refused to let a temperamental composer conduct his own work.

Friml also had a story about *The Donkey Serenade*. He was in New York, and he lived on 165th Street, near a Fox Movie Theater. He would often go there and invariably fall asleep. Once, while about to fall asleep, he thought of a melody—a lullaby. Even while he slept the tune kept repeating itself. Someone passing by his seat awoke him with a start. He was all alone, and the tune haunted him, and so, while in bed that night, he used the black-burnt edge of a match to write the melody of *The Donkey Serenade*.

The next day he played it for Schirmer, and, when asked the name of it, he said, "*In Love*," and dedicated it to Schirmer. It was published as *In Love*. Later on he said to Schirmer that it sounded silly to dedicate a song *In Love* to a man, and so in the next edition it was called *Chanson*.

When Paul Whiteman recorded *Chanson* as a fox-trot, it was given the name *Chansonette*.

Many years later, Stromberg (a producer) called Friml to listen to a script read by Jeanette MacDonald and Nelson Eddy and company. It was a Spanish revolution story, and Friml couldn't understand how his *Firefly* music (an Italian story) would fit.

A couple of young writers got the idea of a [new] lyric and rhythm for *The Donkey Serenade* from *Chansonette*, and the rest is history. Now Friml asked, "What will it be called next?"

Friml's start was in Prague, Bohemia. He was brought in to play for the ballet at the state opera. His predecessor was a violinist, and Friml played all the ballet rehearsals from a violin part and faked the harmonies. This was quite a novel start for a young pianist. He became a favorite with the ballet girls and later wrote numbers for them.

The conductor, impressed by Friml's talent, secured a scholarship for him at the state conservatory, where Antonin Dvořák was head of harmony and composition. Friml studied with Dvořák for four years, but Dvořák was more interested in his own compositions than in his pupils.

Dvořák often rebuked him, but admitted Friml had talent. Dvořák repeated often, "Develop your melody always." Dvořák did not care for too many harmonic tricks. He was set on the classic form and development. Friml came to America, when he was twenty-two years old, as a pianist for Kubelik, the sensationally advertised violin technician, etc.—a modern Paganini.

Since 1928, when Friml wrote the *Three Musketeers*, he has written practically nothing of consequence. Sixteen years later, I met him in Hollywood. He was living with two Chinese ladies who take care of his needs. He has two sons from his first marriage. One of them started a dance band, much to Friml's annoyance. This young fellow wanted to study music. Friml asked me to recommend a teacher.

I chose Alexandre Tansman, a highly capable man, with an international reputation. The price for a lesson was set for $15. Friml thought it too high. Tansman was ready to compromise, but evidently Friml wanted free lessons.

I went to Friml's house twice. He would put on some long-playing records of compositions he had written. He played them for hours, and I became bored. His natural spontaneity of youth was gone. He had written himself out. After the second visit I avoided him.

ELIZABETH TAYLOR, MARGARET O'BRIEN AND BUTCH JENKINS

While with MGM, I was working with three child performers: Elizabeth Taylor, Margaret O'Brien and the little boy Butch Jenkins. Elizabeth

Taylor's bungalow was next to mine. She was a lovely little girl and a fine actress.

Margaret O'Brien, about six years old, was a child prodigy. Her memory was phenomenal. She not only could hear her lines once and speak the words without a mistake, but often would prompt the other actors in their lines.

Butch was a little fellow whose expression was endearing to the public. During the mornings he would speak his lines fairly well, but after lunch he was tired and sleepy. It was very hard to get him to pay attention. Sometimes it was impossible to get him to act in the afternoon.

THE GENESIS SUITE AND WERNER JANSSEN

When I visited my friend Rex Schepp in Indiana, we traveled a good deal. I asked people what records they would enjoy the most, and invariably it was the Bible. This gave me the idea of starting the Bible at the beginning: Have the text read and write music to help the beauty of the text. I decided to call the record album the *Genesis Suite* [begun 1944; music recorded 1945] and to finish the first album with the Babel story.

I picked six stories: Creation, Adam and Eve, Cain and Abel, Noah's Ark, the Covenant, and Babel. For a prelude I commissioned Arnold Schoenberg. Igor Stravinsky wrote *Babel. Creation* was my contribution; Darius Milhaud, *Cain and Abel*; *Adam and Eve* by Alexandre Tansman; the *Covenant* by Ernst Toch; and *Noah's Ark* by Mario Castelnuovo-Tedesco. I had tried to get Richard Strauss and Manuel De Falla but they were too old or too busy.

Tansman immediately finished his work, and it was a wonderful score. Milhaud came through with a sparkling work. Tedesco and Toch did their assignments with fine musicianship. My piece, *Creation*, was well received by the audience.

Stravinsky, in his neat and carefully worded manner, was not easy to talk to. Tansman, a friend of Stravinsky, was with us at the meeting. I gave Stravinsky the text of Babel, and after he read it he announced that he would compose a cantata. I told him that I did not want the words sung. My main idea for the listener was to clearly hear the story of the Bible. Singing often made the text indistinct, especially when sung by a chorus. We argued for a while, and, seeing that I was getting nowhere with him, I suggested that we call a carpenter in to decide whether God's words must be spoken or sung.

Stravinsky, in his prim manner was really startled at my request. He asked, "Why a carpenter?"

"Well," I answered, "many years ago a carpenter called Jesus knew God better than anyone in the world."

Stravinksy sat looking at me for a while, and then said, "I will do it. However, the words of God will be sung by a Greek chorus." He announced this as if he were proclaiming a great judgment. His fee: $1000.

In contrast to Stravinsky's neat and elegant house, Arnold Schoenberg was sitting in a room cluttered with music, clad in easy clothes, and his two young children were running around, laughing and making noise, without regard for me, a visitor. In fact, while I was talking to Schoenberg, the little boy, with a small hammer in his hand, hit me a sharp whack on my knuckles. It did not bother Schoenberg; he barely noticed it.

I asked him to write the *Prelude* for the *Genesis Suite*—a composition depicting a feeling of the time before God created the world—sort of a void atmosphere. Schoenberg at first said, I thought hesitatingly, that he would have to think about it.

When I got to my room, I heard the phone ringing. It was Arnold Schoenberg on the phone. He wanted to write the *Prelude*, and he sounded enthusiastic. I went to see him, and I offered him $750. He (or rather his wife) asked for $1000. I agreed, but since I had five other composers to deal with, I asked him for a complete release, so that I could allow recording and radio performances of the *Genesis Suite* without getting permission from all the composers.

He and his wife said that it was against their principles to sign a complete uncontrolled agreement. I asked them what their principle was worth. They said $500. I agreed to their figure. When I spoke to Schoenberg, he told me that, after thinking my ideas over, the possibilities of a *Prelude* came to him, and he would enjoy composing the work.

Knowing that Stravinsky might hear of the $1500, I came back to him and told him that I would increase my offer $500, so that both he and Schoenberg would receive the same fee. Stravinsky thanked me effusively and said it was the nicest gesture ever offered him.

I asked him to sign a new contract. He had insisted upon his attorney writing the first contract, and now he wanted his attorney to write the new contract.

I was careless in not reading the new contract, and instead of getting what I asked for, the attorney had put in a clause that did not give me the license I needed to control the work. That was the thanks I received for being nice and fair.

Werner Janssen, a friend of mine, was conducting a series of symphonic concerts with his own orchestra. He asked me to give him the privilege of being the first conductor to perform the *Genesis Suite* for his Friday and Sunday concerts.[2] The concerts were to feature a Sibelius symphony and the *Genesis Suite*, with Edward Arnold as the narrator.

When Werner Janssen had his last rehearsal for the *Genesis Suite*, a young lady critic for a newspaper came into the hall and asked how I handled Schoenberg and Stravinsky in the same room, since they had, for many years, debated their opposite views about music.

I told her that I knew about their rivalry, and so I had maneuvered to keep them apart during rehearsals. In the meantime Stravinsky was hogging the rehearsal time and leaving very little time for Toch, Milhaud, Tansman, Tedesco and me. I had figured at least one hour between Stravinsky and Schoenberg. Well, I was wrong.

As Stravinsky was calling Janssen's attention to some detail, Arnold Schoenberg walked into the room. With his poor eyesight, Schoenberg could hardly find his place. The lighted stage and the dark hall did not help matters. He walked down the middle aisle and then, as he neared the stage, turned left and walked right into the same row of seats in which Stravinsky was sitting. They contacted each other. Schoenberg did not recognize his rival. However, Stravinsky looked at Schoenberg but did not greet him. A few minutes later Stravinsky left. There was just enough time left to rehearse Arnold Schoenberg's *Prelude*. Schoenberg listened but did not offer any suggestions to Werner Janssen.

Since it was the last day of rehearsal before the concert, I figured it would be sort of a dress rehearsal. After all, Janssen had rehearsed thirty hours so far. The time allowed for the rehearsal was three hours: One and a quarter hours for the Sibelius symphony, fifteen minutes rest, and the balance of the time for the seven compositions of the *Genesis Suite*. The time for the *Genesis Suite* was to be divided into twenty minutes for Stravinsky's *Babel Cantata*, forty minutes for five of the composers, and thirty minutes for Schoenberg's *Prelude* (the most difficult number).

However, it ended with Stravinsky taking one hour on *Babel*, five minutes of rest, and twenty-five minutes for Schoenberg. The other five composers received no rehearsal. There was no use trying to talk to Stravinsky. One cannot argue with a successful genius.

Stravinsky spent a good deal of time with the so-called Greek chorus (male), trying over and over again to have them sing with an exaggerated stress on the syllables and prolonged and sustained vowels. I thought the effect poor at the rehearsal, and I still think so when listening to the record of *Babel*. It is impossible to understand the text. As he said at our first meeting, "God's words must be sung and not spoken." I say, whether sung or spoken, the words must be clearly enunciated and plainly understood.

The concert went over well. After the concert, Janssen wanted permission to record the suite. He claimed that his contract with RCA Victor allowed him to pick his own recordings. He wanted to start recording immediately and have it ready for the Victor manager who would arrive within a week. He asked me to lay out one half of the expense, and said the Victor would repay us whatever it cost to record the suite.

There was a special price for symphonic recordings of $28 per man for a two-hour recording. Janssen engaged one hundred men. Since he had rehearsed for thirty-three hours for his concerts and had played two concerts, I figured that in two hours he could record all ten sides.

We were recording for two different results: one on film and one on wax [records]. Somehow, because of Victor's inability to get two types of recording simultaneously, we were getting very poor results. In three hours we did not even get one side recorded. There was only one thing to do: make some new arrangement with the musicians' union. Our expenses were $2800 for the first two hours, and then the union jumped to $28 for the next hour, therefore, making our cost for the three hours $5600, with not even one side recorded. The union officials gave us a new price, $10 per man per hour, and that came to $10,000 for one hundred men for ten sides. So instead of the album expense amounting to $2600, it now came to $15,600, not counting the studio and other expenses.

After the orchestral recording, we had to add Edward Arnold's narration and the chorus. This meant more cost. Stravinsky, in his contract, had the privilege of okaying the *Babel* music. He insisted on rehearsing the Greek chorus. (Male voices forcibly pronounced the words, "go to, Let," etc., with the emphasis on the syllables and prolonged length on the vowels.)

Personally, I did not care for his Greek chorus idea, but, after all, he had insisted, and due to my respect for his genius, I let him have his way. Finally, the expense of the recordings amounted to over $20,000.

Janssen had really not told the truth about his Victor contract. The truth was that they had the privilege to accept or refuse his recordings— they refused the album.

Janssen wanted to start a recording company and refused an offer of another company to pay our expenses and work on a royalty contract. And so he started his recording company with his income tax agent in charge of the newly formed recording company.

Soon after that Janssen had to leave for a winter symphonic engagement in Seattle and left the recording business to his agent. He returned to Los Angeles after the winter concert season and inquired about the finances of his recording venture. He was told by his accountant that there was no profit. There had been over ten thousand albums sold, but promotion had consumed the profits.

My son Arthur and Janssen went over the accounts and found discrepancies. They ordered the agent to show his books, and he refused. Not only that, but he would not surrender the masters. After a good deal of fussing, the masters were secured for a sum. Capitol Record Company was interested. They proposed to supplant Edward Arnold's voice with Franklin D. Roosevelt or Winston Churchill's narration. This failed because they were both too busy. Finally, the Capitol executive who was enthusiastic for the album joined the NBC staff, and the man who took his place was less enthusiastic over the project. He found a minister to narrate the stories.[3] His voice was poor, and the promotion was weak. They sold some albums, but it never paid much—not enough to pay our lawyer.

TOMMY DORSEY AND THE TROMBONE CONCERTO

Writing long classical music is difficult for a composer. It takes a good deal of time, effort and expensive copying for the orchestral parts, plus an endless amount of time to interest symphonic conductors enough to perform the work. There is often the demand of prima donna conductors for the first performance.

Even if you are fortunate enough to get a performance, you are faced with refusal for future performances due to the fact that someone different had already performed the work. Unless a new work is a sensational success, it is almost impossible for a new composition to receive a second or third playing.

Tommy Dorsey was searching for a trombone concerto. He had several well-known composers submit their works, and mine was accepted [1942]. While he was doing an MGM picture, using a fairly large orchestra, he rehearsed my concerto. At first I orchestrated the *Concerto for Trombone* for a standard symphonic orchestra [1943]. Tommy asked me to orchestrate it for his orchestra that contained strings, saxophones and brass, so that he could rehearse it while traveling. That meant a new score and new orchestral parts to be copied. It consumed a lot of time, work and money.

About six months later, Leopold Stokowski walked into our MGM studio and asked me if I could show him the score of my *Concerto for Trombone*. I did not connect Tommy Dorsey and Stokowski. I gave him the score. A little while later Stoky was asking for orchestral parts. He was in New York, and he wrote that he wanted to play it with Tommy Dorsey and his youth orchestra for his children's concert at City Center.

Tommy Dorsey played it for a concert [February 1945], and it was a huge success. I was asked to come to New York, because Stokowski and Tommy were to record for the Victor Company. Dorsey was especially anxious for me to come because he said Stoky did not get the American idiom necessary, etc. I was on a few pictures at MGM and wrote to both of them to wait until they came back to Hollywood.

In the meantime, Werner Janssen offered Tommy Dorsey ten performances[4] of the concerto and a handsome sum for me to allow the performances. Tommy refused on the grounds that he was too busy.

The next summer [1945] Stokowski and Dorsey were in Hollywood. Stoky wanted Tommy to do two concerts at the Hollywood Bowl and then record the concerto at the RCA Victor studio. He offered Tommy's manager $500. Tommy's manager asked for $2500. There was a good deal of haggling. In the meantime, Tommy married one of the MGM minor actresses, and she wanted to take a trip to Mexico. Between his wife and his manager, Tommy was in a quandary.

Stokowski called me up and told me that the Bowl concerts were almost due. He was not as annoyed with Tommy as with his manager. Could I get another trombone player to take Tommy's place? The concerto is difficult, but after a lot of searching I found a young fellow, Mr. Bohannon, who was in the army. He could get leave to do the rehearsals and the two concerts.

The two concerts went fairly well, and Stokowski wanted to record the concerto with the new player. He set a date for the recordings, but I objected, because I wanted Tommy Dorsey to be the soloist.

While in New York in 1947, Tommy wanted me to conduct the work with him at the Victor, but I asked if I could find a few more resting spots for the concerto. This was before tape recording, where a number could be cut up and pasted together. I got an idea of adding a piano solo part and having the piano divide some of the trombone solos.

I went to the Philharmonic Orchestra at the stadium, where José Iturbi was soloist. I asked him if he knew Tommy Dorsey, and he replied, "Oh, yes. He is a wonderful player." I asked him if he would mind playing and sharing a record with Tommy. Iturbi said, "I would like to hear the concerto." Luckily, I had a record (acetate), and, with that and my score, I met him at his hotel. It is necessary to explain the work.

The first movement was in classic form, but in the middle I introduced a fugue, partly in jazz form, and near the end I wrote the main theme in fox-trot rhythm. The second movement was melodious and partly spiritual. For the third movement, I composed the whole piece with a boogie-woogie rhythm and called it *Perpetual Motion*.

Iturbi liked the work, especially the boogie-woogie movement. I promised to reorchestrate the work and write a piano solo part worthy of his consideration. Between Iturbi's commitments and Dorsey's busy schedule there were delays. Finally, a date was set to record the concerto at the Victor studio. The two artists were called. Iturbi said, "Fine, I'll be there."

Tommy said, "Nat, I'm sorry, but my MCA agent just signed a Decca recording contract. I cannot work at the RCA Victor studio."

After all my trouble and various orchestrations and copying expense I was disgusted. I dropped the whole matter. Later I recorded the concerto with Wilbur Bradley and the piano soloist Leonard Pennario. I did not engage a symphony orchestra. I orchestrated the concerto for a string quintet and percussion. The recording was not good, but the soloists did a wonderful job. We recorded in a room too small for a grand piano. The room was okay for a small dance combination, but Pennario's crisp and solid tone overpowered the room.

I hope to have it recorded properly someday, but it will be hard to find a great trombonist with Tommy Dorsey's reputation. The above shows the impediments a classic composer goes through: time, effort, expense and the frustrating period to find conductors willing to play new works. Bradley had the technique and tone. In fact, he was a better musician than Dorsey, but Tommy had a tone and style that was unique; besides, he was quite a character, and his reputation meant more audience acceptance.

COMMENTS ON STOKOWSKI

I want to state that I admired Leopold Stokowski very much. He was our greatest and most successful symphonic recording artist—perhaps greater financially than Arturo Toscanini. He was always interested in improving record sound. Another great trait of his was that he was, and still is, an eager student of new music. Toscanini stuck to the established program repertoire. Stokowski braved criticism. He believed that an audience must be made to listen to new music, whether they liked it or not. That was the way to get them accustomed to new sounds. He played and recorded music like Schoenberg's *Gurrelieder*, a tremendous work that no other American conductor would dare to perform in record form at that time. For years he has been the forerunner of new music, both symphonic music and avant-garde composers' operas. He is a controversial figure. In fact, you can admire him and dislike him at the same time.

I attended two of his concerts in Hollywood. I cannot remember where the concerts took place, but with all the trimmings and lights, I felt like I was attending a circus.

The first concert was mostly Bach organ music arranged for a symphonic orchestra. Whether you prefer the original organ or an orchestration for a symphony is not what I am trying to call attention to. The effect of the glorious sound of his performance was thrilling, and I was enthralled. Then came the second concert, an all Wagnerian program. After the second number, I walked out because of his exaggerated romantic efforts in the love music. It got on my nerves, and I walked out.

I also admire Stokowski for his attitude toward other conductors. I never heard him criticize or say a disparaging word about another musician. That is a rare trait for a musician. Leopold Stokowski has done a great deal for music, especially for America.

VINCENTE MINNELLI

I worked with Vincente Minnelli on a pilot radio program. He wrote the script and rehearsed the singers and acts. This was before he became one of the great directors for MGM. His knowledge was uncanny; he was a genius. The show he produced was far ahead of the programs of that time, and it was not accepted.

HEITOR VILLA-LOBOS

Werner Janssen told me an amusing experience with Heitor Villa-Lobos, a composer with remarkable talent. Janssen's symphony orchestra gave regular concerts for a few seasons in Hollywood, and Janssen engaged Villa-Lobos to conduct his works for two concerts [1944].

Lobos was in Brazil and offered to come but needed money for his trip. Janssen sent him the required sum for Lobos and his wife. It turned out that the lady was not his wife, and so she could not enter the United States.

After a good deal of fuss, Lobos and the lady were allowed in. He arrived in Los Angeles and demanded the most expensive suite in a very expensive hotel. For his compositions he needed special percussion instruments. They could not be hired at any instrument factory. They had to be built to order at the fancy cost of $1000.

The rehearsals started; and, out of eight rehearsals, Lobos appeared one or two hours late twice. The third time he did not appear at all. With ninety men getting union prices, this was an enormous bill. In the meantime, Lobos and his lady were living in a lordly fashion—special meals, champagne, etc.

The two concerts were performed, but Lobos and his friend stayed on and on at the hotel while Werner Janssen was getting the bills. This went on for three weeks, and at this point, Janssen put his foot down. He told Lobos to leave, and Lobos said, "I would leave, but I have no money."

Werner gave him enough money to get back to New York and told Lobos that from tomorrow on he would not give Lobos one cent. Lobos stayed on for a few days, but, instead of living in the expensive suite, changed to the cheapest and smallest room in the hotel.

RKO-PATHÉ

I stayed with MGM from 1942 until the middle of 1946. I received a letter from Mrs. Shilkret that she had met Herman Fuchs of RKO-Pathé in New York City, and he wanted me to work on the series *This is America* that I had started in 1942. It was a good offer, and I signed with Mr. Fuchs. I stayed with RKO-Pathé from 1946 until 1953. The company only produced one- and two-reelers, and I composed hundreds of scores for them. By 1953, on account of double features, the one- and two-reelers almost disappeared from the movie theaters.

In 1946 I was in New York. I did quite a few transcription dates for SESAC, besides my RKO-Pathé pictures. I found time to write two one-act operas and two ballets, plus quite a few songs.

GRUENBERG AND LAWRENCE TIBBETT

Before I proceed with my New York activities, I want to write about some things I have neglected to mention. I would like to tell you about Louis Gruenberg and his accomplishments. When I was six years old, my brother Lew and I studied piano with him. Gruenberg's brother Jack was a remarkable young pianist, and he made the first trip to New Orleans with Pinto's New York Boys' Orchestra. Louis went to Europe and studied piano and composition with the famous Ferruccio Busoni. He was described as the master for years. Coming back to America, he composed quite a few works that brought him into prominence. Lawrence Tibbett was featured in his opera *Emperor Jones* at the Metropolitan Opera House, and it was successful. It was Tibbett's greatest role, but it had a dreadful effect on him. The role is both physically and vocally a strain on the artist, since he is clad in just light swimming trunks: The role is part singing and part loud declamation, and the Met stage is drafty. It finally affected Tibbett's voice, and I doubt if he fully recovered from its harmful results.

Gruenberg went to Hollywood and scored a few pictures, and his works were well received. Engagements, now and then, are never steady. There were some classical composers used in the studios, but most of the successful scorers were not considered classical.

ARNOLD SCHOENBERG

There was a chance to hire Schoenberg, Stravinsky and Prokofiev in Hollywood, but they never scored a picture for one reason or another.[5]

I must relate a Schoenberg story. MGM was ready to score the *Good Earth* picture [1937]. Irving Thalberg, the well-known producer, felt that this great picture needed an unusual musical score. He asked Nat Finston, who was in Hollywood, who he considered to be a great composer. Nat, thinking he was just asking a cultural question, mentioned that Arnold Schoenberg, a musician of international fame, had just arrived in Hollywood.

Thalberg, not knowing anything about Schoenberg's style of music, wanted an interview with the master. Schoenberg was contacted and asked to meet Thalberg at the MGM studio.

Schoenberg was a rather short man, a bit dumpy, and could have been taken for a grocer or tailor in appearance. He arrived at the studio and noticed a group of people. He thought that they were to meet him, and so he joined them. There was a guide who marched the group all over the lot. Schoenberg, whose English was not too clear at that time, wondered why he was being walked around the lot.

Finally, he grew suspicious that he did not belong with the guided tour, walked over to the guide, and showed him his pass to see Thalberg. In the meantime, Thalberg, Finston and others interested in the *Good Earth* were sitting in the dining room awaiting the appearance of Schoenberg.

Almost an hour passed, and they were ready to give up when Schoenberg came in while lunch was being served. Thalberg, in his best dramatic manner, told the story of *Good Earth*. His description of the Chinese refugees, the suffering of the women and children, the bombings, the fires and the harrowing locust avalanche was given in the most gruesome detail. When Thalberg was through he said to Arnold Schoenberg, "Now that you have heard this great story and heard of the people's suffering, you as the greatest composer in the world, I think it is just the picture for you to write your greatest music."

Schoenberg, realizing that Thalberg knew nothing of his works and the effects his music had on people, thought for some time. Finally, he looked up and said, "I realize the suffering of these people. It was truly terrible, and so I refuse to do the music. They have suffered enough." This story was told to me by Nat Finston.

This reminds me of my dealings with Arnold Schoenberg about five years before. I was on the General Motors broadcast, and I was approached to have Schoenberg as a guest. I knew him as a composer, but I wondered whether he would conduct. He said yes. He selected a movement of Gustav

Mahler, his teacher. I then asked him to also conduct one of his own compositions. He chose a part from his *Gurrelieder*. This needed a contralto singer.

I recommended Rose Bampton. I told him that she had worked with Leopold Stokowski. He stopped me; he said, "Don't mention Stokowski. He recorded my *Gurre Lieder* for the Victor Company. Why did he not come to me when he was in Vienna and have me show him the correct tempo," etc.

I begged him to hear Rose Bampton, and when he heard her he was delighted with her voice. We were at the Gotham Hotel, on 55th Street at Fifth Avenue. Schoenberg seemed more anxious to talk about Hitler than about the concert. He had been forced to leave Europe on account of the Nazis. This was about 1933, and he declared that he would devote his time to persuading the American people, especially the youth of the country, to stop the menace of Hitler and his Nazi party.

Finally, I invited him to lunch. It was cold, and he must have had a touch of asthma. Knowing that he wanted to eat lightly, I proposed Schrafft's on 57th Street. Although it was a cold day, the sun was shining brightly. As we came into the street, Schoenberg took out a large scarf, put it on his head, and then jammed his derby down over his ears. I had to hold his arm to guide him, and, as luck would have it, I met quite a few people as I marched with the heavy veil up Fifth Avenue.

Schoenberg at that time was looking for some connection with musical establishments that would want his great services. He spoke in derogatory terms of Curtis, Juilliard and other well-known schools of music. I warned him that, if he really wanted to find a proper position, he should tone down his caustic remarks about prominent musicians. Whether he took my advice or not I do not know. Later on he went to Hollywood and was given a post at UCLA. In fact, a hall is now named after him.

I met Schoenberg in Los Angeles. He was a simple man with great ideas, and his atonal system (if you can call it that) has revolutionized our modern music.

GAMBLING

Ronnie, you asked me about Hollywood and gambling. I found Hollywood musicians (mostly composers) not all the same, but it seemed that their job, golf, sex and gambling were quite prevalent. Of course, that does not mean all of them. As for myself, I never gambled in New York. In Hollywood, poker and gin rummy are the things to do. Besides that there was betting on horse races and fancy gambling clubs.

When I started to play poker, we would meet at Nat Finston's house. Not knowing much about the game, I lost several thousands of dollars. Nat Finston told me to quit, saying that I was not sharp enough to play with seasoned players. For a while I stopped and watched each player. I noticed that, at about 1 a.m., certain players received telephone calls from their wives. If they were ahead, they excused themselves, saying that their wives needed help. If they were losing, they would continue playing.

One man in particular never played his cards unless he had a pat hand (a sure winning hand). I noticed that Nat Finston was a good player, but reckless, and that a phrase like "try and beat me" thrown at him would be enough to entice him, even if he should have thrown his cards away. Max Steiner, who had bad eyesight at a near distance, could read cards at a distance, and so cards held carelessly were an advantage for him.

One had to be careful of doctors and lawyers, who were really card sharks and earned more money gambling than in their own profession.

I started to play again, and this time I won more that I had lost previously. My reputation as a poker player rose, and I was told that I was a very fine player.

I left Hollywood for six years[6] and never played poker during that time. When I was back in Hollywood, I started to play again. I never started at the beginning of a session. I would attend a concert or a picture house and arrive at the game at about midnight.

One experience made me quit poker forever. We had played all night, and in the morning, about 10 a.m., George walked in with his young child and said, "What a bunch of idiots, playing poker all night; and now it is a sunny, beautiful day, and you are still at it. I am glad I quit."

An hour later he was back and said, "Just for a little while and for the fun of it, I'll play." Then he added, "Nat, give me $200 worth of your chips. I'll pay you back soon." I gave him the $200. Pretty soon he asked for $200 more. We played on all day and into the night. By 3 a.m. he (George) owed me over $3000.

I knew that he would never pay me back all that money, and so I waited for the time to help him. One seldom gets a perfect hand. We were playing a kind of poker called Low Hand. The best combination for the five cards is A, 2, 3, 4, 5. Twice in that long session I received this combination. One may play for years and never get this hand.

With this pat hand, I thought I could help George. I opened the pot, and George raised me. The other player was Frank, who was doing a lot of beefing but was not losing much. After George, Frank raised. I followed with a raise. The rule allowed raising three times.

By this time I figured that they both had very good hands. In fact, I was sure that, since George was such a large loser, he must have a splendid hand. Then came the drawing of the cards. I stayed pat, and, to my surprise, both George and Frank asked for one card. In other words, they were betting on a chance to better their hands.

We continued. Again I bet; George raised me, and so did Frank. Naturally, I was sure that they had bettered their hand, and I was sure that George must have the better hand. Despite my having the perfect hand, I threw my hand down and said I was bluffing, hoping that George would recover some of his losses. Well, believe it or not, George was bluffing with a poor hand and Frank gathered in the money.

Again the same thing happened. I guess George, by this time, was desperate and hardly playing with any sense. It was ridiculous to continue, and so I asked George, "Do you know what you owe me?"

He said, "I've got some idea. I know it is quite a sum."

I told him it was over $3000. I asked, "What do you have in chips?"

He said, "About $350."

I then told him, "Give me your chips and you do not have to repay me. Just forget the whole thing." Of course, if I had lost that sum, I would have paid. This game finished me with poker. I have not played since then.

As for the stock market, that is too much to write about. It had its ups and downs. In 1929, I asked my secretary to phone my broker to sell my stocks two days before the crash. Frank Crumit was my connection with the brokers. Those were the days of margin buying. I had $135,000 in cash for about $350,000 worth of stocks. The day of the crash, I was conducting a large orchestra, a fifty-singer mixed chorus and soloists. In the middle of the date the news of the crash was announced by one of the musicians. That was almost the end of the recording date.

I had received my mail but had not had a chance to read any of it. With the sad news, I opened my mail expecting to congratulate my good fortune of having sold all my stocks two days ago. What happened was pretty bad. My broker bought instead of selling. I found myself with about $700,000 worth of stocks and only $35,000 in cash. Between Frank Crumit and my secretary, I never found out who was responsible. As for the brokerage firm, they were in such a panic that it was no use even trying to find out from them who was responsible. It was never cleared up. Naturally, I took quite a loss.

A few years later, during the depression time, I went to my broker to buy 2000 shares at $80 a share. He was so sure that it would decline, that he convinced me that I should play AT&T short. What a mistake. It was a calamity. I would have made a fortune, if I had stuck to my own idea. My son now takes charge of my stocks, and he has done a fine job.

Ronnie: *"Did you go broke?"*

Oh, no! I managed to end up in a pretty good financial position. I wish my son had been old enough to manage my business affairs when my earnings were large. But enough of these questions.

NOTES

1. The 1943 two-reeler *Heavenly Music* won an Academy Award for best short musical. The musical score was by Nat, along with Gregory Stone; Max Terr provided incidental music. Sam Coslow was associate producer. Although Johnny Green did not, as best we can tell, participate in the making of this motion picture, it seems likely that this is the picture to which reference is made.

2. On page 203 of his autobiography Werner Janssen writes that it was Nat who asked Werner to conduct the première of the *Genesis Suite*.

3. Inferior quality records were recorded by Artist Record Company in 1946. Unsold records were destroyed in 1950 to allow the release of the recording by Capitol.

If Roosevelt was considered for narration, it must have been before Edward Arnold was chosen, since Roosevelt died in April 1945. An unsigned contract from Capitol for publishing *Genesis*, dated June 13, 1946, substantiates the statement in the autobiography that Capitol was interested in *Genesis* prior to the issue of the album by Artist records.

A September 13, 1951, royalty statement from Capitol includes the statement "One half of $500.00 fee paid to Ted Osborne for narration."

4. Correspondence from Werner Janssen to Nat in 1943 indicates that Tommy Dorsey cancelled a contracted appearance to play the *Concerto for Trombone* on February 6, 1944. The possibility of a second concert had been considered prior to the cancellation.

Liner notes to Decca LP Album DL5370, *Ecstasy*, by Tommy Dorsey and Victor Young, state that Tommy Dorsey had played the *Concerto for Trombone* with an orchestra led by Werner Janssen. Considering that the correspondence from Werner to Nat included a copy of a letter from Werner to Arthur Michaud, manager of the Tommy Dorsey Orchestra, threatening a lawsuit if Werner's advertising and other expenses for the cancelled concert were not reimbursed, it seems unlikely that Tommy Dorsey played the *Concerto for Trombone* with Werner Janssen. At any rate neither Nat's nor Werner's autobiography mention such a performance, and neither Werner Janssen's son nor Tommy Dorsey archivist Walter Scott were aware of any such performance.

5. More precisely, they never scored a picture in Hollywood. Prokofiev scored several pictures in the Soviet Union, beginning with *Lieutenant Kije* in 1934.

6. The "six years" is almost certainly the four and one-half years from March 1938 to August 1942.

CHAPTER 9

THE SKINNER TOUR

Friday, Jan. 11th [1952]: Horrible getaway from N.Y., making a 9:30 [a.m.] train. . . . At five we had an orchestra call, and Nat called the routines for the well-meaning but untalented boys. The piano was immense, and placed at the extreme left of the pit. I had a terrifying time with page turns, as there was a big rack. I used it instead of more sensibly placing the music flat on top. . . .

After a hasty hamburger with Nat I returned to the theater, where the orchestra assembled, sans piano, in the ladies' can, a location to which it was eminently suited. There we rehearsed till twelve. I discovered there that Nat uses no orchestral score when conducting a show; he prefers a piano book. This had never been mentioned, so there was no complete piano book for him. Consequently, he rehearsed partly from scores and partly from memory, with me throwing Cornelia's cues to him. . . .

Afterwards, as Nat was plannning to work all night on a score for his picture date, I went to his tiny, ice-cold room and worked on cues in the orchestra parts till nearly four.

—**Kay Swift**, *personal diary,*
during the first road trip of Paris '90

In 1952 I went on a tour with Miss Cornelia Otis Skinner on her one-woman show. The stories she had written about Paris in the 1890 period centered around Toulouse-Lautrec.[1]

She was superb, and it was a gratifying experience to be part of the show. We started a tour that took us to sixty-five cities in the United States

211

and Canada.

Kay Swift, a splendid composer, wrote the music, and Russell Bennett arranged it for eleven men. We opened at Schenectady for two Saturday shows to break in the act. By Monday we were due in Boston. Outside of Kay Swift, as pianist, and a violinist [Irving Becker] we expected to fill in the other players from the cities we were to visit.

We arrived in Schenectady Friday night and started a rehearsal. Some of the musicians were from Troy and some were from Albany. Since I had seen very little of the music, this was an opportunity for me to get acquainted with the score. For the first hour it seemed impossible to get a fairly decent performance out of the group.

I had hesitated in hiring Miss Swift as pianist, because a composer and conductor relationship often does not work out. Well, I was glad to have her services because of her knowledge of the music. With a good deal of patience, we finally decided to take a chance on using the orchestra for the two Saturday performances. Somehow we did very well on Saturday, and by this time I knew the score by heart.

The Boston orchestra was splendid, except for the cellist. In most cities the union assigns a contractor to a certain theater. Often the contractor will engage another contractor or a relative, regardless of their ability. Since the conductor, as a visitor, must receive an okay from the local union, he is in no position to complain. Should he accuse a player of being incompetent, he would probably end up paying a fine. It is best to get along with the local musicians as amiably as possible.

My reason in mentioning the cellist is to show why I hesitated to hire Miss Swift. Well, Monday and Tuesday went by, and by this time I was conducting the show without looking at the music.

During the Wednesday matinee Miss Swift turned to me and said, "You are picking on me." I told her that I was trying to prevent the cellist (sitting next to her) from making mistakes. She did not believe me.

Then I said, "Well, I can't smile when the music is badly played."

I used my usual way of putting my orchestra men in their place. I never argue; I just exaggerate my point. We started the second act, and I had arranged the orchestra to skip Cue #30 and Cue #34. Miss Swift had not been told of the skipped numbers.

We came to Cue #30. We did not play, and Miss Swift looked at me, but I turned away from her. Then came Cue #34, and again we remained silent. Miss Swift, with a distorted face and tears coming from her eyes, turned to me. I sweetly said, "Now you smile." That did it. She got the point, and from then on we got along fine.

This reminds me of a time I engaged Milton Rettenberg as my top pianist. He had a habit of playing too loud. He was used to playing solos and wanted to hear himself above the orchestra. Despite my warnings, he still kept on playing too loud.

One day, before Milton came in for the rehearsal, I asked the orchestra men not to laugh, no matter what I said. Of course, they knew how often I had asked Milton to play softer. We started rehearsal, and, in a little while, I said, "Milton, you are not playing. I don't hear the piano." He shrugged his shoulders. Again I stopped and asked Milton if he was tired and why I could not hear the piano. He looked at me with a perplexed look. For the first time, I was asking him to play louder. As I stopped for the fifth time he really became angry and he stood up and said, "Look at my hands. They are bleeding." The boys went into hysterics, and, at last, Milton Rettenberg got the point. From then on he improved as an orchestral pianist.

Well, back to our tour. We were in Atlanta, Georgia, and one of the musicians from that city was a young drummer who said he could not read music, but with one rehearsal he could memorize his part. I watched him at the rehearsal, and he was a natural-born talent and his technique was flawless. Not only did he perform beautifully, but he even added some cute effects of his own. When the week was up he offered to stay with us without salary. Of course, we couldn't accept that, and, besides, it was against union regulations.

We asked him what he had done in the past. He told us a very unusual story. He had been in the army and had been shell shocked, which resulted in amnesia. He was in a hospital, in the care of a nurse. While he was convalescing, the nurse took him to a nightclub where Benny Goodman and his band were featured. For some time he listened to a few numbers, and then he asked the nurse if she would allow him to speak to Goodman. She said okay, and he walked up to the platform and asked Benny Goodman if he would allow him to play the drum for the next number. Benny, seeing a boy in uniform, said, "Alright, I'll let you play one number." The boy sat down and did such a clever job that Benny let him play two more numbers.

Coming back to the nurse, he told her that he was cured. He remembered his name and that he had been a drummer before he joined the army. It was an unusual story, and he was so sincere and naive that we believed him. When we left Atlanta the next morning, he tearfully bid us good-bye. If it were not against our union laws, I believe we would have taken him along.

Another drummer in Memphis was a very old man. He must have been a good drummer in his early days, but now he was practically deaf. He came to the rehearsal with the largest bass drum I ever saw. We were performing in an armory, since no theater was available. During the rehearsal he managed to get along through his experience, but for the two performances I had warned Ronnie to watch him and help him from making too many mistakes. In fact, cue him in at the right moments.

Miss Skinner was nearing the end of a story. It was at a quiet spot and, in the midst of a tense and dramatic moment of the Dreyfus story, Ronnie turned around to prepare the old drummer to get ready for a crash chord at the end of the story. The old man thought that Ronnie was giving him a cue, and suddenly he came in with a tremendous bass drum crash that almost shattered the armory. Miss Skinner must have jumped out of her seat. Later on she thought that an explosion had hit the building. It was then that we were informed that the old fellow was deaf and got by the rehearsal by instinct and experience.

In touring sixty-five cities I met many local musicians. About two out of three men managed to meet expenses by working in other occupations. Their musical activities supplemented their earnings. Some were music teachers in schools and colleges, some in their own business, while others worked in jobs such as real estate, automotive mechanics and office work.

Miss Skinner sang three songs in a sketch of a famous Parisian singer that Toulouse-Lautrec had immortalized in his caricatures, Yvette Guilbert. I tried to play the piano myself, because the hired pianists were afraid to attempt the part. It seemed strange that even the fine pianists shied away from a rather simple piano part.

Ronnie asked me if I knew the great trumpet soloist Mendez. I said that he had played under me at MGM. He asked, "Would he give me a lesson?"

I said, "I think so. I'll speak to him when we get to Hollywood." Mendez not only gave Ronnie a few lessons but refused to accept money.

We had two weeks vacation at Los Angeles, and then we performed at Pasadena, San Diego, and San Francisco. Our next stops were Seattle, Portland and Vancouver. Then we headed east to Milwaukee and Chicago. In Chicago the union officials would not let us use our two musicians. They insisted on eleven men from Chicago. My two musicians remained idle for two weeks.

While in Montreal, I boarded a bus to see the rural part. I rode to the end of the line and took a walk. When I decided to return to Montreal, I inquired as to where I could find the proper bus. No one understood me in English or my poor French. Finally, I saw two men who did not look like natives. I walked over to them and they seemed to be having a heated argument. As I came up to them I realized they were speaking Yiddish.

During our tour I made many visits to radio and TV stations. Most of them had my records in their library. I also visited libraries and folk music students and gathered lots of material for my country music collection. Often people would come to me and say that they remembered my radio shows and were collectors of Victor recordings.

Miss Skinner was a delight to be with—gracious, without temperament, and always pleasant. At times her husband, Mr. Alden Blodget, joined us.

He was her manager, and he was a jolly lovable man.

He had a wooden leg that was caused by a wound obtained while hunting. A mistake by a doctor infected his limb, and, in time, it required amputation. He seemed proud of his substituted leg, and he told a story. Arturo Toscanini and his retinue were at Mr. Blodget's home on Long Island, and the talk centered around how some people could stand extreme pain. Toscanini's manager said that Mr. Blodget could stand any pain without flinching. Toscanini wanted it proved.

Blodget pulled up his pants on the artificial leg side and exposed his perfect looking limb, and the manager took a sharp knife and plunged it into the wooden leg. Miss Skinner told me that Arturo Toscanini almost fainted. I am sure most of us would have done the same.

Ronnie, you asked me about conducting without a score. I have a peculiar memory. In my busy routine, most of my scores were given to me at the last minute. Do you remember our last visit to William Revelli, head of the Michigan band? He had 250 players, and he cut it down to 125—mostly pupils, but some teachers. There were twelve young ladies playing the flute. Mr. Revelli asked me to conduct the band, and I asked, "Without a rehearsal?"

He showed me three scores, two by Russell Bennett and an overture by Kabalevsky. I looked the scores over for a few minutes and said, "I will not guarantee results, but I'll try to conduct the three numbers without the scores." Knowing Mr. Revelli's reputation as an instructor, I expected a fair performance, but not such a rich sounding band. I had played with Sousa, Pryor and Goldman and recorded many famous Victor bands, but these 125 ladies and men were the finest.

NOTE

1. *Paris '90* was first performed on a road trip that began on January 11, 1952. Nat directed an orchestra consisting of Kay Swift playing piano, Irving Becker playing violin and the remaining musicians hired locally in each city. The complete sound track was recorded on March 4, 1952, and issued by Columbia as LP 4619. The show played on Broadway from March 4 through April 19, 1952 at the Booth Theater and from April 21 to May 17, 1952 at the John Golden Theater, for a total of 84 performances. On a second tour of 57 cities from September 1952 through April 1953, Nat directed and played piano, and Ronnie Modell played trumpet. Again the remainder of the musicians were hired locally. The archival edition of this work includes an article contributed by Ronnie Modell.

CHAPTER 10
CONCLUSION

As Recording Manager and Director of Light Music for the Victor Talking
Machine Company of Camden, New Jersey, Nathaniel Shilkret's influence
on popular music in America must have been considerable, particularly in
the Twenties and Thirties, but he was to die almost forgotten.

—**Peter Cliffe**, *The Historic Record
and AV Collector Quarterly, July 1993*

RETIREMENT

During 1953 I recorded many transcription dates. In 1954 Mrs. Shilkret
became ill, and between our vacations in Florida and California, I managed
to record and compose. By 1957 she grew worse. It was high blood pressure,
and on April 13, 1958, she passed away. From then on I was retired. If you
asked, "are you able to be happy and not be active," I would answer that I
really do not miss conducting to the point of being unhappy about it. I get
occasional requests to perform, but I really do not care whether I perform
or not. I enjoyed many years of conducting, but it is not a craving.

This reminds me of my clarinet playing days. I quit playing the instrument about 1915. Twelve years later, the Eveready program featured me
in Mozart's clarinet quintet—I played the clarinet with the London String

Quartet. For the first two movements I was fairly comfortable. By the third movement I was tired, and in the fourth movement I was suffering and wondering why I had put myself in such a position. My lips were bleeding because I had used both of my lips, and the pressure of my teeth on my lips was raising havoc. Somehow, I managed to get through.

After that I would be asked by one of the clarinet players to try their new instrument. For a time I received compliments—then polite remarks, and, by 1935, it was "stick to your conducting!" I have not played since then.

FINAL THOUGHTS

I sometimes wonder why conductors who reach eighty years still want to conduct. Is it pride or pleasure? Luckily a conductor is not like an actor. The change in his appearance does not hamper him, and his skill remains undiminished. It was not for the money, yet Toscanini, Stokowski[1] and Pierre Monteux work until the end. I can understand composers writing and creating up to their last breath, but conductors? I approached De Falla and Richard Strauss to write my *Genesis Suite*, but they both refused for the same reason: They wanted to complete what they thought would be their last work. Bartók refused because he was too ill.

There has been a great change in the attitude of the American public and certain critics concerning popular music. In the early 1900s Victor Herbert was dismissed as conductor of the Pittsburgh Symphony Society board of directors for composing successful operettas. They considered it sacrilegious for a classic conductor to associate and contaminate himself with light music—I mean popular music in a broad sense.

They were not interested in whether the music was good or bad. Popular music was considered cheap and vulgar, regardless of its merit. In those days, Leonard Bernstein would have shared Victor Herbert's fate because he wrote his excellent score for the *West Side Story*. Today Bernstein is accepted, despite his writing in both popular and classical fields.

In the early days musicians were restricted to either the classical or the popular field. Even the playing and mixing of instruments in the woodwind section was considered injurious to the lips. An oboe or flute or clarinet player never mixed two different instruments. By the 1920s and 1930s, the American musicians often played flute, clarinet, oboe and bassoon—sometimes four different instruments—and became proficient in all, and they were familiar with both classical and popular music.

Do not misunderstand me; not all classical players can play jazz or vice versa. However, there are many examples of the American versatility. To-day European musicians have followed our American musicians. Of course, there is quite a difference between the classical and jazz tone and phrasing.

I am not expert on the musicians of yesterday or today or on their financial outlook. However, I had experience as a player and later engaged many musicians. It has been a period of many years and many changes.

From 1900 to 1920 music was heard in cafes, restaurants, theaters and party affairs in all societies, all using live musicians. Then came record com-panies paying $1.25 an hour for musicians and 2 cents royalty for composers and lyric writers and also paying a royalty to publishers.

Between 1920 and 1930 radio became important. It led to the devel-opment of the American musicians, both in popular jazz and symphonic music. It was a good period financially. Union prices increased, and there was lots of work. The movie houses employed large orchestras, and radio stations engaged live musicians.

Up to this time a father worked up to a certain time and, when he grew older, he expected his children to work. Exceptionally fine players might work until they became too old or too sick.

By 1930, with the electrical recording, synchronized music and pictures developed. For two years NBC and RCA Victor were busy day and night turning out musical scores on records. Hollywood built their studios to accommodate the sound movies. This practically eliminated the musicians from the theaters. In the theaters, only musicals employed live musicians.

By 1940 disc jockeys started using records and, slowly but surely, live musicians stopped being used on radio. Then came TV, with very few live musicians.

There are still quite a few cities with symphony orchestras, but, in my tour of about sixty-five cities in the United States and Canada, I found many musicians supplementing their earnings with other endeavors. They do not mind their wives working.

Today musicians are college graduates, and they find positions in schools and colleges as teachers and conductors.

Now small combinations, with their amplified equipment, can fill a large hall with more sound than a regular orchestra four times their number. And many more combos are made up of young people, teenagers, some talented and others untrained and amateurish. With so many young people singing and striving for expression, some new form of art may develop, just as strolling minstrels did in Europe, especially in Germany.

With the rapid changes today, it is not difficult to foresee new scientific developments in art and industry. Electronic music may come into vogue. Will it rival standard symphonic scores? Will the new sounds become popular? Who can tell? Will live musicians adopt music as a hobby and not as an avocation? How long will symphony concert recitals and operas continue?

At the present time in America, there are more symphonic societies, opera companies and school groups forming. The arts receive federal aid. Will it become bureaucratic?

Recently I attended a meeting of the directors which dealt with whether or not to apply for federal aid for their symphony orchestra. The board was not sure. They were about 50 percent in favor, but there were many objections heard.

They feared interference, but they thought that many sponsors would expect the federal government to cover most of the expenses and relieve the sponsors of their responsibilities. Will it be similar to our foreign aid to some countries who get used to receiving money, as if it were the lenders' obligation and would help the "haves" as well as the "have nots?"

There is no doubt that art is being considered more and more important in Washington, D.C., and this will require a good deal of money spent on music in all its various forms. With this added expense, how long will it be before it results in political wrangling?

EPILOGUE (Editors' Note)

Nat Shilkret lived with Arthur (his son, Barbara's husband, and Niel's father) and Barbara Shilkret in their home from 1956 until his death on February 18, 1982. Less than a year later, on September 26, 1982, Arthur died.

The two one-act operas referred to in the section RKO-PATHÉ are *The Fur Coat* and *Gently Down the Stream*, both with libretto by impresario-singer Jimi Beni (David Madaleva) who, we believe, performed at least the *Fur Coat* in Rome, Italy in May 1958. Nat Shilkret wrote a third one-act opera, *The Work of Art*, the libretto for which was never completed.

In 1963, he traveled to Mexico to do some orchestration for Rex Schepp; this was Nat Shilkret's last paid work. He wrote some musical compositions and arrangements and prepared copy for his son's publishing business through the 1960s.

Even in the late 1960s he visited the arranger Bill Challis in Massepequa (on Long Island) for lessons. He always had a high opinion of Challis's work.

Nat Shilkret's health gradually declined in the 1970s.

NOTE

1. Stokowski died in 1977. When Nat's autobiography was completed, around 1965, Stokowski was over eighty years old, which might well have prompted the description that Stokowksi would "work to the end."

APPENDIX A
COMPOSITIONS AND
ARRANGEMENTS

The public does not hear songs or see them in written form until arrangements of the songs have been made. Songs usually require some development by arrangers, whose efforts may vary from mere transposition of keys and elaboration of chord structures to more creative work. ... Arrangers have often been lauded as being more important to the success of a popular record than the original writers.

—**M. William Krasilovsky**, *This Business of Music*

Listed below are compositions and arrangements of Nathaniel Shilkret with most incidental music excluded. Pieces for which a separate copyright was found are marked. Copyright dates for music that appeared in motion pictures, with copyright only for the motion picture as a whole, is not marked. Entries not marked with copyright are not necessarily in the public domain. Copright dates, when available, are used and sometimes differ from publication dates. *Skyward*, for example, was copyright in 1934, even though it had already been recorded by 1929. Some works that are arrangements may not be explicitly labeled. Arrangements that first appeared as part of a motion picture or radio broadcast are only marked as being from that motion picture or broadcast, not as being an arrangement.

When all information is available, the entries are in the form

Title/description (if needed)/composer (for arrangements)/lyricist (if any)/co-composer(s) (if any)/name written under (if not Nat Shilkret or Nathaniel Shilkret)/indication that the piece is an arrangement/year of copyright or publication.

The following abbreviations are used: l for lyrics by, arr for arrangement, © for copyright and an asterisk for pieces for which there is written music but no evidence of publication.

Nat published most of his work under the name Nathaniel Shilkret, with Nat Shilkret being the most common variation. He seems to have experimented with several pseudonyms prior to 1925. Three published pieces appeared under the name "N. Hilbert" and another under the name "Ned Arthur." One of his early pieces had the name "Arthur Harold" (his son's first and middle name) crossed out of the 1915 draft when it was revised in the 1960s. The name Mack Fenton (from his brother-in-law's name Mack Finston) was used for two pieces published in 1941, and some of his later work was published under the name Niel Hallett.

Adeste Fideles (Joy to the World), for Rosa Ponselle and Metropolitan Chorus, by J. F. Ward, arr.
*African Love Song.
African Serenade, l H. de Costa, © 1930.
*African War Song.
Album Leaf, from *Winterset,* 1936.
*Alhambra Serenade, ?from *Africa—Land of Contrasts,* ?1934.
All I Want Is You, My Darling, When I Come Home Again, l G. O'Hara, © 1942.
*April, April, l W. Watson, as Nat Schildkret, ca 1915.
April Showers Bring May Flowers, with J. Shilkret, l L. Wood, © 1920.
Arabian Fantasy, cello solo.
Arkansas Traveler, trad., arr.
At Twilight Time, l W. Heagney, © 1929.
Auld Lang Syne, from *That Girl from Paris,* 1936.
Autumn Poem, from Season Poems.
Ay, Ay, Ay, by Friere, modern version: l H. Lawrence, music by Nathaniel Shilkret, 1939.
Ay Que Me Vengo, l L. W. Gilbert, paraphrased, © 1937.

Baby's Blue.
Ballet Eternelle, from *Shall We Dance,* 1936.
Beautiful Blue Danube, see *Blue Danube Waltz.*

A Beautiful Day, as Niel Hallett, ca 1950.
Beer Is Here.
Believe It or Not, 1 C. Tobias, © 1929.
La Bella Sorentia, from *Woman Rebels*, 1936.
Betty, theme song of *Synthetic Sin*, © 1928.
Bible Stories for Children, background music for record album, 1948.
Blue Bonnets, from *Mary of Scotland*, 1936.
Blue Danube Waltz, from *That Girl from Paris*, 1936.
*Blue Tint, from 2nd Movement of Concerto for Trombone.
Blue Waters, 1 N. Washington, © 1929.
Bohemian Girl, main title of *Bohemian Girl*, © 1936.
La Boite a Joujoux, by C. DeBussy, arr, 1952.
Boy Meets Dog, from *Boy Meets Dog*, 1938.
Braided Man's Song.
*Brazilian Love Song, arr.
*Breezing Along, as Niel Hallett.
Bridge Love Song, from *Winterset*, 1936.
A Busy Day (In a Soprano's Life), written for Rosa Ponselle, but never
    used, 1 P. Johnstone, © 1944.
*Buttonwood Tree, 1 H. Richardson, 1955.
By Myself, 1 G. Delworth, with K. McLeod, © 1929.
By-U By-O, as Mack Fenton (name Fenton does not appear on sheet
    music), © 1941.

Carmen Fantasy, cornet solo.
Carmen Selections, by Bizet, arr, by 1940.
*Catch Song, as Niel Hallett, ca 1960.
Chanson Triste, by A. Gretchaninoff, arr, © 1929.
Chant D'Amour, by A. Gretchaninoff, arr, © 1929.
Charmed.
Chasing Rainbows, main title from *Bonefish and Barricuda*, 1955.
Christmas Overture, © 1940.
Cielito Lindo, arr, 1939.
*Ciribiribin, arr, by 1938.
Clarinet Entr'acte, as Niel Hallett, ca 1950.
Clarinet Quintet, ?1939.
Closer to Me, L. W. Gilbert, © 1929.
Comic Polka, as Niel Hallett, ca 1950.
Concerto for Horn, with H. Shilkret, 1952.
Concerto for Trombone, © 1942.
Constant Love, © 1929.
*A Country Dance, as Niel Hallett.
*Cradle Song, ?1915.

The Crazy, Cool Musician in Between, from the 3rd Movement of the
  Concerto for Trombone, 1953.
Creation, from Genesis Suite, © 1945.
Cuban Eyes, with J. Shilkret, 1 I. Caeser, © 1921.
La Cucaracha.
Cuckoo Waltz, Norwegian folk song, arr, ca 1940.

Dance of the Toy Regiment, with J. P. Green, © 1922 (also 1925).
Dancing in a Dream, 1 A. J. Neiburg and S. Mysels, © 1938.
Dancing Stars, xylophone solo, with J. Green, ?1927.
Dancing Tonight, 1 J. Owens, © 1956.
Dancing with an Angel, 1 L. W. Gilbert, © 1935.
Days of Hearts and Flowers, by T. M. Tobani, arr, © 1925.
Death and Final Chords, from Toast of New York, 1937.
Deck the Altar, from The O'Flynn, 1935.
Desire, from Toast of New York, 1937.
Divertissement for Clarinet, see Sextet for Clarinet.
Dorina.
Dorothy and the Wizard of Oz, new music for record album, 1949.
Down the River of Golden Dreams, 1 J. Klenner, © 1929.
Dreamy Rivers, 1 S. Lerner.
Drinking Song, from The O'Flynn, 1935.
Drums of All Nations.
Drunken Song, from The O'Flynn, 1935.

*An Easy Goin' Feller, ?1915.
Eili, Eili, arr, © 1934.
Electricity (March), © 1929.
Ellen, Sweet Ellen, love song for Lady of the Lake, 1 M. Ryskind, © 1929.
Emotional Conflict, for RCA Magic Key, 1939.
Espana Cani, from There Goes My Girl, 1937.
*Eve, from 2nd Movement of Concerto for Trombone.
Eveready Battery Suite, from the The Eveready Hour.
*Exotic Waltz, originally as Nat Hilbert, ca 1915.

*Fancy Free, as Niel Hallett.
*Fantasy, as Niel Hallett.
Farewell Malihini, previously copyright as Salute to Beautiful Hawaii, ©
  1936.
Fate (Tango Valentino), 1 D. MacBoyle, © 1927.
*Feeding the Pigeons and Squirrels.
Feliz Compleaños, Niel Hallett, ca 1950.
Fern der Heimat, 1 J. Frank, © 1926.

Fiddle on the Griddle, ?arr.
The Fight, from *RCA Magic Key*, 1939.
Firefly Scherzo, violin solo.
The First Time I Saw You, from *Toast of New York*, 1937.
First Time in Love, based on Grieg's *Letzter Frühling*.
Die Fledermaus Selection, by J. Strauss, Jr., arr.
Flirtation, from *Toast of New York*, 1937.
Flowers of Springtime, from *It Happened in Paris*, © 1932.
Folk Song, by R. Schumann, arr, 1939.
For He's a Jolly Good Fellow, from *Shall We Dance*, 1936.
For Old Atlantic, from *The Big Game*, 1936.
For You Are Love, from *Walking on Air*, 1936.
Fragrance Waltz, dedicated to Harry James, 1943.
French Ballet Class, from *Shall We Dance*, 1936.
*Friendly Gathering, as Niel Hallett.
Fun in the Sun, see *Snappy Weather*.
Funny Business.
The Fur Coat, one act opera, 1 D. Madaleva (aka J. Beni), 1958.

Der Galizianer Batchen, 1 L. Gilrod, with J. Feldman, © 1922.
The Garden Rose, for *Rogue Song* on *The Palmolive Beauty Box Theater*, 1934.
Gavotte, by Gossec, arr, © 1937.
Genesis Suite, see *Creation*.
Gently Down the Stream, one act opera, 1 D. Madaleva (aka J. Beni), 1958.
Gershwin Memorial Album, by G. Gershwin, arr, 1938.
Ginger Polka, dedicated to Pal, 1942 (?used earlier in 1935 Fitzpatrick travelogue).
Go Get a Bite to Eat, fox-trot, originally the finale to the first act of an *Eveready Hour* broadcast, 1 A. Miller, ca 1927.
*Go Your Way, with J. Shilkret, as J. and N. Hilbert.
*Golden Bells, from *Messer Marco Polo*, 1 H. Wey.
Graceful and Elegant, from *Shall We Dance*, 1936.
*Graceful Waltz, as Niel Hallett.
*Grandfather's Schottische, 1956.
Great American Home (several subtitles) from *Yankee Doodle Home*, 1939.
Green Eyes, Russian folk song, used in *Rogue Song* on *Palmolive Beauty Box Theater*, 1934.
*Gypsy Campfire Song, as Niel Hallett.
Gypsy Vagabond, see *My Gypsy Vagabond*.

Hail to Our Royal James, from *The O'Flynn*, 1935.
Halfwit, from *Winterset*, 1936.
Happy and Light of Heart.
Happy Farmer Op 68 No 10, by R. Schumann, arr, 1939.
Hark! The Years, background music for record album, 1950.
Harvesters' March.
Have You Forgotten, l L. Robin, by D. Suesse and L. Spier, based on
    Syncopated Love Song by D. Suesse and N. Shilkret, 1931.
The Heart Bowed Down, from *Bohemian Girl*, © 1936.
Heart of a Gypsy, l R. Shayon, © 1936.
Hearts and Flowers, see *Days of Hearts and Flowers.*
He's Mine, l Gene Austin, © 1947.
Hindenburg March.
Hippolyte et Aricie, by J. Rameau, arr.
A Home, a Rainbow and You, l P. Cunningham, © 1950.
Home Sweet Home, from *That Girl from Paris*, 1936.
Horn Concerto, see *Concerto for Horn.*
***Humoresque**, clarinet and string quartet.
Humoresque Op 101, No 7, by A. Dvořák, arr, © 1931.
The Hundred Pipers, from *Mary of Scotland*, 1936.
Hunting Song, by R. Schumann, arr, 1939.
Hurdy Gurdy Effect, from *Winterset*, 1936.
Huskin Bee Dance, traditional, arr, 1925.
Hymn to the Sun, Peruvian tunes by D. Roble, arr, 1926.

***I Do Not Think Where 'Er Thou Art**, ca 1915.
I Dreamt I Dwelt in a Marble Hall, from *Bohemian Girl*, 1936.
I Found the Old Gold Locket, l N. Cogane and S. Mysels, © 1940.
I Get a Happy Feeling.
I Hate to Go Home Without You, l C. Gaskill, © 1932.
I Know It All, as Niel Hallett, © 1952.
I Love You More Than Life, Dear, 1941.
I Love You Truly, from *That Girl from Paris*, 1936.
I Rosen Doft, arr, 1925.
I Spoke to the Moon, as Mack Fenton, 1941.
I Will Give You the Keys to Heaven, arr.
Iceland, transcribed, © 1925.
If I Should Send a Rose, l R. Shayon, © 1935.
I'll Be Close to You, l S. Coslow, with B. Shefter, © 1940.
I'll Be Seeing You, see *I'll Be Close to You.*
I'll Dream of You, with J. Shilkret, © 1927.
I'm A-Rockin' in the Saddle, l F. Luther, © 1937.
I'm Dancing with an Angel, see *Dancing with an Angel.*

Impression Hebraique, 1920.
*Impromptu, cello solo, ?ca 1915.
*In a Pensive Mood, as Niel Hallett, 1960.
In a Whimsical Mood, as Niel Hallett, ca 1950.
In the Gypsy Life, from *Bohemian Girl*, © 1936.
In the Lane, Russian folk dance, from *Relaxation Time*, 1939.
In the Woods, Russian folk dance, from *Relaxation Time*, 1939.
*The Indian Summer, originally titled *Spring*.
*Infant Joy, ?1915.
Irish Melody, as Niel Hallett, arr, © 1954.
It Looks Like Rain.
Italian Airs, medley, arr, © 1938.
Italian Street Song, from *Mary of Scotland*, 1936.
It's a Brand New Flag, also labelled *Our Flag Patrol*.
It's Better to Be Fancy Free, from *The O'Flynn*, 1935.

Jasbo Brown, l De Bose Heyward, for the *Eveready Hour*, revised 1935.
Jealous Ballerina, © 1948.
Jealousy, from *Toast of New York*, 1937.
Jeannine, I Dream of Lilac Time, l L. W. Gilbert, © 1928.
*Jenny Kissed Me, ca 1915, revised ca 1960.
John Brown's Body.
John Nesbitt's Passing Parade, arr.
Joy to the World, see *Adeste Fidelis*.
The Jumping Frog, 1951.
Just a Bit of Sunshine, from *It Happened in Paris*, © 1932.
Just a Romantic Fool, with L. Erdody and J. Klenner, © 1933.
Just a Spot on the Horizon, l S. Rich and R. Brody, 1952.
Just a Sweetheart, with J. Pasternak and D. Dreyer, © 1928.
Just Another Kiss, with J. Shilkret, as J. and N. Hilbert, © 1919.
*Just Dance Your Troubles Away.

*The Keen Stars Were Twinkling, ca 1915, revised ca 1960.
Keep It Dark.
Kiddie Kapers, with L. Pollack and A. Sherman, © 1928.
Kije's Wedding, by Prokofiev, arr.
King of the Road, from *Music for Madame*, 1937.
*Kingdom of the Sea, with Rex Schepp.
Kiss 'n Miss, originally titled *The Kissing Cigarette*, ?revised 1952.
Kodak Signature, l H. J. Colwell, © 1930.
Koenigskiller.
Kol Nidre, arr, © 1934.

Ladies of Paree, from *It Happened in Paris,* 1932.
Lady Divine, theme song of *Lady Divine,* 1 R. Kountz, © 1929.
*The Lamb, ca 1915.
Laurel and Hardy Waltz, from *Bohemian Girl,* 1936.
Let Us Sing Our Song of Gladness, R. Schumann, arr, 1939.
Letter Song, from *The O'Flynn,* 1935.
Licorice Bunny, 1 A. Sydney, as Niel Hallett, © 1954.
Liebesfreund, by F. Kreisler, arr.
*Life, ca 1915.
*Life Is But an Empty Dream.
Light and Funny.
Light Regimental, from *Bohemian Girl,* 1936.
Lips Like a Rose, also called *Temptation Waltz,* from *Toast of New York,*
    1937.
*A Little Overture.
Lively Sailors, arr, © 1938.
Loneliest One in Town.
Lonesome Road, 1 G. Austin, 1927.
Look Down That Lonesome Road see *Lonesome Road.*
The Lord Is My Shepherd (23rd Psalm), Biblical lyrics, with M. Terr,
    1942.
Lord Lovat's Lament, from *Gunga Din,* 1939.
Love at First Sight, from *It Happened in Paris,* 1932.
Love Clouds, with L. W. Gilbert and M. Chamlee, © 1935.
Lovely Interlude, 1 R. Jacobs, with B. Shefter, © 1939.
Love's Extasy–Theme Song, "Associated Banks," arr.
*A Love Song, ?1915, ?revised 1930.
*Lullaby.
Luxury, from *Toast of New York,* 1937.

Mad About a Man, also titled *Once There Was A Man* from *Toast of
    New York,* 1937.
Magic of the Dawn, 1 N. Fleeson, © 1931.
March Militaire.
March of the Gnomes, © 1929.
Marching Song of Fair Poland.
Marionette in Motley, by M. Gould, arr, © 1932.
Marseillaise.
Melodramatic, from *Bohemian Girl,* 1936.
*Melody from the 5th Symphony, by P. Tchaikovsky, arr.
*Melody of a Portrait, as Niel Hallett.
*A Memory, 1915, as N. Schildkret, revised ca 1960.
*Memory Hither Come, ?1915, revised ca 1960.

Merry Wives Frolic, adopted from Nicolai's *Merry Wives of Windsor*, as Niel Hallett.

Metropolitan Echoes, main title.

Mexican Moonlight, l K. Gannon, with R. Parker, 1939.

Mimi, Russian folksong, arr, ⓒ 1937.

Minnesota Polka.

***Minuet and Allegro**, solo for clarinet and piano, as N. Schildkret, November 1914.

Moments with You, l J. Yellen, ⓒ 1928.

La Montagnards Sont, from *Swiss Miss*, 1938.

Monterey Country Dance, 1936.

A Mood in Blue, with M. Pollock, ⓒ 1928.

Moon in the River.

Moon Nocturne, piano composition, ⓒ 1933.

Morning Song, from *Boy Meets Dog*, also titled *Reg'lar Fellers*, 1938.

***The Mouse Ran Up the Clock**, originally titled *Monotony*.

***Move On!**

***Music Room**, trio for flute, cello and harp or piano, as N. Schildkret, April 1916.

My Gypsy Vagabond, as Niel Hallett, ca 1950.

My Heart's in the North, from *Mary of Scotland*, 1936.

My Heart's on the Trail, from *The Last Outlaw*, l F. Luther, ⓒ 1936.

My Tears Are Blue, l A. Sydney, as Niel Hallett, ⓒ 1954.

Nancy Lee March, medley, ⓒ 1938.

Negro Spirituals Paraphrase, tone-poem, ⓒ 1938.

The New Champion, from *RCA Magic Key*, 1939.

New York 1910, arr, ca 1950.

New York Ballet '20, by 1942.

New York Sketches, 1920.

***The Night Has a Thousand Eyes**, l W. Bourdillon, as Nat Schildkret, ca 1915, revised ca 1960.

***Nina**, by G. B. Pergolesi, arr, ?ca 1950.

No, No, from *It Happened in Paris*, 1932.

The Northlanders Longing for Home, Swedish folksong, arr, ⓒ 1924.

Norway Folk Tunes, arr, ca 1950.

Nothing to Do, as Niel Hallett.

Now Take Off Your Glasses and Drink Your Fill, from *The O'Flynn*, 1935.

The Nymphs, 1914.

Ode to Victory, overture to *Ode to Victory*, © 1945.
Ola Vienna Gems, with Lanner, as Niel Hallett.
Old Colonel March, © 1928.
The Old Gold Locket, see *I Found the Old Gold Locket.*
On the Meadows, Russian folk dance, 1939.
Once There Was a Man, see *Mad About A Man.*
Once upon a Time, as Niel Hallett, © 1954.
Ooh La La, from *Toast of New York*, 1937.
The Operetta Sequence, from *The Woman I Love*, 1937.
The Organ Grinder, from *Winterset*, 1936.
Original Greek Blues, 1928.
Our Flag Patrol, see *It's A Brand New Flag.*
Out West Where the North Begins, 1 L. W. Gilbert, © 1931.
Overture, from *Bohemian Girl*, 1936.

Painted Desert, with N. Feinstock, 1939.
La Paloma (The Dove), new version and lyric with H. Lawrence.
La Palomita Tango, arr.
Parade of the Wooden Soldiers, by L. Jessel, for the *Mobiloil Concert*,
    ca 1931.
Paris 1890, as Niel Hallett, arr, ca 1952.
Parting Song, from *The O'Flynn*, 1935.
Pennsylvania Special, railroad song, 1927.
Perfume, as Niel Hallett, ca 1950.
Perpetual Motion, from 3rd Movement of *Concerto for Trombone.*
The Pest, as Niel Hallett, ca 1950.
Petite Serenade, as Niel Hallett.
*Piping Down the Valley, ?1915.
*Pizzicato Pluckers, as Niel Hallett.
Plantation Dance, a southern humoresque, © 1930.
Pledge Song, from *The O'Flynn*, 1935.
Poem No. 1 (Summer), © 1923.
Poems, see *Autumn Poem* and *Poem No. 1.*
Polite Society, © 1929.
*Polonaise Grandioso, as Niel Hallett.
Pop Goes the Weasel, traditional, with R. Wilkinson, arr, by 1938.
Precocious Child, © 1928.
Prelude, cello solo, 1915.
Prelude and Dance, with R. Schepp.
A Pretty Little Lassie, ?ca 1915, ?revised ca 1960.
Prisoner's Song, © 1936.
Puss in Boots, two songs for voice and piano, 1 R. Shayon, © 1932.

The Quarrel, with A. Gretchaninoff.
Queen Mary, from *Shall We Dance*, 1936.
Quintet for Clarinet, see *Clarinet Quintet*.
Quintopland, main title, © 1938.

Radio Fanfare, from *Walking on Air*, 1936.
*Rambling Thoughts, piano solo with orchestra.
*Retort, ?1915, ?revised ca 1960.
Ricca-Ricca, from *Woman Rebels*, 1936.
The Riding Club March, ca 1929.
Rigaundon et Musette, by J. P. Rameau, arr.
Road of Romance, l S. Lerner, © 1930.
Romance, by P. Tchaikovsky, arr.
*Rondo Capriccioso, as Niel Hallett.
Route Solitaire.
Row, Row, Row Your Boat, paraphrase with I. Szathmary, © 1938.
Rule Brittania.
Russian Arabesque, flute solo, as Nat Schildkret, ?1915, revised 1943.

Sad Comic, from *Bohemian Girl* and *General Spanky*, 1936.
Salut! Mios Amigos, as Niel Hallett.
Sand Dance, with R. Schepp, ca 1945.
Sass (Sarsaparilla), for Hire's broadcast, ca 1926.
Saturday Night Dance, traditional, arr, ca 1950.
*Say It Again, and Again, as Niel Hallett.
Scaramouche, by J. Sibelius, arr, ca 1950.
A Sea Mist.
Season Poems, see *Autumn Poem* and *Poem No. 1 (Summer)*.
See the Train, from *Toast of New York*, 1937.
*See You Pale Flower, ca 1915.
*Serenade, as Niel Hallett.
Serenade Rhapsodic, ca 1943.
Sextet for Clarinet, ?based on Mozart.
Shilkret Review, (entry based on a list written by Nat Shilkret).
Shortnin' Bread, by J. Wolfe, arr.
Sidewalks of New York, see *Welcome to New York Overture*.
Silence the Lady Moon, from *Bohemian Girl*, 1936.
*Skip Along, as Niel Hallett.
Skyward, © 1934.
Smartest Girl in Town, from *Smartest Girl in Town*, 1936.
Snappy Weather, also called *Fun in the Sun*, © 1929.
*So We'll Go No More A-Roamin', ca 1915.
Soaring (Flight), polka, solo for cornet, 1930.

Soldier's March, by R. Schumann, arr, 1939.

Some Sweet Day, theme song of *Children of the Ritz*, 1929.

Somebody Like You, from *Love Letters*, l H. Rogers, with J. Shilkret, 1920.

*Somewhere, as Nat Schildkret, ?February 1915.

*A Song, ?1915.

Song of the Bayou, by R. Bloom, arr, © 1929.

*Song of the Talley Ho, for *Quality Street* but not used, 1937.

Song of Vengeance, for *Rogue Song* on the *Palmolive Beauty Box Theater*, 1934.

*Spanish Dance.

Spanish Song, from *The O'Flynn*, 1935.

Sparks, as Niel Hallett, 1962.

Specie Americano, based on 3rd movemment of *Concerto for Trombone*, arr by P. Moore, © 1944.

Spinach Song, used in *Puss in Boots*, 1930.

Spring, as Nat Schildkret, ca 1915.

*A Spring Lilt, ca 1915, revised ca 1960.

Stephen Foster Album, paraphrase No. 5, S. Foster, arr, 1938.

Street Sketches, as Nat. Schildkret, © 1916.

*Strolling through the Park, as Niel Hallett.

Stuart Song, from *Mary of Scotland*, 1936.

Summer Poem, see *Poem No. 1*.

Sweet Carmen, as Ned Arthur, 1923.

Sweet Lady Walk with Me?, from *The O'Flynn*, 1935.

Sweet Thoughts, based on R. Schumann's *Little Study*, 1939.

Swing Crazy, from *Walking on Air*, 1936.

*Swiss Music Box, as Niel Hallett.

Syncopated Love Song, with D. Suesse, © 1930.

Take Care, for Acne Care commercial, 1959.

Take Off, background music for *Aviation Sketch* of *RCA Magic Key*, 1939.

*Tangerine Moon Song, originally titled *Dancing in the Moonlight*.

Tango Valentino, see *Fate*.

Tannhauser Overture, from *Music for Madame*, 1937.

Tannhauser Venusberg, from *Music for Madame*, 1937.

Tea Leaves, as Niel Hallett.

Temptation Waltz, see *Lips Like a Rose*.

Theme of Justice, from *Winterset*, 1936.

Then You'll Remember Me, from *Bohemian Girl*, 1936.

This Is Our Day, Beloved, l H. Richardson and M. Ortden, 1955.

Three Blind Mice, traditional, with I. Szathmary, arr, © 1938.

Through the Blue, melody from *Moonlight Nocturne*, 1945.

La Touraine, march, © 1929.
Trammin' at the Fair, with B. Shefter, © 1939.
Traumerei, Op 15, No 7, by R. Schuman, arr, © 1931.
Trial of the Banjo, on a Kodak broadcast on WABC, by J. L. O'Keefe,
     ?arr.
*Tricks.
Trombone Concerto, see *Concerto for Trombone*.
Twilight Mood, from 3rd Movement of *Clarinet Quintent*, 1939.
Two Guitars, Russian Gypsy song, arr, by 1926.
*Two Jolly Trumpeters, as Niel Hallett.
The Two Sentries, as Niel Hallett, ca 1950.

The Ugly Duckling, as Niel Hallett, © 1954.
Una Furtiva Lagrima, from *That Girl from Paris*, 1936.
Una Voce Poco Fa, from *That Girl from Paris*, 1936.
Up and Down the Stairs, from *Walking on Air*, 1936.

Valleys and Hills, from *Bohemian Girl*, 1936.
*Valse Bluette.
Vanilla Blossoms, tango, ?used in *Holland in Tulip Time*, by 1927.
Vanity, from *Toast of New York*, 1937.
Victor March, see *Victory*.
Victory, for Victor demonstration (1925 and 1929) and signature song for
     radio shows *Victor Radio-Record Revue* (1931–1932) and *His Mas-
     ter's Voice* (1932–1933), 1925.
Vienna Bouquet, medley of Viennese favorites, as Niel Hallett, ca 1950.
Vienna Cabmen Song, arr, © 1938.
A Vision, flute solo, 1938.
Vive la Femme, from *It Happened in Paris*, 1932.

*Wake Up, Wake Up, Dear Molly, as Niel Hallett.
Waltz, from *Bohemian Girl*, 1936.
Waltz, from P. Tchaikovsky's *Serenade for Strings*, arr, by 1940.
Was It So, folk lyric, January 24, 1967.
Wee Bit O' Heart, for violin with piano, © 1922 and 1925.
Welcome Chorus, from *The O'Flynn*, 1935.
Welcome to New York Overture, six movements: 1) New York Hurry
     Theme; 2) East Side, West Side (Sidewalks of New York); 3) Wel-
     come to New York and Times Square Overture; 4) In Old New York;
     5) The Bowery; 6) Sidewalks of New York, 1st and 3rd Movements
     by Nat Shilkret, for *RCA Magic Key*, 1939.
We're All Together Again.
Western Waltz Ballet, 1963.

*What a Glorious Day, as Niel Hallett.
*Wherefore, Wherefore?, as Arthur Harold, ca 1915.
Whirlwind Polka, with J. Green.
*Who Knows?, ca 1915.
Why?, as Niel Hallett.
Why Dream About Tomorrow, never finished.
Wie Ayaÿ Leibt a Keinik (How Does a King Live), l J. Feldman, melody
     adapted and arr by J. Feldman and N. H. Shilkret © 1922.
Wig Wag, with B. Shefter.
Winter in My Heart, from *The O'Flynn*, 1935.
Winterset, from *Winterset*, 1936.
Wipin' the Pan, l W. Robison, with A. Baer, © 1928.
Wistaria, as Niel Hallett, 1959.
Wizard of Oz, see *Dorothy and the Wizard of Oz*.
A Work of Art, one act opera, libretto never completed.

Yankee Doodle, theme and scherzo variations, from Toast of New York,
     1937.
*Young Ballerina's Dream, originally titled *A Little Ballerina's Dream*.
You're My Bit of Sunshine, see *Just a Bit of Sunshine*, 1933.

APPENDIX B
SELECTIVE RECORD
DISCOGRAPHY

Prepared with the assistance of Brian Rust and Harry Friedland

Recordings are by Victor unless stated otherwise. The format for entries, when applicable and the data are available, is

Title (Foreign Language) ⟨Author(s)⟩, Album Number, Matrix Number, Record Catalogue Number, Year, Month/Day, Recording Artist(s).

The following abbreviations are used: acc NS-piano for accompanied by Nathaniel Shilkret on the piano, acc (King's) O/NS for accompanied by (King's) orchestra directed by Nathaniel Shilkret, arr for arranged by, Int'l Nov O for International Novelty Orchestra, O for Orchestra, Vic for Victor and NS Vic O for Nat Shilkret and the Victor Orchestra.

1. Earliest documented recordings by Nat Shilkret:

Cavatina (French) ⟨Gounod⟩, —, trial, 1917, 4/18, Miss O. Belloy, acc NS-piano.

Sérénade Française (French), —, trial, 1917, 4/18, Miss O. Belloy, acc NS-piano.

Zoo ik ware een vogel klein (Flemish), —, trial, 1917, 4/18, Miss O. Belloy, acc NS-piano.

Vaagn af din Slummer (Norwegian), 20277-3, rejected, 1917, 8/8, Carsten Woll, acc NS-piano.

Vaagn af din Slummer (Norwegian), 20277-6, rejected, 1917, 8/9, Carsten Woll, acc NS-piano.

Ales Bam Fetter (Jewish) ⟨Louis Friedsell⟩, 20975-2, rejected, 1917, 11/13, Jacob Jacobs, acc King's O/NS.

'O Volontario (Italian) ⟨Prof. Cav. A. Salmaggie-E. G. Pasqualotto⟩, 20178-6, rejected, 1917, 11/20, Prof. Cav. A. Salmaggie, acc King's O/NS.

Rispetti All'Antica (Italian) ⟨Armando Gill-M. Testa⟩, 20179-4, rejected, 1917, 11/20, Prof. Cav. A. Salmaggie, acc King's O/NS.

Primavera Di Baci (Italian) ⟨Ferrara Correra-P. E. Fonzo⟩, 20180-6, rejected, 1917, 11/20, Prof. Cav. A. Salmaggie, acc King's O/NS.

Le Drapeau De Carillon (French) ⟨Octave Cremazie-Ch. W. Sabatier⟩, 21100-2, rejected, 1917, 11/20, Joseph Martel, acc King's O/NS.

Ko Dan Se Zaznava (Slovak), 21105-2, rejected, 1917, 11/22, Milka Schneid, acc King's O/NS.

In Pădurea (Roumanian), 21106-2, rejected, 1917, 11/22, Milka Schneid, acc King's O/NS.

Noćhi Strazari (Serbo-Croatian), 21107-2, rejected, 1917, 11/22, Nikola Zaninović, acc King's O/NS.

Ma Te Mislim (Serbo-Croatian), 21108-2, 72754, 1917, 11/22, Nikola Zaninović, acc King's O/NS.

Šta Cutiš Srbine Tužni (Serbo-Croatian) ⟨L. Jenks, arr Slavoljub Lzicar⟩, 21109-1, 69985, 1917, 11/22, Nikola Zaninović, acc King's O/NS.

I Should Worry (Jewish) ⟨Louis Friedsell⟩, 21110-2, 69999, 1917, 11/22, Anna Hoffman-Jacob Jacobs, acc King's O/NS.

Hot Nit Chosena (Jewish) ⟨Lillian⟩, 21111-2, rejected, 1917, 11/22, Anna Hoffman-Jacob Jacobs, acc King's O/NS.

---

2. The earliest recordings now in the Nathaniel Shilkret Archives, kindly transferred and audio engineered for us by Timo Wuori and the Finnish Institute of Recorded Sound:

Kullan Ylistys (Finnish) ⟨traditional⟩, 21303-2, 72768, 1917, 12/26, Elli Soukas, acc King's O/NS.

Iloa Ja Surua (Finnish) ⟨traditional⟩, 21304-1, 72768, 1917, 12/26, Elli Soukas, acc King's O/NS.

---

3. The first recording of a commercial electrically made record:

Joan of Arkansas ⟨Gilpin⟩, 32160-2, 19626, 1925, 3/16, Mask and Wig Club Double Male Quartet, acc O/NS.

---

4. Grammy award winning recordings: Nat Shilkret conducted all of the recordings listed below but was the recipient of the Grammy Award only for *An American in Paris*; the awards for the other recordings were given to the artist named on the label.

Rhapsody in Blue ⟨George Gershwin⟩, A30173-4, 35822, 1927, 4/21, piano: George Gershwin. *Note:* Whiteman is listed on the label; Nathaniel Shilkret conducted.

My Blue Heaven ⟨Whiting-George Donaldson⟩, 39179, 20964, also 24573, 1927, 9/14, Gene Austin, acc O/NS.

An American in Paris ⟨George Gershwin⟩, 49710–49713, 35963–35964, 1929, 2/4, Vic Symphony O, piano: George Gershwin.

Ballad for Americans ⟨Earl Robinson⟩, P20, BS047035-1 to BS047038-1, 26516–26517, 1940, 2/9, Paul Robeson, acc O/NS.

---

5. An All Star Orchestra recording with a truly all-star list of personnel, including, as Stockdale [1995] wrote in his discography, "two trombonists and a clarinetist who would go on to become big names in the thirties record[ing] together for the first [and we believe the only] time." We quote below Stockdale's entry, which shows more detail than other entries in this discography:

Victor, New York, N.Y., March 21, 1928
ALL STAR ORCHESTRA
Nat Shilkret (ldr) Ray Lodwig, Fuzzy Farrar, Jimmy McPartland (tp) Tommy Dorsey, Glenn Miller (tb) Dudley Fosdick (mel) Benny Goodman (cl) Max Farley (cl, as) Fud Livingston (cl, ts) Joe Venuti, Lou Raderman (vn) Milt Rettenberg (p) Carl Kress (bj, g) Joe Tarto (bb) Chauncey Morehouse (d, vib) Scrappy Lambert (vcl)

BVE 43384-2 I'm More Than Satisfied vSL (TD solo)
    78: Victor 21605
    LP: Broadway BR103
BVE 43385-1 Oh, Baby! vSL (TD solo)
    78: Victor 21423
    LP: Sunbeam SB112
BVE 43385-2 Oh, Baby! vSL (TD solo)
    LP: RCA (F) FXMI-7283

6. The following recordings conducted by Nat Shilkret made the No. 1 position on the charts (source: Whitburn [1986] for charting position; Rust and record labels otherwise):

Tonight You Belong to Me, 36989-2, 20371, 1926, 12/1, Gene Austin, acc O/NS.

Forgive Me, 38172-2, 20561, 1927, 3/15, Gene Austin, acc O/NS, pianos: Jack Shilkret and Milton Rettenberg.

My Blue Heaven ⟨Whiting-Donaldson⟩, 39179, 20964, also 24573, 1927, 9/14, Gene Austin, acc O/NS.

Ramona ⟨Wayne⟩, 42584-3, 21334, 1928, 4/2, Gene Austin acc O/NS.

Jeannine (I Dream of Lilac Time) ⟨L. Wolfe Gilbert-N. Shilkret⟩, 45297-3, 21564A, 1928, 6/26, Gene Austin, acc O/NS.

Carolina Moon ⟨Burke⟩, 48447-2, 21833, 1928, 12/10, Gene Austin, acc O/NS.

When It's Springtime in the Rockies, 58599-2, 22339A, 1930, 2/24, Hilo Hawaiian O, vocal: Frank Luther and Carson Robison, whistling: Carson Robison.

Dancing with Tears in My Eyes ⟨Burke-Dubin⟩, 62218-2, 22425, 1930, 5/12, NS Vic O, vocal: Lewis James.

---

7. Albums and longer recordings (see also "4. Grammy Award Winning Recordings" for Album P20 and "8. Shilkret conducts Shilkret" for Albums P218, Aztec 248, Capitol Albums DBS 92 and 94, ECD3047 and T2334):

Caucasian Sketches: In the Village ⟨Ippolitow-Iwanow, arr N. Shilkret⟩, 27602-2, 68633A (in U.S.: 68632), 1923, 2/17, International Concert O.

Russian Dances: Russkaya i Trepak ⟨Rubinstein⟩, 28522-2, 68633B (in U.S.: 68632), 1923, 8/31, International Concert O.

1812 Overture, Parts 1 and 2 ⟨Tschaikowsky, Op. 49⟩, 26552-6 and 26553-13, 35729A–B, 1923, 6/1 and 9/26, Vic Symphony O.

The Music of Victor Herbert, Vol. 1, C1, 9145–9149, 1927, 10/10–12/29, Vic Salon Group, Vic Concert O and Vic Light Opera Company, acc O/NS.

Fairy Hill Overture, Parts 1 and 2 ⟨Fr. Kuhlau⟩, 68727A–B, Vic Symphony O.

Raymond Overture, Parts 1 and 2 ⟨Thomas⟩, 45155-2 and 45156-2, 35924A-B, 1928, 5/21, Vic Symphony O.

Die Fledermaus ⟨Johann Strauss⟩, 45158-2 and 55160-3, 35956A-B, 1928, 5/21, Vic Symphony O.

The Music of Stephen Foster, C2, 9246–9249, 1928, 6/13–6/29, Vic Salon Group, and NS Vic O with the Jubilee Singers.

An Hour with Schubert, C3, 6927–6928 and 9307–9308, 1928, 11/16–1929, 1/17, John McCormack and the Vic Salon Group and Vic Salon O.

The Music of Ethelbert Nevin, C5, 9478–9482, 1929, 6/27–8/26, Vic Salon Group.

New Year's Eve in New York (Werner Janssen), 53482-5, 53483-5 and 53484-2, 35986A-35987A, 1929, 7/17 and 7/31, Vic Symphony O. *Note:* **Skyward** is on 35987B; records 35986–35987 were also issued with the numbers 36157–36158. As of this writing, this is the only recording of this important work by Werner Janssen.

Zampa, Parts 1 and 2 (Herold), 55656-3 and 55657-2, 35985A–B, 1929, 8/28, Vic Symphony O.

The Music of Rudolf Friml, C9, 9649–9653, 1929, 11/29–1930, 3/18, Vic Salon Group.

Sérénade Mélancolique (Tchaikovsky), 63295-2 and 63296-2, 7744A–B, 1930, 8/25, Mischa Elman, acc O/NS.

The Music of Victor Herbert, Vol. 2, C11, 9903–9907, 1930, ?10/29–11/2, Vic Salon O and Vic Salon Group.

Skyscrapers (John Alden Carpenter), M130, 11250–11252, 1932, 5/1, Vic Symphony O.

Gems from Romberg Operettas, C24, 11792–11796, 1935, 4/27–5/11, Nathaniel Shilkret and the Vic Light Opera Company.

My Man's Gone Now (from album **Highlights from Porgy and Bess**), C25, 11881B, 1935, 10/23. *Note:* The remaining five sides of the album were conducted by Alexander Smallens; the album label is our source of information.

Most Beloved Songs, C27, 4366-4371, 1937, 6/24–7/2, Nelson Eddy.

Gershwin Memorial Album, C29, 12332-12336, 1938, 7/10, Jane Froman, Felix Knight, Sonny Schuyler and the Vic Salon Group.

The Music of Victor Herbert, Vol. 2, C33, 12589–12593, 1939, 7/10, Vic Salon Group and Vic Concert O. *Note:* Nat Shilkret's third Herbert album not only duplicated the labeling "Vol. 2," but also some of the songs are the same as in Volume 1 and the original Volume 2; as noted in chapter 7 of the autobiography, the recordings were all new. Reissues of album C33 were labelled "Vol. 1."

I Hear America Singing, M777, 18009-18010, 1940, John Charles Thomas, acc I.L.G.W.U. Radio Chorus (directed by Simon Rady) and Vic Symphony O.

Tschaikowsky Program, 046471–76, P15, 26486–26488, 1940, 1/19, Vic Salon O.

Sibelius Melodies, P23, 26583–26585, 1940, 4/2, Vic Salon O.

Ziegfeld Follies Hits, 051227–32, P45, 26777–26779, 1940, 6/15, Vic Salon O.

Let's Dance, 051827–32, P37, 26679–26681, 1940, 7/9, Troubadours.

Robin Hood, P35, 26698–26700, 1940, Victor Junior Programs Opera Company.

Hansel and Gretel, P38, 26701–26704, 1940, Victor Junior Programs Opera Company.

Viennese Gayeties, 056100–05, P44, 26774–26776, 1940, 9/11, Vic Salon Group.

Paris '90 (Kay Swift), produced and performed by Cornelia Otis Skinner, Columbia ML4619, 1952, 3/4.

---

8. Shilkret conducts (or plays) Shilkret (see also "11. The SESAC Transcriptions" for twenty-six additional recordings, some composed using the pseudonym Niel Hallett).

Kuutamo ⟨arr N. Shilkret⟩, 23681-5, 1920, 2/18, quartet, clarinet: N. Shilkret.

Dance of the Toy Regiment ⟨Joe Green-N. Shilkret⟩, 26694-2, 73438A, 1922, 7/17, Int'l Nov O, xylophone: Joe Green. *Note:* This was also issued as record number 73947.

Sweet Carmen-Tango ⟨N. Shilkret⟩, 27463-2, 73927B, 1923, 2/7, Int'l Nov O.

Wee Bit 'O Heart ⟨N. Shilkret⟩, 28750-1, 19538A, 1923, 10/16, Michael Gusikoff (violin), acc O/NS.

Ay, Ay, Ay ⟨Osman Pérez Freire, arr N. Shilkret⟩, 32471-4, 19703A, 1925, 4/24, Vic Salon O, extra celeste: Leroy Shield.

Dance of the Toy Regiment ⟨Joe Green-N. Shilkret⟩, 33346-4, 19849A, 1925, 8/26, Vic Salon O, xylophone: Joe Green.

Days of Hearts and Flowers ⟨Jack Mahoney-Theodore Tobani-N. Shilkret⟩, 33361-7, 19790, 1925, 9/15, Whiteman O, dir N. Shilkret.

Paulina-Polka ⟨arr N. Shilkret⟩, 34183-4, 78494B, 1925, 12/29, International Novelty Duo, piano: N. Shilkret.

Mountain Beauty-Waltz ⟨arr N. Shilkret⟩, 34184-4, 78494B, 1925, 12/29, International Novelty Quartet.

Fate (Tango Valentino) ⟨N. Shilkret⟩, 36934-1, 20454B, 1926, 11/15, Int'l Nov O.

Hearts and Flowers ⟨Theodore Tobani, ?arr N. Shilkret⟩, 2328-12, 35922, 1927, 1/14, Vic Concert O.

Lonesome Road ⟨Gene Austin-N. Shilkret⟩, 39188-2, 21098, 1927, 9/16, Gene Austin, acc O/NS.

Moments with You ⟨Jack Yellen-N. Shilkret⟩, 42446-3, 21327B, 1928, 2/16, NS Vic O (as Troubadours), vocal: The Silver-Masked Tenor.

Original Greek Blues ⟨Tetos Demetriades-N. Shilkret⟩, 43304-, 68978, 1928, 3/1, Int'l Nov O, vocal: Tetos Demetriades.

Original Greek Blues ⟨N. Shilkret⟩, ?43363-2, V-41A, ?1928, ?3/15, Int'l Nov O.

Betty ⟨Harold Christy-N. Shilkret⟩, 49173-1, 21838B, 1928, 6/12, NS Vic O, vocal: Franklyn Baur.

Jeannine (I Dream of Lilac Time) ⟨L. Wolfe Gilbert-N. Shilkret⟩, 45297-3, 21564A, 1928, 6/26, Gene Austin, acc O/NS.

Kiddie Kapers ⟨Pollack-Sherman-N. Shilkret⟩, 46324-3, 21588B, 1928, 7/19, Arden-Ohman O.

Jeannine (I Dream of Lilac Time) ⟨L. Wolfe Gilbert-N. Shilkret⟩, 46613-3, 21572A, 1928, 7/27, NS Vic O, vocal: Franklyn Baur.

Just a Sweetheart ⟨Dreyer-Pasternack-N. Shilkret⟩, 47487-2, 21700B, 1928, 9/23, Lewis James with Shilkret's Rhyth-Melodists, piano: Rettenberg, organ: Krumgold.

Jeannine (I Dream of Lilac Time) ⟨L. Wolfe Gilbert-N. Shilkret⟩, 47776-1, 35945B, 1928, 10/22, Vic Salon Group, directed by Leonard Joy, vocal: Frank Munn, Scrappy Lambert.

Just a Sweetheart ⟨Dreyer-Pasternack-N. Shilkret⟩, 47784-3, 21771A, 1928, 10/25, Arden-Ohman O as NS Vic O, cel: N. Shilkret, voc: Frank Munn.

Wipin' the Pan ⟨Willard Robison-Abel Baer-N. Shilkret⟩, 48137-1, 21835B, 1928, 11/9, Troubadours (as High Hatters), vocal: Lewis James, James Melton, Elliot Shaw, Wilfred Glenn.

Jeannine, I Dream of Lilac Time ⟨L.Wolfe Gilbert-N. Shilkret⟩, 48179-1, 1360B, 1928, 11/19, John McCormack, acc O/NS.

Blue Waters ⟨Ned Washington-N. Shilkret⟩, 49339-3, 21822, 1928, 12/14, Hilo Hawaiian O, vocal: The Four Rajahs.

Some Sweet Day ⟨Lew Pollack-N. Shilkret⟩, 49931-3, 21896B, 1929, 2/7, vocal: Franklyn Baur.

Lady Divine ⟨Richard Kountz-N. Shilkret⟩, 49997-2, 21896A, 1929, 2/27, NS Vic O, vocal: Franklyn Baur.

Lady Divine ⟨Richard Kountz-N. Shilkret⟩, 49998-, 21898A, 1929, 2/27, NS Vic O, issued as Paul Oliver, vocal: Frank Munn.

Some Sweet Day ⟨Lew Pollack-N. Shilkret⟩, 51641-3, 21990, 1929, 4/18, Johnny Marvin, acc O/NS.

The Lonesome Road ⟨Gene Austin-N. Shilkret⟩, 51296-2, 21996A, 1929, 4/26, NS Vic O, vocal: Willard Robison.

Skyward ⟨N. Shilkret⟩, 55658-1, 35987B, 1929, 8/28, Vic Symphony O. *Note:* This was also issued as record number 36158B.

Victor March ⟨N. Shilkret⟩, 56986-3, 22390B, 1929, 11/2, NS Vic O, vocal: Lewis James, James Melton, Elliot Shaw and Wilfred Glenn.

Syncopated Love Song ⟨Dana Suesse-N. Shilkret⟩, 58105-2, 22410A, 1929, 12/13, Vic Salon O.

A Mood in Blue ⟨Muriel Pollock-N. Shilkret⟩, 58107-1, 22410B, 1929, 12/13, Vic Salon O.

Road of Romance ⟨Sammy Lerner-N. Shilkret⟩, ?, 58646A, ca 1930, ?, Mobiloil Concert O, v: Lewis James. *Note*: This record was produced for Mobil Oil to motivate their sales people. A sample broadcast is included in the record, and the broadcast begins with *Road of Romance*.

Down the River of Golden Dreams ⟨John Klenner-N. Shilkret⟩, 58598-1, 22339B, 1930, 2/24, Hilo Hawaiian O, vocal: Johnny Marvin.

The Riding Club March ⟨N. Shilkret⟩, 59640-2, 22390A, 1930, 3/19, NS Vic O.

Down the River of Golden Dreams ⟨John Klenner-N. Shilkret⟩, 59769-3, 22418, 1930, 4/29, Johnny Marvin, acc O/NS.

African Serenade ⟨Harry De Costa-N. Shilkret⟩, 63605-4, 22529A, 1930, 9/9, NS Vic O, vocal: Frank Luther.

Plantation Dance (A Southern Humoresque) ⟨N. Shilkret⟩, 63181-1, 24093A, 1930, 10/29, violin solo: Lou Raderman.

Syncopated Love Song ⟨Dana Suesse-N. Shilkret⟩, (?Shilkington) transcription, JGB 518-3, ?1931, ?, O/NS.

Snappy Weather/Vanilla Blossoms ⟨N. Shilkret⟩, 81995-1, 24856, 1934, 3/31, Vic Salon O.

If I Should Send a Rose ⟨Robert Shayon-N. Shilkret⟩, air check from *The O'Flynn*, Part 2, 1935, 3/1, Milton Watson, acc O/NS.

If I Should Send a Rose ⟨Robert Shayon-N. Shilkret⟩, BS99516, ?, 1935, 6/24, Richard Crooks, acc O/NS.

Christmas Overture ⟨N. Shilkret⟩, ?air check from *Ruppert Relaxation Hour*, —, ?1938, 12/23, Nat Shilkret's O.

Gotham Overture ⟨arr N. Shilkret⟩, air check from *RCA Magic Key*, Side 2, 1939, 7/31, O/NS.

Cuckoo Waltz ⟨Jonasson, arr N. Shilkret⟩, 051831-1, P37, 26681B, 1940, 7/9, Troubadours, novachord: Ted Steele.

Ode to Freedom ⟨N. Shilkret⟩, Associated (= Muzak) ZZ-4114, 60709A, Track 3, ?ca 1944, Nat Shilkret and His O.

Nathaniel Shilkret's American Banjo Album ⟨N. Shilkret, Rex Schepp, et al.⟩, P218, 1946, 10/16, banjo solo: Rex Schepp.

Concerto for Trombone ⟨N. Shilkret⟩, Aztec 248, EK-KP-8472, 1947, 11/12 and 17, solo trombone: Will Bradley, piano: Leonard Pennario.

Banjo Novelties ⟨reissue of Nathaniel Shilkret's American Banjo Album⟩,
Aztec 248, EK-KP-0150, 1946, 10/16, banjo solo: Rex Schepp.
Bible Stories for Children (background music: N. Shilkret), Capitol
DBS 92 and 94, 25015–25016 and 25019–25020, 1947, 12/14,
narrator: Claude Rains, acc O/NS.
Dorothy and the Wizard of Oz (background music: N. Shilkret), Capi-
tol ECD3047, 89-30111–89-30113, ?1948, acc O/NS.
Hark! The Years! (background music: N. Shilkret), Capitol T2334,
1950, narrator: Frederick March, acc O/NS.

---

9. Miscellaneous: Two award-winning songs, a song introduced by Nat
Shilkret on radio, and a song whose only recording is by Ethel Merman, with
Nat Shilkret conducting. Other items of note, for which we omit details,
include two 1921 fox-trots by the Shilking Orchestra, where Shilking is a
shortened version of (Nat) Shilkret-(Eddie) King, nineteen recordings with
the Sousa Band between 1923 and 1925, and eight re-recordings in 1932 of
an orchestral track dubbed onto Caruso recordings.

Song of the Bayou ⟨Rube Bloom⟩, 46385-3, 36000, 1928, 12/7, Vic Salon
Group, vocal: Lambert Murphy, Lewis James, James Melton,
Charles Harrison, Elliot Shaw, James Stanley, Wilfred Glenn
and Frank Croxton.
Two American Sketches ⟨Thomas Griselle⟩, 49241-2, 36000, 1928, 12/8,
Vic Concert O.
Jazz Nocturne ⟨Dana Suesse⟩, 72590-1, 24028, 1932, 5/17, Vic Concert
O.
Satan's Li'l Lamb ⟨Harburg-Mercer-Arlen⟩, 73710-1, 24145, 1932, 9/29,
Ethel Merman, acc O/NS, pianos: Jack Shilkret, Roger Edens.

---

10. Recordings of Shilkret compositions by others: The most widely
recorded work of Nat Shilkret is *Lonesome Road* which has been recorded
by more than a hundred top artists. *Jeannine (I Dream of Lilac Time)* was
Nat Shilkret's second most popular work, with more than eighty recordings
being made, and *The First Time I Saw You* ranks third, with Whitburn
listing two recordings as having a peak ranking in the top ten. *Down the
River of Golden Dreams* ranks fourth; however, Whitburn only shows Nat's
own recording of this, with the Hilo Hawaiian Orchestra, as making the top
ten on the charts.

We include here discographic entries for the only two twentieth-century
recordings of *Genesis Suite*. A December 2000 recording is listed in Appendix C.

Genesis Suite (Shilkret, Tansman, Milhaud, Castelnuovo-Tedesco, Toch, Stravinsky, Schoenberg), Artist 1101–1110, music recorded: 1945, 12/11, Werner Janssen conducting; narration by Edward Arnold dubbed ca June 1946.

Genesis Suite (same composers as Artist album), Capitol P8125, P8125Y-Z, music recorded: 1945, 12/11, Werner Janssen conducting; narration by Ted Osborne dubbed December 1950.

---

11. The SESAC Transcriptions: Nat Shilkret recorded at least 260 transcriptions for SESAC in the late 1940s and well into the 1950s. They were intended for distribution to radio stations. These recordings are historically significant because they show clearly the heart of Nathaniel Shilkret's talent: to arrange and conduct a wide variety of music in a way that makes it come alive with the distinctive Nathaniel Shilkret sound. As Nat explained to Leonard Liebling for an article in the *Musical Courier* (May 5, 1934, reproduced in Plate D-95 of the archival edition of this work), "You see, occasionally it is necessary to make a piece sound better than it is." The SESAC recordings included more than twenty pieces composed or arranged by Nathaniel Shilkret, some under the name Niel Hallett. The transcriptions are all the more important because they are a widely diversified collection of recordings made with recent enough technology to convey the full beauty of the music Nathaniel Shilkret created.

SESAC stopped distributing these recordings about 1970, and when SESAC was sold in 1990, Alice Heinecke Drescher (then Alice Heinecke Prager), daughter of founder Paul Heinecke (see the section JAMES MELTON in chapter 5), retained control of the SESAC transcription library. The release by the Nathaniel Shilkret Music Company of a CD containing a portion of these recordings marks the first time since they were made more than fifty years ago that these recordings have been made available to the public.

While working at SESAC from 1951 to 1956, Richard Flusser was the producer for many SESAC transcriptions, including many of those by Nat Shilkret. In a conversation with us (the editors) in February 2001 he said, "we worked well together," indicating that Nat was easy to get along with and that they became personal friends. It was Richard who provided the wealth of musical background information for the program notes. He also provided the English libretto to some of the foreign works. He gave us further information about the recordings: Nat Shilkret selected all the songs and arranged them when necessary. He "invented things useful to radio." Some of the material used consisted of poor quality orchestrations of opera music which Nat, with the help of a staff under his direction, "made attractive." Top people were hired to perform. Most of the recording was done at Columbia Records with an orchestra consisting of up to thirty people. One of the pieces of music in the transcriptions was *Paris 1890*, from the play of the same name written and performed by Cornelia Otis Skinner. She objected to the inclusion of the piece and initiated a lawsuit which was eventually settled to the satisfaction of all parties.

The exact dates of these recordings are not currently available from the Nathaniel Shilkret Archives, and these recordings are listed alphabetically by title. A list of most of these, alphabetized by composer, appears in Appendix L of the archival edition of this work.

The recordings were first issued as records C901–C952. A number such as "927 2" following the title and composer indicates the recording was Track 2 of C927.

Abu Hassan Overture ⟨C. von Weber⟩, 944 1.

Allegro Con Brio ⟨H. Markworth⟩, 941 1.

American Gavotte ⟨B. Reisfeld⟩, 907 3.

Amigos ⟨H. Schubert⟩, 914 4.

Apparition No 2 ⟨F. Liszt⟩, 933 2.

Arkansas Traveler ⟨arr N. Shilkret⟩, 907 1.

At the Lake of Wallenstadt ⟨F. Liszt⟩, 910 2.

Avanti el Tango ⟨P. Mendoza⟩, 940 1.

Bad'ner Mad'ln, I ⟨K. Komzak⟩, 913 4.

Bad'ner Mad'ln, II ⟨K. Komzak⟩, 915 4.

A Beautiful Day ⟨N. Hallett⟩, 927 2.

The Beggar's Opera, I ⟨C. Pepusch⟩, 937 3, tenor: John Druary, soprano: Arlyne Frank.

The Beggar's Opera, II ⟨C. Pepusch⟩, 939 3, tenor: John Druary, soprano: Arlyne Frank.

The Beggar's Opera, III ⟨C. Pepusch⟩, 941 3, *Modes of the Court Are So Common Grown*: John Druary, Raymond Keast and Norman Myrvik, *In the Days of My Youth*: Arlyne Frank, Jimi Beni and Norman Myrvik.

Belle of Bagdad ⟨Morgan-Johnson⟩, 921 3, tenor: John Druary, soprano: Sara Carter.

A Bird Comes Flying, I ⟨S. Ochs⟩, 931 5.

A Bird Comes Flying, II ⟨S. Ochs⟩, 934 5.

Boccaccio, I ⟨F. von Suppe⟩, 911 3, tenor: Jon Crain, baritone: Jimi Beni, soprano: Yvonne Ciannella.

Bohemian Girl, I ⟨M. Balfe⟩, 920 3, vocal: Lee Cass.

Bohemian Girl: I Dreamt I Dwelt in Marble Halls ⟨M. Balfe⟩, 926 3, soprano: Yvonne Ciannella.

Bohemian Girl: Then You'll Remember Me ⟨M. Balfe⟩, 931 3, tenor: John Druary.

Brazilian Beguine ⟨C. de Begnac⟩, 905 4.
Braziliana ⟨E. Ettore⟩, 939 1.
Bresilienne ⟨B. Godard⟩, 948 2.
Brothers In Love: Overture ⟨G. Pergolesi⟩, 905 1.
Burleske, I ⟨R. Strauss⟩, 918 1, solo piano: Aurora Mauro-Cottone.
Burleske, II ⟨R. Strauss⟩, 919 5, solo piano: Aurora Mauro-Cottone.
Burleske, III ⟨R. Strauss⟩, 922 5, solo piano: Aurora Mauro-Cottone.
Butterfly Waltz ⟨R. Friml⟩, 911 4.

Canon ⟨C. Lefebvre⟩, 909 4.
Caprice ⟨J. Sibelius⟩, 902 3.
The Carman's Whistle ⟨W. Byrd⟩, 929 2.
Cavalry Trot ⟨A. Rubinstein⟩, 904 5.
Chick's Ballet ⟨M. Moussorgsky⟩, 948 1.
Children's Suite ⟨B. Bartok⟩, 942 2.
The Chimes of Normandy, I ⟨J. Planquette⟩, 924 3, baritones: Raymond Keast and Jimi Beni, soprano: Yvonne Ciannella.
The Chimes of Normandy, II ⟨J. Planquette⟩, 925 3, baritone: Raymond Keast.
The Chimes of Normandy, III ⟨J. Planquette⟩, 928 3, baritone: Jimi Beni, tenor: John Druary.
Chromatic Etude No 3 ⟨I. Moscheles⟩, 943 1, solo piano: Sherman Frank.
Clarinet Entr'acte ⟨N. Hallett⟩, 923 2, solo clarinets: Alfred Gallodoro and Jimmy Abato.
Come With Me (Ay Come Vengo) ⟨traditional⟩, 904 1.
The Comic ⟨N. Hallett⟩, 917 1.
Cossack Dance ⟨A. Dargomijsky⟩, 951 5.
Curtain Time ⟨E. Fischer⟩, 910 5.
Czech Rhapsody ⟨J. Weinberger⟩, 908 5.

Dance of the Bayaderes ⟨A. Rubinstein⟩, 905 3.
Dance of the Princesses ⟨I. Stravinsky⟩, 908 4.
Dancing Until Dawn ⟨P. Allen⟩, 906 4.
Demon Ballet, I ⟨A. Rubinstein⟩, 912 1.
Demon Ballet, II ⟨A. Rubinstein⟩, 914 2.
Divertimento: Finale ⟨M. Trapp⟩, 952 1.
Divertimento: Scherzetto ⟨M. Trapp⟩, 949 3.
Divertimento: Serenata ⟨M. Poot⟩, 945 4.
The Drum Major's Daughter: Overture ⟨J. Offenbach⟩, 932 1.

The Eagle ⟨E. MacDowell⟩, 902 2.
Eight Nocturnes: Juliet ⟨J. Holbrooke⟩, 936 4.

The Elixer of Love: **Dulcamara's Monologue** ⟨G. Donizetti⟩, 923 3, bartione: Jimi Beni, English lyrics: Richard Stuart Flusser.

The Elixer of Love: **How He Loved Me** ⟨G. Donizetti⟩, 930 3, baritone: Jimi Beni, soprano: Yvonne Ciannella, English lyrics: Richard Stuart Flusser.

The Elixer of Love: **Thank You, Thank You** ⟨G. Donizetti⟩, 932 3, tenor: John Druary, baritone: Jimi Beni, English lyrics: Richard Stuart Flusser.

Erminie, I ⟨E. Jakobowski⟩, 927 3, baritone: Ray Keast, contralto: Beatrice Krebs.

Erminie: Dark Is the Hour ⟨E. Jakobowski⟩, 929 3, baritone: Ray Keast.

Evening in Vienna ⟨F. Schubert⟩, 901 4.

Exotic ⟨S. Runyon⟩, 912 2, saxophone: Jimmy Abato, flute: Arthur Fora.

Fantasia in D Minor ⟨W. Mozart⟩, 940 2, solo piano: Warner Shilkret.

The Faun ⟨V. Andrieff⟩, 901 5.

Faust: Introduction and Song of the Golden Calf ⟨C. Gounod⟩, 933 3, vocal: Lee Cass.

Feliz Cumpleanos ⟨N. Hallett⟩, 918 5.

Festival Music ⟨G. Handel⟩, 909 1.

Fiddle Frolic ⟨A. Coleman⟩, 923 1, solo saxophone: Jimmy Abato.

Forest Murmers ⟨C. Bohm⟩, 925 4.

The Fortune Teller: Romany Life ⟨V. Herbert⟩, 945 3, soprano: Yvonne Ciannella.

The Fortune Teller: Slumber Song ⟨V. Herbert⟩, 946 3, baritone: Raymond Keast.

Four Sketches: Alameda ⟨D. Milhaud⟩, 938 4.

Francois Villon Suite No 1: Prologue ⟨E. Fischer⟩, 922 4.

Gay Music Suite: Intermezzo ⟨S. Muller⟩, 952 2.

H.M.S. Pinafore: Bell Trio ⟨Gilbert-Sullivan⟩, 948 3, baritones: Raymond Keast and Ted Hart, soprano: Yvonne Ciannella.

Habitant Sketches ⟨V. Archer⟩, 930 5.

Here Comes the Rodeo Parade ⟨A. Robinson⟩, 939 5.

Hippolyte Et Aricie ⟨J. Rameau⟩, 942 1.

Hora ⟨Y. Edel⟩, 936 1.

Hungarian Capriccio ⟨E. Zador⟩, 946 5.

Hungarian Rhapsody No 6 ⟨F. Liszt⟩, 907 5.

Huskin' Bee Dance ⟨arr N. Shilkret⟩, 924 5.

Hymn to the Sun ⟨N. Rimsky-Korsakoff⟩, 903 3.

I Know It All ⟨N. Hallett⟩, 930 1.

I Pagliacci, I ⟨R. Leoncavallo⟩, 913 2.

I Pagliacci, II ⟨R. Leoncavallo⟩, 915 3, tenor: Jon Crain, English lyrics: Richard Stuart Flusser.

If I Were King, Overture, I ⟨A. Adam⟩, 931 1.

If I Were King, Overture, II ⟨A. Adam⟩, 933 1.

Improvisation Blue ⟨F. Piket⟩, 904 4.

In a Whimsical Mood ⟨N. Hallett⟩, 927 5.

In Autumn, At an Old Trysting Place ⟨E. MacDowell⟩, 916 5.

Introduction and Allegro, I ⟨B. Godard⟩, 917 2, solo piano: Sherman Frank.

Introduction and Allegro, II ⟨B. Godard⟩, 921 1, solo piano: Sherman Frank.

Invocation ⟨H. Markworth⟩, 939 2.

Irish Melody ⟨N. Hallett⟩, 934 2.

Israeli Dance ⟨Y. Edel⟩, 937 5.

Italian Airs ⟨traditional⟩, 904 3.

Jealous Husband, Overture ⟨G. Pergolesi⟩, 915 1.

Jerry of Jericho Road ⟨P. Clark⟩, 914 3, tenor: John Druary, baritone: Jimi Beni, sopranos: Sara Carter and Yvonne Ciannella.

Jerry of Jericho Road, II ⟨P. Clark⟩, 935 3, tenor: John Druary, baritone: Jimi Beni, soprano: Christine Palmer.

Jumping Frog ⟨N.Shilkret⟩, 916 1.

Kamennoi Ostrow: Part I ⟨A. Rubinstein⟩, 950 5.

Kamennoi Ostrow: Part II ⟨A. Rubinstein⟩, 952 5.

Kapriziose Tarentalle ⟨H. Mietzner⟩, 952 3.

Keys of Heaven ⟨traditional⟩, 913 3, tenor: John Druary, soprano: Sara Carter.

Kije's Wedding ⟨S. Prokofiev⟩, 908 3.

Kiss 'N Miss ⟨N. Shilkret⟩, 914 1.

Kitty Waltz ⟨G. Faure⟩, 910 3.

Konzertstucke: Finale ⟨C. von Weber⟩, 947 5, solo piano: Norman Secon.

Konzertstucke: March ⟨C. von Weber⟩, 945 5.

La Boheme, I ⟨G. Puccini⟩, 905 2, tenor: Jon Crain, soprano: Yvonne Ciannella, English lyrics: Hoyt John Burt, Jr.

La Boheme, II ⟨G. Puccini⟩, 907 2, soprano: Yvonne Ciannella, English lyrics: Hoyt John Burt, Jr.

La Boheme, III ⟨G. Puccini⟩, 909 3.

La Boheme, IV ⟨G. Puccini⟩, 916 3, tenor: Jon Crain, soprano: Yvonne Ciannella, English lyrics: Hoyt John Burt, Jr.

La Forza Del Destino: In This Solemn Hour ⟨G. Verdi⟩, 943 3, tenor: John Druary, baritone: Jimi Beni.

La Gioconda: Furlana ⟨A. Ponchielli⟩, 938 1.

La Jolie Parfumeuse, Overture ⟨J. Offenbach⟩, 922 1.

La Perichole, I ⟨J. Offenbach⟩, 938 3, baritione: Jimi Beni, sopranos: Yvonne Ciannella, Arlyne Frank and Saramae Endlich, English lyrics: Richard Stuart Flusser.

La Perichole, II ⟨J. Offenbach⟩, 940 3, tenor: John Druary, soprano: Saramae Endlich, English lyrics: Richard Stuart Flusser.

La Perichole: Letter Song ⟨J. Offenbach⟩, 942 3, soprano: Saramae Endlich, English lyrics: Richard Stuart Flusser.

Laendler ⟨J. Bayer⟩, 937 4.

The Lee Rigg ⟨R. Goldman⟩, 906 3.

Little Comedy Suite: Anxiety ⟨H. Wunsch⟩, 951 2.

Little Comedy Suite: Happy Ending ⟨H. Wunsch⟩, 950 1.

Little Orchestra Suite: Alla Breve ⟨F. Siebert⟩, 951 3.

Little Orchestra Suite: Finale ⟨F. Siebert⟩, 950 4.

Little Orchestra Suite: First Movement ⟨F. Siebert⟩, 949 2.

Love Tango ⟨G. Ginzel⟩, 943 4.

Lucia Di Lammermoor, I ⟨G. Donizetti⟩, 922 3, tenor: Jon Crain, soprano: Yvonne Ciannella, English lyrics: Hoyt John Burt, Jr.

Lucia Di Lammermoor: Sextet ⟨G. Donizetti⟩, 918 3, Lucia: Yvonne Ciannella, Elgar: Jon Crain, Lord Henry Ashton: Jimi Beni, Raymond: Lee Cass, Alice: Beatrice Krebs, Lord Arthur Bucklaw: John Druary.

Magic Fiddle ⟨G. Schaefer⟩, 917 3, solo violin: Tosha Samaroff.

A Maiden's Wish ⟨F. Chopin⟩, 927 4.

Marriage of Figaro, The: If Dancing Is My Highness' Pleasure ⟨W. Mozart⟩, 944 3, baritone: Jimi Beni, Egnlish lyrics: Richard Stuart Flusser.

Mary Had a Little Lamb, I ⟨E. Ballantine⟩, 920 1.

Mary Had a Little Lamb, II ⟨E. Ballantine⟩, 921 5, solo piano: Sherman Frank.

A Masked Ball: Prelude ⟨G. Verdi⟩, 935 2.

Meistersinger, Die, Act II, Quintet ⟨Wagner-Shilkret⟩, 948 4.

Merry Wives Frolic ⟨N. Shilkret⟩, 913 1.

Midnight ⟨traditional⟩, 903 4.

Mimi ⟨traditional⟩, 903 2.

Minka ⟨G. Eggeling⟩, 928 2, solo piano: Sherman Frank.

A Minor Piano Concerto ⟨E. Grieg⟩, 908 1, solo piano: Sherman Frank.

Momento Capriccioso ⟨C. von Weber⟩, 927 1.
Morning Pastoral ⟨C. Busch⟩, 906 2.
My Gypsy Vagabond ⟨N. Hallett⟩, 933 4.
My Tears Are Blue ⟨Hallett-Bove⟩, 917 4.

Nabucco, Overture, I ⟨G. Verdi⟩, 924 1.
Nabucco, Overture, II ⟨G. Verdi⟩, 925 1.
Narcissus ⟨E. Nevin⟩, 952 4.
New York 1910 ⟨arr N. Shilkret⟩, 915 5, solo xylophone: Irving Farber-
        man.
Night of Romance ⟨E. Fischer⟩, 901 2.
Nightingale ⟨Alabieff-Liszt⟩, 928 4.
Nina Tre Giorini ⟨G. Pergolesi⟩, 925 2.
Nocturne on the Praire ⟨B. Reisfeld⟩, 909 2.
Norway Folk Tunes ⟨arr N Hallett⟩, 935 5.
Nostalgic Waltz No 4 ⟨R. Finney⟩, 932 2.
Nuances, Gentle ⟨C. Haubiel⟩, 919 4.

Oh Marieta ⟨J. Merino⟩, 928 5.
Oh! Doctor ⟨P. Clark⟩, 919 3, *The Drinking Song*: Lee Cass, *Island of
        Dreams*: Jouhn Druary and Sara Carter.
Once Upon a Time ⟨N. Hallett⟩, 918 4.
Open Spaces, I ⟨A. Coleman⟩, 923 5, solo piano: Sherman Frank.
Open Spaces, II ⟨A. Coleman⟩, 925 5, solo piano: Sherman Frank.
Opera Profile No 1: Leonora ⟨G. Verdi⟩, 929 5.
Opera Profile No 2: La Gioconda ⟨A. Ponchielli⟩, 939 4.
Opera Profile No 3: Aida ⟨G. Verdi⟩, 943 2.
Ostinata No 3 ⟨H. Cowell⟩, 929 4.

Paris 1890 ⟨arr N. Shilkret⟩, 909 5.
Pasillo ⟨Cervantes-Sequeira⟩, 911 2.
Pasquinade ⟨A. Siegel⟩, 902 1.
Pastoral in Blue ⟨J. Dallin⟩, 920 4.
Perfume ⟨N. Hallett⟩, 921 2.
Perpetual Motion ⟨J. Strauss⟩, 920 5.
Persian March ⟨J. Strauss⟩, 902 5.
Personal Message ⟨K. Zorlig⟩, 942 4.
The Pest ⟨N. Hallett⟩, 935 1.
The Plague of Love/Come Let's Be Merry ⟨T. Arne⟩, 940 4.
Polka ⟨S. Rachmaninoff⟩, 901 1.
Polonaise, Op 89 ⟨L. van Beethoven⟩, 926 1.
Pop Goes the Weasel ⟨traditional⟩, 906 5.
Portraits: The Hunt/Wedding Music ⟨V. Thomson⟩, 936 2.

Prairie Dawn ⟨J. Dallin⟩, 915 2.
Prelude in C Sharp Minor ⟨S. Rachmaninoff⟩, 902 4.
Preludes 3 and 4 ⟨P. Bowles⟩, 941 4.
Preludes 5 and 6 ⟨P. Bowles⟩, 912 4.
The Prophet: Ballet Excerpt III ⟨G. Meyerbeer⟩, 934 1.
The Prophet: Ballet, IV, Galop ⟨G. Meyerbeer⟩, 928 1.
Punch Polka ⟨R. Nelson⟩, 941 5.

Quartet No 14, Op 131, Scherzo ⟨L. van Beethoven⟩, 926 5.
Queen of Sheba: Entrance March ⟨K. Goldmark⟩, 929 1.
Queen of Sheba: Veil Dance ⟨K. Goldmark⟩, 930 2.

Resignation and Dreams ⟨F. Hummel⟩, 941 2.
Reverie ⟨J. Wynert⟩, 938 2.
Rigaudon ⟨J. Raff⟩, 932 5.
Romance ⟨J. Sibelius⟩, 904 2.
Romantic Dance ⟨F. Siebert⟩, 936 5.
Romantic Fantasy ⟨L. Calbi⟩, 932 4.
Romantik ⟨E. Fischer⟩, 912 5.
Rondo a Capriccio ⟨L. van Beethoven⟩, 917 5.
Rustle of Spring ⟨C. Sinding⟩, 950 3.

Saturday Night Dance ⟨arr N. Shilkret⟩, 940 5.
The Saucy Hollandaise ⟨P. Bliss, Jr⟩, 912 3, baritone: Jimi Beni, tenor:
    John Druary, soprano: Sara Carter.
The Saucy Hollandaise, II ⟨P. Bliss, Jr⟩, 934 3, baritone: Lee Cass.
The Saucy Hollandaise, III ⟨P. Bliss, Jr⟩, 936 3, baritone: Jimi Beni,
    contralto: Beatrice Krebs.
Saxophone Concerto: Serenata ⟨J. Holbrooke⟩, 951 4, solo saxophone:
    Jimmy Abato.
Scaramouche ⟨J. Sibelius⟩, 910 4.
Scenes From the Czardas: Hejre Kati ⟨J. Hubay⟩, 944 5, solo violin:
    Tosha Samaroff.
Scherzo in E Minor ⟨F. Mendelssohn⟩, 901 3.
Scottish Legend ⟨H. Beach⟩, 923 4.
Second Mazurka ⟨B. Godard⟩, 938 5.
Seguidilla ⟨I. Albeniz⟩, 913 5.
Serenade for Strings, Op 12, No 4: Canzonetta ⟨V. Herbert⟩, 944 2.
Serenade No 2: Gavotte ⟨F. Siebert⟩, 930 4.
The Serenaders ⟨N. Hallett⟩, 931 4.
Shining Moon Medley ⟨traditional⟩, 903 1.
Sierra Serenade ⟨G. de Micheli⟩, 908 2.

Silhouettes, La Coquette ⟨A. Arensky⟩, 924 2, solo violin: Tasha Samaroff.

Sixth Sonata: Adagio ⟨A. Corelli⟩, 937 2.

Sonata for a Windy Day ⟨J. Wallowitch⟩, 946 1.

Sophisticated Tap Dance ⟨J. Dallin⟩, 911 1.

The Sorcerer: My Name Is John Wellington Wells ⟨Gilbert-Sullivan⟩, 947 3, baritone: Ted Hart.

South of the Alps, I: In a Harbor City ⟨E. Fischer⟩, 945 1.

South of the Alps, II: Balcony on the Sea ⟨E. Fischer⟩, 947 4.

South of the Alps, III: Boulevard of Flowers ⟨E. Fischer⟩, 946 2.

South of the Alps, IV: Tarentella ⟨E. Fischer⟩, 948 5.

Spanish Sketches: Furioca ⟨N. Dostal⟩, 921 4.

Spanish Sketches: Habanera ⟨N. Dostal⟩, 926 4.

Spanish Sketches: Seguidilla ⟨N. Dostal⟩, 919 2.

Sparks ⟨N. Hallett⟩, 951 1, solo piano: Sherman Frank.

Star Spangled Banner ⟨arr N. Shilkret⟩, 949 5.

Stettiner Polka ⟨W. Schlichtung⟩, 903 5.

String Fever ⟨A. Borodkin⟩, 942 5, includes Abraham Borodkin on cello.

St. Luke ⟨H. Markworth⟩, 944 4.

Suite for Kathryn: Andantino ⟨F. Potamkin⟩, 931 2.

Suite for Two Pianos: Romance ⟨A. Arensky⟩, 950 2.

Suite in B Minor: Minuet and Badinerie ⟨J. Bach⟩, 945 2, solo flute: Julien Baker.

Suite No 12: Gavotte and Andante ⟨D. Scarlatti⟩, 934 4.

Symphony No 1, 4th Movement ⟨Y. Wohl⟩, 919 1.

Symphony No 13: 3rd Movement ⟨F. Haydn⟩, 916 4.

Symphony No 13: 4th Movement ⟨F. Haydn⟩, 914 5.

Tango-Lullaby ⟨V. Thomson⟩, 907 4.

Tarantella Napoli ⟨traditional⟩, 905 5.

Tea Leaves ⟨N. Hallett⟩, 947 2.

Tender Message ⟨R. Friml⟩, 916 2.

Third English Suite, Sarabande ⟨J. Bach⟩, 920 2.

Toy Soldiers ⟨A. Panufnik⟩, 943 5.

Trepak ⟨A. Rubinstein⟩, 910 1.

The Tryst ⟨J. Sibelius⟩, 949 4, solo trumpet: Harry Friestadt, solo violin: Tosha Samaroff, solo oboe: William Arrowsmith.

Twilight Serenade ⟨Jacobs-Marks⟩, 918 2, solo saxophone: Jimmy Abato.

The Two Cuckoo Clocks ⟨L. Scarmolin⟩, 911 5.

The Two Sentries ⟨N. Hallett⟩, 933 5.

Ug-A-Ly Duckling ⟨N. Hallett⟩, 926 2.

Venezia e Napoli: Tarentella ⟨F. Liszt⟩, 949 1, solo piano: Milton
    Rettenberg, second piano: Sherman Frank.
Vienna Bouquet ⟨N. Hallett⟩, 924 4.

Waltz in A Flat ⟨F. Chopin⟩, 906 1, solo piano: Sherman Frank.
Waltzes, Op 39, Nos 15, 6, and 4 ⟨J. Brahms⟩, 935 4, solo piano:
    Sherman Frank.
Warrior's Dance ⟨L. Spohr⟩, 937 1.
Well Tempered Clavier, Prelude and Fugue ⟨J. Bach⟩, 947 1.
With a Violet ⟨E. Grieg⟩, 946 4.
The Wizard, II ⟨J. Holbrooke⟩, 922 2.

APPENDIX C
CD DISCOGRAPHY

The composition *Lonesome Road* has been included in more than thirty CDs, and more than a hundred CDs include other work conducted or composed by Nathaniel Shilkret.

Original recordings from which the tracks listed below are taken are by Victor unless indicated otherwise. Roman numerals in the track numbers refer to the disc number in a set with more than one CD. Items mistakenly identified on CDs as by Nat Shilkret are marked with an asterisk (*). The format, with most data taken from the CD tracklists, is

Title of CD, artist, company: CD number, date of CD.

Track no.: *Title* (composer), matrix no., record no., year, month/day

CONDUCTED BY NATHANIEL SHILKRET

Ballad for Americans and Great Songs of Faith, Love and Patriotism, Paul Robeson, Vanguard: VCD-117/18, 1990, 4/5.

Track 22: *Ballad for Americans* (Robinson), 47035–47038 (all -1), 26516–26517, 1940, 2/9

Batwing Melodies, compilation, Phono-Cut: PH1002, 2002, January.
Track 19: *Swanee River Moon*, 26229-6, 18882A, 1922, 3/17

Beniamino Gigli–Complete Operatic Recordings, Vol. 3, IDI-Italian
Discographic Society: 317–318, 1999, 6/22.
Track 6: *Sadko: No. 4, Song of the Indian Guest* (Rimsky-Korsakov),
BSHQ72832-1, 1570A, 1932, 5/31

Beniamino Gigli–The Complete Victor Recordings, Vol. 1, Beniamino Gigli, Romophone: 82003, 1996, 5/14.
Track I, 10: *Santa Lucia Luntana* (Mario), B25017-6, 64975, 1921, 4/29
Track II, 4: *Canto del Cigno* (Saint-Säens), B28018-2, 1025A, 1923,
5/21
Track II, 7: *Fumiculi Funiculà* (Denza), B31457-3, 1064A, 1924, 11/26
Track II, 8: *Povero Pulcinella* (Buzzi-Peccia), B31477-2, 1064B, 1924,
11/26
Track II, 18: *Quanno 'a Femmena Vo'* (De Crescenzo), BVE33882-1,
1925, 4/10
Track II, 19: *Maria, Mari* (Di Capua), BVE28019-4, 1134A, 1925, 4/10

Beniamino Gigli–The Complete Victor Recordings, Vol. 2, Beniamino Gigli, Romophone: 82004, 1996, 6/11.
Track I, 6: *Torna, Amore* (Buzzi-Peccia), 1243B, 1926, 12/9
Track I, 7: *Stornelli Marini* (Mascagni), 1403B, 1926, 12/9
Track I, 8: *Santa Lucia Luntana* (Mario), 6925, 1926, 12/9
Track I, 9: *Rondine al Nido* (De Crescenzo), 1243A, 1926, 12/9

Beniamino Gigli–The Complete Victor Recordings, Vol. 3, Beniamino Gigli, Romophone: 82005, 1996, 8/13.
Track 17: *Marta* (Simons), BSHQ72534-4, 1570B, 1932, 5/3
Track 18: *Quisiera Olvvidar tus Ojos* (Albéniz), BSHQ72535-2, 1646A,
1932, 5/3
Track 19: *Eres Tu* (Sandoval), BSHQ72536-2, 1646B, 1932, 5/3
Track 20: *Triste Maggio* (De Crescenzo), BSHQ72831-1, 1973, 1932,
5/31
Track 21: *Sadko: no. 4, Song of the Indian Guest* (Rimsky-Korsakov),
BSHQ72832-1, 1570A, 1932, 5/31

Beniamino Gigli—His Greatest Hits on Radio, Beniamino Gigli, Enterprise: 59, 1996, 6/18.
Track 1: *Rondino Al Nido* (De Cresenzo)
Track 2: *Triste Maggio* (De Cresenzo)
Track 5: *Non ti Scordar di me* (Bixio)
Track 18: *Santa Lucia luntana* (De Curtis)

Beniamino Gigli–O Sole Mio, Beniamino Gigli, 2 CD set, EMD/EMI Classics: 63390, 1990, 3/20.

Track ?11: *Triste Maggio* (De Crescenzo)
Track ?14: *Stornelli Marini* (Mascagni)
Track ?16: *Rondine al Nido* (De Crescenzo)
Track ?33: *Santa Lucia Luntana* (Mario)
Track ?36: *Deux Lettres De'enfants* (Menasce)

Best Loved Bands of All Time, compilation, 4 CD set, Reader's Digest Music: RB7-002, 1996.

Track II, 16: *Dancing With Tears in My Eyes* (Dubin-Burke)

Caruso: The Complete Electrical Re-Creations, Enrico Caruso, 2 CD set, Pearl: 9030, 1993.

Track I, 1: *La Forza Del Destino: Solenne in quest'ora* (Verdi), CS74802-2 (using C3179, 1906, 3/13), unissued, 1932, 12/3 (baritone: Antonio Scotti)

Track I, 3: *I Pagliacci: Recitar, mentre preso dal delirio; Vesti la giubba* (Leoncavello), CS58966-1 (using C4317-1, 1907, 3/17), 7720, 1932, 8/15

Track I, 4: *Rigoletto: La donna è mobile* (Verdi), BS71800-1 (using B6033, 1908, 3/16), 1616, 1932, 12/3

Track I, 10: *Aida: Se quel guerrier io fossi; Celeste Aida* (Verdi), CS74803-1 (using C11423, 1911, 12/27), 7770, 1932, 12/3

Track I, 13: **Hosanna* (Granier), (Nathaniel Shilkret incorrectly cited as conductor of the London Symphony Orchestra; recorded in 1937)

Track II, 6: *'O Solo Mio* (diCapua), BS58967-1A (using B17124, 1916, 2/5), 1616, 1932, 8/15

Track II, 9: *Les Percheurs De Perles: A cette voix; Je crois entrendre encore* (Bizet), C74804-1 (using C18822-3, 1916, 12/7), 7770, 1932, 12/3

Track II, 10: *Marta: M'appari tutt'amor* (Flotow), CS58965-1A (using C3100-2, 1917, 4/15), 7720, 1932, 8/15

Track II, 18: *A Dream* (Bartlett), BS71799-1 (using B24466-3, 1920, 9/16), 1658, 1932, 12/3

The Charleston Era, compilation, ASV Living Era: AJA5342, 2000, 8/6.

Track 16: *Ain't She Sweet* (Yellen-Ager), 38171-3, 20568A, 1927, 3/15

Charleston: Great Stars of the 1920s, compilation, Past Perfect, 1998.

Track 11: *Hallelujah*, 38347-1, 20599, 1927, 4/14

Chart-Toppers of the Thirties, compilation, ASV Living Era: AJA5293, 1999, 1/19.

Track 2: *Dancing With Tears In My Eyes* (Dubin-Burke), 22425, 1930, 5/12

Chart-Toppers of the Twenties, compilation, ASV Living Era: AJA5292, 1998.

Track 19: *My Blue Heaven* (Whiting-Donaldson), 39179-2, 20964, 1927, 9/14

Track 21: *Ramona* (Gilbert-Wayne), 42584-3, 21334 and 24573, 1928, 4/2

Track 23: *Carolina Moon* (Davis-Burke), 48447-2, 21833, 1928, 12/10

A Christian Celebration, John McCormack, Pearl: GEMM 9990, 1992, 10/30.

Track 8: *Holy Night (Nacht und Traume)* (Collin-Schubert), CVE49237-3, 6926B, 1928, 12/6

Track 12: *Bread Angels (Panis Angelicus)* (Franck), CVE38733-1, not issued, 1927, 5/6

Track 17: *The Palms (Les Rameaux)* (Baptiste-Faure), CVE36606-1, 6607B, 1926, 10/4

Track 18: *Christ on the Mount of Olives* (Huber-Beethoven), CVE58684-1 and CVE58685-1, not issued, 1930, 2/27

Christmas Legends, compilation, Pro-Arte: 844, 1989.

Track 7: *Parade of the Wooden Soldiers* (Jessel), 26372-6, 80674, 1928, 1/25

The Complete Studio Recordings, Russ Columbo, 2 CD set, Taragon Records (BMG): TARCD 1103, 2003, 8/26.

Track I, 3: *I Don't Know Why*, 70210-1, 22801B, 1931, 9/3

Track I, 4: *Guilty*, 70211-1, 22801A, 1931, 9/3

Track I, 5: *You Call It Madness, But I Call It Love*, 70212-1, 22802A, 1931, 9/3

Track I, 6: *Sweet and Lovely*, 70224-2, 22802B, 1931, 9/9

Track I, 7: *Time on My Hands*, 70281-1, 22826B, 1931, 10/9

Track I, 8: *Goodnight, Sweetheart*, 70282-1, 22826A, 1931, 10/9

Track I, 9: *Prisoner of Love*, 70283-1, 22867B, 1931, 10/9

Track I, 10: *You Try Somebody Else*, 70953-1, 22861B, 1931, 11/18

Track I, 11: *Call Me Darling*, 70954-1, 22861A, 1931, 11/18

Track I, 12: *Where the Blue of the Night*, 70955-1, 22867A, 1931, 11/18

Track I, 13: *Save the Last Dance for Me*, 71207-1, 22903A, 1931, 12/29

Track I, 14: *All of Me*, 71208-1, 22903B, 1931, 12/29

Track I, 15: *Just Friends*, 71218-1, 22909A, 1932, 1/12

Track I, 16: *You're My Everything*, 71219-1, 22909B, 1932, 1/22

Dancing with Tears in My Eyes, Nat Shilkret, ASV Living Era: AJA5389, 2002, 8/13.

Track 1: *Dancing With Tears in My Eyes* (Dubin-Burke), 62218-2, 22425, 1930, 5/12

Track 2: *Honey Bunch* (Friend), 34681-4, 19995, 1926, 3/4

Track 3: *The Doll Dance* (Brown), 38134-4, 20503, 1927, 3/3

Track 4: *Hallelujah!* (Robin-Grey-Youmans), 38347-1, 20599, 1927, 4/14

Track 5: *Ain't That a Grand And Glorious Feeling* (Yellen-Ager), 38893-3, 20732, 1927, 6/9

Track 6: *It's a Million to One That You're in Love* (Davis-Akst), 39689-1, 20837, 1927, 7/21

Track 7: *Why Do I Love You?* (Hammerstein, II-Kern), 41170-2, 21215, 1927, 12/13

Track 8: *The Sidewalks of New York* (Lawler-Blake), 45611-2, 21493, 1928, 6/7

Track 9: *That's My Weakness Now* (Green-Stept), 45609-3, 21497, 1928, 6/7

Track 10: *Dusky Stevedore* (Johnson-Razaf), 45647-2, 21515, 1928, 6/19

Track 11: *Jeannine (I Dream of Lilac Time)* (Gilbert-N. Shilkret), 46619-3, 21572, 1928, 7/7

Track 12: *Softly As in a Morning Sunrise* (Hammerstein, II-Romberg), 47767-3, 21775, 1928, 10/18

Track 13: *Parade of the Wooden Soldiers* (Jessel), 26372-2, 80674 and 12-80674 and V25, 1928, 1/25

Track 14: *The Man I Love* (Ira and George Gershwin), 42418-3, 35914, 1928, 2/7

Track 15: *Broadway Melody* (Freed-Brown), 49958-2, 21886, 1929, 2/15

Track 16: *You Were Meant For Me* (Freed-Brown), 49959-3, 21886, 1929, 2/15

Track 17: *Pagan Love Song* (Freed-Brown), 51012-2, 21931, 1929, 3/7

Track 18: *Some Sweet Day* (Pollack-N. Shilkret), 51641-2, 1929, 4/18

Track 19: *Wake Up, Chill'un, Wake Up* (Robison), 51926-2, 21976, 1929, 4/26

Track 20: *Lonesome Road* (Austin-N. Shilkret), 51927-2, 21996, 1929, 4/26

Track 21: *Am I Blue?* (Clarke-Akst), 53433-1, 22004, 1929, 5/23

Track 22: *Chant of the Jungle* (Freed-Brown) 57514-1, 22203, 1929, 10/31

Track 23: *The Perfect Song* (Breil-Lucas), 57154-3, 22214, 1929, 4/18

Track 24: *Bolero* (Ravel, arr Salinger-N. Shilkret), 63669-2, 22571, 1930, 10/3

Elman: Tchaikovsky and Wieniawski Violin Concertos, Mischa Elman, Naxos: 8.110912, 2002.

Track 4: *Sérénade Mélancolique*, 62395-2 and 62396-2, 7744, 1930, 8/25

The Eternal Mother (Di Eybike Mama): Women in Yiddish Theater and Popular Song, 1909–1925, Wergo (Schott Music): SM1625-2, 2003.

Track 13: *Where Is My Yukel (Vu Iz mayn Yukel) [from operetta Di Amerikaner rebetsin]* 27575-2, 73743A, 1923, 2/26 (Sholom Sekunda and either Anshel Schorr or Louis Stein, Bessie Weisman)

Track 18: *Sabbath Holiday and the New Moon (Shabes, yontef un roshkhoydesh) [from operetta Shulamith]* (Abraham Goldfaden), 31261, 45485, 1925, 1/27 (Mme. Bertha Kalish)

Favorite Songs of the Roaring Twenties, compilation.

Track 1: *That's My Weakness Now* (Green-Stept), BVE45881-2, 21557, 1928, 7/16

Fred Astaire and Ginger Rogers at RKO, compilation (original movie sound tracks), 2 CD set, Rhino Entertainment Company: R2 72957, 1998.

Track II, 1: *Swing Time: Pick Yourself Up* (Kern), 1936

Track II, 2: *Swing Time: The Way You Look Tonight* (Kern), 1936

Track II, 3: *Swing Time: Waltz in Swing Time* (Kern), 1936

Track II, 4: *Swing Time: A Fine Romance* (Kern), 1936

Track II, 5: *Swing Time: Bojangles of Harlem* (Kern), 1936

Track II, 6: *Swing Time: Never Gonna Dance* (Kern), 1936

Track II, 11: *Shall We Dance: Slap That Bass* (Gershwin), 1937

Track II, 12: *Shall We Dance: (I've Got) Beginner's Luck* (Gershwin), 1937

Track II, 13: *Shall We Dance: They All Laughed* (Gershwin), 1937

Track II, 14: *Shall We Dance: Let's Call the Whole Thing Off* (Gershwin), 1937

Track II, 15: *Shall We Dance: They Can't Take That Away From Me* (Gershwin), 1937

Track II, 16: *Shall We Dance: Shall We Dance* (Gershwin), 1937

George Gershwin Memorial Concert–September 8, 1937, Nathaniel Shilkret, et al., 2 CD set, North American Classics: NAC 4001, 1998.

Track I, 2: *An American in Paris* (Gershwin), with the The Los Angeles Philharmonic Orchestra

George Gershwin–Orchestral Works, compilation, The Glass Gramophone Company (Past Perfect).

Track ?: *An American in Paris* (Gershwin), 35963–35964, 1929, 2/4

Track ?: *Rhapsody in Blue* (Gershwin), 35822, 1927, 4/21 (Whiteman listed, Nathaniel Shilkret conducted)

Gershwin Plays Gershwin, Gershwin, Pearl: 9483, 1992, 8/27.

Track 1: *Rhapsody in Blue* (Gershwin), 35822, 1927, 4/21 (Whiteman listed, Nathaniel Shilkret conducted)

Track 21: *An American in Paris* (Gershwin), 35963–35964, 1929, 2/4

Gershwin: 'S Wonderful, complilation, Avid: 1998, 12/15.

Track 16: *Of Thee I Sing* (Gershwin), (vocal: Froman and Schuyler)

Gigli in Song, Beniamino Gigli, Pearl: GEMM 9915, 1992, 8/28.

Track 15: *Stornelli Marini* (Mascagni), 1403B, 1926, 12/9

Track 16: *Rondine al Nido* (De Crescenzo), 1243A, 1926, 12/9

Track 21: *Marta* (Simons), 1570B, 1932, 5/3

Track 22: *Hojasdealbum, Op. 165 Espanaino Tango in D Major* (Albéniz), 1646A, 1932, 5/3

Track 23: *Eres Tu* (Sandoval), 1646B, 1932, 5/3

Track 24: *Triste Maggio* (De Crescenzo), 1973, 1932, 5/31

Giovanni Martinelli: The Complete Acoustic Recordings (1912–1924), Giovanni Martinelli, 3 CD set, Romophone: 82012-2, 1999, 2/9.

Track III, 8: *Guillame Tell: Troncar Suoi di* (Rossini), C27392-2, not issued, 1923, 1/23

Track III, 9: *Guillame Tell: Troncar Suoi di* (Rossini), C27392-4, 95213, 1923, 1/23

Track III, 10: *Guillame Tell: O Muto Asil* (Rossini), C27426-2, 74800, 1923, 2/1

Track III, 11: *Giovinezza* (Gasteldo), C27527-2, 74809, 1923, 2/1

Track III, 17: *La Juiva: Dieu, Que Ma Voix* (Halevy), C31363-2, not issued, 1924, 12/3

Track III, 18: *La Juiva: Rachel, Quand du Seigneur* (Halevy), C31364-2, not issued, 1924, 12/3

Giuseppi De Luca, Vol. 1, Giuseppi De Luca, 3 CD set, Pearl: 9159, 1995, 10/24.

Track 60: *Guilliame Tell* (Rossini)

Greatest Hits From Sigmond Romberg, compilation, Pearl: 9761, 2000, 7/25.

Track 2: *Maytime–Waltz Medley* (Romberg), 36030, 1930, 10/15

Track 9: *My Maryland: Introduction, Dixie, Boys in Grey, Mother, Silver Moon, Your Land Is Mine* (Romberg), 12954, ca April 1935

Track 12: *Nina Rose–Your Smiles, Your Tears* (Romberg), HMV DA 1559 1936, 9/21

Historic Gershwin Recordings, compilation, 2 CD set, BMG-RCA: 63276-2, 1998, 10/13.

Track I, 2: *An American in Paris* (Gershwin), 49710–49713 (all -2), 35963–35964, 1929, 2/4

Track I, 12: *Rhapsody in Blue* (Gershwin), 30173-8 and 30174-6, 35822, 1927, 4/21 (Paul Whiteman and His Orchestra directed by N. Shilkret)

The History of Pop Radio, 10 CD set, compilation, International Music Company (Germany): 205598-202 through 205607-202, 2001.

Track I, 2: *When My Sugar Walks Down the Street*, 19585 (vocal: Gene Austin and Aileen Stanley)

Track I, 15: *Rhapsody in Blue*, Paul Whiteman O, 35822

Track I, 18: *Lucky Lindy*, 20681

Track I, 20: *Lonesome Road* (Austin-N. Shilkret), 21098 (vocal: Gene Austin)

Track II, 1: *My Blue Heaven*, 20964, (vocal: Gene Austin)

Track II, 5: *The Voice of the Southland*, 21714 (vocal: Gene Austin)

Track II, 9: *Carolina Moon*, 21833 (vocal: Gene Austin)

Track II, 12: *Makin' Whoopie*, 21831 (vocal: Eddie Cantor)

Track II, 20: *Ramona*, 21334 (vocal: Gene Austin)

Track IV, 6: *Prisoner of Love*, 22867 (vocal: Russ Columbo)

Track V, 7: *Frankie and Johnny*, 24650 (vocal: Helen Morgan)

Track VI, 12: *Ah! Sweet Mystery of Life*, 4323 (vocal: Jeannette Mc-Donald and Nelson Eddie)

Track VIII, 1: *Donkey Serenade*, 4380 (vocal: Allan Jones)

The title of the CD set is deceptive: The tracks are mastered from commercially issued records, and nothing in the liner notes makes any specific connection between the records and radio broadcasts.

I Get a Kick Out of You, Ethel Merman, Pavilion Records (Flapper): PAST CD7056, 1995, 3/21.

Track 4: *How Deep Is the Ocean (How High Is the Sky?)* (Berlin), 73708-1, 24146, 1932, 9/29

Track 5: *Satan's Li'l Lamb* (Harburg-Mercer-Arlen), 73710-1, 24145, 1932, 9/29

Track 9: *I Gotta Right to Sing the Blues* (Koehler-Arlen), 73711-1, 24145, 1932, 9/29
Track 20: *I'll Follow You* (Ahlert-Turk), 73709-1, 24146, 1932, 9/29

Irish Nightingale, Morton Downey, ASV Living Era: AJA5173, 1996, 1/23.
Track 4: *I'll Always Be in Love with You* (Stept), BVE49670, 21860, 1929, 1/21

Legendary Three Tenors, Enrico Caruso, Beniamino Gigli, John Mc-Cormack, BMG-RCA: 68534, 1996, 7/16.
Track 11: *Marta* (Simons), 1570B, 1932, 5/3

Love Me Forever, Grace Moore, Pearl: GEMM 9116, 1994, 7/25.
Track 1: *Music Box Revue: Tell Her in the Spring Time* (Berlin), 31661-10, 19613A, 1925, 2/26
Track 6: *The Dubarry: I Give My Heart* (Leigh-Millöcker), BS74708-2, 1614A, 1932, 12/19
Track 7: *The Dubarry: Without Your Love* (Leigh-Millöcker), BS74707-2, 1615B, 1932, 12/19
Track 8: *The Dubarry: The Dubarry* (Leigh-Millöcker), BS74709-2, 1614B, 1932, 12/19

Love's Old Sweet Song: 25 Great Singers in Popular Ballad, compilation, ASV Living Era: AJA5130, 1994, 7/26.
Track 14: *Song of Songs* (vocal: Richard Crooks)

Lucrezia Bori: The Victor Recordings (1914–1925), Lucrezia Bori, 2 CD set, Romophone: 81016-2, 1995, 9/29.
Track II, 8: *La Bohème: Quando M'en Vo' Soletta Per la Via* (Puccini), 28620-5, 1053A, 1923, 9/28
Track II, 9: *L'Amico Fritz: Son Pocchi Fiori* (Mascagni), 28622-2, 967A, 1923, 9/28
Track II, 10: *L'Amico Fritz: Non Mi Resta Che el Piante* (Mascagni), 28624-3, 967B, 1923, 9/28
Track II, 20: *The Little Damozel* (Novello), 33478-3, 1162A, 1925, 11/21
Track II, 21: *La Bohème: Donde Lieta Usci' al Tuo Grido D'Amore* (Puccini), 33476-5, 6561A, 1925, 11/21
Track II, 22: **La Bohème: Son Andati? Fingevo di Dormire* (Puccini), 33943-3, 8068A, 1925, 11/24 (The liner notes credit both Nathaniel Shilkret and Rosario Bourdon with conducting this track; Bourdon actually conducted.)

Lucrezia Bori–The Victor Recordings (1925–1937), Lucrezia Bori, 2CD set, Romophone: 81017, 1996, 4/9.

Track II, 7: *Don Giovanni: Batti, Batti o Bel Masetto* (Mozart), 14614A, 1937, 7/22

Track II, 8: *Don Giovanni: Vedrai, Carino* (Mozart), 1846B, 1937, 7/22

Track II, 9: *Le Nozze Di Figraro: Deh Vieni Non Tardar* (Mozart), 14614B, 1937, 7/22

Magic Key Program: Gems From Gershwin, Jane Froman, Sonny Schuyler, and Felix Knight, vocalists; Nathaniel Shilkret conductor, BMG-RCA: 09026 63275-2, 1998. (Originally issued as Album C33.)

*The Magnificent Gigli, Beniamino Gigli, Pickwick Group: GLRS 102, 1993. (The liner notes list Nathaniel Shilkret as director on some unspecified tracks. To the best of our knowledge, none of the tracks were directed by him.)

Mary Garden—The Complete Victor Recordings (1926–1929), Mary Garden, Romophone: 81008, 1996, 1/10.

Track 20: *Carmen: En Vain Pour Éviter les Résponses Amères* (Bizet), 1539B, 1929, 6/5

Masters of the Xylophone, George Hamilton Green and Joe Green, Xylophonia Music: XMC001, 1993.

Track 15: *Dance of the Toy Regiment* (J. Green-N. Shilkret)

McCormack in English Song, John McCormack, Pearl: GEMM 9970, 1993.

Track 13: *Through All the Days to Be* (Hope), BVE33820, not issued, 1925, 10/27

Track 14: *The Holy Child (Away in the Manger)* (Martin), BVE37149-2, not issued, 1926, 12/17

Track 15: *Tick, Tick, Tock* (Hamblen), BVE38732-2, not issued, 1927, 5/6

McCormack in Song, John McCormack, Nimbus: 7854, 1998, 3/17.

Track 14: *Norah O'Neale* (arr Hughes), 1929

Track 15: *Rose of Tralee* (traditional), 1930

Music for Moderns, Paul Whiteman Concert Orchestra, NAXOS: 8.12.5.0, 2000.

Track 6: *Rhapsody in Blue* (Gershwin), (conducted by Nathaniel Shilkret)

The Music of Broadway, compilation, 2 CD set, Encore Productions: ENBO-CD2 #9/94, 1994.

Track I, 2: *I Can Do Wonders With You*, 56719-3, 22185, 1929, 9/26
Track I, 24: *Of Thee I Sing: medley*, 12332, 1938, 7/10
Track II, 1-3: *Music in the Air*, 39001, 1932
Track II, 4: *The DuBarry* (Millöcker), BS74709-2, 1614B, 1932, 12/19
Track II, 5: *Without Your Love* (Millöcker), BS74707-2, 1615B, 1932, 12/19 (not credited)
Track II, 6: *I Give My Heart*, (Millöcker), BS74708-2, 1614A, 1932, 12/19
Track II, 22: *Begin the Beguine*, Gladys Swarthout, 1943

My Heart Speaks, Jane Froman, Jasmine Records: JASCD 107, 1998.

Track 6: *Summertime/It Ain't Necessarily So* (G. and I. Gershwin-Heyward), 024013-1, ?12334A, 1938, 7/10
Track 9: *Maybe/Do Do Do/Clap Yo Hands/Someone to Watch Over Me* (G. and I. Gershwin), 024015-1, ?12335B, 1938, 7/10
Track 10: *The Man I Love* (G. and I. Gershwin), 024011-1, ?12333A, 1938, 7/10
Track 21: *Who Cares/So Am I/I Got Rhythm* (G. and I. Gershwin), 024010/12/14/17, 1938, 7/10

My Wild Irish Rose, John McCormack, BMG-RCA: 68668, 1997, 2/11.

Track 1: *Ireland, Mother Ireland* (O'Reilly), BVE56192-4,1928, 1/13
Track 15: *Rose of Tralee* (Glover), BVE58586-2, 1930, 2/19

Nat Shilkret and His Victor Orchestra, The Hot Dance Sides 1926 to 1930, Nat Shilkret and the International Novelty Orchestra, Swing Time: 9912, 2000, 6/6.

Track 1: *Honey Bunch*, 34681-4, 19995, 1926, 3/4
Track 2: *Sweet Thing*, 36932-2, 20352, 1926, 11/16
Track 3: *Look Up and Smile*, 37548-2, 20456, 1927, 1/19
Track 4: *Zulu Wail*, 39619-2, 20926, 1927, 7/1
Track 5: *Headin' for Harlem*, 40110-2, 20976, 1927, 9/23
Track 6: *Get Out and under the Moon*, 43699-3, 21432, 1928, 5/3
Track 7: *That's My Weakness Now*, 45609-3, 21497, 1928, 6/7
Track 8: *Dusky Stevadore*, 45647-2, 21515, 1928, 6/19
Track 9: *When Sweet Suzie Goes Steppin' By*, 45648-1, 21515, 1928, 6/19
Track 10: *Susianna*, 49024-4, 21996, 1929, 1/25
Track 11: *There Is a Happy Land*, 50934-2, 21913, 1929, 3/13
Track 12: *Why Can't You?*, 51132-3, 21953, 1929, 4/8
Track 13: *Hitting the Ceiling*, 51193-3, 21969, 1929, 4/19

Track 14: *Wake Up, Chillun, Wake Up*, 51926-2, 21976, 1929, 4/26

Track 15: *Am I Blue*, 53433-1, 22004, 1929, 5/23

Track 16: *I'm the Medicine Man for the Blues*, 53475-2, 22055, 1929, 7/15

Track 17: *Waiting at the End of the Road*, 55642-1, 22073, 1929, 7/30

Track 18: *Bottoms Up*, 55661-2, 22109, 1929, 8/30

Track 19: *Bigger and Better Than Ever*, 55662-2, 22109, 1929, 8/30

Track 20: *Georgia Pines*, 56787-1, 22195, 1929, 10/17

Track 21: *Chant of the Jungle*, 57514-1, 22203, 1929, 10/31

Track 22: *That Wonderful Something*, 57516-1-2, 22203, 1929, 10/31

Track 23: *Blue, Turning Grey Over You*, 58621-1, 22332, 1930, 1/24

Nipper's Greatest Hits–The 20s, compilation, BMG-RCA: 2258-2-R, 1990.

Track 2: *My Blue Heaven* (Whiting-Donaldson), 39179-2, 20964, 1927, 9/14 (uncredited)

Track 6: *Lucky Lindy* (Gilbert-Baer), 38844-3, 20681 1927, 5/26

Track 12: *Makin' Whoopie* (Donaldson-Kahn), 49001-3, 21831, 1928, 12/18

Track 20: *Rhapsody in Blue* (Gershwin), 30173-8 and 30174-6, 35822, 1927, 4/21 (Paul Whiteman and His Orchestra directed by N. Shilkret)

Oscar Hammerstein–The Legacy, compilation, Pearl: GEM0131, 2000.

Track 1: *Music in the Air: The Song Is You* (Kern), 74653, 1612, 1932, 12/8

Track 3: *Rose Marie: Rose Marie* (Stothart-Harbach-Friml), 92708, HMV DA 1664, 1935, 12/31

Track 7: *Rose Marie: The Mounties* (Stothart-Harbach-Friml), 97207, HMV DA 1464, 1935, December

Track 9: *Rose Marie: Indian Love Call* (Harbach-Hammerstein-Friml), 97847, HMV DA 1537, 1936, 9/17

Track 21: *Music in the Air: And Love Was Born* (Kern), 74656, 1612, 1932, 12/8

Tracks 14 and 22 were conducted by Nathaniel Finston.

Our Grandparent's Music, complilation.

Track 6: *Nola* (Arnst)

Paris '90, Cornelia Otis Skinner, accompanied by orchestra directed by Nathaniel Shilkret, DRG: 19034, 2003, 2/11. (Original soundtrack of the complete Broadway show.)

Prime Voce–Giovanni Martinelli, Giovanni Martinelli, Nimbus: 7804, 1989, 11/14.

Track 6: *Guilliame Tell: Asil Héréditaire* (Rossini)
Track 7: *Aida: Celeste Aida* (Verdi)

Prime Voce–John Charles Thomas, John Charles Thomas, Nimbus: 7838, 1992, 10/26.

Track 4: *Trees* (Kilmer), 1525, 1931, 5/26
Track 6: *Swing Low, Sweet Chariot* (Negro spiritual), 2168, 1941, 3/19
Track 10: *Home on the Range* (Guion), 1525, 1931, 5/26
Track 11: *Show Boat: Ol' Man River* (Kern), 2168, 1932, 5/19
Track 12: *Ev'ry Time I Feel de Spirit* (Negro spiritual), 2168, 1941, 3/19
Track 20: *Sylvia* (Scollard), 571, 1932, 5/19

Prima Voce–Lawrence Tibbett: From Broadway to Hollywood, Lawrence Tibbett, Nimbus: 7881, 1996.

Track 11: *The Rogue Song: The Rogue Song* (Grey-Stothart), 58187-1, 1446, 1930, 1/13
Track 12: *The Rogue Song: The Narrative* (Grey-Stothart, arr Lehár) 58188-3, 1446, 1930, 1/13
Track 13: *The Rogue Song: The White Dove* (Grey-Stothart), 58196-3, 1447, 1930, 1/15
Track 14: *The Rogue Song: When I'm Looking at You* (Grey-Stothart), 58195-2, 1447, 1930, 1/15
Track 15: *The Prodigal: Without a Song* (Eliscu-Youmans), 67492-2, 1507, 1931, 3/6
Track 16: *The Prodigal: Life Is a Dream* (Eliscu-Youmans), 67493-2, 1507, 1931, 3/6

Prima Voce–Legendary Baritones, Lawrence Tibbett, et al., Nimbus: 7867, 1995, 4/7.

Track 17: *Barbiere de Siviglia: Largo al Factotum* (Rossini), CVE59753-4, 7353, 1930, 4/15

Prime Voce–Martinelli, Vol. 2, 1913–1923, Giovanni Martinelli, Nimbus: 7826, 1991, 10/22.

Track 16: *Gugliemo Tell: Troncar Soui di* (Rossini), 95213, 1923, 1/23
Track 20: *Gugliemo Tell: Giovinezza* (Rossini), 74809, 1923, 2/1

Prima Voce–Miguel Fleta, Miguel Fleta, Nimbus: 7889, 1997, 11/25.

Track 13: *Amapola: De Amor en los Hierros de Tu Rejá* (Lacalle), 1073, 1925, 1/6

Prima Voce–Sampler, compilation, Nimbus: 1430, 1994, ?/4.
Track 12: *Norah O'Neale* (Troll), 1929

Prima Voce–Tibbett in Opera, Lawrence Tibbett, Nimbus: 7825, 1991.
Track 4: *Un Ballo in Maschera* (Verdi), 1930, 4/15
Track 5: *Il Barbiere di Seviglia* (Rossini), 1930, 4/15
Track 6: *Faust* (Gounod), 1930 4/15
Track 7: *Tannhäuser* (Wagner), 1934, 4/20

Prisoner of Love, Russ Columbo, ASV Living Era: AJA5234, 1997.
Track 1: *Prisoner of Love*, 70283-1, 22867B, 1931, 10/9
Track 5: *I Don't Know Why*, 70210-1, 22801B, 1931, 9/3
Track 6: *Guilty*, 70211-1, 22801A, 1931, 9/3
Track 7: *You Call It Madness, But I Call It Love*, 70212-1, 22802A, 1931, 9/3
Track 8: *Sweet and Lovely*, 70224-2, 22802B, 1931, 9/9
Track 9: *Time on My Hands*, 70281-1, 22826B, 1931, 10/9
Track 10: *You Try Somebody Else*, 70953-1, 22861B, 1931, 11/18
Track 11: *Call Me Darling*, 70954-1, 22861A, 1931, 11/18
Track 12: *Where the of the Night*, 70955-1, 22867A, 1931, 11/18
Track 13: *Save the Last Dance for Me*, 71207-1, 22903A, 1931, 12/29
Track 14: *All of Me*, 71208-1, 22903B, 1931, 12/29
Track 15: *Just Friends*, 71218-1, 22909A, 1932, 1/12
Track 16: *You're My Everything*, 71219-1, 22909B, 1932, 1/22
Track 23: *Goodnight, Sweetheart*, 70282-1, 22826A, 1931, 10/9

The Radio Years–George Gershwin Memorial Concert, Enterprise, 1995, April.
Track 3: *An American in Paris* (Gershwin), 35963–35964, 1929, 2/4

Ravel: Bolero, compilation, BMG-RCA: 63670, 2000, 6/6.
Track 5: *Bolero* (Ravel), 63669-2, 22571, 1930, 10/3

Richard Crooks–19 Operatic Arias, Richard Crooks, Fone (Ita): 9016, 1993, 5/25.
Track 8: *Manon: En Fermant les Yuex* (Massonet)
Track 19: *Jocelyn, Op. 100: Ah!, Ne T'eveille Pas Encor "Berceuse"* (Goddard)

A Richard Crooks Serenade, Richard Crooks, ASV Living Era: AJA5240, 1998, 2/17.
Track 1: *Serenade: Overhead the Moon Is Beaming* (Donnelly-Romberg), 54858-4, 1930, 7/7

Track 2: *Ah, Sweet Mystery of Life* (Young-Herbert), 43734-3, 1928, 4/28

Track 3: *The Song of Songs* (Lucas-Moya), 43735, 1928, 4/28

Track 4: *When You're Away* (Blossom-Herbert), 49043-4, 1929, 2/11

Track 5: *Rio Rita* (Tierney-McCarthy), 58185-3, 1930, 1/10

Track 6: *Only a Rose* (Friml), 58186-2, 1930, 1/10

Track 7: *Because* (Teschemacher-D'Hardelot), 62275-2, 1930, 6/14

Track 8: *I Bring a Love Song* (Hammerstein II-Romberg), 63621-2, 1930, 9/3

Track 12: *Macushla* (MacMurrough-Rowe), BS75509-3, 1933, 5/11

Track 13: *Smilin' Through* (Penn), BS78826, 1933, 12/18

Track 14: *If I Should Send a Rose* (Shayon-N. Shilkret), BS99516, 1935, 6/24

Richard Crooks, Tenor, compilation, 2 CD Set, Delos: DE5501, 1997, 5/20.

Track II, 11: *Love's Old Sweet Song* (Bingham-Molloy), BS87394-1, unissued, 1935, 1/17

Rossini–The Supreme Operetta Recordings, ?, Pearl: 88, 2000, 7/25.

Track 8: *Guilliame Tell* (Rossini)

Track 10: *Guilliame Tell* (Rossini)

Runnin' Wild, compilation, ASV Living Era: AJA5017, ?1991.

Track 16: *Without That Gal* (Donaldson), 22739, 69929-1, 1931, 6/11

Shake That Thing! compilation, ASV Living Era: AJA5002, ?1999.

Track 13: *Just a Night for Meditation*, 21547, 1928, 7/12

Shall We Dance, Fred Astaire, Ginger Rogers and Mantan Mooreland, EMI: EMTC-102. (Track list not known; cf. **Fred Astaire and Ginger Rogers at RKO**.)

Shall We Dance, Fred Astaire, The Glass Gramophone Company (Past Perfect), 1994. (Track list not known; cf. **Fred Astaire and Ginger Rogers at RKO**.)

Skyscrapers: Symphonic Jazz, Nathaniel Shilkret, Naxos: 8.120644, 2002, September.

Track 1: *Skyscrapers* (Carpenter), CS72607-1, CS72608-1, CS72610-1, CS72611-1, CS72613-1, CS72614-1, 11250–11252, 1932, 5/1

Track 2: *Manhatten Serenade* (Alter), 43303-3, 35914, 1928, 3/1

Track 3, 4: *Two American Sketches* (Griselle), 49241-2, 36000, 1928, 12/28

Track 5: *Song of the Bayou* (Bloom), 46385-3, 36000, 1928, 12/7
Track 6: *New Year's Eve in New York* (Janssen), 53482-5, 53483-5, 53484-2, 35986A and B, 35987A, 1929, 7/17 and 7/31
Track 7: *Skyward* (N. Shilkret), 55658-1, 35987B, 1929, 8/8
Track 8: *Jazz Nocturne* (Suesse), BS72590-1, 24028, 1932, 5/17
Track 9: *Manhattan Moonlight* (Alter), CS72592-1, 36067, 1932, 5/17
Track 10: *Buffoon* (Confrey), CS72591-1, 24028, 1932, 5/17

So This Is Love, Grace Moore and Richard Crooks, ASV Living Era: AJA5257, 1999, 5/18.
Track 9: *The Dubarry: Without Your Love* (Millöcker), 1615B, 1932, 12/19
Track 10: *The Dubarry: I Give My Heart* (Millöcker), 1614A, 1932, 12/19

The Song Is ... Harold Arlen, compilation, ASV Living Era: (UPC) 743625515923, 1995, 9/19.
Track 10: *Last Night When We Were Young*, 11877A (vocal: Lawrence Tibbett)

The Song Is You, compilation, Memoir Classics: 427, 1995, 3/21.
Track 2: *Music in the Air: The Song Is You* (Hammerstein II-Kern), BS74563, 1612, 1932, 12/8
Track 3: *Music in the Air: And Love Was Born* (Hammerstein II-Kern), BS74656, 1612, 1932, 12/8
Track 4: *The Prodigal: The Southerner: Without a Song* (Eliscu-Youmans), BVE67492, 1507, 1931, 3/6 (vocal: Tibbett)
Track 5: *The Prodigal: The Southerner: Life Is a Dream* (Freed-O. Strauss), BVE67493, 1507, 1931, 3/6
Track 6: *The Rogue Song: The Rogue Song* (Grey-Stothart), BVE58187, 1446, 1930, 1/13
Track 7: *The Rogue Song: The Narrative* (Grey-Stothart, arr Lehár), BVE58188, 1446, 1930, 1/13
Track 8: *The Rogue Song: When I'm Looking at You* (Grey-Stothart), BVE58195, 1447, 1930, 1/15
Track 9: *The Rogue Song: The White Dove* (Grey-Stothart), BVE58196, 1447, 1930, 1/15
Track 16: *Road to Mandolay* (Kipling-Speaks), CS95371, 11877, 1935, 4/20
Track 17: *In a Persian Garden: Myself When Young* (Khayyam-Lehmann), CS74704, 1706, 1932, 12/16

The Songs of Victor Herbert, compilation, ASV Living Era: AJA5340, 2000, 8/8.

Track 1: *Naughty Marietta: Ah Sweet Mystery of Life* (Young-Herbert), BVE 43734-3, 1928, 4/28 (vocal: Richard Crooks)

Track 6: *Red Mill: The Day Is Done ... Moonbeams* (Blossom-Herbert), BVE 49942-2, 1929, 2/11

Track 9: *Naughty Marietta: 'Neath the Southern Moon* (Young Herbert), BVE 89306-2, 1935, 3/11 (vocal: Nelson Eddy)

Track 10: *Naughty Marietta: Tramp Tramp Tramp* (Young-Herbert), BS89303, 1935, 3/11 (vocal: Nelson Eddy)

Track 23: *Naughty Marietta: Ah Sweet Mystery of Life* (Herbert), OA97848, 1936, 9/17 (New York) (vocal: Nelson Eddy and Jeanette McDonald)

Sousa Marches Played by the Sousa Band, John Philip Sousa, et al., 3 CD set, Crystal: 461, 2000, 1/18.

Track I, 12: *High School Cadets* (Sousa), 19871B, 1925, 10/22

Track II, 16: *The Chantyman's March* (Sousa), 19400A, 1924, 5/14

Track III, 9: *Ancient and Honorable Artillery Company* (Sousa), 19400B, 1924, 6/19

Star Spangled Rhythms, compilation, 4 CD set, BMG (Smithsonian): RD-111 DMC-4-1450, 1997.

Track I, 11: *Mr. Gallagher and Mr. Shean, Parts 1 and 2* (Gallagher-Shean), (26703-4, director unknown, and) 26728-2, 18941, 1922, (7/20 and) 8/18

Track II, 7: *Indian Love Call*, PBS97847-2, 4323A, 1936, 9/17 (vocal: Jeannette MacDonald and Nelson Eddy)

These Were Our Songs: The Early 30s, compilation, 7 CD set, Reader's Digest Music, 1989.

Track III, 5: *Prisoner of Love*, (vocal: Russ Columbo)

Three Historic Tenors, Beniamino Gigli, ?, ?, Pearl: 9776, 1992, 8/28.

Track 4: *Rondino al Nido* (De Crescenzo)

Track 13: *España*

Track 16: *Marta* (Simons)

Track 20: *Quann'a Femmena Vo'* (De Crescenzo)

Three Tenors: Enrico Caruso, Richard Crooks, Walter Widdop, Enrico Caruso, Richard Crooks, and Walter Widdop, Claremont (SAF): GSE785052, 1995, 5/2.

Track 5: *Pagliacci: Vesti la Giubba* (Leoncavalla), DB1802, 1932, 8/15 (vocal: Enrico Caruso; with 1907 voice track; uncredited)

Track 6: *Marta: M'appari* (Flotow), DB1802, 1932, 8/15 (vocal: Enrico Caruso; with 1917 voice track; uncredited)

Track 9: *Manon: Le Rêve* (Massenet), DB2093, 1933 (vocal: Richard Crooks)

Titanic: Melodies from the White Star Music Book, compilation, Pearl: 7822, 1998, 1/20.

Track 9: *Salut d'amour, Op. #12* (Elgar), 67731, 22599, 1930, 12/21

Tito Schipa–The Complete Victor Recordings, 2 CD set, Romophone: 82014, 1999, 4/13.

Track I, 6: *Chi Se Nne Scorda Occhui!* (Bartholémy), 66117, 1922, 11/3

Track I, 7: *Serenata Napulitanata* (Costa), 66121, 1922, 11/3

Track I, 10: *A Grenada* (Palacios), 74838, 1923, 5/31

Track I, 11: *Il Barbiere di Siviglia: Ecco Ridente in Cielo* (Rossini), 66192, 1923, 5/31

Tito Schipa–Favorites, Tito Schipa, ASV Living Era: AJA5248, 1999, 4/20.

Track 6: *Chi Se Nne Scorda Occhiu!* (Barthélemy), BVE27115-6, 1922, 11/3

Tunes from the 'Toons, compilation, Pro-Arte Digital: CDD 3400, 1991.

Track 7: *Buffoon* (Confrey), 1932, 5/17

20 Gramophone All-Time Greats, Vol. 2, ASV Living Era: AJA5133, 1994, 7/25.

Track 10: *Songs My Mother Taught Me* (Dvorak, arr Mcfarren), (vocal: Rosa Ponselle)

*25 Continental All-Time Greats, compilation, ASV Living Era: AJA5129, 1994.

Track 1 : **Louise* (Robin-Whiting), BVE 50942-2, 1929, 3/14 (The liner notes state accompanying orchestra is conducted by Nat Shilkret; the original sheets at Victor say Leonard Joy.)

Under the Double Eagle–The Marches of John Philip Sousa, compilation, Pearl: GEMM 9249, 1996, 7/16.

Track 1: *Under the Double Eagle* (Wagner), 355-12, 19871, 1925, 10/22

Track 2: *High School Cadets* (Sousa), 243-14, 19871, 1925, 10/22

Track 20: *The Chantyman's March* (Sousa), 30101-1, 19400, 1924, 5/14

Track 21: *Ancient and Honorable Artillery* (Sousa), 30505-3, 19400, 1924, 6/19

A Victor Herbert Showcase, compilation, Flapper: PAST CD9798, 1992.

Track 1: *March of the Toys* (Herbert), 9148, 1927, 11/2

Track 13: *Eileen: Medley* (Herbert), 9904, 1930, ca 11/1

Track 15: *'Neath the Southern Moon* (Herbert), 4781, 1935, 3/11

Vol. 1: Favourites, John McCormack, NAXOS: 8.120504, 2000.

Track 2: *The Rose of Tralee* (Spencer-Glover), 58586-2, 1452, 1930, 2/19

Track 3: *A Pair of Blue Eyes* (William Kernell), 58588-1, 1453, 1930, 2/19

Track 6: *Sonny Boy*, 48178-3 (Jolson-deSylva-Brown-Henderson), 1360, 1928, 11/19

Track 8: *Silver Threads among the Gold* (Rexford-Danks), 11834-4, 1173, 1925, 12/23

Track 11: *Little Boy Blue* (Field-Nevin), 58595-2, 1458, 1930, 2/21

Track 12: *All Alone*, 31523-2 (Irving Berlin), 1067, 1924, 12/17

Track 15: **Jeannine, I Dream of Lilac Time* (Gilbert-N. Shilkret), 48179-1, 1360, 1928, 11/19 (director: Leonard Joy)

Track 17: *Just for Today* (Partridge-Seaver), 36363-1, 1281, 1926, 9/28

Track 18: *Ireland, Mother Ireland* (O'Reilly-Loughborough), 56192-4, 1452, 1930, 2/21

Wanda Landowska, The Early Recordings, Wanda Landowska and Alessandra Scarlatti, Biddulph Piano Series/LHW: 16, 1998, 3/19. (*The track list in the liner notes credits accompaniment by Nathaniel Shilkret on all tracks; the text of the notes makes clear that the accompaniment is at most on Tracks 7–11.)

Track 7: *Don Giovanni: Minuet* (Mozart)

Track 8: *Suite For Harpsichord in E Minor Tambourin* (Rameau)

Track 9: *Pièces de Clavecin For Harpsichord, 1st Book Le Coucou* (Daquin)

The Wibbly Wobbly Walk, compilation, Saydisc: 350, 1985.

Track 18: *Parade of the Wooden Soldiers* (Jessel), 26372-6, 80674, 1928, 1/25

Yes Sir, That's My Baby, compilation, New World: 80279-2.

Track 12: *My Blue Heaven* (Whiting-Donaldson), 39179-2, 20964, 1927, 9/14

COMPOSED OR ARRANGED
BY NATHANIEL SHILKRET

See also these CDs listed above: **Dancing with Tears in My Eyes, The History of Pop Radio, Masters of the Xylophone, A Richard Crooks Serenade, Skyscrapers: Symphonic Jazz** and **Vol. 1: Favourites.**

Nathaniel Shilkret's composition, *Concerto for Trombone*, was recorded on July 8, 2004, by the Colorado Symphony Orchestra, under the direction of Jeff Tyzik, with James Pugh as trombone soloist, and on August 4 and 5, 2004, by the São Paulo Symphony Orchestra, under the direction of John Neschling, with trombone soloist Christian Lindberg. Both soloists will include their recording in a CD consisting of their trombone solos, with NAXOS issuing the Lindberg recording as BIS-CD-1448, with estimated release in August 2005.

Anita O'Day: Young Anita, 4 CD set, Anita O'Day, Proper Records: P1183, 2001.

Track III: 7: *Lonesome Road* (Austin-N. Shilkret), 1945, 2/10 (acc Nat King Cole Trio; p: Cole; g: Oscar Moore, b: Johnny Miller; MacGregor Transcriptions, Los Angeles)

Australia's Queen of Song, Gladys Moncrieff, EMI (Australia): 814651-2.

Track 1: *Jeannine (I Dream of Lilac Time)* (Gilbert-N. Shilkret)

The Best of Paul Whiteman: The Columbia Years, Paul Whiteman, Collectors' Choice Music: A61240, 2002.

Track 10: *Just a Sweetheart* (Dreyer-Pasternack-N. Shilkret), Columbia W147142, 1630D

The Best of "The Capitol Years," Nelson Riddle, Capitol: 0777 7 8918929, 1993.

Track 13: *Jeannine (I Dream of Lilac Time)* (Gilbert-N. Shilkret)

Better Than That, Pilgrim Travelers, BMG (Specialty): 7053-2, 1994.

Track 15: *Lonesome Road* (Austin-N. Shilkret), 1953, 7/2 (previously unissued take-2)

Bill's CD Collection, Vol. IV, Preservation Hall Jazz Band, William A. Gill (?), 199?.

Track 4: *Lonesome Road* (Austin-N. Shilkret)

British Dance Bands, Vol. 3, compilation, NAXOS: 8120656, 2003, 3/31.
Track 16: *The First Time I Saw You* (Wrubel-N. Shilkret)

Classical Columbia and OKeh Recordings of Joe Venuti and Eddie Lang, 8 CD set.
Track III, 13: *Jeannine (I Dream of Lilac Time)* (Gilbert-N. Shilkret), Columbia 147013-2, 14362D, 1928, 9/17 (vocal: Eva Taylor [Irene Gibbons])
Track III, 15: *Jeannine (I Dream of Lilac Time)* (Gilbert-N. Shilkret), Okeh 41134, 401158-C, 1928, 9/27 (guitar: Eddie Lang)

Country Legends, Floyd Cramer, BMG-RCA (Buddha): 74465 99775, 2001.
Track 13: *Lonesome Road* (Austin-N. Shilkret), 1959, 7/8 (Nashville, TN, piano: Floyd Cramer, bass: Bob Moore, guitar: Ray Edinton and Hank Garland, drums: Buddy Harman, trumpet: Karl Garvin, producer: Chet Atkins)

Darin at the Copa, Bobby Darin, Atco (Time Warner): 82629-2, 1994.
Track 1b: *Lonesome Road* (Gilbert-N. Shilkret), original release in 1960

Def Trance Beat (Modalities of Rhythm), Steve Coleman, Novus (BMG): 01241, 1995, 3/14.
Track 7: *Jeannine's Sizzling (from Frire Revisited and Jeannine I Dream of Lilac Time* (Coleman and Gilbert-N. Shilkret), 1994, 6/14–17.

Down to Earth, Stevie Wonder, Motown: 3746351662.
Track 8: *Lonesome Road* (Austin-N. Shilkret), ?1966

Encore–Detroit Symphony Orchestra, conducted by Neeme Järvi, Chandos: CHAN 9227, 1993.
Track 6: *Humoresque Op. 101, no. 7*, (Dvorak, arr N. Shilkret), 1991, 11/9

Favourites, Gracie Fields, Pegasus (Prestige Records, United Kingdom): PGN CD 809, 2000.
Track 5: *The First Time I Saw You* (Wrubel-N. Shilkret), 1937, 11/18

Feel So Good, Storyville Stompers, Rugalator.
Track 6: *Lonesome Road* (Gene Autry [sic]-N. Shilkret)

Frances Faye Sings Folk Songs, Frances Faye, Avenue Jazz (Bethlehem): R2 75807, 1999.

Track 2 : *Lonesome Road* (Austin-N. Shilkret), 1957, Feb or March

Track 14: *Lonesome Road* (Austin-N. Shilkret), 1957, Feb or March (stereo)

Frankie Valli and the Four Seasons: 25th Anniversary Collection, Frankie Valli, Rhino: 72998, 1987.

Track III: 1: *Lonesome Road* (Austin-N. Shilkret)

Frankie Valli and the Four Seasons: Anthology, Frankie Valli, Warner: OP5508, to be issued.

Track ?: *Lonesome Road* (Austin-N. Shilkret)

The Genesis Suite (creative director: Nathaniel Shilkret), Werner Janssen and the Janssen Symphony Orchestra of Los Angeles, chorus directed by Hugo Strelitzer, narrated by Ted Osborne (label incorrectly says narrated by Edward Arnold), Angel Records: 67729, 2001, 11/6.

Track 2: *Creation* (N. Shilkret), 1945, 12/11

The Genesis Suite (creative director: Nathaniel Shilkret), Rundfunk Sinfonieorchester Berlin, directed by Gerard Schwarz, featuring the Ernst Senff Chor, Naxos: 8.559442, 2004, 9/21 (recorded at the Jesus Christus Kirche, Berlin, December 2000, producer: Wolfram Nehls, recording engineer: Martin Eichberg, mastering engineer: Tom Lazarus, recording supervisor: Paul Schwendener).

Track 2: *Creation* (N. Shilkret), (narration: Tovah Feldshuh, Barbara Feldon, David Margulies, Fritz Weaver and Isaiah Sheffer)

The Harmonious Hits of the Merry Macs, Merry Macs, Collectors' Choice Music: CCM0025-2, 1996.

Track 2: *By-U, By-O* (Owens-Fenton), Decca 4023, DLA2760, 1941, 9/12 (written by Nathaniel Shilkret as Mack Fenton)

Have Tangy Guitar Will Travel, Duane Eddy, Jamie Guyden: 4007, 1999 3/2.

Track 1: *Lonesome Road* (Austin-N. Shilkret)

How High the Moon, Sonny Stitt, Chess (GRP Records): 0005, 1998.

Track 7: *Lonesome Road* (Austin-N. Shilkret), MCA 13692, 1958, 8/1

In Love in Vain, Frank Stallone with the Sammy Nestico Orchestra, Simba: 18827-7305-2, 1998.

Track 9: *Lonesome Road* (Austin-N. Shilkret), 1998, 1/3 or 1/4

The Jazzworthy Ted Lewis, Ted Lewis, Retrieval Records (Germany): RTR79014, 1997.

Track 2: *Lonesome Road* (Austin-N. Shilkret), 149758-2, 1930, 1/10 (personnel included cornet: Muggsy Spanier, trombone: Harry Raderman, clarinet: Jimmy Dorsey)

Joy to the World, Hoyt Axton, Fourmatt: JAY CD 005, 2002.

Track 6: *Lonesome Road* (Austin-N. Shilkret)

Julie ... At Home/Around Midnight, Julie London, Liberty (EMI, United Kindom): NBR 724385454226, 1996.

Track 2: *Lonesome Road* (Austin-N. Shilkret)

***Kickin' the Clouds Away; Gershwin at the Piano**, Klavier, 2001, 2/6.

Track 12: **Make Believe* (Shilkret) (track list says Nat Shilkret, but it is composed by Jack Shilkret)

Kiss of Fire, Louis Armstrong, Past Perfect, 2001.

Track 12: *Jeannine, I Dream of Lilac Time* (Gilbert-N. Shilkret), L5662, Decca 28076, 1951, 11/28

Lilac Time, Jimmy Rowles, Kokopelli Records: KOKO1297, 1994.

Track 15: *Jeannine (I Dream of Lilac Time)* (Gilbert-N. Shilkret)

A Lonesome Road, Paul Robeson, ASV Living Era: AJA 5027, 1984.

Track 24: *Lonesome Road* (Austin-N. Shilkret), accompanied by orchestra directed by Ray Noble, Bb17551-2, HMV B3146, 1929, 8/30

The Mighty Wurlitzer, Ann Leaf and Gaylord Carter, New World Records: 80227-2, 1988.

Track 6: *Jeannine (I Dream of Lilac Time)* (Gilbert-N. Shilkret)

Mitch Miller and the Gang, Mitch Miller, 3 CD set, Sony: 15242, 1996.

Track II, 2: *Jeannine, I Dream of Lilac Time* (Gilbert-N. Shilkret)

Muggsy Spanier, 1939–1944, Muggsy Spanier, Giants of Jazz: CD 53222, 1997.

Track 13: *Lonesome Road* (Austin-N. Shilkret), 1939, 12/12 (cornet: Muggsy Spanier, tenor sax: Nick Calazza, trombone: George Brunies, clarinet: Rod Cless, piano: Joe Bushkin, bass: Bob Casey, drums: Al Sidell)

A Musical Marriage, Peggy Lee and Dave Barbour, Jasmine: 355, 1999, March.

Track 17: *Lonesome Road* (Austin-N. Shilkret), 1946, 5/7

My Hour of Need, Dodo Greene, Blue Note: 52442, 1996.
Track 6: *Lonesome Road* (Austin-N. Shilkret), BST 8900, 1962, 4/17 (tenor sax: Ike Quebec, guitar: Grant Green, organ: Sir Charles Thompson, bass: Milt Hinton, drums: Billy Higgins; recorded Van Gelder Studio, Englewood, NJ)

The New Sound, Volumes I and II, Les Paul and Mary Ford, EMI-Capitol: COL2780, 2000.
Track 15: *Lonesome Road* (Austin-N. Shilkret)

The One and Only Tommy Dorsey, Tommy Dorsey, BMG-RCA: CAD1-650, 1987.
Track 2: *Lonesome Road* (Austin-N. Shilkret)

The Original Soul Sister, Sister Rosetta Tharpe, 4 CD set, Proper Records (U.K.), 2002, 11/19.
Track I, 4: *Lonesome Road* (Austin-N. Shilkret), 1938
Track I, 19: *Lonesome Road* (Austin-N. Shilkret), 1941

Outa Sight, Earl Andreza, Capitol: 72434-94849-2-4, 1998.
Track 8: *Lonesome Road* (Austin-N. Shilkret), 1962, March

Paegen Hand, Anni-Frid Lyngstad, EMI: CMCD 6041, 1991.
Track 16: *När Du Blir Min (Lonesome Road)* (Austin-N. Shilkret), 1968 (Swedish lyrics by O. Bergman; Marcos Österdahls Orchestra)

Paul Robeson, Paul Robeson, Pearl: 9382, 1992, 8/26.
Track 15: *Lonesome Road* (Austin-N. Shilkret)

Paul Robeson Sings Ol' Man River and Other Favorites, Paul Robeson, EMD-Angel: 47839, 1987, 1/1.
Track 3: *Lonesome Road* (Austin-N. Shilkret)

Prayer Meetin', Jimmie Smith, EMI (Capitol-Blue Note) CDP7 84164-2, 1988.
Track 7: *Lonesome Road* (Austin-N. Shilkret), 1960, 6/13

The Radio Years–Helen Traubel Rarities on Radio from 1937 to 1944, Helen Traubel, Enterprise–Radio Years (Italy): RY10, 1996, 5/25.
Track 12: *Lonesome Road* (Austin-N. Shilkret), 1944

Rat Pack, Frank Sinatra, Dean Martin and Sammy Davis Jr., United Audio Entertainment (Holland): UAE30492, 1996.
Track 24: *Lonesome Road* (Austin-N. Shilkret), (v: Frank Sinatra)

The Rockin'est, The Collins Kids, Bear Family: BCD16250, 1997.
Track 20: *Lonesome Road* (Austin-N. Shilkret), OB 2002-1, Co 4-41541

St. Louis Blues (from Newport Jazz Festival, 1959, 7/5), Moon: MCDF
028-2, 1990.
Track 5 (middle third of track): *Lonesome Road* (Austin-N. Shilkret)

Satchmo in Style, Louis Armstrong with Gordon Jenkins, Verve:
DL8440, 2001.
Track 3: *Jeannine (I Dream of Lilac Time)* (Gilbert-N.
Shilkret), L5662, Decca 28076, 1951, 11/28

Splendor of the Brass, Jim Manley, Victoria: VC4342, 2000, February.
Track ?: *Lonesome Road* (Austin-N.Shilkret)

Stealin' Apples, Benny Goodman Small Groups, Definitive Records
(Capitol Records): DRCD11110, 1999.
Track 7: *Lonesome Road* (Austin-N. Shilkret), Capitol 394, 1947, 3/7
(piano: Tommy Dodd, bass: Harry Babison, drums: Tommy Romersa)

The Swinging Mr. Lunceford, Jimmie Lunceford, Empress:
RAJCD897, 1998.
Track 5: *The First Time I Saw You* (Wrubel-N. Shilkret), 62345, Decca
1364A, 1937, 7/8

That Old Feeling, Grace Fields, ASV Living Era: 5062, 1989.
Track 20: *The First Time I Saw You* (Wrubel-N. Shilkret), 1937, 11/18

Too Long In Exile, Van Morrison, Polygram: 3145192192, 1993, 6/8.
Track 10: *Lonesome Road* (Austin-N. Shilkret)

Les 24 Merveilles de Monde de la Trompette, Jean-Claude Borelly,
Warner (Delphine): 27036-2, 1990.
Track 9: *Lonesome Road* (Austin-N. Shilkret-Walker)

Two Sides of the Chantays/Pipeline, The Chantays, Repertoire
Records: RR4114WZ, 1990.
Track 14: *Lonesome Road* (Austin-N. Shilkret)

The Velvet Touch of Skitch Henderson, Skitch Henderson, 2 CD set,
Sony: A2 28645, 1997.
Track II, 8: *Jeannine, I Dream of Lilac Time* (Gilbert-N. Shilkret)

APPENDIX D

RADIO BROADCASTS

When all data are available, the format for entries, arranged in order of Nat Shilkret's starting date, is:

beginning date–ending date for Shilkret's appearance

Title of Show, sponsor(s), station or network, beginning year–ending year of show, time and duration of show.

Dates are listed in the form year, month/day. Shows discussed in the autobiography are marked with an asterisk. Additional information about the shows and copies of many sources of information appear in the archival edition of this work.

1925, 1/1–?; 1929, 10/10–1931, 6/28

Victor Talking Machine Hour, The Victor Talking Machine Company, various times, with the show renamed after RCA bought Victor in 1929.

The January 1, 1925, Victor broadcast is the earliest documented Shilkret broadcast. See also 1931–1932, **RCA Victor Radio Record Review**, 1932–1933, **His Master's Voice of the Air** and 1938–1939, **The Magic Key (of RCA)**. Nat Shilkret indicated that he participated for a total of seven years in Victor broadcasts.

*1925 Summer–1930, 12/16
The Eveready Hour, National Carbon Company (maker of Eveready Batteries), NBC Red, (1923–1930 on WEAF for a total of 377 broadcasts) on network 1926–1930, Tuesdays, 9:00–9:30 p.m.

*at least 1926, 1/10–6/23
Hire's Harvesters, Hire's Root Beer, NBC, 1926–1927.

*1926 ?Jul–?1928
The Maxwell House Hour, Maxwell House Coffee, NBC Blue, 1926–1932, Thursdays, 9:00–10:00 p.m.

*?1926–1934
The Smith Brothers, Smith Brothers' Cough Drops, NBC, 1926–1934, NBC Red (and later NBC Blue and CBS), 15 and 30 minute formats. See also 1934, 1/7, **Songs You Love**.

*from 1926; includes 1929, 4/26–5/24; 1930, 3/21–7/25; 1931, 3/27–9/11; 1932, 5/6–9/9
The Eastman Kodak Hour, Eastman Kodak, WABC, Fridays, 9:00 p.m. in 1932.
    The broadcasts also featured young soprano Thelma Kessler and the Kodak male quartet in May 1932.

1926, 9/15
Third Annual Radio Industry Dinner Broadcast.

*?1926 Sep (includes 1926, 12/15 and)–1927, 1/1
Pennsylvania Railroad Hour.

*?1927–1928
General Motors Program, NBC, 1927–1931.

?1928–1929, 7/31
La Touraine (Concert) Hour, ?, WEAF and affliated network, NBC, 1928–1929, Wednesdays, 7:30 p.m.

*1929, 5/18–10/5
The Symphonic Hour, General Electric, NBC Blue, ?1926–1934, Saturdays, 8:00–9:00 p.m.

*1929, 10/8
1929 Library of Congress Festival of Chamber Music Broadcast, October 7–9, 1929, Elizabeth Sprague Coolidge Foundation.

*1930, 1/8–1931, 7/23
Salada Salon Orchestra, Salada Tea Company, NBC Blue, 1930–1931,
Thursdays, 8:30 p.m.

*1930, 1/29–1932, 10/5
Mobiloil Concert, Mobil Oil, NBC, 1929–1932, Wednesdays, 9:30–10:00
p.m. during 1931–1932.

1930, 6/29
Metropolitan Echoes, ?, WEAF, Sundays, 2:00–2:30 p.m.

*1930, 12/23 and 1931, 1/26, 2/18, 3/16
?, Freihofer.

1931–1932
RCA Victor Radio Record Review, RCA Victor, 1931–1932 weekly
15-minute transcribed program.
    This show consisted of transcriptions of approximately the first half of
several Victor records, together with advertising for these records and for
RCA radios.
    The Shilkret composition *Victor March* (also titled *Victory*) was used
as the theme song. On at least one broadcast, Nat Shilkret spoke briefly
and on another broadcast, all music played was by the Shilkret orchestra.
The announcer would name the artist that recorded the advertised disk.

1932, 1/4–1933, 4/20
Music That Satisfies, Chesterfield, CBS, 1931–1945, except Sundays,
10:30–10:45 p.m. EST during 1932.

1932, 1/19
Meet the Artist, WABC, CBS, 5:15 p.m.
    Nat Shilkret was interviewed by Bob Taplinger (see Plate D-79 in the
archival edition of this work).

13 programs prerecorded in September and October 1932
His Master's Voice of the Air, November 1932–February 1933, 15 minutes.
    The show consisted of music by the RCA Victor Concert Orchestra,
conducted by Nathaniel Shilkret, with guest artists that included baritone
Conrad Thibaud.

*?1933
?, Johns Manville, NBC, 1933, 15 minutes.

1933–1934
Wheeler and Woolsey, NBC Blue, 1933–1934, 30 minutes.

Swartz and Reinehr write, "A 30-minute comedy-variety program star-ring the comedy team of Bert Wheeler and Robert Woolsey, with music by the Nat Shilkret Orchestra." The Shilkret Archives contain no independent verification of this.

1933–1935
An Evening in Paris, Bourjois, NBC Blue, 1928–1936.

1934, 1/7–3/25; 1934, 10/4–1935, 3/30
Songs You Love, Smith Brothers' Cough Drops, NBC Blue, 1933–1937, 15- and 30-minute formats.

*1934, 1/7–12/20
Hall of Fame, 1934, Lysol, NBC Red, Sundays, 10:30 p.m.

*1934, 4/3–1935, 7/30
The Palmolive Beauty Box Theater, Palmolive-Colgate, NBC, 1934–1937, Tuesdays, 10:00–11:00 p.m.

*?1934, 9/18–1935, 3/19
The Packard Show, Packard Motor Car Company, NBC Blue, 1934–1938, Tuesdays, 8:30–9:00 p.m. (until October 1935).

*1934, 10/7–1935, 4/21
General Motors Concerts, General Motors, NBC Blue and Red, 1929–1937; for 1934–1935: NBC Blue, Sundays, 8:00–9:00 p.m.

*1934, 12/7–1935, 3/1
The O'Flynn, Esso, CBS, 1934–1935, Fridays, 10:30–11:00 p.m.

The broadcast was an adaptation for radio of the Broadway show of the same name, presented in thirteen one-half hour episodes. Cast: Ray Collins (speaking voice of Flynn O'Flynn), Milton Watson (singing voice of Flynn O'Flynn), Lucille Wall (speaking voice of Lady Benedetta), Viola Filo (singing voice of Lady Benedetta), Peggy Allenby (speaking voice of Fancy Free), Helen Oelheim (singing voice of Fancy Free), Jack Smart (Jacques), John Carmody (Conacher O'Rourke), Louis Hector (Roger Hendrigg). An-nouncer: David Ross. Producer: William A. Bacher. Adaptation: Henry M. Neely.

1935, 8/22
The Star-Bulletin Community Hour (Honolulu), The Honolulu Star-Bulletin, KGU, 7:00–8:00 p.m.

Nat Shilkret was guest speaker on Thursday, August 22, 1935, the night before he finished his vacation in Hawaii. He was interviewed by Earl Wilty and shared time on the hour with the leading local violinist, Robin McQuestar.

*1936, 6/30–9/22
The Camel Caravan, R. J. Reynolds Tobacco Company, CBS, 1933–1954, Tuesdays, 9:30–10:30 p.m. EDT during summer 1936.

The announcer introduces the broadcast with, "An hour starring America's outstanding personalities, with Rupert Hughes as master of ceremonies. ... We have with us, as usual, Nathaniel Shilkret and his concert orchestra and Benny Goodman and his famous swing band."

1937, 9/8
George Gershwin Memorial Concert, service of CBS, 8:00–10:30 p.m.

This tribute to George Gershwin, two months after his death, was broadcast worldwide and featured the key artists who performed Gershwin's work during his lifetime. Nathaniel Shilkret conducted *An American in Paris*. The entire two and one half hour historic broadcast of this concert has been expertly digitized and made commercially available on CD.

?1937
The Firestone Hour, Firestone Tire and Rubber Company, NBC, 1928–1957, Mondays, 8:30 p.m. in 1937.

*at least 1938, 7/10 and 1939, 1/29, 6/11 and 7/3–9/18
The Magic Key (of RCA), RCA, NBC Blue, 1935–1939, Sundays, 2:00–3:00 p.m., then Mondays, 8:30–9:30 p.m. beginning June 26, 1939.

A variety show hosted in summer 1939 by Ben Grauer. The opening number was a musical selection by Nathaniel Shilkret and his orchestra, followed by a comedy segment by Colonel Stoopnagle. The complete set of broadcasts is available at the Library of Congress.

*at least 1938, 9/20–1939, 3/17
Relaxation Time, Knickerbocker, includes WEAF, Tuesdays and Fridays.

13 programs prerecorded in October and November 1938
Song and Story, recorded by the American Bankers Association for resale to individual banks to sponsor on local stations, 15 minutes each. Detailed literature describing the program is reproduced in the archival edition of this work.

The first half of the show featured Nat Shilkret playing three pieces (eleven of the total of thirty-nine pieces were compositions or arrangements of Nat Shilkret), and the second half of the show was a dramatization of the life of "The Whites," and each episode would involve a problem of the White family which banks helped to solve. Cast: Selena Royle, Gene Leonard, Carleton Young, Mitzi Gould. Announcer: Richard Stark.

1939

The Carmen Miranda Show, NBC, 1939, 60 minutes weekly.

Swartz and Rienehr write that it was "hosted by Carmen Miranda, with Judy Ellington and the Rodgers Sisters, with music by the Nat Shilkret Orchestra and the Charlie Barnett Orchestra." The Shilkret Archives contain no independent verification of this.

*1940, 7/22–1940, Nov

The Carnation Contented Hour, Carnation Milk, NBC, 1931–1951, Mondays, 10:00–10:30 p.m. during 1932–1949.

*1940, 11/2–1941, 1/11

Chicago Theater of the Air, MBS, 1940–1955, 10:00–11:00 p.m. EST, Saturdays in December 1940.

Nat Shilkret substituted for Henry Weber for shows featuring *Desert Song* (Claire) on Nov. 16; *Eileen* (Melton) on Nov. 23; *The Countess Maritza* (Gorin) on Nov. 30; *Sweethearts* on Dec. 7; *Rio Rita* on Dec. 14; *Rose Marie* on Dec. 21; *New Moon* on Dec. 28; and *Sari* on Jan. 11, 1941.

at least 1940, 11/26,27,28 and 12/?24,26,27

The Long Man, at least WSGN (Birmingham, AL), 9:00 or 9:30 p.m.

The Birmingham Age-Herald said, "The Long Man program will feature music by Nathaniel Shilkret's orchestra."

1940, 12/4

Pageant of Melody, at least on WGN, 8:30 p.m. CST.

Nat Shilkret, substituting for Henry Weber, conducted *Martha* for singers Helen Jepson, James Melton, Suzanne Sten and (radio baritone) Earl Wilkie.

1941, 2/5

Music Hall, at least WMIN, 2:05 p.m.

This was a specially broadcast transcription. From the St. Paul (MN) Dispatch: "'Ballad for Americans' with Paul Robeson, as soloist, will be the highlight ... Nathaniel Shilkret directs the symphony orchestra."

?1943, 12/2–1944, 6/25
Let's Be Charming, Lewis Howe, MBS, 1943–1944, 1:30–2:00 p.m., Thursdays.

Swartz and Reinehr, include this description: "A 15-minute music and homemakers program hosted by Julia Sanderson and Pat Barnes, with music by Nathaniel Shilkret and the John Gart orchestra." The Shilkret Archives contain no independent verification of this.

Nat's brother Jack had worked with Sanderson and her husband Frank Crumit.

1945, 10/27
Radio Rostrum, Lewis Howe, WLIB, NY, at least 1945.

This series of transcriptions featured one notable conductor on each broadcast, giving a biographical sketch of the guest interspersed with transcribed music conducted or composed by him.

1956, 7/3
The Classical Disc Jockey, Label Bank, KABC AM and FM, Los Angeles, evenings.

The program featured transcriptions of classical music, with Tom Baxter announcing. Nathaniel Shilkret, a special guest on July 3, 1956, was interviewed between musical selections. These selections included the Shilkret recordings *I Hear America Singing* and an excerpt from the third movement of the *Concerto for Trombone*.

APPENDIX E
FILMOGRAPHY

According to Arthur Shilkret, Nat Shilkret estimated that he worked on a total of between 600 and 800 motion pictures. Many of these were one- or two-reelers. A full reel is approximately nine minutes of playing time.

Sources of information used to compile this list include the *Catalogue of Copyright Entries, Cumulative Series, Motion Pictures,* ASCAP author's royalty records, cue sheets, scores in the Nathaniel Shilkret Archives, published motion picture listings, listings made by Nat and Arthur Shilkret, and correspondence to and from Nat Shilkret.

Some motion pictures use existing music written by Nat Shilkret, even though he had no direct participation in the making of the picture. The most noteworthy example is the inclusion of the song *Lonesome Road* in the movie *Show Boat.*

When known, selected songs or cues used in motion pictures are listed. These range from best selling songs, such as *The First Time I Saw You,* to minor cues; lyricists and cocomposers (George Gershwin is among the cocomposers) are not listed.

All motion pictures are black and white with sound, unless indicated otherwise. Copyright dates, not dates of issue, are used when available. Entries which appear in published lists and for which we have no independent corroboration are marked with an asterisk (*).

The following abbreviations are used: r for reel(s), ft for feet, min for minutes, RKO for RKO Radio Pictures, RKO-P for RKO Pathe; MGM for Metro-Goldwyn-Mayer, and m sc and m dir to indicate that Nat Shilkret wrote the musical score or was the musical director, respectively. We write "songs" to indicate compositions written or arranged for a motion picture and "uses" to indicate usage of already existing compositions of Nat Shilkret.

When all data are available, the format for the listings is:

month/day   **Title**, film company, length, form of participation, songs.

1928

9/17   **Lilac Time**, First National Pictures, 11 r, silent, unsynchronzied song: *Jeannine, I Dream of Lilac Time.*

10/17   **Battle of the Sexes**, United Artists, 10 r, m sc, song: *Just a Sweetheart.*

12/11   **Synthetic Sin**, First National Pictures, 7 r, song: *Betty*, theme song.

1929

1/24   **Dancing Vienna**, First National Pictures, 7 r, music: Victor Orchestra on matrixes 42538 through 42555, recorded March 16 and 20, 1928.

2/25   **Children of the Ritz**, First National Pictures, 7 r, sound only on trailer issued 1929, 3/12, song: *Some Sweet Day*, theme song.

3/5   **Wrong Again**, MGM, 2 r.

3/28   **The Divine Lady**, First National Pictures, 12 r, sound only on trailer issued (before the movie) 1929, 3/20, song: *Divine Lady*, theme song.

4/27   **Show Boat**, Universal Pictures, 12 r, uses *Lonesome Road.*

8/12   **Perfect Day**, MGM (Hal Roach Comedy), 2 r, silent, (unsynchronized) m sc.

?   **The Lady of the Lake**, FitzPatrick Pictures copyright in Argentina, m sc, song: *Ellen, Sweet Ellen.*

1930

2/13   **Blotto**, MGM (Hal Roach Comedy), 2 r, songs: *Cuckoo, Frolic.*
*3/26   **The Rogue Song**, MGM, 12 r, conductor.
7/16   **The Laurel-Hardy Murder Case**, MGM, 3 r, m sc.
10/17   **Africa Speaks**, Columbia Pictures, 8 r, motivated composition *African Serenade.*
*?   **The Break Up**, Talking Picture Epic, 53 min, musical arranger.

1931

3/3   **Chickens Come Home**, MGM, 3 r.
8/6   **Guilty Hands**, MGM, 8 r.
?   **Out West Where the North Begins**, ?, 1 r, m sc.
*?   **The Prodigal**, MGM, ? r, conductor.
?   **Radio Salutes**, Paramount, 1 r, appears in the motion picture conducting.

1932

1/?   **Puss in Boots**, Picture Classics, 4 r, m sc, songs: *Puss in Boots, All I Have Is Spinach, A King Can Do No Wrong.*
*8/22   **Romantic Argentina (A FitzPatrick M. G. M. Traveltalk)**, MGM, conductor.
10/13   **Skyscraper Souls**, MGM, 10 r, cues.
10/25   **Three on a Match**, First National Pictures, 7 r, silent, unsynchronized song: *Electricity March.*

1933

*2/20   **Norway—Land of the Midnight Sun (FitzPatrick M. G. M. Traveltalk)**, MGM, 1 r, conductor.

6/17   New Zealand–The White Man's Paradise (A FitzPatrick Traveltalk), MGM, 1 r, cues.

*9/12   Dutch Guiana, Land of the Djuka (A FitzPatrick Traveltalk), MGM, 1 r, conductor.

9/22   The Solitaire Man, MGM, 7 r.

10/31   The Zoo (An Oswald Comedy), Universal Pictures, 1 r, cues.

1934

2/24   The Social Register, Columbia Pictures and Associated Film Producers, 8 r, m dir.

*6/13   Glimpses of Erin (A FitzPatrick Traveltalk), MGM, 1 r, conductor.

7/2   Cruising in the South Seas (FitzPatrick M. G. M. Traveltalk), MGM, 1 r, m sc, uses *Panorama of the Harbor, Funny Face.*

7/6   Citadels of the Mediterranean (FitzPatrick M. G. M. Traveltalk), MGM, 1 r, m sc, songs: *Alhambra Gateway, Ginger.*

7/9   Africa, Land of Contrast (M. G. M. Traveltalk), MGM, 1 r, m sc; songs: *Camel Scene and Hyacinth Field, Cape of Good Hope.*

9/18   Holland in Tulip Time (FitzPatrick M. G. M. Traveltalk), MGM, 1 r, color, m sc, songs: *Boat Scene and Three Dutchman Talking, Dutch Dance, Tulip Scene, Vanilla Blossoms.*

9/28   Our Daily Bread, Viking Productions (released by United Artists), 8 r.

10/2   Switzerland the Beautiful (FitzPatrick M. G. M. Traveltalk), MGM, 1 r, m sc, songs: *Potpourri–Patriotic Medley, Sansouci.*

11/12   Ireland–The Emerald Isle (A FitzPatrick Traveltalk), MGM, 1 r, color, m sc, song: *All Irish Folk Medleys.*

*?1934   Charming Ceylon, MGM, 8 min, conductor.

?1934   Dutch Zealand (M. G. M. Traveltalk), MGM, 1 r, m sc, song: *Panorama of Harbor.*

*?1934   Siam to Korea (FitzPatrick Traveltalk), MGM, 1 r, conductor.

?   Pincushion Man, ?, uses two Shilkret recordings: *Buffoon* (24028) and *Dance of the Toy Regiment* (V-25).

1935

1/3   Zeeland, The Hidden Paradise (FitzPatrick M. G. M.
           Traveltalk), MGM, 1 r, songs: Main Title, *Zeeland, The Hidden Paradise.*
5/4   Los Angeles—Wonder City of the West (A FitzPatrick
           Traveltalk), MGM, 1 r, color, m sc.
*11/12   Honolulu—The Paradise of the Pacific (FitzPatrick Traveltalk), MGM, 1 r, conductor.

1936

*2/5   Sacred City of the Mayan Indians (A James A. Fitz-
           Patrick Traveltalk), MGM, 616 ft, color, conductor.
2/12   The Bohemian Girl, MGM (Hal Roach Comedy), 8 r, m sc;
           songs: *Ballroom Waltz, Bohemian Girl Fantasy, The Heart
           Bowed Down, I Dreamt I Dwelt in a Hall of Marble, In the
           Gypsy Life, The Sad Comic, Silence the Lady Moon, Slow and
           Funny, Valleys and Hills.*
6/18   The Last Outlaw, RKO, 8 r, song: *My Heart's on the Trail.*
7/30   Mary of Scotland, RKO, 14 r, m dir, uses *My Heart's In the
           North,* songs: *Blue Bonnets, The Hundred Pipers, Italian Street
           Song, Stuart Song.*
8/18   The Last of the Mohicans, Reliance Production of California
           (released by United Artists), 10 r, m dir.
8/21   Second Wife, RKO, 7 r, cues.
8/22   Walking on Air, RKO, 8 r, m dir, songs: *Radio Fanfare, My
           Heart Wants to Dance.*
9/21   China Clipper, Warner Brothers and Vitaphone (released by
           First National Production), 10 r.
9/27   Swing Time, RKO, 12 r, m dir.
10/9   The Big Game, RKO, 75 min, m dir, song: *For Old Atlantic.*
10/29   A Woman Rebels, also titled Portrait of a Rebel, RKO, 88
           min, m sc, songs: *Ballroom Echoes, La Bella Sorentia, Ricca-
           Ricca.*
11/27   Smartest Girl in Town, RKO, 6 r, m dir, song: *Bridal Chorus
           (Lohengrin).*
12/3   Winterset, RKO, 8 r, m dir, song: *Album Leaf.*

12/4   **General Spanky**, MGM (Hal Roach Comedy), 8 r, uses *Sad Comic*.

12/31   **That Girl from Paris**, RKO, 12 r, m sc, with Andre Kostelantez, and m dir, songs: *Beautiful Blue Danube, Una Voce Poco Fa*.

1937

1/15   **The Plough and the Stars**, RKO, 8 r, m dir.

1/18   **Racing Lady**, RKO, 6 r, cues.

1/19   **Criminal Lawyer**, RKO, 7 r, m sc.

2/19   **Sea Devils**, RKO, 10 r, m sc.

3/3   **Glimpses of Java and Ceylon (FitzPatrick M. G. M. Traveltalk)**, MGM, 822 ft, color, m sc, songs: *Ceylon Life, High Buddha Temple, Hindu Silk, Java Dance*.

4/9   **Soldier and the Lady** also titled **Michael Strogoff**, RKO, 9 r, m dir, songs: *Tartar Terror, My Campfire, Pity Me*.

4/9   **Way Out West**, MGM (Hal Roach Comedy), 7 r, songs: *Funny and Mysterious, Laurel and Hardy Way Out West, Sad Comic*.

4/22   **Hong Kong, The Hub of the Orient (A FitzPatrick Traveltalk)**, MGM, 721 ft, color, m sc, songs: *Cherry Blossom, Picturesque Hong Kong*.

4/23   **The Woman I Love**, RKO, 10 r, uses: *Ricca Ricca*; song *Operetta Sequence*.

5/7   **Shall We Dance**, RKO, 12 r, m dir, songs: *For He's a Jolly Good Fellow, French Ballet Class, Ballet Eternelle, The Queen Mary, Dance of the Waves Ballet*.

5/12   **Serene Siam (A FitzPatrick Traveltalk)**, Loew's–MGM, 810 ft, color, m sc, songs: *Farewell to Siam, Pilgrims of the Orient*.

5/14   **Behind the Headlines**, RKO, 6 r, cues.

5/21   **There Goes My Girl**, RKO, 8 r, song: *Espana Cani*.

6/4   **Border Cafe**, RKO, 7 r, m dir.

7/14   **Topper**, MGM, 10 r, cues.

7/16   **Super-Sleuth**, RKO, 7 r, m sc.

7/22   **The Toast of New York**, RKO, 12 r, m dir and m sc, songs: *Desire, The First Time I Saw You, Flirtation, Mad About a Man, Ooh La La, See The Train, Temptation Waltz*.

*8/18   **Night 'n Gales (Our Gang Comedy)**, MGM, 1 r, cues.

9/20   **Forty Naughty Girls**, RKO, 7 r, cues.

10/1   **Music for Madame**, RKO, 8 r, m dir, songs: *King of the Road, Tanhauser Overture, Tanhauser Venusberg, Una Furtiva Lagrima.*

10/5   **Keeper of the Lions (An Oswald Cartoon)**, Universal Pictures, 1 r, cues, songs: *The Dumb Cluck, Keeper of the Zoo.*

10/22 **Breakfast for Two**, RKO, 65 min, cues.

10/29 **There Goes the Groom**, RKO, 7 r, cues.

11/5   **Fight for Your Lady**, RKO, 67 min, m sc, uses: *Beautiful Blue Danube.*

11/12 **Living on Love**, RKO, 61 min, cues.

11/18 **The Mysterious Jug (An Oswald Cartoon)**, Universal Pictures, 1 r, m sc, song: *Doxie.*

12/3   **Danger Patrol**, RKO, 9 r, cues.

12/10 **Quick Money** also titled **Taking the Town**, RKO, 6 r, m sc.

12/17 **Hitting a New High**, RKO, 9 r, songs: *Ardon Gl Incensi, Canzonetta.*

12/23 **The Lamplighter (An Oswald Cartoon)**, Universal Pictures, 1 r, cues.

12/31 **Wise Girl**, RKO, 8 r, cues.

1938

1/5   **She's Got Everything**, RKO, 8 r, cues.

1/14   **Everybody's Doing It**, RKO, 7 r, cues.

2/9   **Boy Meets Dog** also titled **Reg'lar Fellers**, 1 r, m dir.

2/23   **Trade Mice (An Oswald Cartoon)**, Universal Studios, 1 r, m sc, songs: *Adventerous Mouse, The Donkey's Lament.*

3/18   **Condemned Women**, RKO, 8 r, cues.

4/4   **This Marriage Business**, RKO, 7 r, uses *The First Time I Saw You.*

4/22   **Go Chase Yourself**, RKO, 8 r, uses *The First Time I Saw You.*

5/3   **Swiss Miss**, Loew's, 8 r, cues; song *La Montagnards Sont.*

5/4   **Law of the Underworld**, RKO, 7 r, cues, uses *The First Time I Saw You.*

5/13   **Bit and Bridle**, Pathe News (Sportscope #6), 10 min, cues.

5/13   **Gun Law**, RKO, 60 min, uses *My Heart's On the Trail.*

6/3   **The Saint in New York**, RKO, 8 r, cues.

6/8   **Blind Alibi**, RKO, 7 r, cues.

6/17   **Blond Cheat**, RKO, 7 r, cues.

7/15   **Brother Golfers**, Pathe News (Sportscope #9), 11 min, cues.
8/12   **Painted Desert**, RKO, 59 min, cues.
11/16   **Sydney, Pride of Australia (James A. FitzPatrick's Traveltalks)**, MGM, 1 r, color, m sc, songs: *Beautiful Beach of Bondi, Bridge Panorama.*
*?   **Di Que Me Quieres**, RKO, 80 min, m dir.

1939

1/27   **Gunga Din**, RKO, 12 r, song: *Lord Lovat's Lament.*
2/24   **One Third of a Nation**, Paramount (Dudley Murphy Production), 8 r, m sc.
3/22   **Glimpses of Australia (A FitzPatrick Traveltalk)**, Loew's-MGM, 1 r, color, m sc.
5/23   **Yankee Doodle Home**, Columbia Pictures of California, 911 ft, m sc and m dir, songs: *Great American Home* and *Skyscraper.*
6/23   **Montmartre Madness**, Columbia (Music Hall Vanities), 1 r, m sc, songs: *Apache Act, In a Montmartre Cellar Cafe.*

1940

8/23   **Wildcat Bus**, RKO, 64 min, cues.
11/29   **Meet the Missus**, Republic Pictures, 7 r, cues.

1941

1/24   **The Saint in Palm Springs**, RKO, 66 min, m sc.
4/4   **Repent at Leisure**, RKO, 66 min, m sc.
5/1   **Citizen Kane**, RKO, 119 m, cues, song: *Una Voce Poco Fa.*
?   **Jungle Cavalcade**, edited from **Bring 'Em Back Alive** (The Van Bueren Corp., RKO, 1932, 6/24), **White Cargo** (?British International Pictures, 1930, 9/6), and **Fang and Claw** (The Van Beuren Corp., RKO, 1935, 12/20, m dir.

*?   **Stolen Paradise**, also titled **Adolescence**, Monogram Pictures,
            64 min, m dir.

1942

?3/27   **Pathe News Issue #61**, Pathe, ? min, uses *Boogie Woogie*.
5/13   **The Falcon Takes Over**, RKO, 63 min, cues.
7/27   **The Big Street**, RKO, 88 min, cues.
?10/15   **Private Smith U.S.A.**, Pathe (This is America), 2 r, cues.
11/23   **The Last Session**, Loew's–MGM, short, songs: Main Title,
            French Village, Victor Hugo Reading Room, Soul of France.
12/15   **Keeper of the Flame**, Loew's–MGM, 10 r, conducted.

1943

1/1   **Seven Miles from Alcatraz**, RKO, 62 min, cues.
?1/18   **Pathe News Issue #41**, Pathe, ? min, song: *An Old Southern
            Town.*
?1/22   **You, John Jones**, Loew's–MGM, short, songs: *In England, Yes
            I Wonder.*
1/25   **Portrait of a Genius**, Loew's–MGM (A Carey Wilson Minia-
            ture), 990 ft, songs: *Why Can't Man Fly* and *The Parachute.*
?1/26   **Pathe News Issue #44**, Pathe, ? min, uses *Ogareff Theme.*
?1/28   **Pathe News Issue #46**, Pathe, ? min, uses *Ogareff Theme;*
            song: *Truth Triumphant.*
1/29   **A Stranger in Town**, Loew's–MGM, ? min, m sc.
2/12   **Journey into Fear**, RKO, 68 min, uses *Halfwit, Tartar Terror;*
            songs: *Gangster, Shadow.*
?2/18   **Pathe News Issue #52**, Pathe, ? min, uses *Building Empires,
            Loch Lomand.*
?2/28   **Pathe News Issue #53**, Pathe, ? min, uses *An Old Southern
            Town.*
3/2   **Plan for Destruction**, Loew's–MGM, 2 r, m sc.
3/17   **Air Raid Wardens**, Loew-MGM, 7 r, m sc, as Nat Shilkret.
4/13   **Calling All Kids**, Loew's–MGM, 996 ft, m sc, with Max Terr.
4/21   **Heavenly Music**, Loew's–MGM, 2 r, m sc, as Nat Shilkret, with
            Max Terr.

5/6 **Presenting Lily Mars**, Loew's–MGM, 11 r, cues.

5/21 **Above Suspicion**, Loew's–MGM, 9 r, cues.

6/8 **That's Why I Left You (John Nesbitt's Passing Parade)**, Loew's–MGM, 862 ft, m sc, with Max Terr.

7/1 **Don't You Believe It (John Nesbitt's Passing Parade)**, Loew's–MGM, 940 ft, m sc, with Max Terr.

7/1 **Trifles That Win Wars (John Nesbitt's Passing Parade)**, Loew's–MGM, 976 ft, m sc, as Nat Shilkret, with Max Terr.

7/2 **Hitler's Madman**, also titled **The Hangman** and **Hitler's Hangman**, Loew's–MGM, 9 r, cues.

7/13 **Nursery Rhyme Mysteries (John Nesbitt's Passing Parade)**, Loew's–MGM, 954 ft, m sc, as Nat Shilkret, with Max Terr.

7/27 **Ode to Victory**, Loew's–MGM, 978 ft, m sc, as Nat Shilkret, with Max Terr.

10/19 **Storm (John Nesbitt's Passing Parade)**, Loews–MGM, 687 ft, m sc, with Max Terr.

10/20 **To My Unborn Son (John Nesbitt's Passing Parade)**, Loew's, 779 ft, m sc, with Max Terr.

12/4 **My Tomato**, Loew's–MGM (A Robert Benchley Miniature), 669 ft, song: Main Title.

1944

*1/4 **Cry Havoc**, Loew's-MGM, 10 r, m dir.

1/4 **Song of Russia**, Loew's–MGM, 12 r, cues.

4/13 **Patrolling the Ether (A Crime Does Not Pay Subject)**, Loew's–MGM, 2 r, m sc.

4/26 **Three Men in White**, Loew's–MGM, 9 r, m sc.

7/6 **An American Romance**, Loew's–MGM, 16 r, color, cues and conductor.

8/22 **Lost in a Harem**, Loew's–MGM, 10 r, cues.

10/3 **Nostradamus IV**, Loew's–MGM (A Carey Wilson Miniature), 999 ft, m sc, with Max Terr.

10/18 **Mrs. Parkington**, Loew's–MGM, 12 r, cues.

11/3 **A Lady Fights Back (John Nesbitt's Passing Parade)**, Loews–MGM, 927 ft, m sc.

11/28 **Nothing But Trouble**, Loew's–MGM, 7 r, m sc.

12/5 **Blonde Fever**, Loew's–MGM, 7 r, m sc.

12/11   **Dark Shadows (A Crime Does Not Pay Subject)**, Loew's–
         MGM, 2 r, cues.
*?   **Return From Nowhere**, ? min, m sc.

1945

1/3   **This Man's Navy**, Loew's–MGM, 10 r, m sc, uses *Skyward*.
3/23   **The Clock**, Loew's–MGM, 9 r, conductor.
9/1   **Our Vines Have Tender Grapes**, Loew's–MGM, 10 r, song:
         Elephant Sequence.
10/5   **She Went to the Races**, Loew's–MGM, 9 r, m sc.
*?   **MGM Christmas Trailer**, MGM, 3 min, m dir, with Axel Stor-
         dahl.

1946

2/4   **The Hoodlum Saint**, RKO, 9 r, m sc.
4/10   **Boy's Ranch**, Loew's–MGM, 10 r, m sc.
4/25   **Courage of Lassie,** also titled **Blue Sierra**, Loew's, 10 r, color,
         cues.
6/4   **Faithful in My Fashion**, Loew's–MGM, 8 r, m sc.
6/19   **Crack Up**, RKO, 93 min, uses *The First Time I Saw You*.
8/27   **No Leave, No Love**, Loew's–MGM, 13 r, cues.
12/13   **Kentucky Basketeers**, RKO-P (Sportscope #4), 8 min, m sc.

1947

4/4   **Wild Turkey**, RKO-P (Sportscope #8), 8 min, m sc.
5/3   **Love and Learn**, Warner Brothers (First National Pictures), 83
         min, uses *Some Sweet Day*.
7/22   **Song of the Thin Man**, Loew's–MGM, 86 min, cues.
11/25   **Out of the Past**, RKO, 97 min, uses *The First Time I Saw You*.
12/21   **Pin Games**, RKO-P (Sportscope #4), 8 min, cues.

1948

1/20	**Alias a Gentleman,** Loew's–MGM, 75 min.
2/6	**Sports Coverage,** RKO-P (Sportscope #6), 8 min, m sc.
3/5	**Teen Age Tars,** RKO-P (Sportscope #7), 9 min, m sc.
4/2	**Doggone Clever,** RKO-P (Sportscope #8), 8 min, m sc.
4/9	**Who Killed Doc Robbin,** Hal Roach Studios, 50 min, color, cues.
5/28	**Muscles and the Lady,** RKO-P (Sportscope #10), 9 min, m sc.
8/20	**Glamour Street,** RKO-P (This is America #11), 16 min, cues.
8/20	**Strikes to Spare,** RKO-P (Sportscope #13), 8 min, cues.
9/11	**Athletic Stars,** RKO-P (Sportscope #3), 8 min, m sc.
12/10	**Girls in White,** RKO-P (This is America #2), 16 min, cues.
12/17	**Fighting Tarpon,** RKO-P (Sportscope #4), 8 min, m sc, song: *Fighting Tarpon.*

1949

6/10	**I Like Soap Because,** RKO-P (Screenliner #9), 9 min, song: *I Like Soap Because.*
6/24	**Kentucky Derby Story,** RKO-P (This is America #9), 17 min, m sc.
7/1	**Rolling Thrills,** RKO-P (Sportscope #11), 8 min, cues.
7/6	**The Great Sinner,** Loew's–MGM, 110 min, cues.
8/5	**Airline Glamour Girls,** RKO-P (Screenliner #11), 9 min, m sc.

1950

3/3	**Expectant Father,** RKO-P (This Is America #6), 16 min, cues.
3/10	**New Zealand Rainbow,** RKO-P (Sportscope #7), 8 min, cues.
4/7	**Horse Show,** RKO-P (Sportscope #8), 8 min, cues.
4/21	**Sunshine U.,** RKO-P (Screenliner #9), 8 min, song: *Sunshine U.*
5/5	**The Bauer Girls,** RKO-P (Sportscope #9), 8 min, cues.
9/8	**It's Only Muscle,** RKO-P (Screenliner #1), 9 min, cues.

1951

3/19   **Lullaby of Broadway**, Warner Brothers, 92 min, color, ?uses *Have You Forgotten.*
3/25   **Flying Padre**, RKO-P (Screenliner #8), 9 min, m sc.
4/6   **Slammin' Sammy Snead**, RKO-P (Sportscope Series #8), 8 min, cues.
5/18   **Florida Cowhands**, RKO-P (Screenliner #10), 9 min, cues.
6/1   **Ted Williams**, RKO-P (Sportscope #10), 8 min, cues.
6/29   **Lake Texoma**, RKO-P (Sportscope #11), 8 min, cues.
7/20   **Ambulence Doctor**, RKO-P (This Is America #11), 16 min, cues.
9/28   **Channel Swimmer**, RKO-P (Sportscope), 9 min, songs: *Diving Dynasty, Skating Lady.*
11/1   **Submarine Command**, Paramount, 87 min.
11/30   **Riders of the Andes**, RKO-P (Screenliner), 8 min, song: *Riders of the Andes.*

1952

5/9   **The Half-Breed**, RKO, 81 min, color, cues.
7/17   **You for Me**, Loew's–MGM, 70 min, cues.
8/3   **Let's Go Fishing**, RKO-P (Sportscope), 8 min, song: *Chasing Rainbows.*
8/13   **Lure of the Turf**, RKO-P (Sportscope), 8 min, cues.
8/15   **Professor F. B. I.**, RKO-P (produced with the cooperation of the F. B. I.), 15 min, cues.
11/21   **Desperate Search**, Loew's–MGM, 71 min, cues.
12/31   **Wild Boar Hunt**, RKO-P (Sportscope), 8 min, song: *State Trooper.*

1953

2/20   **Nostradamus Says So**, Loews–MGM (Prophecies of Nostradamus #1), 11 min, uses *Nostradamus IV*, Main Title.
3/3   **Cry of the Hunted**, Loew's–MGM, 79 min.

3/8   **Seaside Sports**, RKO-P (Sportscope), 8 min, songs: *Mighty Marlin, Teenage Tars.*
4/30   **A Slight Case of Larceny**, Loew's–MGM, 71 min.
6/11   **Let's Ask Nostradamus**, Loews–MGM (Prophecies of Nostradamus #2), 10 min, song: *Nostradamus*, with Eugene Zador.
6/16   **The Beast from 20,000 Fathoms**, Warner Bros., 80 min, uses *Have You Forgotten.*

1954

1/27   **Fire Fighters**, RKO-P (Screenliner), 8 min, song: *Fire Fighters.*
2/21   **Golfing with Demaret**, RKO-P (Sportscope), 8 min, song: *Golfing With Demaret.*
2/25   **Dog Scents**, RKO-P (Sportscope), 8 min, cues.
3/8   **Prisoner of War**, MGM, Loew's–MGM, 81 min, cues.
6/16   **Desert Angelers**, RKO-P (Sportscope), 8 min, cues.
7/6   **Hot Rod Galahads**, RKO-P (Sportscope), 8 min, songs: *College Climbers, Men of Shooting Str, Research Rand.*
10/19   **Alpine Fortress**, RKO-P (Screenliner), 8 min, song: *Alpine Fortress.*

1955

4/22   **Lucky Me**, Warner Brothers, 100 min, color.
10/20   **Bonefish and Barracuda**, RKO-P (Sportscope), 8 min, uses *Chasing Rainbows* as Main Title.

1956

2/5   **Fortune Seekers**, RKO-P (Screenliner), 8 min, uses *Sunshine U.*; song: *You Can Make a Mill.*
3/13   **Canadian Lancers**, RKO (Sportscope), 8 min, uses *Blue Bonnets, Riders of the Andes.*

6/9   **Four Minute Fever**, RKO-P, 9 min, uses *Kentucky Basketeers,
         Sports Coverage*; song: *Hail Notre Dame.*
8/2   **Aqua Babes**, RKO-P (Sportscope), 8 min, uses *I Like Soap Be-
         cause, Skating Lady, Variety Sports.*
11/22   **High Dive Kids**, RKO-P (Sportscope), 8 min, uses *Diving Dy-
         nasty, Slammin Sammy Snead*; songs: *Gold Doctor, Muscles
         and the Lad.*
12/29   **Holland Sailing**, RKO-P (Sportscope), 8 min, song: *College
         Climbers.*

1957

?3/23   **Gyp the Gypsies**, Hal Roach Studios, 30 min, cues.

1962

?   **Tender Is the Night**, 146 min, uses *Jeannine, I Dream of Lilac
         Time.*

1974

?   **California Split**, 108 min, uses *Lonesome Road.*

1998

?   **Yours for a Song**, PBS, made for television, includes excerpt of
         Radio Salutes (1931).

APPENDIX F

NOTED PERSONALITIES

The people listed below are mentioned in the autobiography; those for whom Nat Shilkret describes his personal experience with are marked with an asterisk (*); people listed in more than one category are marked with a dagger (†).

Composers of Light Operettas, Musicals, Movie Scores and Popular Music

Ager, Milton (1893–1979)

Berlin, Irving (1888–1989)

†Bernstein, Leonard (1918–1990)

Carmichael, Hoagy (1899–1981)

Donaldson, Walter (1893–1947)

†Ellington, Duke (1899–1974)

Foster, Stephen (1826–1864)

*Friml, Rudolph (1879–1972)

*†Gershwin, George (1898–1937)

*†Gould, Morton (1913–1996)

*†Grofé, Ferde (1892–1972)

*Gruenberg, Louis (1884–1964)

*Herbert, Victor (1859–1924)

Kern, Jerome (1885–1945)

Korngold, Erich Wolgang (1897–1957)

Lehár, Franz (1870–1948)

Romberg, Sigmund (1887–1951)

*Sousa, John Philip (1854–1932)

Steiner, Max (1888–1971)

Strauss, Johann, Jr. (1825–1899)

*†Waller, Thomas (Fats) (1904–1943)

*Webb, Roy (1888–1982)

COMPOSERS OF CLASSICAL AND AVANT-GARDE MUSIC

Bach, Johann Sebastian (1685–1750)

Bartók, Béla (1881–1945)

Beethoven, Ludwig van (1770–1827)

†Bernstein, Leonard (1918–1990)

Borodin, Alexander (1833–1887)

Brahms, Johannes (1833–1897)

Chopin, Frédéric (1810–1849)

Copland, Aaron (1900–1990)

Debussy, Claude (1862–1918)

Dvořák, Antonin (1841–1904)

*De Falla, Manuel (1876–1946)

*†Gershwin, George (1898–1937)

Gounod, Charles (1818–1893)

Grieg, Edvard (1843–1907)

Haydn, Franz Joseph (1732–1809)

*†Kreisler, Fritz (1875–1962)

Liszt, Franz (1811–1886)

MacDowell, Edward (1861–1908)

*Mahler, Gustav (1860–1911)

Mendelssohn, Felix (1809–1847)

Moussorgsky, Modest (1839–1881)

Mozart, Wolgang Amadeus (1756–1791)

Paganini, Niccolò (1782–1840)

Prokofiev, Sergei (1891–1953)

Puccini, Giacomo (1858–1924)

Rimsky-Korsakov, Nikolai (1844–1908)

Rossini, Gioacchino Antonio (1792–1868)

Saint-Saëns, Camille (1835–1921)

*Schoenberg, Arnold (1874–1951)

Schubert, Franz (1797–1828)

Schumann, Robert (1810–1856)

Sibelius, Jean (1865–1957)

*Strauss, Richard (1864–1949)

*Stravinsky, Igor (1882–1971)

Tchaikovsky, Peter Ilyich (1840–1893)

Verdi, Giuseppe (1813–1901)

Villa-Lobos, Heitor (1887–1959)

Wagner, Richard (1813–1883)

Weber, Carl Maria von (1786–1826)

ARRANGERS

*Bennett, Robert Russell (1894–?)

*Challis, William (1904–1994)

*†Grofé, Ferde (1892–1972)

*Livingston, Fud (1906–1957)

*Satterfield, Tommy (?–?)

OPERA SINGERS

*Alda, Francis (1883–1952)

Althouse, Paul (1889–1954)

*Bori, Lucrezia (1887–1960)

*Caruso, Enrico (1873–1921)

*†Chaliapin, Feodor (1873–1938)

*Crooks, Richard (1900–1972)

*De Luca, Giuseppe (1876–1950)

*†Farrar, Geraldine (1882–1967)

*Galli-Curci, Amelita (1882–1963)

*Garden, Mary (1874–1967)

*Gigli, Beniamino (1890–1957)

*Jeritza, Maria (1887–1982)

*†Lehmann, Lotte (1888–1976)

*McCormack, John (1884–1945)

*Peerce, Jan (1904–1984)

†Pinza, Ezio (1892–1957)

*†Pons, Lily (1898–1976)

*†Ponselle, Rosa (1897–1981)

Tetrazzini, Luisa (1871–1940)

*†Tibbett, Lawrence (1896–1960)

JAZZ AND BLUES ARTISTS

*Beiderbecke, Bix (1903–1931)   Handy, W.C. (1873–1958)
*Dorsey, Jimmy (1904–1957)   *Nichols, Red (1905–1965)
*Dorsey, Tommy (1905–1956)   Venuti, Joe (1904–1978)
†Ellington, Duke (1899–1974)   *†Waller, Thomas (Fats) (1904–1943)
*Goodman, Benny (1909–1986)   *Whiteman, Paul (1890–1967)

BANDLEADERS AND CONDUCTORS
(see also JAZZ ARTISTS)

*Barrère, Georges (1876–1944)   *Mengelberg, Willem (1871–1951)
Barzin, Léon (1900–1999)   Monteux, Pierre (1875–1964)
Beecham, Sir Thomas (1879–1961)   *Ormandy, Eugene (1899–1985)
*Bodanzky, Artur (1877–1939)   *Pasternack, Josef A. (1881–1940)
*†Casals, Pablo (1876–1973)   *Previn, Charles (1888–1973)
*Damrosch, Walter (1862–1950)   *Pryor, Arthur (1870–1942)
*Goldman, Edwin Franko (1878–1956)   *Rapee, Erno (1891–1945)
*†Gould, Morton (1913–1996)   *Safonov, Vassily Ilyitch (1852–1918)
*Hoogstraten, Willem van (1884–1965)   *Sevitzky, Fabien (1893–1967)
*†Iturbi, José (1895–1980)   *Stokowski, Leopold (1882–1977)
*Janssen, Werner (1899–1990)   *Toscanini, Arturo (1867–1957)
*Kostelanetz, André (1901–1980)   *Wallenstein, Alfred (1898–1984)
Lewis, Ted (1892–1971)   *Walter, Bruno (1876–1962)
Lombardo, Guy (1902–1977)   *Waring, Fred (1900–1984)
Lopez, Vincent (1895–1975)   *†Ysaÿe, Eugène (1858–1931)

INSTRUMENTALISTS (see also JAZZ ARTISTS)

*†Casals, Pablo (1876–1973)   *†Kreisler, Fritz (1875–1962)
*Elman, Mischa (1891–1967)   *Minnevitch, Borrah (1903–1955)
*Heifetz, Jascha (1901–1987)   *Segovia, Andrés (1893–1987)
*Horowitz, Vladimir (1904–1999)   *Shaw, Artie (born 1910)
*†Iturbi, José (1895–1980)   *†Ysaÿe, Eugène (1858–1931)

LYRICISTS

*Gershwin, Ira (1896–1983)   Mercer, Johnny (1909–1976)
*Kahn, Gus (1886–1941)   Yellen, Jack (1892–1991)

ACTORS, ACTRESSES, DANCERS, POPULAR SINGERS, PRODUCERS AND DIRECTORS

*Anderson, Judith (1897–1992)
*Arnold, Edward (1890–1956)
*Astaire, Fred (1899–1987)
*Austin, Gene (1900–1972)
*Autry, Gene (1907–1998)
*Bainter, Fay (1892–1968)
*Barrymore, Ethel (1879–1959)
*Barrymore, John (1882–1942)
*Berman, Pandro (born 1905)
*Brice, Fanny (1891–1951)
*†Chaliapin, Feodor (1873–1938)
Chaplin Charlie (1889–1977)
*Cooper, Gary (1901–1961)
Crosby, Bing (1904–1977)
*Dalhart, Vernon (1883–1948)
*Duncan, Isadora (1877–1927)
*Dunne, Irene (1898–1990)
*Eddy, Nelson (1901–1967)
*Etting, Ruth (1896–1978)
*Farmer, Frances (1914–1970)
*†Farrar, Geraldine (1882–1967)
Fokine, Mikhail (1880–1942)
*Fontaine, Joan (born 1917)
*Ford, John (1895–1973)
*Froman, Jane (1907–1980)
*Furness, Betty (1916–1994)
Gluck, Alma (1884–1938)
*Grant, Cary (1904–1986)
Hammerstein, Oscar (1847–1919)
Hardy, Oliver (1892–1957)
*Hepburn, Katharine (1907–2003)
*Hull, Henry (1890–1977)
*Jenkins, Butch (born 1937)
*Jenks, Frank (1902–1962)
*Jolson, Al (1886–1950)
*Kane, Helen (1910–1966)
*Kiepura, Jan (1902–1966)
Laemmle, Carl, Jr. (1908–1979)
Laurel, Stan (1890–1965)
*†Lehmann, Lotte (1888–1976)
*Levant, Oscar (1906–1972)

*Lorre, Peter (1904–1964)
*MacDonald, Jeanette (1903–1965)
*Margo (1917–1985)
McLaglen, Victor (1886–1959)
*Minnelli, Vincente (1903–1986)
*Moore, Colleen (1900–1988)
*Moore, Grace (1901–1947)
Moorehead, Agnes (1906–1974)
*Mordkin, Mikhail (1881–1944)
*Morgan, Helen (1900–1941)
*Mowbray, Alan (1897–1969)
*O'Brien, Margaret (born 1937)
*Oakie, Jack (1903–1978)
*Pan, Hermes (1905(?)–1990)
*Pavlova, Anna (1881–1931)
†Pinza, Ezio (1892–1957)
*†Pons, Lily (1898–1976)
*†Ponselle, Rosa (1897–1981)
*Rathbone, Basil (1892–1967)
*Roach, Hal (1892–1992)
*Robeson, Paul (1898–1976)
*Rogers, Ginger (1911–1995)
Rose, Billy (1899–1966)
*Schipa, Tito (1889–1965)
*Shore, Dinah (1917–1994)
Sinatra, Frank (1915–1998)
*Skinner, Cornelia Otis (1903–1979)
*Small, Edward (1891–1977)
*Smith, Kate (1907–1986)
*Stanley, Aileen (1893–1982)
*Stromberg, Hunt (1894–1968)
*Swanson, Gloria (1899–1983)
*Swarthout, Gladys (1904–1969)
*Taylor, Elizabeth (born 1932)
*Thalberg, Irving (1899–1936)
Thomas, John Charles (1892–1960)
*†Tibbett, Lawrence (1896–1960)
Valentino, Rudolph (1895–1926)
*Vallee, Rudy (1901–1986)
*Wald, Jerry (1911–1962)

APPENDIX G

GENEALOGY

"married" is abbreviated "m"
William Shilkret—Rose Zeiger

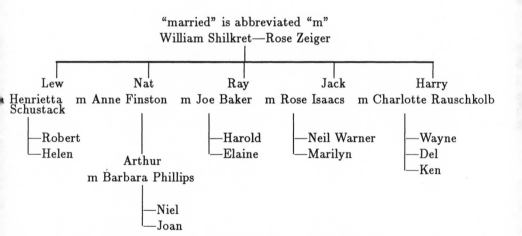

Lew	Nat	Ray	Jack	Harry
Henrietta	m Anne Finston	m Joe Baker	m Rose Isaacs	m Charlotte Rauschkolb
Schustack				

—Robert   —Harold   —Neil Warner   —Wayne
—Helen   Arthur   —Elaine   —Marilyn   —Del
    m Barbara Phillips   —Ken

—Niel
—Joan

Note: The following are name changes other than by marriage:

William Shilkret from Wulf Naftule Schüldkraut
Rose Zeiger Shilkret from Krusel Zeiger Schüldkraut
Nathaniel (Nat) Shilkret from Nathan Schüldkraut (Natan written
for Nathan on birth certificate)
Anne Finston from Anna Finkelstein
Nathaniel Finston from Nathan Finkelstein
Rose Isaacs from Rose Eisig

Neil Warner from Warner Neil Shilkret (anglicized version of his grandfather's name)

Barbara Phillips from Ruth Marie Bauch

Niel Shell from Nathaniel Shilkret

APPENDIX H

CHRONOLOGY

year month/day

—1889	12/25:	Born New York, New York (brother Lew age 3)
—1894		Sister Ray (Baker) born
—1897		Joins New York Boys' Orchestra as clarinet soloist
	10/13:	Brother Jack born (died 6/16/64)
—1898	3/16:	Brother Harry born (died 4/5/75)
—1910	Jun:	Designated alumni, B.A., by CCNY
—1914	6/14:	Marries Anne Finston (Anna Finkelstein)
—1915	3/30:	Son (and only child) Arthur born
	Jun?:	Began working for the Victor Talking Machine Co.
—1924		Composes *Prisoner's Song*; his claim to composition is disputed
—1925		First radio broadcasts; sponsors: Victor, Eveready, and Hire's
	3/16:	Records first publicly released electrically recorded disk
—1927	4/21:	Records Gershwin's *Rhapsody in Blue* (inducted into Grammy Hall of Fame; Whiteman listed as conductor)
	9/16:	Records his composition *Lonesome Road*
—1928	6/28:	Records his composition *Jeannine I Dream of Lilac Time*

1929	1/9:	Conducts first radio performance of *An American in Paris*
	Jan:	RCA buys the Victor Talking Machine Company
	2/4:	Records Gershwin's *An American in Paris* (inducted into Grammy Hall of Fame in 1997)
1934	5/31:	Receives honorary Doctor of Music from Bethany College
1935	11/18:	Becomes RKO music director and head of music dept
1936		Musical director for Astaire-Rogers movie *Swing Time*
		Nominated for Academy Award, best score, for *Winterset*
1937		Musical director for Astaire-Rogers movie *Shall We Dance*
	9/8:	Conducts *American in Paris* at Gershwin Memorial Concert in the Hollywood Bowl
1938	Mar:	Returns to New York to resume radio broadcasting
	Aug:	Cancer symptoms begin to appear
1939	Fall:	Meets Barbara Phillips; she meets Arthur the next year
1940	4/20:	Operation to remove cancer of intestine
	Jul:	Goes to Chicago for radio broadcasts
1941		Spends a year at Beverly Hills Hotel, recuperating from cancer
	9/30:	Son Arthur marries Barbara Phillips
1942	Oct?:	Begins at MGM writing musical scores and conducting
1944	3/4:	Only grandson, Niel, born
1946	Jul?:	Begins at RKO-Pathé scoring one- and two-reelers
1948	2/4:	Only granddaughter, Joan, born
1952	Jan-Jun:	Conducts *Paris '90* on road trip, then Broadway
	Sep:	(through Apr 1953) 57-city *Paris of '90* tour with Skinner
1953		Ends formal commitment to RKO-Pathé
1958	4/13:	Wife Anne dies
1965	(ca):	Completes autobiography
1981	6/3:	Only great-grandchild (girl) Marissa Shell born
1982	2/18:	Dies of heart failure in Franklin Square, New York

BIBLIOGRAPHY

References not explicitly mentioning Nathaniel Shilkret are marked with an asterisk (*). Page numbers on which discussion of Nathaniel Shilkret appears are indicated only when not obtainable from the index of the reference. Some references are made to Internet websites.

ALICOATE, JACK
[1948] *The 1947 Film Daily Yearbook Motion Pictures*, Film Daily, Los Angeles?, pp. 287 and 305ff.

AVRUTIS, ALAN
[1996] *Catalogue of Victor Red Seal 78s*, 2nd edition, unpublished (in the collection of the New York Library for the Performing Arts), pp. 1–3, 15.

BAKER, THEODORE (REVISED BY NICHOLAS SLONIMSKY)
[1984] *Baker's Biographical Dictionary of Musicians*, 7th edition, Schirmer, New York.

BORDMAN, GERALD
[1980] *Jerome Kern: His Life and Music*, Oxford University Press, New York.

BURBANK, RICHARD
[1984] *Twentieth Century Music*, Facts on File, New York.

BUXTON, FRANK, AND BILL OWEN
[1997] *The Big Broadcast 1920–1950*, 2nd edition, Scarecrow Press, Lanham, Maryland.

CHARTERS, SAMUEL B., AND LEONARD KUNSTADT
[1962] *Jazz: A History of the New York Scene*, De Capo, New York.

CLAGHORN, CHARLES EUGENE
[1973] *Biographical Dictionary of American Music*, Parker Publishing, West Nyack, New York.

CLARKE, DONALD (ED.)
[1989] *The Penguin Encyclopedia of Popular Music*, Viking Press, New York.

COLLIER, JAMES LINCOLN
[1989] *Benny Goodman and the Swing Era*, Oxford University Press, New York.

CONNOR, D. RUSSELL, AND WARREN W. HICKS
[1969] *BG on the Record: A Bio-Discography of Benny Goodman*, Arlington House, New Rochelle, New York, pp. 6–7, 162, 164, and 177 (see also p. 427).

COSLOW, SAM
[1977] *Cocktails for Two: The Many Lives of Giant Songwriter Sam Coslow*, Arlington House, New Rochelle, New York.

CRAFTON, DONALD (CHARLES HARPOLE ED.)
[1997] *Film, History of the American Cinema; Vol. 4, The Talkies: American Cinema's Transition to Sound, 1926–1931*, Scribner, New York (indexed as Shildret).

CRAWFORD, DOROTHY L.
[1995] *Evenings On and Off the Roof: Pioneering Concerts in Los Angeles, 1939–1971*, University of California Press, Berkeley, California.

CRAWFORD, RICHARD
[1993] *The American Musical Landscape*, University of California Press, Berkeley, California.

CROCE, ARLENE
[1972] *The Fred Astaire and Ginger Rogers Book*, Galahad Books, New York, pp. 99, 117, 124.

DANIEL, OLIVER
[1982] *Stokowski: A Counterpoint of View*, Dodd-Meade, New York.

DEARLING, ROBERT AND CELIA, WITH BRIAN RUST
[1981] *The Guinness Book of Recorded Sound*, 2nd edition, Guiness Books, London.

DELONG, THOMAS A.
[1980] *The Mighty Music Box: The Golden Age of Musical Radio*, Amber Crest, Los Angeles, California (besides index see inside back cover).

[1983] *Pops: Paul Whiteman, King of Jazz*, New Century, Piscataway, New Jersey.

[1994] *Frank Munn: A Biodiscography of the Golden Voice of Radio*, Sasco Associates, Southport, Connecticut.

[1996] *Radio Stars: An Illustrated Biographical Dictionary of 953 Performers, 1920 through 1960*, McFarland, Jefferson, North Carolina.

DOOLEY, ROGER

[1979] (1948) *From Scarface to Scarlett: American Films in the 1930s*, Harcourt Brace Jovanovich, New York.

DRAKE, JAMES A., AND KRISTEN BALL LUDECKE

[1999] *Lily Pons: A Centential Portrait*, Amedeus Press, Portland, Oregon.

DRIGGS, FRANK, AND HARRY LEWINE

[1996] *Black Beauty, White Heat: A Pictorial History of Classic Jazz, 1920-1950*, De Capo, New York.

DUNNING, JOHN

[1976] *Tune in Yesterday: The Ultimate Encyclopedia of Old-Time Radio 1925-1976*, Prentice Hall, Englewood Cliffs, New Jersey.

[1998] *On the Air: The Encyclopedia of Old Time Radio*, Oxford University Press, New York.

ENGEL, LYLE KENYON

[1964] *Five Hundred Songs That Made the All-Time Hit Parade*, Bantam, New York, p. 167.

EVANS, PHILIP R., AND LARRY F. KINER

[1994] *TRAM: The Frank Trumbauer Story*, Scarecrow Press, Metuchen, New Jersey, p. 88.

EWEN, DAVID

[1936] *The Man with the Baton*, Crowell, New York.

[1956] *A Journey to Greatness: The Life and Music of George Gershwin*, Holt, New York.

[1957] *Panorama of American Popular Music*, Prentice Hall, Englewood, New Jersey.

[1964] *The Life and Death of Tin Pan Alley: The Golden Age of American Popular Music*, Funk and Wagnalls, New York.

[1977] *All the Years of American Popular Music*, Prentice Hall, Englewood, New Jersey.

FEIST, LEONARD (ED.)

[1980] *An Introduction to Popular Music Publishing in America*, National Music Publishers' Association, New York, p. 67.

FREEDLAND, MICHAEL

[1974] *Irving Berlin*, Stein and Day, New York.

GELATT, ROLAND
[1955] *The Fabulous Phonograph.* J. B. Lippincott, New York.*

GEVINSON, ALAN (ED.)
[1997] *American Film Institute Catalog,* University of California Press, Berkeley, California.

GILES, RAY
[1936] *Here Comes the Band,* Harper, New York.

GOLDBERG, ISAAC
[1958] *George Gershwin: A Study in American Music,* Ungar, New York.

GOODMAN, PETER W.
[2000] *Morton Gould: American Salute,* Amadeus, Portland, Oregon.

GRACYK, TIM, WITH FRANK HOFFMANN
[2000] *Popular American Recording Pioneers: 1895-1925,* Haworth Press, New York (besides index see pp. 2, 40, 42, 63, and 92).

GREEN, STANLEY
[1981] *Encyclopaedia of the Musical Film,* Oxford University Press, New York.

GREEN, STANLEY, AND BURT GOLDBLATT
[1973] *Starring Fred Astaire,* Dodd-Mead, New York.

GREENBERG, RODNEY
[1998] *George Gershwin,* Phaidon, London.

GRUNWALD, EDGAR A.
[1939] *Radio Directory, Vol. III, 1939-1940,* Variety, New York, pp. 36, 92, and 251 (see also p. 59).

GUTMANN, PETER
[2000] *George Gershwin and the Rhapsody in Blue,* www.classicalnotes.net/features/gershwin.html

HAENDIGES, JERRY
[1997] *Jerry Haendiges Vintage Radio Logs,* members.aol.com/radiolog4/logp1008.html

HALLIWELL, LESLIE
[1979] *Halliwell's Film Guide,* Granada, London.
[1997] *Halliwell's Who's Who in the Movies,* 13th Edition, Harper, New York.

HAMM, CHARLES E.
[1979] *Yesterdays: Popular Song in America,* Norton, New York.

HARRIS, STEVE
[1988] *Film, Television, and Stage Music on Phonograph Records,* McFarland, Jefferson, North Carolina, Items 3771 and 6033.

HARRISON, NIGEL
[1998] *Songwriters: A Biographical Dictionary with Discographies*, McFarland, Jefferson, North Carolina.

HASSE, JOHN EDWARD
[1999] *Jazz: The First Century*, William Morrow (HarperCollins), New York.

HENEBRY, MIKE
[2000] *International Society of Twenties Orchestras Newsletter Shows*, Mike Henebry, Los Alimitos, California, pp. 14–15.

HESKES, IRENE
[1994] *Passport to Jewish Music: Its History, Traditions, and Culture*, Greenwood Press, Westport, Connecticut.

HICKERSON, JAY
[1996] *The New Revised Ultimate History of Radio Network Programming and Guide to All Circulating Shows*, 3rd edition, Jay Hickerson, Hamden, Connecticut.

HILMES, MICHELE
[1997] *Radio Voices, American Broadcasting, 1922–1952*, University of Minnesota Press, Minneapolis, Minnesota.*

HIRSCHHORN, CLIVE
[1991] *The Hollywood Musical*, Portland House, New York.

HISCHAK, THOMAS S.
[1999] *The American Musical Film Song Encyclopedia*, Greenwood Press, Westport, Connecticut.

HITCHCOCK, H. WILEY, AND STANLEY SADIE
[1986] *New Grove Dictionary of American Music*, Macmillan, London.

HOLMES, JOHN L.
[1982] *Conductors on Record*, Greenwood Press, Westport, Connecticut.

JABLONSKI, EDWARD
[1981] *The Encyclopedia of American Music*, Doubleday, Garden City, New York.
[1996] *Harold Arlen: Rhythm, Rainbows and Blues*, De Capo, New York.
[1998] *Gershwin*, De Capo, New York.
[1999] *Irving Berlin: American Troubador*, Henry Holt, New York.

JABLONSKI, EDWARD, AND LAWRENCE D.STEWART
[1973] *The Gershwin Years*, Doubleday, Garden City, New York.

JANSSEN, WERNER, AND D. BRUCE LOCKERBIE
[ca 1980] *While the Music Lasts*, unpublished, 261 double-spaced typed pages, pp. 44, 128–129, 137, 140, 202–205, 235; see also p. 234.

JOHNSON, J.
[1999] *Judy Garland Movie Songs*, Schirmer, New York.

KARLIN, FRED
[1994] *Listening to Movies: The Film Lover's Guide to Film Music*, Schirmer, New York (besides index see pp. 317, 324–325, 353, 372).

KATZ, EPHRAIM
[1994] *The Film Encyclopedia*, Harper, New York.*

KENNDALL, ALAN
[1987] *George Gershwin*, Universe Books, New York.

KIMBALL, ROBERT, AND ALFRED SIMON
[1973] *The Gershwins*, Atheneum, New York.

KINER, LARRY F.
[1992] *Nelson Eddy: A Bio-discography*, Scarecrow Press, Metuchen, New Jersey, pp. 28–31, 37–38, 43–44, 60–61, 83–85.

KINKLE, ROGER D.
[1974] *The Complete Encyclopedia of Popular Music and Jazz 1900–1950*, Vol. 1–4, Arlington House, New Rochelle, New York.

KNIGHT, ARTHUR (INTRODUCTION)
[1970] *The New York Times Directory of the Film*, Arno Press (New York Times), New York.

KOLODIN, IRVING
[1950] *A Guide to Recorded Music*, Doubleday-Doran, Garden City, New York.

KRASILOVSKY, M. WILLIAM, AND SIDNEY SHEMEL
[2000] *This Business of Music: The Definitive Guide to the Music Industry*, 8th edition, Billboard, New York.*

KRUEGER, MILES
[1977] *Show Boat: The Story of a Classical American Musical*, Oxford University Press, New York.

LACKMANN, RON
[1970] *Remember Radio*, G. P. Putnam's Sons, New York, p. 22, col. 2.

LANGE, HORST H.
[1966] *Die Deutsche "78er" Discographie der Hot-Dance- und Jazz-Muzik 1903–1958*, Colloquium, Berlin.

LARKIN, COLIN (ED.)
[1998] *The Encyclopedia of Popular Music*, Macmillan, New York.

LAX, ROGER, AND FREDERIC SMITH
[1984] *The Great Song Theseaurus*, Oxford University Press, New York, p. 510.

LEVANT, OSCAR
[1940] *A Smattering of Ignorance*, Doubleday, Garden City, New York.*
[1969] *The Memoirs of an Amnesiac*, Samuel French, Hollywood.*

LIMBACHER, JAMES L. (ED.)
[1974] *Film Music: From Violins to Video*, Scarecrow Press, Metuchen, New Jersey.

LOWE, LESLIE
[1975] *Directory of Popular Music, 1900-1965*, Peterson Publishing, Droitwich, England.

THE LYNN FARROL GROUP
[1980] *The ASCAP Biographical Dictionary of Composers, Authors, and Publishers*, ASCAP, New York.

MALONE, BILL C.
[1968] *Country Music U.S.A.: A Fifty Year History by Bill C. Malone*, University of Texas Press, Austin, Texas.

MALONE, BILL C., AND JUDITH MCCULLOH (EDS.)
[1975] *Stars of Country Music: Uncle Dave Macon to Johnny Rodriguez*, University of Ilinois Press, Urbana, Illinois.

MALTIN, LEONARD
[1999] *2000 Movie and Video Guide*, Signet, New York.*

MARCO, GUY A.
[1993] *Encyclopedia of Recorded Sound in the United States*, Garland, New York.

MARTIN, GEORGE WHITNEY
[1983] *The Damrosch Dynasty: America's First Family of Music*, Houghton Mifflin, Boston.*

MARVIN, KEITH
[2000] *The Graham-Paige March*,
www.autohistory.org/feature_2.html

MATTFIELD, JULIUS
[1962] *Variety Music Cavalcade: A Chronology of Vocal and Instrumental Music Popular in the United States 1620-1961*, Prentice Hall, Englewood Cliffs, New Jersey, pp. 405, 438.

MCCABE, JOHN, AL KILGORE, AND RICHARD W. BANN
[1975] *Laurel and Hardy*, E. P. Dutton, New York.

MCCARTHY, ALBERT
[1971] *Big Band Jazz*, Putnam's Sons (Chilton), Philadelphia, Pennsylvania.
[1974] *The Dance Band Era: The Dancing Decades from Ragtime to Swing: 1910-1950*, Chilton, Philadelphia, Pennsylvania.

MCCORMACK, LILY
[1949] *I Hear You Calling Me*, Bruce, Milwaukee, p. 147 and picture before p. 153.

MCNAMARA, DANIEL I. (ED.)
[1952] *The ASCAP Biographical Dictionary of Composers, Authors, and Publishers*, 2nd edition, Crowell, New York (see also The Lynn Farrol Group for newer edition).

MEYER, HAZEL
[1958] *The Gold in Tin Pan Alley*, Lippincott, Philadelphia, Pennsylvania.*

MUNDEN, KENNETH W. (ED.)
[1971] *American Film Institute Catalog of Motion Pictures Produced in the United States: Feature Films 1921–1930*, R. R. Bowker, New York.

NATIONAL TRUSTEES
[1999] *The GRAMMY Awards Webcast–OfficalSite*

OJA, CAROL J.
[1982] *American Music Recordings: A Discography of 20th-Century U.S. Composers*, Institute for Studies in American Music, Conservatory of Music, Brooklyn College of the City University of New York, Brooklyn, New York.

OSBORNE, ROBERT
[1999] *Seventy Years of the Oscar: The Official History of the Academy Awards*, Abbeville Press, New York.

PALMER, JACK
[1999] *Vernon Dalhart*, www.garlic.com/~tgracyk/dalhart.htm

PEYSER, JOAN
[1998] *The Memory of All That: The Life of George Gershwin*, Billboard, New York.

RAYMOND, JACK
[1998] *Show Music on Record from the 1890s to the 1980s*, 2nd edition, Ungar, New York.

RAYNO, DON
[2003] *Paul Whiteman: Pioneer in American Music; Volume 1: 1890–1930*, Scarecrow Press, Lanham, Maryland.

REIS, CLAIRE R.
[1947] *Composers in America*, Macmillan, New York.

RHOADS, B. ERIC
[1996] *Blast From the Past: A Pictorial History of Radio's First 75 Years*, Streamline Press, West Palm Beach, Florida, p. 196 (photo).

RIZZOLI, RICORDI
[1972] *Encyclopedia del Musica*, Rizzoli Editore, Milano.

RUST, BRIAN

[1970a] *Victor Master Book*, Vol. 2, W. C. Allen, Stanhope, New Jersey.

[1970b] *Jazz Records 1897–1942*, Storyville, London.

[1972] *The Dance Bands*, Ian Allan, London.

[1973] *The Complete Entertainment Discography 1890–1942*, Arlington House, New York; unindexed pages too numerous to cite.

[1975] *The American Dance Band Discography 1917–1942*, Arlington House, New Rochelle, New York.

[1978] *The American Record Label Book*, Arlington House, New Rochelle, New York, p. 309.

SADIE, STANLEY (ED.)

[1994] *The New Norton/Grove Concise Encyclopedia of Music*, Norton, New York.

SANFORD, HERB

[1972] *Tommy and Jimmy: The Dorsey Years*, Arlington House, New Rochelle, New York.

SAVILLE, R. RICHARD

[1996] *Nat Shilkret: His Master's Voice*,
mypage.direct.ca/r/rsavill/shilkret.html

SCHULLER, GUNTHER

[1989] *The Swing Era: The Development of Jazz 1930–1945*, Oxford University Press, New York.

SCHWARTZ, CHARLES

[1973] *Gershwin: His Life and His Music*, Bobbs-Merrill, Indianapolis, Indiana.

SETTEL, IRVING

[1967] *A Pictorial History of Radio*, Grosset and Dunlap, New York.

SHALE, RICHARD

[1985] *Academy Awards*, Ungar, New York.

SHAPIRO, NAT, AND BRUCE POLLACK (ED.)

[1985] *Popular Music, 1920–1979*, Vol. 1–2, Oxford University Press, New York.

SHERMAN, MICHAEL

[1992] *The Collectors' Guide to Victor Records*, Monarch Records Enterprises, Dallas, Texas (besides index see pp. 65, 67, 77, 112–115, 143, and implicit mention on 82).

SIMON, GEORGE T.

[1971] *Simon Says: The Sights and Sounds of the Swing Era 1935–1955*, Arlington House, New Rochelle, New York.

[1981] *The Big Bands*, 4th Edition, Schirmer, New York.

SLIDE, ANTHONY
[1982] *Great Radio Personalities in Historic Photographs*, Dover, New York.

SLONIMSKY, NICOLAS
[1971] *Music Since 1900*, 4th edition, Scribner, New York.

SMART, JAMES R.
[1970] *The Sousa Band: A Discography*, Library of Congress, Washington, D.C. (see Index of Conductors).

SMITH, STEVEN C. (ED.)
[1990] *Film Composers Guide*, Lone Eagle, Berverly Hills, California.

SPAETH, SIGMUND
[1948] *A History of Popular Music in America*, Random House, New York.

SPOTTSWOOD, RICHARD E.
[1990] *Ethnic Music on Record: A Discography of Ethnic Recordings Produced in the United States, 1893–1942*, Vol. 1–7, University of Illinois Press, Urbana, Illinois.

STADWELL, WILLIAM E., AND MARK BALDIN
[2000] *The Big Band Reader*, Haworth, New York.

STOCKDALE, ROBERT L.
[1995] *Tommy Dorsey on the Side, Studies in Jazz, No. 19*, Scarecrow Press, Metuchen, New Jersey.

SUDHALTER, RICHARD M.
[1999] *Lost Chords*, Oxford University Press, New York.

SUDHALTER, RICHARD M., AND PHILIP R. EVANS
[1974] *Bix: Man and Legend*, Arlington House, New Rochelle, New York.

SWARTZ, JON D., AND ROBERT C. REINEHR
[1993] *Handbook of Old-Time Radio: A Comprehensive Guide to Golden Age Radio Listiening and Collecting*, Scarecrow Press, Lanham, Maryland.

TERRACE, VINCENT
[1999] *Radio Programs, 1924–1984: A Catalogue of Over 1800 Shows*, St. Martin's Press, New York.

THOMAS, BOB
[1964] *Fred Astaire, The Man, The Dancer*, St. Martin's Press, New York.*

THOMPSON, OSCAR (ED.; ALSO NICOLAS SLONIMKSY)
[1964] *The International Cyclopedia of Music and Musicians*, Dodd-Mead, New York.

WALKER, LEO
[1989] *Jazz, The Big Band Almanac*, 2nd Edition, De Capo, New York.

WALSER, ROBERT
[1999] "Don Redman, Portrait of a Bandleader," *Keeping Time: Readings in Jazz*, Oxford University Press, New York.

WHITBURN, JOEL
[1986] *Joel Whitburn's Pop Memories 1890–1954: The History of American Popular Music*, Record Research, Menomonee Falls, Wisconsin.

WHITE, RAYMOND A.
[1998] *The Gershwin Legacy*, Library of Congress, www.loc.gov/loc/lcib/9809/gershwin.html

WIER, ALBERT (ED.)
[1938] *The Macmillan Encyclopedia of Music and Musicians*, Macmillan, New York.

WOLFE, CHARLES, K.
[2001] *Classic Country: Legends of Country Music*, Routledge, New York, p. 73.

WORTH, PAUL W.
[1997] *John McCormack: Extant Radio Broadcasts 1925–1942*, www.jump.net/-pwworth/radio.html

Abbreviations Used in Index

actr	actor or actress
ancr	announcer
arrg	arranger
arts	artist
auth	author
bass	bass player
bib	author cited in bibliography
bson	bassoonist
busn	business person
cell	cellist
chor	choreographer
clar	clarinetist
cmdn	comedian or comedienne
comp	composer
cond	conductor or band leader
danc	dancer
ddir	dance director
dir	director
educ	educator
flut	flutist
govt	politician, statesman
lyrc	lyricist
md	medical doctor
news	news broadcaster or news columnist
oper	operatic singer
perc	percussionist
pian	pianist
pops	popular or other non-operatic singer
prod	producer
publ	publisher
sax	saxophonist
scie	scientist or inventor
trmp	trumpet player
trom	trombonist
viol	violinist
writ	songwriter or scriptwriter

INDEX

Pages corresponding to section headings are marked in italics. The reader must search the following material, which is not included in this index: all portions of entries in Appendixes A, B and D, which are in bold print; all material in the remaining appendixes, the foreword, the introduction and the photospread.

1812 Overture, 44–45

A&R (Artist and Repetoire) Committee. *See* Victor
Abato, Jimmy (clar), 246–247, 251–252
Academy Award, 209n1
Acne Care commercial, 232
acoustical recordings. *See* mechanical recordings
Adam, Adolphe (comp), 248
Adam and Eve, 196
Adler, Jacob (actr), 2
Aeolian Hall, 51, 58
Africa—Land of Contrasts, 222
agents, 68, *84,* 91, 174, 185, 189, 201
Ager, Milton (comp), 94
AGMA, 52
Ain't She Sweet, 94
Alabieff, Alexander Nicholaevich (comp), 250

Albani, Countess (Olga Medolago) (pops), 143
Albeniz, Isaac (comp), 251
Alda, Francis (oper), 138, 139
Aleichem, Scholom (auth), 39
Algonquin Hotel, 98
All Star Orchestra, 237
Allen, Paul Hastings (comp), 246
Allenby, Peggy (actr), 282
Also Sprach Zarathustra, 10, 17
Althouse, Paul (oper), 182
Altschuler, Jacob (busn), 15
Altschuler, Modest (comp), *14*
American Bankers Association (Associated Banks), 228, 283
An American in Paris, 90, *99,* 172, 283
American People's Chorus, 183
American Romance, 189–192
Americansky, 4
Anderson, Judith (actr), 117

Andrieff, Vasilii Andrieff (comp), 247
Angela Mia, 125
Anthony Adverse, 170
Archer, Violet (comp), 247
Arden-Ohman Orchestra, 241
Arensky, Anton (comp), 252
Arlen, Harold (comp), 243
Arne, Dr. Thomas Augustine (comp),
    250
Arnold, Edward (actr), 170, 177,
    198–200, 209n3, 244
Arnstein, Ira (comp, cond), *157*,
    163n9
Arrowsmith, William (oboe), 252
Arthur, Ned. *See* Shilkret, Nathaniel
    "Nat"
Artist Record Company, 209n3
ASCAP (American Society of Com-
    posers and Publishers), 72–73,
    117, 127, 158, 180n3
Astaire, Adele (danc), 9n1
Astaire, Fred (danc, actr), 9n1, 170–
    177
AT&T, 208
atonal system, 206
Atterberg, Kurt (critic), 100
auditions, 13, 74, *78*, 79, 82, 108, 113,
    128, 144, 150
Auer, Mischa (actr), 170
Austin, Gene (pops, lyrc), *74*, 97, 117,
    226, 228, 237–238, 240–241
Autry, Gene (actr, pops), *113*
Ave Maria, 139
Ay, Ay, Ay, 40, 50
Ayer and Son, 63, 84, 115, 160–161
Aylesworth, Merlin Hall, Esq. (busn),
    122, 124–125, 128, 138, 150
Aylesworth, Mrs., 124
Aztec Record Company, 242–243

Babel, 196, 198–199
Babel story, 196

Bach, Johann Sebastian (comp), 30,
    139, 149, 202, 252–253
Bacher, William A. (dentist, writ,
    prod), *145*, 165, 184–185, 282
Baer, Abel (comp), 234, 241
Bagby morning series, 31
Bainter, Fay (actr), 117
Baker, Julien (flut), 252
Balfe, Michael William (comp), 168,
    245
Ballad for Americans, 183, 285
Ballantine, Edward (comp), 249
Bampton, Rose (pops), 91, 121–122,
    206
The Bankers' Hour radio show (*Song
    and Story*), 63
Baravalle, Victor (cond), 120, 180n5
Barber of Seville, 113, 171
Barnes, Pat (ancr, actr), 285
Barnett, Charlie (cond), 284
The Baron, *11*
Barrère, Georges (flut, cond), 24–25,
    27, 80
Barrymore, Ethel (actr), 98
Barrymore, John (actr), 98
Bartók, Béla (comp), 217, 246
Barzin, Léon (cond), 161
baseball game, 52
Bauer, Harold (pian), 54, 117, 121
Baur, Franklyn (pops), 241
Baxter, Tom (ancr), 285
Bayer, J. (comp), 249
Beach, Mrs. H. H. A. (comp), 251
bear, 71
Because, 50
Becker, Irving (viol), 212, 215n1
Beecham, Sir Thomas (cond), 143
Beethoven, Ludwig van (comp), 17–
    18, 30, 93, 96, 122, 130, 143, 166,
    250–251
    Fifth Symphony, 31, 122
    Ninth Symphony, 18, 56
Beiderbecke, Leon "Bix" (trmp), *115*

Belloy, Miss O. (pops), 235
Beni, Jimi (David Madaleva) (oper), 219, 225, 245–249, 251
Bennett, Robert Russell (comp, arrg), 100, 174, 212
Benton, William (busn), 146
Benton and Bowles Advertising Agency, 84, 145, 147
Berlin, Irving (comp), 40, 60, 89, 117, 144, 158, 171
Berlin Music Inc., 52
Berman, Pandro S. (prod), 169, 172–173, 180n4
Bernie, Ben (cond), 77
Bernstein, Leonard (cond, comp), 43, 73, 217
Bethany College, 159
Beverly Hills Hotel, *186*
Bible, 196
The Big Game, 225
Bizet, Georges (comp), 223
Blaine, James (govt), 33
Bledsoe, Jules (pops, actr), 75
Bliss, Paul Jr. (comp), 251
Blodget, Alden (busn), 214–215
Bloom, Rube (comp), 100, 232, 243
Blue Danube, 171
blues, 171
Blum, J. Everett, 181
BMI, 72–73, 104n4, 127, 158
Bodanzky, Artur (cond), 86, 136–137, 139
Bohannon, Hoyt (trom), 201
The Bohemian Girl, 168, 226–228, 230–233
Bohm, Carl (comp), 247
Bojangles of Harlem, 172
Boldt (busn), 27
Bond Bread, 140
Bonefish and Barricuda, 223
Booth Theater, 215n1
Bori, Lucrezia (oper), 53, 117, 138

Borodin, Alexander Porfirivich (comp), 14, 98
Borodkin, Abe (cell), 121, 252
Borodkin, Herb (cell), 121
borscht circuit, 1
Boston Fidets, 29
Boston Pops, 92
Boston Symphony Orchestra, 151
Boswell, Connie (pops), 131
Boswell Sisters (Connie, Helvetia, Martha), 130–131
Boulanger, Nadia (pian, educ, comp), 100
Bourdillon, Francis William (poet), 229
Bourdon, Rosario (cond), 45
Bourne, Saul (busn), 52
Bove (lyrc), 250
Bowles, Chester (busn), 146
Bowles, Paul (comp), 251
Boy Meets Dog, 229
Bradley, Will (Wilbur Swichtentenburger) (trom), 181, 202, 242
Brady, Alice (actr), 117
Brahms, Johannes (comp), 27, 34, 55, 86, 93, 253
   First Symphony, 55, 93
   Quintet, 27
Brainard, Bertha (busn), 119–120
Brice, Fanny (cmdn), 74
Briskin, Sam (busn), *167*, 173
Bristol (investor), 158
Brody, Roy (lyrc), 227
Brokenshire, Norman (ancr), 115, 130
Brown, Lew (writ), 142
Brown Derby restaurant, 90, 133
Bruch, Max (comp), 137
Bruno (busn), 189
Bruno Company, 47–48
Burke, Joe (writ), 238
Burt, Hoyt John Jr. (lyrc), 248–249
Busch, Carl (comp), 250
Bushman, Mrs. (busn), *83*

Busoni, Ferruccio (pian, comp, cond), 204

Busse, Henry (trmp), 77–78, *116*, 127

Byrd, Richard E. (navy), 86

Byrd, William (comp), 246

Caeser, Irving (lyrc), 224

Cafe Boulevard, 12

Cain and Abel, 196

Cairns, Cliff (busn), 47, 66, 68

Calbi, Luigi S. (comp), 251

Camden studio, *44*, 48, 59, 67, 96, 106
    office, 74
    plant, 108
    sales force, 42

Camel Cigarette radio shows
    Camel Caravan, 165–166
    Camel Pleasure Hour, 115

Candle Lights, 115

cantors, 38

Capitol Record Company, 199, 209n3

Capitol Theatre, 53

Carmichael (busn), 128–129

Carmichael, Hoagland (Hoagy)
    (comp, pian), 116

Carmody, John (actr), 282

Carnation Milk radio show (*The Car-
    nation Contented Hour*), 181, 184

Carnegie Hall, 184

Carnegie Hall Lyceum, 33

Carnival of Venice Variations, 3

Carpenter, John Alden (busn, comp),
    239

Carson, Robison (pops), 72

Carter, Sara (oper), 245, 248, 250–251

Caruso, Enrico (oper), 27, 31, 37–38,
    42, 48–50, 60n5, 66–67, 106, *114*,
    130, 187, 243

Caruso, Rudolfo (oper), *50*

Casals, Pablo (cell, cond), 117, 119

Case, Anna (oper), 20

Cass, Lee (oper), 245, 247, 249–251

Castelnuovo-Tedesco, Mario (comp),
    196, 198, 244

Catskill borscht circuit. *See* borscht
    circuit

Cavaliere, Lina (oper), 21

CBS, 128–130, 158, 185, 189

Century Theater, 26

Cervantes-Sequeira, 250

Chafferelli, A. (clar), 139

Chaliapin, Feodor Ivanovich (oper),
    31, 117, 119–120, 179

Challis, Bill (arrg), 78, 95, 115, 184–
    185, 219

Chamlee, Mario (writ), 228

Chanson, 194

Chansonette, 194–195

Chaplin, Charlie (film cmdn), 64

Chapman, Mr. ("cond"), 31–32

Chapman, Mrs. (busn), 31

Charmaine, 125

Chauve Souris, 40

Chesterfield radio show (*Music That
    Satisfies*), 115, *128*, 131–133

Chez Paree club, 186

Child, Calvin G. (busn), 39, 47, 49,
    138

Children of the Ritz, 232

Childs restaurant, 160

Chinese ambassador, 16

Chloe, 97

Chopin, Frédéric (comp, pian), 30,
    135, 149, 249, 253
    Concerto, 135

Christmas Overture, 181

Christy, Harold (lyrc), 241

church chimes, *111*

Churchill, Winston (govt), 200

Ciannella, Yvonne (oper), 245–249

Cielito Lindo, 40

City Center, 200

City College of New York, 27

Claire, Marion (oper), 284

Clark, Palmer John (comp), 248, 250

Clark, Walter (busn), 66, 72, 96
Cliffe, Peter (auth), 216
Cogane, Nelson (lyrc), 226
Cohen, Irving (oboe), 25, 88
Coleman, Albert (comp), 247, 250
Collins, Ray (actr), 282
Colonel Gimp (Martin "Moe the
    Gimp" Snyder), 132–134
Columbia British Phonograph Com-
    pany, 66
Columbia Pictures, 164
Columbia Record Company, 20, 38,
    47, 59, 66, 73–75, 78, 100, 140,
    167–168, 188–189
  Foreign Department, 38
  prize, 100
  studio, 144, 245
Columbo, Russ (pops), *114*
Colwell, Hobart J. (lyrc), 227
Coming 'Round the Mountain, 131
Concerto for Trombone, 93, 200,
    209n4, 223–224, 230, 232, 285
Congressional Library, 111
Congressional Music Library Concert,
    110
Congressional Music Library Hall, 110
Conrad, Con (comp), 114
The Continental, 114
Conway, Pat (cond), 84
Cooper, Gary (actr), 96–97
Copland, Aaron (comp), 100
Corelli, Arcangelo (comp), 252
Correra, Ferrara (writ), 236
Coslow, Sam (pops, writ, publ), 226
Coulter, Douglas (busn), 85, 87, 160
The Countess Maritza, 284
The Covenant, 196
Cowell, Henry (comp), 250
Crain, Jon (oper), 245, 248–249
Crawford, Jesse (organ), 97
Crawford, Richard (bib), 104n6,
    104n8
Creation, 196

Cremazie, Octave (writ), 236
Croce, Arlene (bib), 180n5
Crooks, Richard (oper, pops), 82, 91,
    117, 160, 242
Crosby, Bing (pops, actr), 39, 75, 77,
    94, 120, 129, 130
Cross, Milton (ancr), 93, 135
Croxton, Frank (pops), 243
Crucifixion, 117
Crumit, Frank (pops), 72, 102, 117,
    208, 285
Cuckoo Waltz, 40
Cunningham, Paul (lyrc), 226
Curtis, Mrs. (socialite), *88*
Curtis Institute of Music, 206

Dalhart, Vernon (pops), 42–43
Dallin, Jacques (comp), 250–252
Damrosch, (Mrs. Walter) Margaret,
    33–34
Damrosch, Walter (cond), 18, 24–28,
    33–34, 45, 80, 93, 99, 123–124,
    179
  Concert Tour, *23*
  dance craze, 35
Dargomijsky, Alexander (comp), 246
Dark Eyes, 40
Davis (busn), 47, 49
Dawes, Charles Gates (govt, busn),
    162n2
de Begnac, Carlo (comp), 246
De Costa, Harry (lyrc), 222, 242
De Falla, Manuel (comp), 196, 217
De Gogorza, Emilio (oper), 126
De Koven, Reginald (comp), *103*
De Leath, Vaughn (pops), 102
De Luca, Giuseppe (oper), 44–45, 51,
    117
de Micheli, Guido (comp), 251
De Pachmann, Vladimir (pian, cond),
    80
The Deacon. *See* Aylesworth, Merlin

Debussy, Claude (comp), 80, 87, 90,
    149, 223
Decca Record Company, 94, 201
DeLong, Thomas A. (bib), 162n6
Delstaiger, Charles. *See* Staigers, Del
Delworth, George (lyrc), 223
Demetriades, Tetos (pops), 241
the Depression, 162n1
Desert Song, 284
Deutsch, Adolph (arrg, comp), 77
Di Blassi (I Tolsch) (trmp), 12
Diane, 125
Ditson's Music Store, 31
Dixieland Jazz Band, 57
Donaldson, Walter (comp), 75, 237–
    238
Donizetti, Gaetano (comp), 247, 249
The Donkey Serenade, 194–195
Dorsey, Jimmy (clar), 78, 80, *93*, 95,
    121–122, 130–131, 171, 173, 181
Dorsey, Tommy (trom), 20, 75, 78,
    88, *93*, 95, 97, 121, 130, 181, *185*,
    200, 209n4, 237
Dostal, Nico (comp), 252
Down River of Golden Dreams, 243
Down the Street, 119
Downey, Morton (pops), 77
Drescher, Alice Heinecke (busn), 244
Dreyer, David (writ), 227, 241
Dreyfus (stage designer), 64
Druary, John (oper), 245–251
Du Bist Mein Herz Allein, 127
Dubin, Al (writ), 238
Duncan, Isadora (danc), 33
Dunne, Irene (actr, pops), 143
Dunning, John (bib), 162n6
Dutschke, Hermann, Sr. (horn), 17
Dvořák, Antonin (comp), 13, 195, 226

Eastman Kodak radio show (*The
    Eastman Kodak Hour*), 63, 82,
    143, 233, 280
Ecstasy, 209n4

Eddy, Nelson (pops, actr), 178, 194,
    239
Edel, Yitzchak (comp), 247–248
Edens, Roger (pian), 243
Edison, Thomas A. (scie), 20, 106
efficiency expert, 67
Eggeling, George (comp), 249
Eggerth, Marta (oper, actr), 187
Eileen, 284
Einstein, Albert (scie), 155
electrical recordings, 35, 47, 57–58,
    66, 111, 114–115, 218, 237
Elijah, 24
Elizabeth Sprague Coolidge Founda-
    tion, 280
Ellington, Edward K. "Duke" (comp,
    cond, pian), 45
Ellington, Judy, 284
Elman, Mischa (viol), 14, 54, 59, *76*,
    79–80, 117, 120, 134, 137, 155,
    239
    father of, 76
Emperor Jones, 2, 204
Endlich, Saramae (oper), 249
Engel, Carl, 110
Erdody, Leo (comp, cond, viol), 65,
    227
Eroica, 118
Esso (now Exxon) radio show (*The
    O'Flynn*), 63, 147–148, 224, 226–
    230, 232–234, 242
Estrellita, 40, 50
Etting, Ruth (pops, actr), 129–130,
    132
Ettore, Eugene (comp), 246
Evans, Philip R. (bib), 104n7
Eveready radio show (*The Eveready
    Hour*), 63, 82, *85*, 87, 216, 224–
    225, 227
Exxon. *See* Esso (now Exxon) radio
    show (*The O'Flynn*)

Farberman, Irving (perc), 250

Farewell Malihini, 165
Farley, Max (clar), 237
Farmer, Francis (actr), 170, 177
Farrar, Fuzzy (trmp), 237
Farrar, Geraldine (oper, actr), 31, 44, 117, 143
Fate (Tango Valentino), 73
Faure, Gabriel (comp), 248
feast or famine, 37, 66, 130
Feder, Willie, 3
Feinsmith, Sam (clar, sax), 80, *131*
Feinstock, Nellie (writ), 230
Feist Company (publishers), 96–97, 158
Feldman, Joe, 225, 234
Fenton, Mack. *See* Shilkret, Nathaniel "Nat"
Fidelio, 135
Fields, Lew (cmdn), 150
Filo, Viola (pops), 282
Fine Romance, A, 172
Finney, R. L. (comp), 250
Finnish Institute of Recorded Sound, 236
Finston (Shilkret), Anne, 36
Finston, Arthur, 163n8
Finston, Mack, 222
Finston, Nathaniel (Nat) (cond, busn), 21, 29, 36, 158, 163n8, 188–191, 205, 207
Finston, Sydney, 164
Firefly, 194–195
Fireside Tales, 118
First National Pictures, 96, 164
The First Time I Saw You, 173, 177, 243
Fischer, Ernst (comp), 246–247, 250–252
Fitzpatrick, James (busn), *158*
Fitzpatrick, Ruth (busn), 158–159
Flashes, 115
Fleeson, Nelson (writ, lyrc), 228
Fleta, Miguel (oper), *50*

Flonzaley Quartet, 27
Floridia, Pietro (comp), 77, *149*, 159
Flusser, Richard Stuart (educ, busn), 244, 247–249
Fokine, M. Mikail (danc, chor), 33
Fontaine, Joan (actr), 170
Fonzo, P. E. (writ), 236
Fora, Arthur (flut), 247
Forbestein, Leo F. (comp), 188
Ford, John (dir), 169, 175
Fosdick, Dudley (melaphone), 237
Foster, Stephen (comp), 98, 101–102, 232, 238
The Four Rajahs, 241
Fox Movie Theater, 194
Fox studio, 188
Fradkin, Frederick (viol), *151*
Frank, Arlyne (oper), 245, 249
Frank, Jvan (lyrc), 224
Frank, Sherman (pian), 246, 248–250, 252–253
Franko, Nahan (viol, cond), 6, *156*
Freire, Osman Pérez (comp), 240
Friedland, Harry, 235
Friedsell, Louis (writ), 236
Friere (writ), 222
Friestadt, Harry (trmp), 252
Friml, Billie (pian), 193
Friml, Rudolf (comp), 101, *102*, *193*, 239, 246, 252
Friml-Shilkret-Donaldson, 193
Froman, Jane (pops), 182, 239
Fuchs, Herman (busn), 204
The Fur Coat, 219
Furness, Betty (actr), 86
Furness, George (busn), 85–86

Galli-Curci, Amelita (oper), 31, 44–45, 47, 117, 166
Gallodoro, Alfred (clar), 246
gambling, *206*
Gannon, Kim (lyrc), 229
Garden, Mary (oper), 117, 143

Gart, John (cond), 285
Gary, Judge (busn), 32
Gaskill, Clarence (writ), 226
Gatti-Casazza, (Mrs. Giulio) Alda, 138
Gatti-Casazza, Giulio (busn), 162n5
Gauthier, Eva (oper, pops), *51*
Gavotte (Gossec), 83
Gelatt, Roland (bib), 60n4, 103n1, 162n1
General Electric radio show, 63, 93
General Foods, 82
General Motors radio shows, 63, 83, 134–135, 141, 205
General Spanky, 231
Genesis Suite, *196*, 209n2, 217, 224
Gently Down the Stream, 219
Georges Barrère Ensemble, *25*
Gerhardt, J. (clar), 10
Gerry, Elbridge (attorney, public advocate), 9n1
Gerry Society, 8
Gershwin, George (comp), 30, 51, 58–59, 77, 86, 89, 99, 126, 142–143, 172–174, 225, 237, 239, 283
album, *182*
death, 177
Piano Concerto, 118
Gershwin, Ira (writ), 173
Gershwin Memorial Concert, 90
Gibbons, Floyd (news), 143, 162n6
Gigli, Beniamino (oper), 117, 124
Gilbert, L. Wolfe (lyrc), 96–97, 222–224, 227–228, 230, 238, 241
Gilbert, Sir William S. (auth, lyrc), 247, 252
Gill, Armando (writ), 236
Gilpin, Charles (writ), 237
Gilrod, Louis (lyrc), 225
Gimp. *See* Colonel Gimp
Ginzel, G. (comp), 249
Glazunov, Alexander (comp), 55, 64
Glenn, Wilfred (pops), 241–243

Gluck, Alma (oper, pops), 138
God Bless America, 60
Godard, Benjamin L. (comp), 246, 248, 251
Goldkette, Jean (cond), 95
Goldman, Edwin Franko (comp, cond), 84, 157, 215
Goldman, Richard (comp), 249
Goldmark, Karl (comp), 251
Goldstein, Manny (viol), 19–20
Goldwyn studios, 173
Good Earth, 205
Goodman, Benny (clar, sax, cond), 80, 166, 181, *185*, 213, 237, 283
Gorin, Igor (oper), 284
Gorman, Ross (clar, sax), 77
Gossec, François-Joseph (comp), 105, 225
   Gavotte, 83
Gotham Hotel, 206
Gould, Mitzi (actr), 283
Gould, Morton (comp, cond), *57*, 183, 228
Gounod, Charles François (comp), 139, 235, 247
Gracyk, Tim (bib), 60n2
Grainger, Percy (comp), 126
Grand Canyon Suite, 127
Grand Street Theater, 2
Grant, Cary (actr), 170
Graphic (newspaper), 142
Grauer, Ben (ancr), 283
Gray, Alexander (oper, actr), 128
Green, George Hamilton (perc, scie), 112
Green, Jack (pian), 64–65
Green, Joe (perc), 112, 224, 234, 240
Green, Johnny (comp, cond, pian, busn), 80, 156, 209n1
Gretchaninoff, Alexander (comp), 223, 231
Grieg, Edvard (comp), 118, 225, 250, 253

Griselle, Thomas (comp), 100, 110, 243
Nocturne and *March*, 100, 110
Grofé, Ferde (arrg, comp), 77–78, *127*, 149
Gruenberg, Jack (pian), 204
Gruenberg, Louis (comp), 100, *189*, *204*
father of, 2
Guilbert, Yvette (pops), 214
Gunga Din, 228
Gurrelieder, 202, 206
Gusikoff, Michael (viol), 240

Hackett (busn), 147–148
Hall of Fame. See Lysol radio show
Hallett, Niel. *See* Shilkret, Nathaniel "Nat"
Hambitzer, Charles (pian, comp, educ), 29–30, 32
Hammerstein I, Oscar (impresario, prod), 193–194
Hampton, Lionel (cond, vibraphone), 112
Hand (judge), 158
Handel, George Frederick (comp), 247
Handy William Christopher "W. C." (comp), 110
Hanna, Mrs. (socialite), 16
Harbach, Otto (lyrc, auth), 193–194
Harburg, Yip (lyrc), 243
Hardy, Oliver (film cmdn), 168
Harling, W. Frank (comp), 57–58
harmonica, 47–48, 69–70
Harold, Arthur. *See* Shilkret, Nathaniel "Nat"
Harrison, Charles (pops), 243
Hart, Philip (auth), 104n8
Hart, Ted (oper), 247, 252
Haubiel, Charles (comp), 250
Hauser (busn), 47–48
Hauser, Franklin (comp), 147
Havrilla, Alois (ancr), *87*

Haydn, Franz Joseph (comp), 96, 252
Hazlett, Chester (clar, sax), 77, 121, 130–131
Heagney, William (lyrc), 222
Hearst, William Randolph (busn), 96
Heavenly Music, 209n1
Hector, Louis (actr), 282
Heidelberg, Paul (flut), 21
Heifetz, Jascha (viol), 54, 59, 76, 79–80, 106, 117, 134, 137, *155*
Heinecke, Alice. *See* Drescher, Alice Heinecke
Heinecke, Paul (busn), 127, 244
Heinrich (trmp), *25*
Hepburn, Katharine (actr), 138, 169
Herbert, Victor (comp, cond), 2–3, 6, *13*, 29, 58, 101–102, 193, 217, 238–239, 247, 251
Herbert album, *182*
Hérold, Ferdinand (comp), 239
Hershman, Mordachay (cantor), 38
Hertz, Alfredo (cond), 19
Heyward, DeBose (auth, poet), 227
Hickman, Art (cond), 41
Higgins, 67
High Hatters, 241
Hilbert, J. and N. (pseudonym), 225, 227
Hilbert, Nat. *See* Shilkret, Nathaniel "Nat"
Hill (ancr), 142
hillbilly songs, *69*
Hillpot, Billy "Trade" (pops, cmdn), 63
Hillpot and Lambert (Smith Brothers team), 63
Hilo Hawaiian Orchestra, 238, 241–243
Hinkel, Florence (oper), 24
Hire's Root Beer radio show (*Hire's Harvesters*), 63, 82, 231
His Master's Voice of the Air. See Victor

Hitler, Adolf, 162n4, 206
Hoffman, Anna (pops), 236
Hofman, Josef (pian), 26
Hohner Harmonica, 48
Holbrooke, Josef (comp), 246, 251, 253
Holland in Tulip Time, 233
Hollywood Bowl, 90, 201
  concert, 187
Hoover, Mrs. Herbert, 110
Horowitz, Mrs. Vladimir, 134
Horowitz, Vladimir (pian), 134–136
horse tricks, 70, 113
Horses, Horses, Horses, 50
Hubay, Jeno (comp), 251
Hughes, Rupert (auth, ancr), 283
Hull, Henry (actr), 117
Hummel, Ferdinand (comp), 251
Hungarian Gypsy Orchestra, 46
Hutscheson, Edward (pian, educ), 118
Hyman, 13

I.L.G.W.U. Radio Chorus, 239
I Hear America Singing, 187n1, 285
I Tolsch, 12
Il Mio Tesoro, 118
In a Little Spanish Town, 97
In a Mist, 115
In Love, 194
In the Dark, 115
Information Please, 90
The Informer, 175, 180n1
International Concert Orchesta, 238
International Music Company, 73
International Novelty Orchestra, 36, 240–241
International Quartet, 39
Ippolitow-Iwanow, Michail (comp), 238
Irish Rhapsody, #4, 102
Isadora Duncan tour, *33*
It Happened in Paris, 225, 227–229, 233

Italian Serenade, 121
Iturbi, José (pian, cond), 201

Jablonski, Edward (bib), 104n11
Jacobs, Jacob (pop), 236
Jacobs, Ray (lyrc), 228
Jaenecke, Bruno (horn), *150*
Jakobowski, Edward (comp), 247
James, Harry (cond, trmp), 225
James, Lewis (pops, oper), 102, 238, 241–243
Jameson, Anne (oper), 182
Janssen, Werner (cond, comp), *196*, 203, 209n2, 209n4, 239, 244
  tax agent for, 199
Japanese Emperor, 38
jazz, 35, 57, 80–81, 115–116, 131–132, 156, 170–171, 185, 201, 217-218
The Jazz Singer, 35n2
Jeannie With The Light Brown Hair, 102
Jeannine I Dream of Lilac Time, *95*, 243
Jenkins, Jackie "Butch" (actr), *195*
Jenks, Frank (actr), 170
Jenks, L. (writ), 236
Jepson, Helen (oper), 91, 139, 284
Jeritza, Maria (oper), 117, 120
Jessel, Leon (comp), 230
John Golden Theater, 215n1
Johnson (writ), 245
Johnson, E. R. Fenimore, Jr. (busn), 46, 96
Johnson, Eldridge Reeves (busn, machinist), *46*, 47, 59, 60n4, 80, 96, 140
Johnstone, Patricia (lyrc), 223
Jolson, Al (pops, actr), 35n2, 39, 41, *52*, 96
Jonasson (comp), 242
Jones, Allen (pops, actr), 126
Joseffy, Rafael (pian), 29
Jospe, Sam (cond), 21

Joy, Leonard (cond), 241
Jubilee Singers, 238
Judson, Arthur M. (busn), 91, 104n8
Juilliard School of Music, 118, 206

Kabalevsky, Dmitri (comp), 215
Kahn, Gus (comp, lyrc), 193
Kane, Helen (pops, actr), 117
Kapp, Jack (busn), 94
Karlin, Fred (bib), 180n2
Keast, Raymond (oper), 245–247
Keltic, 118
Kern, Jerome (comp), 40, 75, 120,
    142, 158, 172
Kessler, Thelma (pops), 280
Kiepura, Jan (oper, actr), 187
King, Dennis (actr, pops), 117
King, Edward T. (busn, perc), 36, 38,
    41, 43–45, 47, 55–56, 66, *67*, 75,
    95, 101, 243
  cymbal, 68
  King's Orchestra, 236
  séance, 67
King, Mrs. Eddie, 67
King Lear, 2
King Lear, part of, 2–3
Klein, Manny (trmp), 121, 130
Klenner, John (lyrc), 224, 227, 242
Knecht, Joseph (cond), 27, 32
Knickerbocker Beer radio Show (*Re-
    laxation Time*), 181, 227, 242
Knight, Felix (pops), 182, 239
Kodak. *See* Eastman Kodak
Kohon, Benjamin (bson), 23
Kohon, Markus (bson), 23
Komzak, Karl (comp), 245
Korngold, Erich Wolfgang (comp),
    170, 187
Kortalasky (viol), 55
Kostelanetz, André (cond), 170–171
Kountz, Richard (lyrc), 228, 241
Krasilovsky, M. William (attorney,
    auth), 221

Krebs, Beatrice (oper), 247, 249, 251
Kreisler, Fritz (viol, comp), 31, 59, 79,
    154, 228
Kress, Carl (guitar), 97, 237
Krumgold, Sigmund (organ), 241
Kubelik, Jan (viol), 195
Kuhlau, Fr. (comp), 238
Kwartin, Sawel (cantor), 38

La Boheme, 139, 149
La Scala, 85
La Scala Opera House Orchestra, 55
La Traviata, 51
Labate, Bruno (oboe), 80
Lady of the Lake, 224
Laemmle, Carl, Jr. (prod), 75
Lambert, Scrappy "Mark" (pops), 63,
    237, 241
Landon, Alfred (govt), *159*
Lang, Phil (cond), 183
Lanner (comp?), 230
Largo al Factotum, 113
Lasky, Jesse L. (prod), 170
The Last Outlaw, 229
Laurel, Stanley (film cmdn), 168
Lawrence, Harold (writ, lyrc), 222,
    230
Le Galliene, Eva (actr), 117
Lebedoff, Aaron (cantor), 38
Lefebvre, Channing (comp), 246
Lehár, Franz (comp), 127, 183, 187n1
Lehmann, Lotte (oper), 135
LeMaire, Rufus, 188
Lemberg, Austria (Lvov, Ukraine), 4
Leonard, Gene (actr), 283
Leoncavallo, Ruggiero (comp), 248
Lerner, Sammy (lyrc), 224, 231, 242
LeRoy, Henri Leon (clar), 27
Letzter Frühling, 225
Levant, Oscar (actr, pian), *89*
Levy (bass), 18
Levy, H. (clar), 10
Lewis, Earl, 91

Lewis, Ted (cond), 77–78
Lhevinne, Josef (pian), 15
Lichtman, Al, 188
Liebestod, 33
Liebling, Leonard, 244
Liederkranz Hall, 58, 112–113
Lieutenant Kije, 209n5
Liff, Henry (cond, viol), 19
Lilac Time, 95–96
Lillian (writ), 236
Lilly, Josiah Kirby (busn), *101*
Lindbergh, 126
Linkletter, Art (radio and TV host),
    52
Lipstone, 188
Lipton, Sir Thomas (busn), *150*
Liszt, Franz (pian, comp), 30, 77, 233,
    247, 250, 253
Little Club, 53
Little Study, 232
Livingston, Fud (arrg, clar), 237
Livingston, Joseph (Fud) (clar, sax,
    arrg, comp), 64, 171, 173
Lobos. *See* Villa-Lobos
Lodwig, Ray (trmp), 237
Lombardo, Guy (cond), 75, 129
London String Quartet, 217
Lonesome Road, 75, 97, 243
Longo, Frank (pian), 28–31
*Look Down That Lonesome Road. See
    Lonesome Road*
Lopez, Vincent (cond), 77
Lorre, Peter (actr), 90
Los Angeles Symphony, 161
Louise–Depuis le Jour, 144–145
Lucas, Nick (pops, guitar), 143
Lucky Strike, 63
Lund, John (cond), 14
Luther, Frank (pops, writ), 72, 226,
    229, 238, 242
Lvov, Ukraine. *See* Lemberg, Austria
Lysol radio show (*Hall of Fame*), 63,
    137–139, 155

Lzicar, Slavoljub (arrg), 236

MacBoyle, Darl (lyrc), 224
MacDermott. *See* McDiarmid, E.
MacDonald, Jeanette (actr), *178*, 194
MacDonough, Harry (pops, busn), 47,
    62–63, 66–68
MacDowell, Edward (comp, pian),
    117, 246, 248
  Opus 45, 118
  Opus 57, 118
  Opus 59, 118
  Piano Concerto, 90
MacDowell, (Mrs. Edward) Marian,
    117–118
MacDowell Colony, 118, 162n3
Mack, Charles E. (cmdn), *73*
Madaleva, David. *See* Beni, Jimi
Madison Square Garden, 84
Magic Key (of RCA). See Victor
Mahler, Gustav (cond), *17*, 206
Mahoney, Jack (writ), 240
Maisch, Charlie (sound engineer), 55
Make Believe, 75
Malone, Bill C. (bib), 60n3, 103n3,
    162n1
Manville radio show, 143
Mapelson's Metropolitan Library, 118,
    179
March, Frederick (actr), 243
Margo (actr), 169
Margulis, Charlie (trmp), 121, 130
market crash, 81, 106, 208
Markworth, Henry (comp) 245, 248,
    252
Marsh, George (film cutter), 176
Marshall, Dan (flut), 29–30
Martel, Joseph (pops), 236
Martha, 284
Martinelli, Giovanni (oper), 44-
    45, *49*, *50*, 117
Martini, Nino (oper), 170, 177

Marvin, Johnny (pops, comp), 72, 117, 241–242

Mary of Scotland, 169, 223, 226–227, 229, 232

Mask and Wig Club, 237

Massey, Guy, 43

Mauro-Cottone, Aurora (pian), 246

Maxwell House Coffee radio show (*The Maxwell House Hour*), 63, 82, 92

MCA, 147, 201

McAlpin Hotel, 157

McAndrew, John (auth), 36

McCormack, John (oper, pops), 39, 41, 44, 47, 54, 82, 97, 101, *102*, 106–107, 117, 179, 239, 241

McCormack, (Mrs. John) Lilly, 107

McDiarmid, E. (flut), 108–109

McLaglen, Victor (actr), 175

McLeod, Keith (writ), 223

McNamee, Graham (ancr), 83, 108–110, 150

McPartland, Jimmy (trmp), 237

McQuestar, Robin (viol), 283

mechanical recordings, 40, 45–46, 48, 53, 55, 60n3, 114

Melton, James (oper, pops), 63, 91, 102, 107, *127*, 182, 241–243, 284

Mendelssohn, Felix (comp), 23, 251

Mendez, Rafael (trmp), 214

Mendoza, David (cond, viol), 53, 91

Mendoza, Pablo (comp), 245

Mengelberg, Willem (cond), 44, 56–57, 84

Menuhin, Sir Yehudi (viol, cond), 155

Mercer, Johnny (lyrc), 116, 243

Meredith, Burgess (actr), 169

Merino, Julio (comp), 250

Merman, Ethel (pops), 243

Merritt, Frank (news), 1

Mesnard, Auguste (bson), 27

Messer Marco Polo, 225

Metropolitan Chorus, 222

Metropolitan Opera House (Met), 12, 17–18, 22, 49, 50–51, 59, 84, 91, 108, 124, 136, 138–139, 144, 147, 157, 179, 182–183, 204

  Association, 162n5

  Chorus, 84

  Ensemble, 85

  Orchestra, 56

Meyer, Hazel (bib), 162n4

Meyerbeer, Giacomo (comp), 251

MGM, 96, 112, 158, 164, 180n4, 188–190, 195, 200–201, 203–205, 214

Michaud, Arthur (busn), 209n4

Midsummer Night's Dream, 15

Mietzner, Heinz (comp), 248

Mighty Lak' a Rose, 117

Milhaud, Darius (comp), 196, 198, 244, 247

Miller, A. (lyrc), 225

Miller, Glenn (trom), 237

Miller, Mitch, 94

Mills, Irving (publ), 104n6

Mills, Jack (publ), 74

Mills Brothers, 129–130

Mills Music Company, 74

Minnelli, Vincente (dir), *203*

Minnevitch, Borrah (harmonica), *47*, 61n5

Miranda, Carmen (actr), 284

Mississippi Suite, 127

Mitchell, Daniel (busn), 37

Mobil Oil radio show (*Mobiloil Concert*), 63, 126–128, 140–141, 230, 242

Modell, Ronnie (trmp), 1–5, 8, 25, 43, 52, 80, 88, 94, 113, 115, 206, 208, 213–215, 215n1

Moe the Gimp. *See* Colonel Gimp

Monteux, Pierre (cond), 217

moonshiners, 70

Moore, Colleen (actr), 96–97

Moore, Grace (oper, actr), 91, *144*

Moorehead, Agnes (actr), 145

Moran, George (cmdn), *73*
Mordkin, Mikhail (danc), 15, 33
Morehouse, Chauncey (perc), 237
Morgan (writ), 245
Morgan, Helen (actr, pops), 120
Morgan, John Pierpont (busn), 66
Moscheles, Ignatz (comp), 246
Moussorgsky, Modest (comp), 14, 246
Mowbray, Alan (actr), *177*
Mozart, Wolfgang Amadeus (comp),
    30, 93, 96, 101, 107, 118, 151,
    216, 231, 247, 249
  Horn Concerto, 151
Muller, Sigrid Walter (comp), 247
Munn, Frank (pops), 241
Muratore, Lucien (oper), 21
Murphy, Lambert (pops), 243
Music Box Revue, 144
Music for Madame, 227, 232
Musical Courier, 244
Muzak, 242
Muzio, Claudia (oper), 20
My Blue Heaven, 75
Myrvik, Norman (oper), 245
Mysels, Sammy (lyrc), 224, 226

N. W. Ayer and Son. *See* Ayer and
    Son
Narcissus, 117
Nat Shilkret and the Victor Orches-
    tra. *See* Victor
Nathaniel Shilkret Music Company,
    244
Naughty Marietta, 193
Nazi party, 206
NBC, 104n10, 107, 121–122, 124–125,
    127–128, 130, 132, 140, 155, 157–
    158, 160, 179, 182, 185, 200, 218
NBC Chorus, 182
Neely, Henry M. *See* the old stager
Negro Spiritual Paraphrase, 110
Neiburg, Al (lyrc), 224
Nelson, Rudo (comp), 251

Nevin, Ethelbert (comp), 101, 117–
    118, 239, 250
Nevin, Mrs. Ethelbert, 117–118
New England Idylls, 118
New Moon, 284
New York Boys' Orchestra, 1, 3–8,
    12–13, 19, 64, 204
New York Conservatory of Music, 13
New York Giants, 52
New York Philharmonic Orchestra
    (including New York Symphony
    Orchestra), 10, 13, *17*, 18, 27–28,
    44, 56, 84, 91, 93, 134, 141, 143,
    159, 182
Newman, Alfred (cond), 188
Newman, Ernest (critic), 100, 107
Nichols, Red (trmp), *116*
Nicolai, Otto (comp), 229
Nietsche, Friedrich (philosopher), 10
Noah's Ark, 196
Nocturne and *March*. *See* Griselle
Nola, 59
Norma, 136
Norse, 118
North Russian Symphony, 156

Oakie, Jack (actr), 170
Obaugh, C. D., 69, 103n2
Obaugh, Walter, 103n2
O'Brien, Margaret (actr), *195*
Ochs, Siegfried (comp), 245
Odeon records, 39
Oelheim, Helen (pops), 282
Offenbach, Jacques (comp), 246, 249
The O'Flynn. *See* Esso radio show
O'Hara, Geoffery (lyrc), 222
O'Keefe, James L. (arrg), 233
Okeh Record Company, 20, 42, 104n3
Ol' Man River, 75
Old Dominion Steamship Line, 6
the old stager (Henry M. Neely)
    (ancr, prod), 148, 282
Oliver, Paul, 241

Olsen, George (drum, cond), *75*
One Night of Love, 144
Ormandy, Eugene (cond), 53, 91, 134
Ortden, M. (lyrc), 232
Osborne, Ted (minister), 200, 209n3, 244
Otello, 22
Owens, Jack (lyrc), 224

Packard radio show, 143
Paganini, Noccolò (comp, viol), 195
Pal (dog), 225
Paley, William S. (busn), *128*, 189
Palmer, Christine (oper), 248
Palmolive-Colgate radio show (*Palmolive Beauty Box Theater*), 145, 147, 225, 232
Pan, Hermes (dance dir), 172, 176
Panufnik, Andrzej (comp), 252
Parade of the Wooden Soldiers, 40
Paramount studio, 96, 187–188
Paris '90. See Skinner Tour
Paris 1890, 245, 250
Park Avenue Hotel, 19
Parker, Ruth (writ), 229
Pasqualotto, E. G. (writ), 236
Pasternack, Josef A. (cond, pian), 12, 44–45, 227, 241
Pathé, 20–21
Pathé Frère, 24
Pauletta, 149
Pavlova, Anna (danc), 15, 33
Peer, Ralph (busn), *72*, 73, 104n3
Peerce, Jan (oper), 182–183
Pelletier, Wilfred (cond), 91
Pennario, Leonard (pian), 202, 242
Pennsylvania Railroad radio show, 63
Pepusch, Christopher (comp), 245
Pergolesi, Giovanni Battista (comp), 229, 246, 248, 250
Perpetual Motion, 201
Petersboro, 118
Petrillo, James C. (union), 140, 184

Pfeiffer, Max (bass), 22
the phantom violinist, 152, 163n8
Philadelphia Symphony Orchestra, 44, 114
Philharmonic Society. *See* New York Philharmonic Orchestra
Piastro, Michel (viol, cond), 55
Piatigorsky, Gregor (cell), *155*
Picasso, Pablo (arts), 80
Pick Yourself Up, 172
Picon, Molly (oper), 38
Piedmont, Italy, 38
Piket, Fred (comp), 248
Pilzer, Maximilian (viol), 79
Pinter (busn), 5–6
Pinto, Alfred (cond, harp), 3–4, 6–7, 12–13, 19, 64
Pinza, Ezio (oper, actr), 120
Pittsburgh Fair, 6
Pittsburgh Symphony Society, 217
Planquette, Jean Robert (comp), 246
Plantation Dance, 82
The Plough and the Stars, 175
Plunkit, Joseph (busn), 64–65
Pollack, Lew (writ), 227, 241
Pollock, Muriel (comp, lyrc, pian), 229, 242
Ponchielli, Amilcare (comp), 249–250
Pons, Lily (oper, actr), 106, 117, 134, 170–171
Ponselle, Rosa (oper), 44, 59, 117, 134, 136–137, 139, 141, 222–223
Poot, Marcel (comp), 246
Pops (*see also* Whiteman, Paul), 78
Porgy and Bess, 172
Porter (busn), 47
Possell, George (flut), 139
Potamkin, F. J. (comp), 252
Prager, Alice Heinecke. *See* Drescher, Alice Heinecke
Prelude (Schoenberg) (*see also* Wagner), 197
Previn, Charles (cond), 115, 160, 188

Prisoner's Song, *42*, 44, 69
Prokofiev, Sergei (comp), 205, 227, 248
Pryor, Arthur (trom, cond, comp), 20, 215
Puccini, Giacomo (comp), 139, 149, 248–249
Puss in Boots, 232

Quality Street, 232

Rachmaninoff, Sergei (comp, pian, cond), 14–15, 54, 250–251
Raderman, Lou (viol), 42, 48–49, 52–55, 65, 82, 87–88, 97, 121, 133–134, 146, 237, 242
Radio Center of the World. *See* Victor
Radio City (Music Hall), 148, 158
Rady, Simon (cond), 239
Raff, Joseph Joachim (comp), 251
Rains, Claude (actr), 243
Rameau, Jean Philippe (comp), 226, 231, 247
Ramona, 96–97
Rapee, Erno (cond, comp), 57–58, 124, *125*, *140*
Rathbone, Basil (actr), 117
Raymond, Gene (actr), 170–171
RCA, 118, 128, 164
RCA Magic Key. See Victor
RCA Victor. *See* Victor
RCA Victor Radio Record Review. *See* Victor
recordings. *See* electrical recordings and *see* mechanical recordings
Red Nichols and His Five Pennies, 116
Reg'lar Fellers, 229
Reiner, Fritz (cond), 132, 134
Reisfeld, Bert (comp), 245, 250
Relaxation Time. See Knickerbocker Beer radio show

Republic Film Corp., 188
Requiem (Brahms), 86
Respighi, Ottorino (comp, pian), 130
Rethberg, Elisabeth (oper), 117
Rettenberg, Milton (pian, attorney), 65, 89, 97, 128, 212–213, 237, 238, 241, 253
Reuter (horn), *17*
The Revelers, 84, 101–102, 117
Revelli, William D. (cond), 215
Rex (dog), 120–121
Rhapsody in Blue, 58, 77, 86, 88, 105n11, 110, 142–143
Rhythm Boys, 77
Rhyth-Melodists, 98
Rice, Gladys (oper), 102, 126, 182
Rich, Selma (lyrc), 227
Richardson, Hal (lyrc), 223, 232
Richman, Harry (pops), *185*
Ricordi (publishers), 149
Riesenfeld, Hugo (comp, prod, busn), 158
Rigoletto, 51
Rigoletto Quartet, 45
Rimsky-Korsakov, Nikolai (comp), 14, 247
Rio Rita, 284
RKO (Radio Pictures), 86, 89, 164–167, *169*, 179, 180n3, 180n4, 189
RKO-Pathé, 188, *204*
Roach, Hal (prod, dir), 168–169
Robbins, Jack (publ), 75
Robeson, Paul (pops, actr, political activist), 75, 143, *183*, 237, 285
Robin, Leo (lyrc), 226
Robin Hood, 103, 187n1
Robin Hood Dell concerts, 92
Robinson, Anne (comp), 247
Robinson, Earl (comp, choirmaster), 183, 237
Robison, Carson (pops), 238
Robison, Williard (pops), 234, 241
Roble, Daniel (comp), 226

Rockefeller, John (busn), 150
The Rodgers Sisters, 284
Rogell (busn), 174–175
Rogers (playboy), *150*
Rogers, Ginger (danc, actr), 170–173,
    175–176
Rogers, Howard (lyrc), 232
Romberg, Sigmund (comp), 40, 239
Romeo and Juliet, 138
Rondo Capriccioso, 151
Roosevelt, Franklin D. (govt), 114,
    200, 209n3
Roosevelt, Theodore (govt), 117
Rosary, 117
Rose, Billy (prod), 75
Rose Marie, 284
Roseblatt, Josef (cantor), 38
Ross, David (ancr), 282
Rossini, Gioacchino Antonio (comp),
    113
Rothafel, S. L. "Roxy" (busn), *57*,
    100, 107, 124–126, 182
Rothier, Léon (oper), 44–45
Round Table, 98
Roxy. *See* Rothafel
Roxy Theater, 125
royalties, 72–75, 91, 97, 117, 125, 140,
    182–183, 199, 218
Royle, Selena (actr), 283
Rubinoff, David (viol), 155
Rubinstein, Anton (comp, pian), 157–
    158, 238, 246, 248, 252
Runyon, Santy (comp), 247
Ruppert, Jacob (busn), 181
Russian Ballet, 64
Russian Symphony, 14
Rust, Brian (discographer), 104n5,
    235, 238
Ryskind, Morris (lyrc), 224

Sabatier, Ch. W. (writ), 236
Safanov, Vassily Ilyitch (cond), 10,
    15, 17, 28

St. Louis Blues, 110
Saint-Saëns, Camille (comp), 151
    Introduction, 151
    Opus 28, 151
Salada radio show, 63
Sales, Charles "Chic" (cmdn), 117
Salmaggie, Prof. Cav. A. (pops), 236
Salon Orchestra. *See* Victor Salon
    Orchestra
Samaroff, Tosha (viol), 249, 251, 252
Sanderson, Julia (pops, ancr), 285
Sandrich, Mark (dir), 172–173, 176
Sanford, Harold (cond, music dir),
    142–143
Sanjek, Russell (auth), 104n6
Sannella, Andy (clar), 97
Sari, 284
Sarnoff, David (busn), 95, 106–107,
    128, 140
Satterfield, Tommy (arrg, pian), 78
Satz, Ludwig (pops, film cmdn), 38
Scarlatti, Domenico (comp), 252
Scarmolin, Louis (comp), 252
Schad (busn), 107
Schaefer, Grant (comp), 249
Scheff, Fritzi (oper, pops), 126
Scheherazade Symphonic Suite, 15
Schendel (pian), *34*
Schepp, Rex (banjo, busn), 82, 92,
    196, 219, 227, 230–231, 242–243
Schillinger, Joseph (comp), 156
Schipa, Tito (oper), 117–119
Schirmer, Gustave (publ), 193–194
Schirmer Music Company, 179
Schlichtung, Wilhelm (comp), 252
Schlossberg, Max (trmp), 28, 30
Schneid, Milka (pops), 236
Schneider, Madame (medium), 69
Schoenberg, Arnold (comp), 54, 90,
    196–198, 202, *205*, 244
Schrafft (restaurant), 206
Schrammel. *See* Victor Schrammel
    Orchestra

Schubert, Franz (comp), 30, 100–102, 107, 239, 247
Schubert, Hugh (comp), 245
Schubert Centennial, 100
Schultz, Leo (cell), 13
Schumann, Robert (comp), 30, 107, 149, 225–226, 228, 232–233
Schumann-Heink, Ernestine (oper), 117, 124
Schuyler, Sonny (pops), 182, 239
Schüldkraut, Wulf. *See* Shilkret, Nathaniel, father of
Scott (handyman), 67
Scott, Walter (biographer), 209n4
Scriabin, Alexander (comp, pian), 14–15
Sea Pieces, 118
séance, 67
Secon, Norman (pian), 248
Segovia, Andrés (guitar), 117
Seligman and Company, J. and W., 60n4, 66, 78, 95
Serenade for Strings, 233
Serenade Rhapsodic, 92
SESAC, 127, 204, 244
Sevitzky, Fabien (cond), 92
Shakespeare, William (playwright), 2, 86, 138
Shall We Dance, 173, 177, 222, 225, 231
Shapiro-Bernstein Publishing Company, 43, 73
Shaw, Artie (clar, sax, cond), 80, 121, *122*, 130–131, 181
Shaw, Elliot (pops), 241–243
Shayon, Robert (lyrc), 226, 230, 242
Shefter, Bert (comp, pian), 226, 228, 233, 234
Shell, Niel (educ), 219
Sherman, Al (writ), 241
Sherry Caterers, 16
Shield, Leroy (cond, pian), 240
Shilking Orchestra, 243

Shilkington Transcriptions, 140, 242
Shilkret's Rhyth-Melodists, 241
Shilkret, Anne, 34, *111*, 113, 118, 120–121, 141, 164–165, 187, 216
Shilkret, Arthur (publ), 34, 37, 52, 157, 164, 180, 183, 187, 187n2, 219
Shilkret, Barbara, 219
Shilkret, Harry (md, trmp), 113, 184, 223
Shilkret, Jack (cond, comp, pian, clar), 53, 93, 222, 224–227, 232, 238, 243, 285
Shilkret, Lew (pian, busn), 4, 8, 204
Shilkret, Nathaniel "Nat" (cond, comp, clar, pian, busn), 1–2, 9n1, 19, 25, 36, 43, 45, 50, 53–54, 56, 59, 60n3, 62, 67, 79, 80, 93, 97–98, 102, 104n11, 106, 113–114, 135, 139, 160–161, 162n2, 164, 180n1, 180n2, 180n5, 187n2, 209n1, 209n2, 209n4, 211, 215n1, 216, 219, 220n1, 222
  Academy (Oscar) Award, 189, 209n1
  Academy (Oscar) Award nomination, 170
  aunt, 4
  cancer, *188*
  cigarette case, from McCormack, 102
  father of (Schüldkraut, Wulf), 2–5, 8, 12
  first public speaking, 64
  Grammy awards, 237
  grandparents of, 4
  honorary doctor's degree, 159
  laughing gas, 113
  Lemberg, Austria, visits, 4
  marriage, 34
  mother of, 4, 6
  pet dogs. *See* Pal and *see* Rex
  pie throwing contest, 21

pseudonym, Arthur, Ned, 222, 232
pseudonym, Fenton, Mack, 222–223, 226
pseudonym, Hallett, Niel, 222–228, 230–234, 244–248, 250–253
pseudonym, Harold, Arthur, 222, 234
pseudonym, Hilbert, Nat, 224
radio shows (*see also* individual sponsors), 62
radio shows, number of, 164
recordings, number of, 37, 164
Red Seal conductor, 45
retirement, *216*
surgery, 181, 187n2
uncle, 4
and Victor Orchestra, 36, 238, 241–242
Shilkret, Niel. *See* Shell, Niel
Shilkret, Warner (Niel Warner) (cond), 247
Shore, Dinah (pops, actr), *184*
Show Boat, 75, 120
Showboat Hour, 145
Sibelius, Jean (comp), 183, 197–198, 231, 239, 246, 251–252
Sidney, Louis K. (busn), 188
Siebert, Friedrich (comp), 249, 251
Siegel, Arsene (comp), 250
Siegfried Idyls, 87
Siegrist, Frank (trmp), 77
The Silver-Masked Tenor, 241
Silvers, Lou (busn), 168
Sinatra, Frank (pops, actr), 75
Sinding, Christian (comp), 251
Sixth (Pathétique) Symphony, 24
Skinner, Cornelia Otis (actr, auth), 1–2, 82, 117, 143, 211, 240, 245
Skinner, Otis (actr), 117
Skinner (*Paris '90*) Tour, 1, 211–215
Skolnik, Gregory (viol), 53
Skyler, Sonny. *See* Schuyler, Sonny
Skyward, 86, 221

Slap That Bass, 176
Small, Edward (prod), 173, 177
Smallens, Alexander (cond), 239
Smart, Jack (actr), 282
Smeck, Roy (guitar), *48*
Smith, Joe (viol), 35
Smith, Kate (pops), 95
Smith, Mamie (pops), 104n3
Smith Brothers (Hillpot and Lambert), 63
Smith Brothers Cough Drops radio show (*Songs You Love*), 63, 82, *121*
Snyder, Martin. *See* Colonel Gimp
Sodero, Cesare (cond), 157
Song and Story. See Bankers' Hour radio show
Song of the Bayou, 100
Songs You Love. See Smith Brothers Cough Drops
Sooy brothers (Charles, Harry O., Raymond R. and one other) (recording engineers), 40
Soukas, Elli (pops), 236
soundproof studios, 58–59, 115
Sousa, John Philip (comp, cond), 2, 6, 14, 20, 29, 117, 215
Sousa Band, 243
Souvaine, Henry (comp, busn), 134–136, 141
Spalding, Albert (viol), 20
Speyer and Company, 60n4
Spier, Larry (writ, publ), 226
Spohr, Ludwig (comp), 253
Sponsor, Mr. (busn), 137–139, 160
Stadium Summer Concerts (Lewisohn), 91
Staigers, Del (trmp), 88
Stainer, Sir John (comp), 117
Stanbury, Douglas (pops), 126
Stanford, Charles Villiers (comp), 102
Stanley, Aileen (pops), 74
Stanley, James (pops), 243

Stark, Ray (agent), 189
Stark, Richard (ancr), 283
Steele, Ted (novachord), 242
Steiner, Max (comp), *166*, 180n1,
    180n2, 180n3, 180n5, 207
Sten, Suzanne (oper), 284
Stephen Foster Hall, 101
Sterling, Sir Louis (busn), *66*, 103n1
Stevens, Risë (oper), 91, 147
Stewart, Lawrence D. (bib), 104n11
Stockdale, Robert L. (auth), 237
Stokowski, Leopold (cond), 44–45,
    81–82, 112, 124, *178*, 200–201,
    202, 206, 217, 220n1
Stone, Gregory (comp), 209n1
Stoopnagle, Colonel Lemuel Q.
    (cmdn), 117, 283
Stradivarius, 121, 151–152
Strand Theatre, *64*, 65, 69, 71
Strauss, Johann, Jr. (comp), 156, 225,
    238, 250
Strauss, Richard (comp), 10, 17, 23,
    196, 217, 246
Stravinsky, Igor (comp), 51, 184,
    196–199, 205, 244, 246
The Street Singer (Arthur Tracy)
    (pops), 130
Stroh, Charles (busn), 60n2
Stroh, John Matthias Augustus (scie),
    60n2
Stroh instruments, 40, 44, 60n2
Stromberg, Hunt (prod), 194
Sudhalter, Richard M. (bib), 104n7,
    162m1
Suesse, Dana (comp), 226, 232, 242–
    243
Sullivan, Sir Arthur (comp), 247, 252
Swanson, Gloria (actr, pops), 143
Swarthout, Gladys (oper, actr), 91,
    145–147
Sweethearts, 284
Swichtentenburger, Wilbur. *See* Brad-
    ley, Will

Swift, Kay (comp), 211–212, 215n1,
    240
Swing Time, 172
Swiss Miss, 229
Sydney, Art (ancr, lyrc), 228–229
Symphony (motion picture), 166
Synthetic Sin, 223
Szathmary, Irving (writ), 231–232

Tabuteau, Marcel (oboe), 25, 27
Talley, Marion (oper), 91, *108*, 117
    mother of, 108
Tammany Boss, 96
Tannhäuser Overture, 56
Tannhäuser, 177–178
Tansman, Alexandre (comp), 195–196,
    198, 244
Taplinger, Bob (ancr), 281
Tarto, Joe (bass), 237
Tauber, Richard (oper, actr), 39
Tavan, 22
Taylor, Elizabeth (actr), *195*
Tchaikovsky, Peter Ilich (comp), 14,
    24, 44, 120, 137, 183, 228, 231,
    233, 238–239
television. *See* TV
Terr, Max (comp), 209n1, 228
Testa, M. (writ), 236
Tetrazzini, Luisa (oper), 194
Thalberg, Irving (prod), 205
That Girl from Paris, 170, 222–223,
    226, 233
There Goes My Girl, 224
theremin, 109
Theremin, Leo (scie), *109*
Thesaurus Transcriptions, 140
Thibaud, Conrad (oper, pop), 281
This Is America, 188, 204
Thomas, Ambrose (comp), 238
Thomas, Bob (bib), 9n1
Thomas, John Charles (oper, pops),
    80, 119, 134, 138, 239
Thomas, Thomas L. (oper), 182

Thompson, J. Walter. *See* Walter
    Thompson
Thomson, Virgil (comp), 250, 252
Three Musketeers, 195
Thurber, Jeannette (dir of conserva-
    tory), 13
Tibbett, Lawrence (oper, pops), 91,
    112, 117, 168, 204
The Toast of New York, 170, 173, 177,
    224–225, 227–228, 230–231, 233
Tobani, Theodore (comp), 224
Tobias, Charles (lyrc, writ), 223
Toch, Ernst (comp), 196, 198, 244
Tolsch (Di Blassi), 12
Top Hat, 171
Toscanini, Arturo (cond), 2, 25, 28,
    44, *55*, 80–81, 124, 134–135, 139,
    141, 143, 149, 151, 159, 161, 170,
    182, 202, 215, 217
Toscanini, Mrs. Arturo, 135
Toulouse-Lautrec, Henri de (arts),
    211, 214
Tours, Frank (comp), 194
Tracy, Arthur. *See* The Street Singer
Tragica, 118
Trapp, Max (comp), 246
Trentini, Emma (oper), 193–194
tricks, horse. *See* horse tricks
Tristan and Isolde, 33, 86
Troubadours, 36, 240–242
TV, 12, 78, 80, 92, 114, 116–117, 140,
    147, 214, 218
Twain, Mark (auth), 39
The Two Black Crows, 73–74

UCLA, 206
Une Voce Poca Fa, 171
Union Carbide, 85
union, 3, 7, 12–14, 27, 35, 81, 92, *122*,
    129–130, *139*, 161, 166, 199, 203,
    212–214, 218
United Artists, 164
Universal, 75, 164, 188

U.S. Steel, 32

Valentino, Rudolph (actr), *73*
    Tango Valentino. See Fate
Vallée, Rudy (pops, cond), *111*, 117
Van Barr (cond), 35
van Hoogstraten, Willem (comp),
    135–136
Vaughn, George (clar, arts, poet), *34*
Venuti, Joe (viol), 77, 237
Verdi, Giuseppe (comp), 22, 249–250
vibraphone, *112*
Victor, 12, 14, 20, 26, 30, 35, 41–43,
    47, 50, 51, 53–55, 57–60, 60n3,
    60n4, 62–66, 68–69, 72, 74, 76–
    78, 80, 86, 88, 91, 95–97, 99–100,
    104n3, 104n4, 104n5, 104n11,
    106–108, 110–114, 116–118, 120,
    124, 127–128, 130, 137–139, 144,
    164–166, 168, 182–183, 187, 189,
    199–201, 206, 214–216, 235
    A&R (Artist and Repetoire) Com-
        mittee, 47, 49, 62–63, 73, *94*, 101
    Black Label, 73, 79
    Blue Label, 73
    Country Records Department, 42
    Dance Department, 94
    Domestic Department, 40, 44–45
    Executive Committee, 80
    Export Department, 37, 42, 44–45,
        50, 72, 94, 111
    Foreign Department, 37–38, *41*,
        44–45, 72, 94
    German Department, 58
    Green and Purple Labels, 73
    Hillbilly Department, 44–45, 72, 94
    His Master's Voice of the Air radio
        show, 233
    Magic Key of RCA radio show, 90,
        182, 224–225, 229, 232, 242
    prize, 100
    Race Department, 42, 44, *45*, 57,
        72, 94

Radio Center of the World, 106

RCA Victor Division, 96, 108, 112, 122, 140, 165, 178, 198, 201, 218

RCA Victor Radio Record Review radio show, 233

Red Seal (operatic) Department, 12, 38, 42, 44, 47, 73, 94, 106, 187

Semi-classical Department, 94

Victor Concert Orchestra, 238–240, 243

Victor Junior Programs Opera Company, 240

Victor Light Opera Company, 238–239

Victor March, 60, 281

Victor Salon Group, 238–241, 243

Victor Salon Orchestra, *40*, 44, 47–48, 51, 54, 59, 64, 77, 97, 101, 108, 112, 162n2, 239–240, 242

Victor Schrammel Orchestra, 39

Victor Symphony Orchestra, 44, 104n11, 238–239, 241

Victor Talking Machine Company. *See* Victor

Victrola, 59, 76, 114

Vidor, King (dir, prod), 189–193

Viennese Gayeties, 187n1

Villa-Lobos, Heitor (comp), 54, *203*

Volpe, Arnold (cond), 15

von Suppe, Franz (comp), 245

Wagner, Richard (comp), 17, 33, 56, 77, 87, 107, 120, 149, 177, 249

Prelude, 33

Wald, Jerry (prod, writ), 142

Waldorf-Astoria Hotel, *26*, 34, 138

Walking On Air, 225, 231–233

Wall, Lucille (actr), 282

Wallenstein, Alfred (cell, cond), 141, *159*

Wallenstein Ensemble, 160

Waller, Thomas "Fats" (pian, pops, comp), *97*

Wallowitch, John (comp), 252

Walt Whitman Hotel, 108

Walter, Bruno (cond), 134, 141–142

Walter Thompson Agency, 84

Waltz in Swingtime, 172

Ward, J. F. (arr), 222

Waring, Fred (cond), 75

Warner, Neil. *See* Shilkret, Warner

Warner Brothers, 96, 188

Washington, Ned (lyrc), 223, 241

Watson, Milton (pops), 242, 282

Watson, W., 222

The Way You Look Tonight, 172

Wayne, Mabel (writ), 238

WEAF (New York), 87

Webb, Roy (comp), 168–170, 174, 180n3

Webb, Theodore (oper), 145

Weber, Carl Maria von (comp), 149, 245, 248, 250

Concertino, 14

Weber, Henry (cond), 284

Weber, Joe (cmdn), 150

Weber, Marek (cond), 39

Weber and Fields, 150

Weinberger, Jarimar (comp), 246

West Side Story, 217

Western Electric Company, 59

WGN (Chicago), 184

When My Sugar Walks Down the Street, 74

Whitburn, Joel (auth), 238, 243

White, David (busn), 126, 141

Whiteman Orchestra, 240

Whiteman, Paul (cond) (*see also* Pops), 40–41, 44, *57*, 63, 66, 76, *77*, 88, 104n11, 116, 127, 153, 156, 194, 237

The Whites, 283

Whiting, George (writ), 237–238

Who, 75

Whyte, Gordan (busn), 85, *87*
Wielage, R. P. (busn), 47, 67
Wien du Stadt meine Traume, 96
Wilkie, Earl (pops), 284
Wilkinson, Ralph, 230
William Tell Overture, 6, 21
Willow Grove Park, 6–7, 20
Wiltshire Hotel, 89
Wilty, Earl (ancr), 283
Winchell, Walter (news), 143
Winterset, 169, 222–223, 226, 230, 232, 234
Witmark Publishers, 29
Wohl, Yehuda (comp), 252
Wolf, Hugo (comp), 107, 121
Wolfe, Jacques (comp), 231
Woll, Carsten (pops), 235–236
The Woman I Love, 230
A Woman Rebels, 223, 231
Wood, Leo (comp), 222
Woodin, William Hartman (govt), *114*
Woolcott, Alexander (writ), *98*
WOR (Newark, New York), 161
The Work of Art, 219
Wreck of the Old '97, 42–43

wrestling, 12, 80
Wright (md), 184, 189
Wruble, Allie (lyrc), 177
Wunsch, Hermann (comp), 249
Wuori, Timo, 236
Wynert, Johnny (comp), 251

Yale University, 111
Yankee Doodle, 70, 137
Yankee Doodle Home, 225
Yellen, Jack (lyrc), 94, 229, 241
Yellow Ticket, 129
Young, Carleton, (actr), 283
Young, Victor (comp, cond, viol), 209n4
Ysaÿe, Eugène (viol, cond), 32

Zador, Eugen (comp), 247
Zaninović, Nikola (pops), 236
Zayde, Jascha (viol), 55, 64, 121, 137
Ziegfeld Follies, 13, 183, 240
Ziegfeld Follies Hits, 187n1
Zigeunerweisen, 155
Ziporkin, Leon (bass), 83
Zirato, Bruno (busn), 37
Zorlig, Kurt (comp), 250

ABOUT THE AUTHOR
AND EDITORS

This work is the autobiography of Nathaniel Shilkret, with editing, a preface, an introduction, appendixes and a bibliography written by Barbara Shilkret and Niel Shell.

Barbara Shilkret became Nathaniel Shilkret's daughter-in-law when she married his son Arthur Shilkret in 1941. When Arthur was drafted into the U.S. Army in 1942, Barbara took an active role in operating the Nathaniel Shilkret Music Company, and currently she is the owner of this company.

Niel Shell is the grandson of Nathaniel Shilkret. Since 1971, he has been Professor of Mathematics at the City College of New York, the same school where Nathaniel Shilkret, class 'ex1910, is an alumnus. Niel's office sits on the hallowed former grounds of Lewisohn Stadium, where George Gershwin made his conducting première. Gershwin conducted his work *An American in Paris*, using the première recording (still readily available after seventy-four years!) by Nathaniel Shilkret to rehearse with. Niel is author or editor of four books and thirty research articles, published in eight countries spread over four continents.

NATHANIEL SHILKRET AND THE SYMPHONIC POPS

1. **SCHERZO IN E MINOR**, by Felix Mendelssohn (2:36)
2. **CAPRICE**, by Jean Sibelius (2:21)
3. **ARKANSAS TRAVELER**, arr. Nathaniel Shilkret (2:11)
4. **A BEAUTIFUL DAY**, by Niel Hallett (2:35)
5. **UG-A-LY DUCKLING**, by Niel Hallett (2:15)
6. **TEA LEAVES**, by Niel Hallett (2:20)
7. **PARIS 1890**, by Kay Swift, arr. Nathaniel Shilkret (2:32)
8. **CLARINET ENTR'ACTE**, by Niel Hallett (2:22),
   solo clarinets: Alfred Gallodoro and Jimmy Abato
9. **POP GOES THE WEASEL**, arr. Nathaniel Shilkret (2:18)
10. **ABU HASSAN OVERTURE**, by Carl Maria von Weber (3:13)
11. **IF I WERE A KING, OVERTURE, I**, by Adolphe Charles Adam (2:51)
12. **APPARITION No. 2**, by Franz Liszt (2:37)
13. **FAUST: INTRO. AND SONG OF THE GOLDEN CALF**, by Charles Gounod (3:35)
14. **MY GYPSY VAGABOND**, by Niel Hallett (2:24)
15. **THE TWO SENTRIES**, by Niel Hallett (1:55)
16. **THE PROPHET: BALLET EXCERPT**, by Giacomo Meyerbeer (2:40)
17. **IRISH MELODY**, by Niel Hallett (2:43)
18. **THE SAUCY HOLLANDAISE, II**, by Paul Bliss Jr. (2:36),
    baritone: Lee Cass
19. **SUITE No. 12: GAVOTTE AND ANDANTE**, by Domenico Scarlatti (2:06)
20. **A BIRD COMES FLYING, II**, by Siegfried Ochs (3:09)
21. **THE PEST**, by Niel Hallett (2:12)
22. **A MASKED BALL: PRELUDE**, by Giuseppe Verdi (3:10)
23. **JERRY OF JERICHO ROAD, II**, by Palmer John Clark (3:03),
    tenor: John Druary, baritone: Jimi Beni, soprano: Christine Palmer
24. **WALTZES, Opus 39, Nos. 15, 6, 4**, by Johannes Brahms (2:28),
    solo piano: Sherman Frank
25. **NORWAY FOLK TUNES**, arr. Niel Hallett (2:18)
    In honor of these times of great national pride:
26. **THE STAR SPANGLED BANNER**, arr. Nathaniel Shilkret (2:52)
    Total time: 69:23